Mainlines, Blood Feasts, and Bad Taste

A Lester Bangs Reader

Lester Bangs *edited by* **John Morthland**

From 1969 until his death in 1982, Lester Bangs was one of the most prolific rock critics in America, writing for *Creem, The Village Voice, Rolling Stone* and pretty much every other music-oriented publication in the known world.

John Morthland, coexecutor of the Bangs literary estate, was a colleague of Bangs from 1969 until the author's death. He was editor of *Creem* in 1974–75. He is a writer at large for *Texas Monthly.*

Also by Lester Bangs

Psychotic Reactions and Carburetor Dung
edited by Greil Marcus

Mainlines, Blood Feasts, and Bad Taste

Mainlines, Blood Feasts, and Bad Taste

A Lester Bangs Reader

Edited by **John Morthland**

ANCHOR BOOKS
A Division of Random House, Inc.
New York

An Anchor Books Original, August 2003

 Published in the United States by Anchor Books, a division of Random House, Inc., New York, and simultaneously in Canada by Random House of Canada Limited, Toronto.

Owing to limitations of space,
permissions appear at the end of the book.

Library of Congress Cataloging-in-Publication Data
Bangs, Lester.
Mainlines, blood feasts, and bad taste : a Lester Bangs reader /
edited by John Morthland.
p. cm.
ISBN 0-375-71367-0 (pbk.)
1. Rock music—History and criticism. I. Morthland, John. II. Title.
ML3534.B314 2003
781.66'09—dc21 2003040392

Book design by Rebecca Aidlin

www.anchorbooks.com

Printed in the United States of America
10 9 8 7 6

For Ben, Midge, Karen, Tom, and Matty

Contents

\\\ ///

RAVING, RAGING, AND REBOPS

Introduction and Acknowledgments

Though I loved and respected his writing as much as anyone, when Lester Bangs died, basically of a Darvon overdose, in 1982 I mourned the loss of a great friend more than that of a great writer. Truth is, I never read his work critically; I liked what I liked and if something else he wrote didn't engage me, I just moved along to the next thing without giving it much thought. Hardly a day has passed since that I haven't thought of Lester, but the hole his death left in my personal life dwarfs the loss I feel as a reader and colleague of Lester.

Yet here I have been these last few months, reading him very critically, making judgments right and left while agonizing to determine what I considered most worthy of inclusion in this book that hadn't already appeared in *Psychotic Reactions and Carburetor Dung* (Alfred A. Knopf, 1987), the posthumous anthology Greil Marcus edited. I wish I could now give you the magic formula I used, but there isn't one; it's a highly subjective matter, after all. I tried to pick the best-written pieces that I felt reflected the range of Lester's themes—make that, his passions—and I tried to group and order them in a way that created a feel rather than a timeline (Greil having already done the latter so well). In the process, I rediscovered, for me, two key points about his work.

The first was his ability to move his most electric thoughts from the brain to the page without interruption. As a music writer myself, I've heard great improvisational players declare that when they're at their best, they don't create music so much as music passes through them and out their instrument. Having shared an office with Lester, I can remember sitting there in awe, watching him write, literally, as fast as he could type. Of course, this sometimes created inferior as well as superlative work, and of course, I can also picture him (albeit less frequently) slumped head down on typewriter, trying to think of what to say next, and how to bend the language to his will. But surely this ability accounts for the sheer rollin'-and-tumblin' energy of his work. It also explains how he could write such a delightfully scathing putdown of an album, such as the MC5 review that appears in this book, only to decide later that the same LP is an all-time classic, and be equally credible both times; how he can use the same criteria to praise the Miles Davis of the Seventies that he'd earlier used to condemn that very same music; that's also why he was so unselfconscious about making so many confident predictions that have, with time, turned out to be so wrong (plenty of them occur in these pages). And it's why I wanted to bunch together a few of his pieces involving travel; to my mind, some of his most spontaneous and explosive writing came when Lester was plopped down in a relatively new or foreign place and simply turned loose to record what he saw and heard. In that situation, his sense of wonder could elevate the obvious into revelation, translate the ordinary into the extraordinary, launch into amazing moral and ethical tangents, and find humor in the most serious places and/or a dark underbelly where humor was intended. And do it all so breathlessly it left a reader with jet lag.

The second point concerns how rock writing has changed since the days when these pieces were done. This subject is debated virtually any time two or more rock critics wind up in the same room, especially if they're at an industry event like South By Southwest; the arguments usually revolve around the fact that there are so many more music writers than ever before; around the way it's become a recognized profession in such a short time, and geared, not coincidentally, toward consumerism and the music industry's notion of publicity rather than toward journalism and/or criticism; around how much more difficult it's become, and the concessions a writer has to make to the PR machine, to get face time with interview subjects; around how effortlessly music journalism mutated into celebrity journalism. These are all good and true insights, and I've made them myself at various times, but the single factor that strikes me most after months of immersion in Lester's work is that rock critics don't fantasize these days. Period. 'Nuff said.

Nearly all the previously published writings collected here first appeared in publications that were outside—and often *way* outside—the publishing mainstream at the time, and that mainstream has become even narrower since (to the extent that some of these pieces probably couldn't even get published in today's fringier periodicals). At the time of his death, after about thirteen years as a professional writer, Lester's name was known only in fairly small circles. Since then, as what's acceptable from a writer has come to be defined ever more conservatively, Lester's own stature has risen, proving once again that you don't miss your water til your well runs dry, and that the vision and value of troublesome types can seldom be celebrated until they're no longer troublesome. He has been the subject of a biography and appeared in songs by artists such as R.E.M., Bob Seger, and the Ramones. I thought Philip Seymour Hoffman got Lester's 'tude, at least, down pretty well in *Almost Famous,* Cameron Crowe's paean to his own days as a young rock writer. Rock critics today routinely cite Lester as their greatest influence, though it's usually hard to detect said influence in their work.

All of this has, finally (and thankfully), made it possible for American culture to take Lester more seriously as a writer. But that's come at a price, and it's one that Lester himself often wrote about. The best-known, bull-in-a-china-shop Lester—who was always dangerously loaded, who could be so insulting and malicious as well as self-destructive, who could be oblivious to the people around him, who was a Falstaffian clown and then grimly serious most of the time—the kind of guy, in short, some unfortunates like to live through vicariously—has stuck in the public fancy. The Lester who could stay up hours calmly giving or taking personal advice, who could be deferential and accommodating and even accept rebuke and try to act on it constructively, who seemed neither doomed nor damned though certainly driven, who had an expansive lust for life and a sense of humor and (sometimes even, and for no apparent reason) cheerfulness to match it, who could actually be *counted on,* dammit, has become even more obscure than he was while alive. To some extent this is inevitable, especially in someone as contradictory and conflicted as Lester. And certainly nobody in his right mind could minimize the former Lester; he was there for everyone to see, is well documented in these pages, and did, make no mistake, manage to kill himself accidentally at age thirty-three. But if nothing else, I hope that making so much of his work available again will, in addition to reconfirming that he was one of the most worthy chroniclers of his times, illuminate once again the Lester who made a pretty good friend. And as long as he's receiving all this added recognition, I'd like it to extend to his work again, too. Given that one of his pet themes concerns romanticizing, or reducing to their most colorful caricature, pop figures (especially those who die young) rather than looking harder at the totality of their lives and the work that brought them to prominence in the first place, it's the very least a book such as this should do. Especially for those readers who weren't around at the time.

/// \\\

More than a few of Lester's friends and fans were instrumental in bringing this anthology to fruition. Ben Catching, who is Lester's nephew and the executor of his estate, signed the necessary documents to make it happen and then, as always, turned me loose to handle it as I saw fit. Ben and his wife Midge, their daughter Karen Hildebrandt and her husband Tom and their son Matty, have all been good friends and good hosts to me when I visited, and I've also come to know Lester even better through them. As the estate's literary coexecutor (along with myself), Billy Altman has helped handle Lester's affairs for two decades now and likewise pitched in on various aspects of this project.

As editor of Lester's first posthumous collection, Greil Marcus is a mighty tough act to follow. But he made my job easier by providing all manner of practical advice and encouragement and serving as a conscientious sounding board when that was what I needed.

Many of the pieces in this book were first gathered by Greil from various sources when he began compiling *Carburetor Dung* back in the Eighties, and he thanked those people in the Introduction and Acknowledgments to that book; since I used 'em too, I second that emotion. Quite a few more of Lester's writings have been unearthed in the years since then, and for getting those manuscripts and letters to me or putting me in touch with people who had them or helping me to find the right person from whom to get permission to use them, I thank Gil Asakawa, Bill Bentley, David Browne, Jean-Charles Costa, Jim DeRogatis, Holly George-Warren, Ellen Gibbs, Barney Hoskyns, Robert Hull, Miriam Linna, Alan Niester, Andy Schwartz, Greg Shaw, Bill Stephen, Vinny Testa of Testa Communications, and Dolly Zander.

Others provided editorial counsel that helped me determine which articles I would ultimately use or offered other forms of insight, advice, and help with niggling little details. They are Chuck Eddy, Ben Edmonds, Bill Holdship, Jaan Uhelszki Kaufman, Dave Marsh, Michael Ochs, RJ Smith, Carol Schloner Swanson, and Queenie Taylor. A few did double duty. University of Texas journalism student Dana Centola without fail met deadlines on inhuman amounts of inputting and added useful editorial input. Georgia Christgau not only provided incisive editorial counsel but also did some inputting herself. And *Texas Monthly* assistant editor Katy Vine also offered considerable, and considered, editorial insights: along with *TM* editorial assistant Jennifer Olsen, she supervised the magazine's UT student interns Andy Buck, Quincy Collins, Erin Donnelly, Allison Gray, Michelle Morris, and Chamlee Williams in the inputting of numerous pieces. Since Lester did all his writing in the precomputer era, there was a lot of inputting to do, and I was damn lucky to get it done by people who did not treat it like drudge work for even one line.

Andrew Halbreich and Rick Triplett helped with some vexing legal questions. Sam Staples kept me from falling apart by whacking some sense back into my computer whenever it started messing with me.

Jeri Pamp gamely negotiated and helped ease the solitude and the full gamut of, er, mood swings that this project brought out in me, hanging in there even when it must have seemed to her like *I* was barely there.

Theron Raines of Raines and Raines was Lester's agent when he was alive, and has continued in the same capacity for the estate. Edward Kastenmeier of Random House was the first editor to see the original proposal for this book, and jumped on it right away.

/// \\\

In as few instances as possible, where there were references I felt some readers might not understand because Lester's work was so of the moment, I have added explanatory footnotes. But because I believe that even with all the time that has elapsed Lester's work still stands on its own, I usually haven't tried to introduce individual pieces or put them in a context. But I would like to explain briefly the sole exception, which is the three pieces gathered in the opening section called Drug Punk. That was also the title of an autobiographical book the teenage Lester wrote before he was ever published anywhere except in his high school newspaper and literary magazine. It's a maddeningly erratic manuscript, but pure Lester in so many respects, and some of its best moments set up the rest of *this* book so effectively. So please, have at it.

—John Morthland
Austin, Texas
June 2002

\\\ ///

DRUG PUNK

/// \\\

from Two Assassinations and a Speedy Retreat into Pastoral Nostalgias

Today Andy Warhol was assassinated—well, I shouldn't say "assassinated," he was shot by some chick who *wanted* to murder him, and right now he's in critical condition, 50-50 chance or so they say. I was over at my girlfriend Andy's today listening to my new William Burroughs album for the first time (it just came in the mail) when suddenly they shouted for me from the bedroom. When I went in Andy's mother told me the news. Somehow I got the feeling they were expecting me to get distraught or something, so I faked this bunch of guffaws. Actually the news had no effect on me, at least no kind that could be measured positively or negatively, except that kind of vibration that sudden real-life surrealism sets off in you. It blew my mind is what I meant to say. When you say "Blow my mind," you don't mean anything to do with sadness or happiness, you mean WHAM!, the sudden impact of something outrageous, incredible, unthinkable, and I guess you could say that that's a positive feeling. Andy's mother went on to say blandly: "Some New York woman art critic shot him. Blew his whole head right off."

"*What?!* Is he dead then?"

Andy started to laugh. Her mother corrected her own surrealism (Burroughs had just been saying on the phonograph, "Trak news service. . . . We don't report the news we write it"): "No, he's just in the hospital in critical condition." I went back into the living room and wrote on the paper slipcover from inside my Burroughs album: "June 3,

1968—Day Andy Warhol was assassinated." It looked better that way than if I'd wrote "Day Andy Warhol was shot."

Maybe I should be more concerned. Warhol used to be one of my heroes. Of course, I didn't know a damn thing about him, hadn't seen any of his movies or very many of his paintings, but I'd seen a TV show on him with the Velvet Underground playing that blew my mind, and I read what I could here and there in the magazines. Somewhere along in there I bought a giant poster with his face and sunglasses on it, and kept the thing up for months. It's not much to look at, or rather it wasn't, it's dead now. . . . I mean it wasn't one of these psychedelic-rococo things you can stare at for hours. As a matter of fact it was ugly, downright, and after a while the only reason I kept it up was that I wanted pictures on my wall and it was big. Back when I first got it I kept it right across from my bed and at night in the darkness I would stare at the face, trying to simulate perceptual drug experience, until it changed. But the changes never had much definition, not much showed in that face, it was just a famous face, incredibly blank and perhaps that was its claim to fame. Without the sunglasses he looked like a typical fey faggot, but with shades he achieved this rubbery cement look, a cement wall. Gradually over the months I began to find out that Warhol had little or nothing to do with the movies under his name. Roger met Warhol (or an imposter, as has been rumored since) and Paul Morrissey, who seems to be the real man responsible for the films, when they came to lecture at San Diego State. I wasn't there, but again Warhol came across as a catatonic if anything. When I moved to Broadway the poster went up in the living room there, and one night when they were all on acid and all equally bum-tripped, Jerry Luck fastened his paranoia on the Warhol poster: "I can't stand that guy, he's always looking at me! Ugh, that face!"

"The cat hassling you?" I sympathized.

"Man, I can't stand it! I'd like to rip that fucker into a million pieces! All the time I feel him staring at me, every motherfucking time I look around I see him staring at me like that, an' I hate the fucker, I hate 'im!"

I was in a very ironic/sarcastic mood that night, so I said: "Well, man, if he bothers you that much, rip the shit out of him! The poster belongs to me and I don't mind. Go ahead . . . fuck 'im up!"

"Really? I can?"

"Shore, go right ahead, have a ball!"

Everybody else made noises of disgust or told Luck to cool it. For a brief moment there was an odd suspenseful lull, and then he sprang at the poster and ripped it off the wall with a gurgling cry. Flopping about on the floor like a beached octopus, he tore it into a scattered litter of small pieces, snarling. Then he sat up, scratching his head, and looked around the room dazedly. I looked at him curiously. The others had made even more disgusted noises. Someone told him to clean up the mess, and he grumbled just like he did the night that he and Dan and Roger stole a chicken from some neighbor and he cleaned and plucked it on our kitchen floor, taking a bite from its bloody crotch to prove his Class.

But to get back to the assassination; when I got home that night my mother met me at the door with the news. She said he had been shot by his "girlfriend." Later Roger came over, and was predictably shocked when I dropped the bomb, gasping wide-eyed and staggering around the room a moment with his hand to his head. I don't think this was so much an indication that Warhol held some dear place deep in his heart, as an example of his typical response when his mind is blown.

/// \\\

Yesterday Andy Warhol was shot in his New York office, today Robert Kennedy in an L.A. hotel lounge just as he was finishing his victory speech after winning the California primary. And just two months ago, almost to the day, Martin Luther King, a far better man than either of the other two, was murdered in Memphis by a hired assassin who still eludes the FBI. Who next? *What* next? Andy and I were sitting in the den about half past midnight browsing a state college catalog when her mother shouted from the bedroom, "Andy! Come quickly! Bobby Kennedy's been shot!" We ran down the hall to sit dazedly watching the strange milling mélange on the screen, nervous confused newscasters their voices breaking as they interviewed witnesses most of whom had differing stories, cameras blurring in and out of focus again and again, pandemonium, a harried cop shouting for everyone to clear the room but breaking off in mid-sentence as he saw a CBS man two feet away holding his microphone out to a witness, muddy charcoal semidarkness on the screen as they doused the lights in the lounge in an unsuccessful attempt to clear it, hearing an account later of the tense moments right after the shooting when photographers and reporters and bystanders crowded in so close over Kennedy and the two other wounded individuals that the senator (prone on the floor with blood all over his face, hands, and hips) finally had to cry out for some air, his mob was suffocating him . . . saw the would-be assassin dragged out surrounded by a tough contingent of a couple dozen cops pushing through the crowd, their captive barely glimpsed between trunks of cops as he hung half-limp yet his muscles tightened trying to roll himself almost into a fetal ball with arms defensively over the crown of his head . . . another supposed assassin got away . . . Andy was sobbing. Her mother clucked about "This country, I don't know . . ." and said to Paul: "Paul, let's move to Australia." Andy declared fiercely through her tears: "I'll bet it was one of those *McCarthyites!*" She is, predictably, a fanatical Kennedy supporter. I'm for McCarthy. Earlier in the evening, she had been crying, "nearly distraught" as she herself put it at the prospect, which seemed quite likely then according to network projections, of Kennedy's defeat. I watched the TV coverage of the immediate aftermath of his shooting with my jaw hanging, stupefied and shocked in the same way I'd been those interminable leagues of moments that I sat in the Angels' living room watching the progress of their gang rape.

The data on the TV began to repeat itself: no new developments. I said good night to Andy and drove to Valley Liquor to pick up some Ezerase typing paper for the philosophy paper I'd planned to write on this all-night speed session. As I paid for it I casually said to the clerk, "Dja hear the news about Bobby Kennedy?" and he said, passing time of day with customer, "Yeah . . . they're gonna hafta stop doing those things."

/// \\\

Andy called me to report through tears that Senator Kennedy was still on the operating table, seven hours since the shooting, she says they got him through the shoulder, neck, and one big corner clipped off the skull behind an ear, three bullets through the smiling young presidential hopeful, and she has sat all night in front of the TV speeding and crying, while I've sat puffing panting with the sustained sex joy of plumbing this my Mainline, jugular vein of memories, convictions of the head and reachings-out of heart all years for some crystalline totality, and this is it, I can't cry this morning, even though America is disintegrating with a rapidity that's even shocking some of the dissidents, with an immutable beam-cracking ruination exceeding the wildest projections of those wooly insurgents America internalized from Tom Paine Franklin and the rest, as I feel the total tornado of the cosmos whirling 'round me "like a Jacuzzi Whirlpool Bath," as all the Grossmont Junior College speakers used to say muckraking at tournaments until poor wop Jacuzzi's millions-maker became a cliché representing the very epitome of our American "decadence," I feel ecstatic chills swirling up and pouring down my limbs and trunk as a day and night of methedrine slowly flakes from me like dried paint flakes from the barnacled bow of a gargantuan ocean liner, all night these mounting hours Senator Robert Kennedy slowly dying on L.A. operating table of sterile stainless steel I've been plumbing this Mainline's depths, new literature aborning in here my recent speed sessions, when that methedrine's in my blood and that blood is in my head, something new, I keep returning in allusions to the Velvet Underground, no, specifically, Lou Reed, mind made it out of New York maelstrom halfway intact, now I pick up his messages thanx to the R&R Renaissance the massive push of record companies hustling like mad beetles after hog-slopping troughs brimful of dollar bills, remember Grand Guy Grand's trick and people diving shamelessly into the massive vat of shit and piss and blood and pus and snot and come etc. after seasoning of U.S. greenbacks in the filth, everything flows in and lawd we're all sittin' pretty have been how long now? But confidentially although it shore ain't no secret I feel the lid's about to blow. Driving Andy to school. Suddenly, after half our transit done in silence, she says: "America is disintegrating, Les."

"I know it," I say. "I've known it for a long time. . . . All anybody has had to do for the past year or so was read the editorials in magazines like *Life,* or the *Post,* and they would've known the whole thing was falling apart." When sheets like that start predicting imminent apocalypse and monstrous social earthquakes, you *know* the keg's about to blow, because those mags are part of the Greater American Mainline at present, they shoot right out to reach in one way or another a majority of the populace every week, and the last thing they want to do is alarm Mr. and Mrs. America unnecessarily, to set the reactionaries to cleaning their '76 muskets or alarm the milk-and-sports-page millions securely ensconced in their stucco dugouts with unfounded rumors of indigenous explosions expected to rip out the quiet keep-off-the-grass parks, the shady cement sidewalks leaf strewn cross the illusions of permanence in the initials of lovers now friends walking precincts on Desenex feet and varicose veins for the Republican party and the Next President of the United States (as is obvious by today, since last night) Richard M. Nixon, no, these serene town centers proudly perpetuating quiet cracker images from 1853 must not be torn up madly out of that storied earth like the vertebrae of some ironically smiling Jesus of brilliantine halo, after all, this isn't France!

I said to Andy that I'd foreseen the seam-ripping of America's frayed old frock coat, and I added: "I supposed it couldn't be otherwise. . . ." and she said "Democracy won't work, it's a shame but it just won't work" and I said, "The reason it's falling apart this way is that the people of America have been living in the past too long. . . . For too long we've broadcasted the American Dream on all networks as gospel and everybody's been content . . . living in the past. . . . The nation is falling now because its people haven't been able to face it when the granite thunderbolt plows square into their upper plates, that the American Dream is only a dream, and that the American Reality is imperative, a powder-keg situation."

She started crying again. I put my hand on hers where it lay on the seat and she pulled it away abruptly, with the first touch. "Oh, don't try to comfort me, you, I know that you don't understand . . . it's the people like you . . . and that *shit* you read—"

"You mean the *Free Press,* and like that?"

"That *crap,* that *filthy lying crap,* and the crap those *Right*-Wingers put out, that's what's destroyed America!"

I won't deny it, for all I know she's pretty right, in fact I'm *sure* she is, those hysterical paranoid Left-er New Left idiots are just as much to blame as anybody. America, which is essentially *our universe,* is having earthquake-sized convulsions, choking, spitting up blood, reeling dizzily into some crumpling limp falldown of terminal disease, weaving back and forth on its knees moaning and clutching itself tightly in one wounded area after another, raving like a wood-grain-alcoholic crashing in the Bowery on his Last Go-Round, and I don't have any answers, or even very many *opinions* right now, seems like all the factions in the brawl are starting to look like the very thing they're opposing so desperately, so that even semilucid and halfway rational New Leftists who can *see* in reasonably complete clarity the disastrous turn their politics and political organizations down to the last one have taken, must still sit tight keep their chops gritted and be ready for the impending fight, no matter what the consequences, perhaps because they've never really conceived of America falling into a continent of burning junk piles and primitive local control by brute force, meaning that perhaps they're just bored with the same old scene, day after day, month after month, everything secure, bolted down, in order, safe for the cowering rodent-citizenry of elm-lined tract homes, maybe these cats just wanta see the entire structure fall or at least get shaken to its quick for once simply because it's never happened before and, you know, man, like with their Che caps and half-ass homemade Mollies, why, they're a Revolutionary Insurgent Liberation Army, *can*-you-dig-it?, ready to get out there by God and do some fucking Liberating! No matter if the cat's never seen blood in his life before outside the movies, man, he will fight with the strength of twenty flabby imperialist racist middle-class WASP head of human cattle because he has the pure true Fire in his heart, and not only that he's taken lots of acid! He's strong! No, man, he sure ain't gonna turn tail and run when he charges toward hand-grenade blasts which blow small bits of the flesh and blood and entrails of a woman and her three small children his way, what the fuck, what's a little splatter of blood and guts on your sleeve?; and he won't run when the cops come in with *their* guns blazing or even machine guns turning slowly in that street storefront wall to storefront wall; but he MAY run when he walks up to some big Jimmy Brown Quarterback-type Black Militant spade boppin' down the street of smoke and fire and death and he sez, "Hey, man, whaddya say, ain't the revolution *outasight,* how about, hey you want some grass?" and that big spade just slowly swivels his pumpkin-size head to take in this stupid eager-faced Honkey Hippy coming on like such a White Tom and pretty soon the spade sez: "Split, what boh, fo' ah bus' yo' haid." Real calm but real obvious in his sincerity too, just kinda standin' there all lordly and amused hands on his hips legs spread and smilin' easy but radiating a blistering solid blast of white hot hate out from his red eyes through those impenetrable shades designed to tell the person confronted nothing at all. Now if you think that white ex-Love neo-Political Longhair cat is gonna stand there and try to reason that thing out with that big spade, you're just plain stupid, as stupid as ninety percent of the Hip and New Left Community (and I mean those that've been around long enough that they should know better, not these little high school punks just picked up on grass & acid last month) has gotten right now. And anybody lets themselves get that stupid is doubly dangerous: dangerous first to themselves, because they're liable to get their heads busted, and dangerous to every single one of the rest of us, as dangerous as Lyndon Johnson or (yes, perhaps this is no time to say it but it was true) Bobby Kennedy before he was shot or General Hershey or J. Edgar Hoover. They are dangerous to every one of us precisely because they are at this very moment playing with fire, I mean insurrection, when they don't have the slightest idea how to control it or what it means or even that they are exacerbating the probability that a great many of us, certainly including them, are going to experience disruptions in our lives from which we may never recover, which we may not even survive.

The shooting of Kennedy last nite was something in the way of a final straw for me. I can see the great storms coming, but at this point I've given up hope on finding any sort of even temporarily pacifying solution. McCarthy is almost certainly out of the Democratic running for the presidency. Humphrey will most probably run against Nixon, & the latter will almost certainly win. Whatever else happens, I'm thru combing magazines and papers and pamphlets and what not in that vain effort to figure out what is going on in all those regions of darkness around. Fuck 'em all, squares on both sides. I am the only complete man in the industry. I'm going to write as much as I can, this is what I want to do, take you on a guided tour of my Mainline, trying to make the frescoes imprinted on my own skull's inner walls as comprehensible to you as possible, with as little oldtime speedflight wordsperm bullshit, to create at last and for once for me a real old-time *book,* which is its own world and simultaneously represents my own inner world to as high a degree of satisfaction as I can give myself, although the form is jumbled and random and flawed and excessive and self-indulgent, yes, at least at last to make my soul soil comprehensible & truly personal a splash and splatter between duration of intermittent straight statement maybe I can attain what I sense budding here & get real expression to radiate from these white and empty faces for once this summer if never another time fore or aft.

from Part 1 (Prologue), Chapter 1
Previously Unpublished, 1968

A Quick Trip Through My Adolescence

Growing up with ease and comfort, but *fast,* about as fast as you could imagine short of some primitive tribe's brutal confirmation, using LSD as a rite of passage like you're supposed to be able to use the army, things sometimes get a bit complicated. Brain befogged in the halls of wisdom, Elements of Civilized Communication hammered home on chains of bleary-eyed mornings by mechanical-minded profs with a mania for grammar and gentle lady Grade Eleven romanticists who believe in youth and poetry and tearing out some proof of basic competence from each of their pupils for one furious, feverish month before disembarking with them for isles of Hawthorne and Longfellow and tender hothouse flowerings of student poem and story. Which for me was a snap, but I was still eternally hung up. Desperately I wanted my writing not to ring true, because if it rang true it was adolescent and that was seven leagues below hack. Rare flashes of insight all but lost in python coils of muscular, crepuscular verbiage, but how those clumsy image-clusters would zing like crystal arrows straight and true from my heroic pinnacles to stand all smooth and apple-cheeked and rustless on the page, grinning there in total imbecilic self-confidence like Disney archetypes, cute piglike little Fans spawned by Hercules galoots slopping sperm into backseat blondes who once upon a springtime's incognito wailed like saxophone sirens and stole their future husband slaves away from Elysium's prom/game whirl, drawing them to bedroom corners where they spread themselves in musky lust of joy-blundering boys finally entering that frothy twilight world where slow rivers of a delicious stench gushed and groaned outpouring from underground grottoes holding the sacred mystery of all those years, all o'erhung with tangles of soft brown brush, an ecstatic raving jungle whose interior we plumbed coming some when each of us to learn it bit by bit as we plunged eyes or hands or finally cocks in from so many afternoons, went foraging in the thighs and wombs and brought back sizzling jewels and smoky dreams to give our art some shape and ballast, for that was how it always was: I'd seldom start a writing session without a spiritual recharge from my secret Grove Press muses beforehand, some mad laughter or an apocalyptic tantrum and then *to work!,* wham, bam, slashing away at my typewriter until occasionally a great clot of keys would become hopelessly entangled, would refuse to untwist and fall back into their berths from the action of my whiplash fingertips and my energy would explode in fists pounding on the frame of the machine, which bore up admirably under the frenzies of the years—I'd write for love, with an artificial energy that betrayed all of puppy love's sickly fatigue, each day at least one outpouring of confusion and desire and violence, and then I'd shove it in the drawer with all the others, and then perhaps I'd drag my weary satisfaction to the bathroom, snatching a stray magazine along the way in hopes of encountering some slim filly squatting palms-to-chest in a girdle advertisement, and once inside I'd lock the door, tear down my pants, turn half around and lift the toilet's lid, finally to sit myself down on my throne and commence jacking off triumphantly, one hand clenched around my cock while the other mauled the open arm's-length magazine's curl of pages folded back and my eyes jerked up and down to my left hand's rhythm between that nameless postpubescent model's Sears catalog–wholesome moue and her primly shielded boyish chest, down her pale arms to where her unattainable thighs were suffocating for me within that ugly girdle's prism, locked away like distant record bins for all the times I came and for all my quick-breathed supplications, so my eyes would roll then down her usually lithe and luscious legs if such were possible, that is, if they weren't folded under her leaving only squashed-out calves and slimlined thighs in view, and hitting bottom I'd let my vision lick her person in ascent once more, clicking into each strap to dig wildly at its impregnable wall.

A life without complications: no lover to be responsible to between times, just annals of sperm sagas set down on toilet paper or Kleenex or spit straight from my pendulous rod into the void, no formulations for the future except fantasies where I tramped the sloping sidewalks of North Beach or Greenwich Village a poet madman king in dada-colored castoff rags, no concept of writing as anything but a sacred squawking Aztec exorcism, no satisfactory concept of existence not bequeathed by mad bums, junkies, perverts, gray old "existential" misanthropes, or charlatans in scriptures almost memorized, no need for movement or action or social hangups apart from the daily high school gauntlet because home was a dizzy hive glutted with books and records and reams of type-jammed paper, once past living room skirmishes with an oldtime Bible mother declaiming her ailments, and on weekends there was the Kingdom Hall for me to stew in, Friday nights and Sunday nights pressure-cooking my torpid, squandered rage, while Saturday was swallowed by TV and long lawn-wallowings the motley number of us in the neighborhood's combined comic book collections until at last Great God CHICKS and a series of juicy Witness-slut girlfriends for easing adolescent virility hangups with long luscious afternoons in grass and hammocks and old couches in the shady patios behind their parents' houses where we'd lie wrapped around each other like two clumsy cubs but man it felt better than any drugtrip I've ever had and a good deal of the sex since because our delight was unalloyed and ignorant, gleefully experimental like pygmies as I'd try to force my tongue down her throat and feel her nails scuffing semisuccessful attempts to claw my back like in the movies, and all those ball-breaking unrelieved erections, countless hernias as the heavy panting petting stretched on and on across the hours two animalistic adolescents obsessively embracing grinding cloth-walled groins together sliding calves in leglocks (her bare soft pink calves making my balls burn so I wanted to grab her leg and take a bite) Frenching fanatically in dusky backseats late-nite rooftops green Saturday gardens we mauled and tugged and tore at each other's flesh hungry pubescents frantic for orgasm-surrogates, because they would never touch my cock with their hands and had fucked no more than I. A succession of Lindas with ratted hair formed a healthy counterpoint to the rabid scrawl-sessions and hours of yellow-visaged broodings cloistered in my stuffy lair where I dreamed of Love long insomniac nights painting raga-choirs of black-mascara'd hip-avant goddesses dressed in motley streaming rags all across my ceiling, because I knew that somewhere (Greenwich Village, my city in the sky) there lounged lovely sidewalksfull of strange sleek dementedly beautiful females capable of appreciating my holy madness and the scriptures it spewed. Little did I dream I'd fall in love with Gina, a counterfoil from the most hated hives of the patriotic masscult middle class, the only chick who came forth to challenge my Madman hype. No, I didn't know myself, but I knew my textbooks well, and so continued brooding lonely toward the day I'd meet my Madwoman, languishing in my room and rereading Patchen's *The Journal of Albion Moonlight* wishing mad planetoids and torn rhinoceroses would rain from *my* sky, waiting for apocalypse or high-school graduation, when I would forsake my solitude and journey Eastward, a mad notebook pilgrim seeking the land of pot and street poets, where my Rimbaudian light would be appreciated.

And when in my junior year I finally poked my fuzzy snout and small pink eyes from my burrow, it really didn't mean much, although my whole façade made a 360-degree retrack—having braved and transcended the cold fires of existential nihilism, I was ready now to be everybody's hyperstimulated hypergregarious Enfant Terrible Guru, grinning big and brassy as a po' Nigger who's just inherited a million bucks and can start edging other folks' feet into the cakewalks of his own ragtime soul. Now that the puberty-ovens of solitary penance had been served, I was ready to set the Sucker world (heads, college professors, Aware students, and dilettante esthetes) on its ear. Granted, I started at the very top of the San Diego totem, by God, with college hipster parties at which I was always the youngest one, and yes indeed I held my own admirably, being somewhat new to alcohol though not to pot—joyfully drunk, astoundingly gregarious after a couple of warm-up glasses of wine, I circulated from one group to another spouting spontaneous poetry and impressing the pop-eyed hell out of all of them, always doing things like raising wine bottles over my head and saying, "Ah, the golden flowing river of sunshine joy!" giant-smiling, ecstatic, like the electric disciples of that Love-and-Joy politic destined to flourish three years later, for Christ's sake! But I guess I was just ahead of my time because I got hit more than once with snarls like the one from a really Beat (I know she wasn't straight because she had straight extra-long hair, wire-rim glasses, sandals, and esoteric duds) chick sitting near me on the night of the golden sunshine outburst, who responded: "Cool it, man!"

But of course I didn't cool it, I never cooled it, because alcohol always turned me into a Zen lunatic. It was really all involuntary, I was just hip from the core of my sixteen-year-old soul to the jigsaw-jumping charge of joyous jive that vibrated around me as I moved from room to room flashing teeth in that nonstop smile and commanding all to recognize me by the gleam of archangelic enlightenment blazing in my eye as I ad-libbed motley flatulent streams of "poetry," so that more than one 5-foot-7 tweedsheathed bearded philosophy major was seen to let fall his mask of haughty cynicism during one of my poetic reveries, the mask replaced on his countenance by a slowly spreading expression of dreamy, bemused warmth. The schmucks. One of them tried to match me one night by shooting some spontaneous poeticisings back, but I nailed the sonofabitch to the wall: he had stolen it, nuance for cadence, off a Dylan Thomas record.

But that look they would get on their faces when I'd shift into my routine! It's that stupid expression which signifies that its wearer has suddenly been reminded of one of the most precious, uncontaminated, uplifting areas of existence, the kind of expression you see on people when they're holding a puppy in their hands which is almost too cute to look at, although in this case the response was never that peculiar vocalism, equal parts verbal vomit, drool, and mucus, which people seem to reserve exclusively for little animals and babies. That is not to say that it shouldn't have been, however. I was being cute in much the same way that a dog or a baby is cute, taking people on insubstantial little trips, mostly centered around things of nature like rivers of the sun's highways, electric gray clouds, black-browned thunderskies raining soot and the like, trips awakening in them sensations of innocence and the "purity" of esthetically beautiful imagery which, like much of my writing then, wasn't about a damn thing.

I was, after all, something new in their experience—about all that happened at these parties was that the males made with a lot of intellectual talk in hopes that the chicks would be so impressed with the quality of their minds that they'd wanna ball them that very night. A few made good that way but on the whole the folks just didn't seem cheerful or eased-up enough even when they were full of booze to warrant any kind of sweeping generalizations, other than that just about everybody (me included, natch) seemed to be polishing up some kind of routine. Lots of beard-strokers and lots of people with the exact same high nasal way of articulating. I always used to see Ben Warston there with his perennial trappings—a dollar gallon of red wine in one hand, his everlasting suede jacket, and a tough little high school chick two-thirds his age, generally some floozie he'd pick up as she was hitchhiking to Jack in the Box or something—as a semiliterate grass-smoking dropout, he was set up straight to take those liberals and artsies for all they were worth. He'd read enough Henry Miller and could drop enough philosophers' names to intimidate the living hell out of the whole natty bunch when he showed up half-stoned with that sardonic smile on his face. The result was that he got drunk free on the best stuff every weekend.

Most of the others didn't have it so cushy. I recall one exceedingly esoteric cat with beard sitting straddle-legged on a chair in front of the heater, drinking beer incessantly and eyeing almost everyone, especially the women, with smoldering suspicion until at 4 A.M., satisfied I suppose that he'd beat all of 'em that counted, he dropped his last bottle and slumped dead, his chin thudding on the top rim of the chair's back. *His* routine. I wonder if it ever got him laid.

The only other thing they did at those hip-cool get-togethers was dance. Of course, there were always one or two profs and their wives, discoursing learnedly over precise mixed drinks, making the kids feel simultaneously nervous at the presence of a great mind that all the chicks thought was sexy because of his waxed mustache, and at the same time important because he'd come to *their* party instead of one with other learned faculty members where he would've been able to discourse even more learnedly. As for the professors themselves, the vast majority that I encountered then and later who really tried to "get down to where the students live" came across almost to a man as essentially sheepish figures, struggling to assert themselves among the young generation with wooden attempts at "coolness," dropping all the latest hip/New Left clichés, coming on strong about drugs and "deconditioning" when they really detested them, making little jokes in whatever fashion was current. Misfits. The dazed, socially atrophied little college professor caught up helplessly in a hated lover of a dream in which he scoffs at the cliché identity of cloistered myopia even as he lives it to the hilt, dropping into classrooms to rattle off the rote of years, spilling facts like tickertape, then scurrying back from the bell to his office, where he might be seen on any day of the week thrashing about in a sea of books and papers and pamphlets and magazines, digging down toward prehistoric strata or snatching publications out of the air to keep ever up. My first semester in college I asked an English teacher of mine what he thought about a current literary movement. He had never heard of it: "Right now I'm engaged in a reinvestigation of Greek drama. I never read anything less than 30 years old, because you can't tell what's of value that's being written today, and anyway there are too many other things."

I asked him where he found the time to pursue his own studies as heavily as he seemed to and still grade papers, keep up with the news, read magazines, and all that.

"Oh, papers don't bother me—haven't you noticed how few written assignments I've given in this class? It's not necessary if you read the words in the textbook and take notes on my lectures and our class discussions. I find plenty of time to study literature—in fact, it's all I do. I keep up with the news in a marginal way—I just don't care about it enough to do more than that. And magazines and all that sort of thing . . . do *you* read magazines?"

Yes, I said, all the time.

That seemed to put him out a little bit. He said that magazines were a waste of my time if I wanted to be a writer, that I should be studying literature "even if you just read through the Great Books of the Western World as you'd read any trivial book . . . because you know that no matter how many classes in literature you take, it won't mean a damn thing. You've got to educate yourself or you'll end up just like all these other know-nothings with degrees."

I thought longingly of my weekly comic book, *Life,* of my always irresistible *Time* and *Newsweek* which I hated and read with some mad compulsion almost weekly, of my twice-a-month *Beat* and my monthly *Hit Parader,* both rock 'n' roll rags and both absolutely essential, I thought of the weekly hippie papers which were my life's blood at the time, the *East Village Other,* the L.A. *Free Press,* and the San Francisco *Oracle,* and finally I saw my supreme favorite among all the periodicals I lived by, *The National Close-Up,* the most gutbucket proletarian yellow sheet I've ever read, the belovedly recalled cover of the first issue of it that I ever bought, one night when I was stoned on Romilar and wine and Benzedrine, that ugly red tabloid banner split-second exploding like a blinding flashbulb before my mind's eye:

INSANE VIRGIN MURDERS TO "HAVE SEX WITH GOD"

"Nothing personal," she sez

and below that:

MARIJUANA IN THE PENTAGON!

But of course he was right—you *can't* fuck around with a lot of jive and madness and expect to get a first-rate education. I asked him if his social contacts didn't suffer by his marriage to literature.

"Of course they do, in fact they've practically become nil. But, I don't know, I don't really miss them."

I'd see him in his office occasionally, days I happened by, bent over his desk, furiously twisting back and forth, pen in hand, paperback on his right and gilt-flecked old tome his left, notebook in the center, the atmosphere therein vibrating like that in the Elysian orgone box dreamed of by smokers of de Quincey and Burroughs. I never saw him in the halls but he was rushing between his two stations, bent forward by the propulsion of his peculiar distracted intensity, and should we meet he never failed to chide me for the omnipresent tabloids, comic books, "undergrounds," and rock mags under my arms, which never failed to give me a twinge of guilt. It had not yet occurred to me on a conscious level that in reading slick journalism, hippie pulp, and obscenely amusing articles like "Insane Virgin Murders to Have Sex with God" I was preparing just as surely for a literary life quite different from that of the days when a young writer first practiced writing short stories in the style of Hemingway, then Faulkner, then Fitzgerald, etc. etc. etc., in the meantime reading the classics for background. I was just beginning to realize that I was coming up in the dawning days of a new era when literature would turn to toilet paper, daily news would become surrealistic, and artists of all stripes everywhere would feel blissfully free to cut themselves loose from their heritage, or even not learn that heritage, because there was more relevance to be found in the splashy trash of the popular press, in the open-throated yawps and mechanical twangs of rock 'n' roll, in the chaotic inner jungles which all of us hurled ourselves into with every type of drug imaginable; and engaging in all this willful and apparently self-destructive abuse to the sensibilities for the purpose of finding each of us for ourselves the raw endlessly disguised essence which had to be sought outside all schools, methods, social mechanisms, and popular self-help devices. In other words, we had to fuck up before we could stand up, and nothing was more relevant than the apparently irrelevant, and nothing less relevant than the Eternal Verities enclosing this 2,000-year-old consciousness like a box. The consciousness of all of this was a vague cloud distantly forming then, but I followed my as-yet-masked muse even so, by reading trashy tabloids instead of enduring literature, and spending much more time under my headphones filling my shimmying soul with rock 'n' roll than I spent reading anything, by smoking grass and attending acid as a guidance counselor, by writing eight to twelve hours in a row on innumerable allnite binges, piling up reams of raving bullshit but honing my talents all the time and publishing this straight-ahead improvisatory style month after month, until at last I began to speak in a Voice almost my own, to gain effortlessly a progressive mastery of words, tossing off adolescent woodshed epiphanies in white-hot eruptions of inspiration, even though the influence of William Burroughs still shows. I suppose I'm not a truly dedicated artist, whatever that is, and I don't want to be. I'll probably never produce a masterpiece, but so what? I feel I have a Sound aborning, which is my own, and that Sound if erratic is still my greatest pride, because I would rather write like a dancer shaking my ass to boogaloo inside my head, and perhaps reach only readers who like to use books to shake their asses, than to be or write for the man cloistered in a closet somewhere reading Aeschylus while this stupefying world careens crazily past his waxy windows toward its last raving sooty feedback pirouette.

Part 1 (Prologue), Chapter 4
Previously Unpublished, 1968

from The Great El Cajon Race Riot and Two Friday Night Parties

I don't know what kind of sociopsychological implications I was looking for, but they weren't there. It was merely another night at the Hell's Angels', where cruelty and violence and the degradation of women is taken for granted. Several people were markedly bored. It *was* boring, in a way. No, not boring—it seemed almost as if time had come to a stop. Despite the rising and falling intermittent hubbub of conversations, there seemed to be a peculiar kind of silence in the air that made itself felt like a heavy purple blanket, a thick undersea atmosphere in which all motion was slowed in *effect* though not in sight . . . in every part of the room, every aspect of the surroundings, all my perceptions were suffused with a strange, almost tangible stillness. But perhaps it is time to begin at the beginning.

It was a dull Friday evening in early March. Gina had a play rehearsal at school immediately after dinner, so I rode up with her, intending to listen to a record I'd seen in the Listening Library a few days before called *The Sounds of Harlem.* Unfortunately I had forgotten that the library was closed on Friday nights, so I spent the time watching the play rehearsal, although I had already seen it three times. After a few minutes I slipped out for a moment and took three Libriums at the water fountain. The drama kids invited us to a party afterwards, and my boredom-and-Librium-deadened heart lifted at the pleasant expectation that perhaps I'd be able to do a little drinking.

It was quite a party. Our thoughtful hostess had provided a wonderful selection of Coke & 7-Up, to go with our cake, and after an old war movie starring Richard Widmark in the Casbah we played charades. Ah, these drama people, how they love to perform. The Librium just kept dragging on and the boredom began to turn into a kind of indiscriminate lull. I was starting to feel somewhat like a cross between a mushroom and a toad sedated into a clammy haze, so finally I just reached into my shirt pocket and, against my better judgment (since I knew that group scenes and speed just don't mix for me), popped the single benny I'd been saving for the morrow's projected Norwich stone into my mouth. A few minutes later the toady lull had turned to a state of mild nervous alertness. The charades began to irritate me. Excusing myself to make the head, I pushed in the lock on the door and turned on the faucet to drown out the squeak of hinges as I opened the medicine cabinet to look for likely pills in prescription vials. The old babe had a large jar of Darvon! I scooped out a dozen or so and was pleasantly surprised to find two solitary, peculiar-colored capsules—barbituates! I had never seen pills that looked like this before, but somehow you just know these things.

After the party, Gina took me home and I walked in to find all my friends slumped in their usual non-high poses of dejected boredom. That benny still had me kind of nervous, so I made it to a darkened corner and lay back in an old chair, hoping for no hasslement or bullshit from anyone, staring dully into the dark space behind the couch, too speeded to sleep or read but not nearly speeded enough to write, in a kind of depression which made me decide against using any of the Darvons or barbituates, fidgeting slightly and dreaming of a bottle of vodka.

Suddenly Silly Willy burst thru the front door in a shortie Japanese-type bathrobe, eyes gleaming, and said, "Hey, you fuckers! How-would-jew-like-to-rip-yerselves-off A NICE JUICY FUCK TONIGHT?"

Mutt immediately perked up. "What?"

"We got a broad over here and she's fuckin' with *every*body, man! I already got mine, an' some o' the guys are goin' *twice!*"

I didn't particularly relish the idea of being something like sixteenth man in line at an Angel gang bang, and even if I *were* that flipped-out and horny, the Benzedrine I'd taken earlier would have made it pretty near impossible for me to partake in the festivities anyway. However, it didn't take much perceptivity to know that Willy was drunk, well-soused, and anyway I wanted to observe one of these celebrated good-time-slop Angel gang bangs for once, so I stood up saying "Hey man, can I get in on this too?" figuring that in all the confusion nobody would notice that I'd missed my turn in line to go in the kitchen and tank up.

"*Sure,*" yelled Willy, "Come one, come all!" Mutt was already practically out the door.

Outside, hurrying down the rutty road in the dark, Willy explained the situation. "We got this broad over here, man, an' she's jus' puttin' out for everybody. . . . She'll do anything you want but most ever'-body's gettin' blow jobs now, cause that ole cunt gits kinda *nasty,* y'know, after it's had about five guys pumpin' it right in a row. . . . Course, if you really wanna git *nasty.* . . ." In my mind I pictured some dumb scroungy mama laying in the middle of the floor scratching the bugs out of her hair with a distracted look in her eyes while some big greasy hog of an Angel lay on top of her whumping and grunting toward his impatiently-pushed-for Come, the rest of the club lined up behind with their trousers partly pulled down and their cocks hanging, waiting like a line of kids outside the Saturday afternoon box office of a theater. When we got up to the door Willy whirled around suddenly and asked me, neither overly serious nor laughing, but matter-of-factly as a doorman at some semiexclusive club, "By the way, just one thing: are you eighteen?"

"Sure, I'm eighteen."

"Okay." And I followed him in. I glanced around for a moment, wondering where the big attraction was. Suddenly I saw it, there in a corner, a chunky slit-eyed aging (21 or so) Juvenile Delinquent type sitting at the end of the couch, with a naked girl crouched in front of him, huddled on the floor and up against his legs, her tangled hair the only part of her head that was visible as her face was jammed down into his lap, sucking his cock. I looked up at the guy she was servicing again. His face held no expression at all, gave no sign of feeling or emotion, except for the tight-lipped scowling half-sneer so many of these Junior Hoodlum type guys affect in exact carbon copy of each other.

Looking back around the room, I saw most of the Dago Angels slumped in drunken repose, occasionally mumbling at each other or croaking hoarsely at someone across the room. Nobody seemed to be asleep, but everybody looked pretty drunk. On the second couch in the room sat T. R., swilling Colt 45 and raving drunkenly at various people around the room, sometimes at no one in particular, his volume rising and falling from ragged roar to throaty alcoholic muttering. About half of what he said was intelligible; the rest was lost in animal drunken growls and various inchoate noises from his booze-thickened vocal chords. He was certainly talkative tonight. His woman Charlotte hovered erratically round him, a strange figure of a female in Angel denim "colors" and a head of hair that was incredibly straggly even for one of the mamas, sticking out in weird jagged tangles like black steelywires. Somehow her whole appearance reminded me of Archy's alley cat Mehitabel,[1] or some other classic straggly black alley cat of New York slums. Turning to Willy, I said, "Say, man, is there any booze left?"

"Nah," he laughs, eyes twinkling like Santa Claus, beaming with expansive benevolent beer-joviality, "we drank it all up, 'cep' ol' T. R. there's got his private stash o' Colt in the kitchen. . . . I don't think he's got but a coupler three cans left, butcha kin ask 'im anyway . . ."

I decided against that, looking around for a place to sit. Except for

[1] The cockroach Archy and the alley cat Mehitabel were created in the light verse of New York newspaper columnist and humorist Don Marquis (1878–1937). These characters then appeared in the 1954 album *Archy and Mehitabel,* songs written by Joe Kleinsinger and Joe Darion and sung by Carol Channing and former silent-movie comedian Eddie Bracken. That album became the basis for *Shinbone Alley,* a 1957 Broadway musical written by Mel Brooks, which in turn led to the obscure 1970 animated Hollywood film *Archy and Mehitabel,* by English animator John David Wilson.

the floor, the only place was a space of couch at T. R.'s left side. With only a slight inner tremor of nervous hesitation, I walked over and sat down there, thinking that even if T. R. *should* flip out in drunken dinosaur rage and start to rend me limb from limb, the others would intercede and save me.

Superficially, though, I absorbed it all like a true pop journalist, open-mouthed mumble-moaning "Wow, wow, wow" over and over, all I could say eyes riveted to the cringing naked girl who blew sixteen of them that night her face a waxy mix of blood and pus and tears and come. No, I never flinched, I watched them all thru Benzedrine and the peripatetic joint that circled the room as she moaned in the center of the floor like the ruined hub of this crazily turning wheel the joint passed from Willy to Bob to Sammy to Funky to Charlotte to T. R. to me to the two nameless stony postadolescent hoods with reptilian faces who sat the far couch slowly chewing their gum with slit-eyes unblinking never widening as they played their cool gangster mannikinisms to the frozen hilt unmoving save when the Mex snapped his fingers and pointed one slow index finger at his crotch signaling the softly sobbing by-now-dazed victim that it was his turn, she must do all for he is only a rock with a cold vicarious half-registered orgasm, she crawls over undoes his pants unzips his fly pushes a dumb half-sleeping hand into his BVD's extracting a limp rubbery tube on which she lays her face her head starts bobbing barely up-down zombielike as I look around and see Bob and Willy shooting the shit, Sammy the hardworked Angel mama sprawled splay-legged against a wall staring dishwater-eyed at absolutely nothing, Funky on the floor head back against the wall contemplating dark blue space in ceiling shadows of an adjacent room a slightly melancholy look on his face, T. R. growling and muttering in unintelligible drunken confusion half-filled can of Colt 45 tilting from his left hand at a precarious angle while his seldom-glimpsed eyes perhaps roll back behind his omnipresent impenetrable sunglasses and he never registers his old lady Charlotte's concentrated attempts to bring some life into his cock as she kneels on the floor in front of him hair a straggly mass that flashes me again of Archy's Mehitabel and sucks on his cock gargling vain half-coherent imprecations out of the side of her mouth up at him while the record player blares the same records again and again a collection of old Motown hits and an Otis Redding album. Otis is moaning "I've been loving you a little too long" as I look back to where the sobbing girl is still working on the Mex who is beginning to get pissed off saying "What kinda half-ass creep job is this" and T. R. comes out of his stupor momentarily saying "Clout that bitch upside the head, mothafucka, tell 'er she better give you some proper fuckin' head or I'm 'on make damn straight she ain't alive to see the sun come up" and the Mex replies "Ahhh she no good, just fuckin' tease ain't even give half-ass try" and T. R. lashes out suddenly with his booted foot kicking the girl in the cunt, once, twice, back of the neck, raving at her in heavy medium-tempoed slurred anger of advanced intoxication "I said give that boy some *head* mothafucka an' do it right or you ain't gonna live long!" She sobs out something unintelligible with the Mex's cock still in her mouth. T. R. rises suddenly, unsteady, tottering, stumbles over to her, leans, yanks her hair savagely pulling her head out of the Mex's lap, lifts his boot high and brings it down hard in her face, hard enough to bruise and pain but not so hard she can't go back to sucking cocks, he gives her another kick, the base of the spine, she hardly makes a sound, this has been going on for several hours now after all. . . . T. R. drops her head, she returns to the Mex's lap, T. R. lumbers back to his seat, Charlotte reaching immediately for his fly, I hear Otis crying and whining through the haze which by now has turned to static, the joint is passed to me once again, I inhale and hand it to the Mex who as before merely accepts it without even acknowledging my presence, holding my breath I float out for a moment, losing track of place and time and sense, fade back in to banal telegraphy of Bob's and Willy's chitchat, open my eyes and look in the opposite direction from the girl and the Mex, Sammy has gone to sleep, Bob strokes his mustache as he banters with Willy: "Yeah, she was pretty good, took her a little while to get goin' but at the end she was all there good and solid."—It took forty-five minutes of steady sucking for this girl to make Bob come. Now in his corner Funky is engrossed in a crossword puzzle book, his gnarled pencil making soft scratching noises in the little boxes, T. R. is mumbling to himself a subdued raving, head fallen back against the wall, Colt .45 can on its side by his side and around it a big dun-colored smear on the couch, Charlotte sits at his feet on the floor with her hands resting in her lap, head wobbling slightly, a dazed abstracted look in her eyes, the Mex's junior-gangster buddy sits just as he sat when I first came in, epitome of coolness, slit-eyes unreadable, hands folded in his lap, mouth at rest in a prim shuttered line which could with utmost simplicity convert to a sneer but never does, a true man of stone, I look back across the room and though those on the other end have not changed from when I last regarded them I now catch something I never noticed before, a tattered vintage copy of *Uncle Scrooge* from my collection lying open on the carpet, so random fates of real life make this literary symbology complete by their cynical grace, and I've taken the whole scene in at last, nothing more to add.

from Part 2, Chapter 12
Previously Unpublished, 1967–8

\\\ ///

HYPES AND HEROICS

/// \\\

The MC5: *Kick Out the Jams*

Whoever thought when that dirty little quickie *Wild in the Streets* came out that it would leave such an imprint on the culture? First the Doors (who were always headed in that direction anyway) grinding out that famous "They-got-the-guns-but-we-got-the-numbers" march for the troops out there in Teenland, and now this sweaty aggregation. Clearly this notion of violent, total youth revolution and takeover is an idea whose time has come—which speaks not well for the idea but ill for the time.

About a month ago the MC5 received a cover article in *Rolling Stone* proclaiming them the New Sensation, a group to break all barriers, kick out all jams, "total energy thing," etc. etc. etc. Never mind that they came on like a bunch of sixteen-year-old punks on a meth power trip—these boys, so the line ran, could play their guitars like John Coltrane and Pharoah Sanders played sax!

Well, the album is out now and we can all judge for ourselves. For my money they come on more like Blue Cheer than Trane and Sanders, but then my money has already gone for a copy of this ridiculous, overbearing, pretentious album, and maybe that's the idea, isn't it?

The set, recorded live, starts out with an introduction by John Sinclair, "Minister of Information" for the "White Panthers," if you can dig that. The speech itself stands midway between *Wild in the Streets* and Arthur Brown. The song that follows it is anticlimactic. Musically the group is intentionally crude and aggressively raw. Which can make for powerful music except when it is used to conceal a paucity of ideas, as it is here. Most of the songs are barely distinguishable from each other in their primitive two-chord structures. You've heard all this before from such notables as the Seeds, Blue Cheer, Question Mark and the Mysterians, and the Kingsmen. The difference here, the difference which will sell several hundred thousand copies of this album, is in the hype, the thick overlay of teenage-revolution and total-energy-thing which conceals these scrapyard vistas of clichés and ugly noise.

"Kick Out the Jams" sounds like Barrett Strong's "Money" as recorded by the Kingsmen. The lead on "Come Together" is stolen note-for-note from the Who's "I Can See for Miles." "I Want You Right Now" sounds *exactly* (down to the lyrics) like a song called "I Want You" by the Troggs, a British group who came on with a similar, sex-and-raw-sound image a couple of years ago (remember "Wild Thing"?) and promptly disappeared into oblivion, where I imagine they are laughing at the MC5.

Rolling Stone, April 5, 1969

Charlie Haden: *Liberation Music Orchestra*

Charlie Haden is one of the most hypnotically inventive bassists in contemporary jazz. Maturing in Ornette Coleman's revolutionary quartet of the early Sixties, he revealed early (in pieces like "Lonely Woman") highly developed improvisational abilities and a bent for strange, moving harmonies. Now he has formed his own group for the purpose of presenting his furiously humanistic musical polemics to the world. The results are not the most innovative sides to emerge from the new jazz, but are certainly among the most earthy and impassioned.

Too many of this decade's jazz pathfinders are so intent upon cutting across all barriers to break on through to the other side that they've forgotten to play with their *hearts* as well as their fingers, minds, and nervous systems. This record, with its recurrent mournful Spanish sonorities and sudden interludes of pure piercing song, should do much to balance the situation. The songs are all anthems of various revolutions past and present; they range from Bertolt Brecht's "Song of the United Front" to "Los Quatros Generales" (a fiery Andalusian folk anthem from the Spanish Civil War) to Ornette's starkly beautiful "War Orphans." Whatever one may think of the vaguely defined politics and somewhat labored New Leftist atmosphere of the undertaking, the music all speaks for itself as a raw multivoiced cry for the ever-distant prize of true freedom.

The musicians include some of the new jazz's most eloquent and innovative voices: Don Cherry, Mike Mantler, Roswell Rudd, and Gato Barbieri, who plays the most searingly pure tenor saxophone that I have heard in some time, as pregnant with consuming love and painfully articulate suffering as Charles Mingus's best work. But all involved comport themselves with single-minded discipline and that impassioned restraint whose subtlety and control makes a musical soul-baring that much more convincing. Like Pharoah Sanders' *Karma,* this record suggests a new maturity in the camps of the jazz avant-garde, a weathered internalization of all reckless experiments which allows the artists to submit the revelations encountered out on all those limbs to clearly defined and relatively directed musical purposes. Thus, the relatively familiar and unadventurous framework of brooding flamenco, rather than being a hackneyed musical strait-jacket stifling woolly ramblers, proves a firm foundation for exalted, heart-swelling statements by turns lyrical and dissonant. Haden's bass work is especially superb, throbbing and droning with a restless yet understated intensity expressing perfectly the pulsebeat of lives like those in the Spanish Resistance, lived in eternal fear and the fiercely nurtured strength of brave dreams. The arrangements by Carla Bley are miracles of dynamics, rising and falling in volume and velocity and the awe-inspiring balance of collective ensembles improvising freely through swellings and contractions of individual voices entering and leaving the mysterious swirling circle of simultaneous songs as diverse as the number of performers yet never lacking the kind of transporting telepathic unity that makes this multiplicity of musical lines such a far cry from the chaos of the charlatans in other sections of the avant-garde hiding under the mantle of these geniuses.

Rolling Stone, February 21, 1970

Canned Heat: *The New Age*

Hey kids and bluesbusterbrowns of all ages, guess who's back? No, not the Plaster Casters Blues Band—it's Canned Heat! The originators of Boogie in the flesh! And it sure is refreshing to see 'em too, what with all these jive-ass MOR pseud-dudes like John Lee Hooker ripping off their great primal riffs and milking 'em dry.

How did we love Canned Heat? Let's count the ways. We loved 'em because they scooped out a whole new wrinkle in the monotone mazurka; it wasn't their fault that a whole generation of ten zillion bands took and ran it into the ground *sans finesse* after Canned Heat had run it into the ground so damned good themselves. We loved 'em because they've always held the record for Longest Single Boogie Preserved on Wax: "Refried Boogie" from *Livin' the Blues* was forty-plus minutes of real raunch froth perfect for parties or car stereos, especially if they got ripped off—and a lot of it was even actually listenable. We loved 'em because Henry Vestine was an incredible, scorching motherfucker of a guitarist, knocking you through the wall. And we loved 'em because Bobby Bear was so damned weird you could abide his every excess.

But Canned Heat disappeared from the sets for a while there, just sorta flapped up and boogied into the zone and what was really sad was that nobody missed 'em. Even though they were always real fine journeymen, they never made a *wholly and entirely* good album, of course, but they've consistently had their moments. And *The New Age*, which of course is no new age at all, has just as many of 'em as any of the others. There's "Keep It Clean," a happy highho funk churn like unto their cover of Wilbert Harrison's "Let's Work Together," which means it could very well be hitbound. There's "Rock 'n' Roll Music," Bear Hite's obligatortilla in deference to the traditions, his utter lack of imagination, and all that. He's been listening to some old New Orleans r&b this time, so it's OK even if he does still sing like a scalped guppy.

"Framed" is just a reprise in new drag of their classic about being busted in Denver that was on *Boogie with Canned Heat,* and that was just a new drag on old Bo Diddley and "Jailbait" riffs. "Election Blues" is the required slow blues chest retch. "So Long Wrong" is one more lowdown blackboned gutgrok funk-lurking album closer boogie just like lotsa their other yester highlights. Vestine still knows how to play so's to make you feel like ringworms are St. Vitusing in your heartburn, and Hite scrapes your intestines widdat bass good as Mole Taylor ever did. "Lookin' for My Rainbow" even has Clara Ward and her jive bombers just for a tintype taste of authenticity, but it's boring as old View-Master slides and most of the rest of the songs are just some kinda nondescript clinkletybonk tibia-rattling in pursuit of yeehah countryisms so let 'em dry rot in the grooves.

Buy this album if you've gotta lotta money or don't care much what you blow your wad on, but don't pass up any of the really cosmic stuff like the Stooges for it or the shadow of Blind Lemon Jefferson will come and blow his nose on your brow every night.

Rolling Stone, June 7, 1973

Dandelions in Still Air: The Withering Away of the Beatles

Name me one Sixties superstar who hasn't become a zombie. Dylan doesn't count, because he's been revivified, at least in terms of being a hot contender, by *Blood on the Tracks.* And Lou Reed is a professional zombie who can cackle in the grooves instead of up his sleeve. But Mick Jagger, Joe Cocker, Steve Stills . . . they're all washed-up, moribund, self-pitying, self-parodying has-beens. And the more I thought about it, the more it seemed to me that the four splintered Beatles may well have weathered the pall and decay of the Seventies the worst.

One by one, in order of descending credibility: Paul McCartney makes lovely boutique tapes, resolute upon being as inconsequential as the Carpenters which in itself may be as much a reaction to John's opposite excesses as a simple case of vacuity. You could hardly call him burnt out—*Band on the Run* was, in its rather vapid way, a masterful album. Muzak's finest hour. Of course he is about as committed to the notion of subject matter as Hanna-Barbera, and his cuteness can be incredibly annoying at times. If he was just a little more gutsy, he might almost be Elton John.

Lennon, as ever, seems Paul's antithesis. He'll do *anything,* reach for any cheap trick, jump on any bandwagon, to make himself look like a Significant Artist. His marriage to Yoko was culture-climbing that revealed a severe and totally unexpected inferiority complex. Of course,

John's been staying drunk a lot, making a public spectacle of himself with such shameless élan that Lou Reed is gonna have to hustle his ass or lose the crown: Kotexes on the forehead, standing on tables in nightclubs screaming "I'm John Lennon! I'm John Lennon!" disrupting the stage acts of his peers in a manner more befitting Iggy Pop or perhaps the famous Lenny Bruce–Pearl Bailey incident in Vegas.

Somehow you have to feel affection and even a curious sort of admiration for John as he engages in these escapades. In spite of the fact that they amount to a stance that might best be summed up as I Am Pathetic, Therefore I Am Charismatic (lifestyle is Art, said John and Yoko, so now he's Fatty Arbuckle, having left his Coke bottle on the train in *A Hard Day's Night*), which itself has become trite in these dunced-out and depleted times, there is a curious mangled echo of the Olden Spirit of Beatle Mischief in all this public idiocy.

His records, of course, are something else again. Paradoxically, in spite of his lurching stabs at social significance, he moves closer to Paul's mode of technically clean, spiritually piddling hackwork with each album. He sings about scars in his face on the barroom floor, but without much conviction anymore, and his instrumental surroundings are more blandly competent every time out. *Walls and Bridges* constituted a schlocky parody of the tortured artist writhing in a sterile sanitarium of his own design, and the fact that it reached Number One and spawned hit singles is disheartening in that it will certainly not encourage him to strive for anything that might be transcendent in the way that the "Mother"–"Working Class Hero" album, for all its embarrassing infantilism and freelance spite, had a certain gauche and wretched majesty.

George Harrison belongs in a daycare center for counterculture casualties, another of those children canceled not (so much?) by drugs this time but something perhaps far more insidious. His position seems to be I'm Pathetic, But I Believe in Krishna, which apparently absolves him from any position of leadership while enabling him to assume a totally preachy arrogance toward his audience which would be monumental chutzpah if it weren't coming from such a self-certified nebbish.

Ringo is beneath contempt. He used to be lovable because he was inept and knew it and turned the whole thing into a good-natured game. Now he is marketing that lameness in a slick Richard Perry–produced package, and getting hits via the stratagem, but the whole thing reeks. It is a bit as if Peter Max were designing stage sets for *Hee Haw*'s Archie Campbell.

So the moptops have ended up mopping the floor of the supermarket, which is keeping them from bankruptcy and no doubt reassuring them that they still Matter on some level, but they do not and never will again give off a glint of the magic they used to radiate with such seeming effortlessness. That magic is currently one of the hottest items in the Woolworth's where Sixties nostalgia is peddled like bric-a-brac—in spite of the *Sgt. Pepper* Broadway bomb. Elton John was characteristically shrewd in releasing a cover looking back at "Lucy in the Sky with Diamonds."

On the other hand, I am constantly hearing people say, with minor perplexity, that they can still play early Stones albums, but old Beatle records (like old Dylan records), and particularly *Sgt. Pepper*, gather dust on the shelves. As with Dylan singing about Hattie Carroll, the Beatles celebrating the explosion of Love as a Way of Life amounts now to an artifact, just as today's Heavy Statements will prove to be just about as ephemeral. Somebody told me the other night that people would still be listening to Led Zeppelin's "Stairway to Heaven" a hundred years from today, and *Sgt. Pepper* as well. He's full of shit, of course, because "Stairway to Heaven" is not for the ages in the sense that Duke Ellington, say, might be, and as previously stated there aren't that many here among us who listen to *Sgt. Pepper* even eight years after it exploded on the pop world and, as prophesied by Richard Goldstein,[2] proceeded to all but ruin the rock of the next few seasons

[2] The *New York Times* pop critic who was nearly universally reviled for being one of the few to actually pan *Sgt. Pepper.*

by making rank-and-file musical artisans even more self-conscious and pretentious than dope already had.

The center of any pop aesthetic has even less chance of holding than the last administration of this country had. Rock 'n' roll will *not* necessarily stand; currently it seems to be jaywalking on its knees. But maybe that's a good reason to dig out all those musty Beatles albums and see if we perhaps can find in them, if not the bouncy mysticism that once seemed our staff of life, at least a good time. And perhaps in doing this we can discover the roots of the four separate styles of disintegration we're currently witnessing.

I have this theory, which has gotten me into minor fracases on a couple of occasions, that the Beatles' initial explosion was intimately tied up with the assassination of President John F. Kennedy. In fact, I have been known to say that JFK's killing was a *good* thing, historically speaking. A man died in an ugly fashion, he happened to be a man that people who didn't know anything about corporate politics considered the leader of the "free world," it was a national tragedy, etc. But on another level it was good because it opened a lot of things up. When Kennedy was in office we were living in a national dream world, the New Frontier as panacea, the illusion of unity. Underneath it all things were just as shitty as ever, but patriotism in those days seemed viable even for many of the avant-deviant-opposition fringes of our society. That misconception was shattered with the president's skull: the dream was over, and we were left with fragmentation, disillusionment ("I don't believe in Jesus, I don't believe in Elvis," etc.), cynicism, hostile factions.

All of which was fine. People began to look inside themselves, instead of toward a popstar of a president, for their definition of America. Out of this forcible introspection erupted the New Left, acid, all those alternative lifestyles which by now have of course become even more oppressive than the delusions of the Kennedy era. So in that sense it was healthy for the body politic that we lost that mythological leader; it forced us to contemplate a whole new set of options.

It also left us with a gnawing void which forced us to find new leaders, of a new kind or any kind at all, and fast. Thus the Beatles, exploding across America from Ed Sullivan's stage and several different record companies, just weeks after the shot was fired. They were perfect medicine: a sigh of relief at their cheeky charm and a welcome frenzy to obliterate the grief with a tidal wave of Fun for its own sake which ultimately was to translate into a whole new hedonist dialectic.

I can remember the first time I ever heard the Beatles as distinctly as, I suppose, everyone else in the Western world. Walking home from school, I stopped off at the local record shop to check on the latest jazz, and there they were, "I Want to Hold Your Hand" spinning around and engulfing that shop with warm swelling waves of something powerfully attractive yet not quite comprehended, not yet. I wasn't much of a rock fan at the time, but there was some unmistakable stunning blare to that record that set it completely apart from what had come before in spite of its seemingly rudimentary form. It was that high droning scream they hit you with on "Iwannaholdyour—*haaaaaaaaaand!*" and "I get *hiigh,*" something that connected with broader concepts and idioms than any previous rock, like a muezzin's cry almost, and I stood in awe and thought: "The Beatles in the sky." That was where that cry, on the last brilliantly resonant syllable of each of those lines, seemed to be coming from.

Celestial and the boys next door all in one cheery, impudent package—Jesus, no wonder they were lapped up so greedily. Even better, there were four of them, filling the leadership gap with a new kind of junior (and equally illusory) democracy that gave the phrase "rock 'n' roll group" a whole new meaning and inspired a whole generation, blah blah blah. But the point is that in spite of the fact that each had his fanatical adherents, they were never John, Paul, George, and Ringo half so much as they were the Beatles, and *that* stood for something that they never could achieve apart, or even separately within the band. To search for the roots of their current degeneration in those early records is probably fruitless, in spite of odd parallels and contradictions: cosmic peace 'n' love George used to write (at least for the band) almost nothing but bitter put-downs like "Don't Bother Me" and "Think For Yourself." John could be as hateful then as now (from "You Can't Do That" to "How Do You Sleep" is not so far), and Paul was always a closet schmaltzmeister ("Michelle").

But the main thing that emerges from the career of the Beatles is the rise and fall of the concept of the *group*, which began to give way in rock to the ascendance of the solo artist at about the time they released their White Album, which has often been criticized for being a collection of songs by four separate individuals instead of a unified statement. Not to get too pretentious, but the Beatles' decline also parallels the decline of the youth culture's faith in itself as a homogenous group, for the proof of which we need look no further than the very corniness of a phrase like "youth culture" when you encounter it upon the page. That ain't no fuckin' culture no mo', the blacks even started imitating whites imitating blacks, and the adjourned Beatles, like most of their peers and contemporaries, have by now finally settled for imitating themselves.

To listen to early Beatles albums, or any Beatles albums up to the White Album, is to listen to collective enterprise, and of course the banality of the early songs becomes doubly ironic when you consider that "love" in the "I Want to Hold Your Hand" sense became transposed into "LOVE" as in flowers and beads grubbily handed to you on street corners and all you need is a little crystalline surcease of sorrow, the whole confused mess driving you crazy as John Lennon yelps out "Gimme Some Truth" and Paul responds from suburbia with "Another Day," perhaps his most topical solo venture ever. Impotent flailings vs. the celebration of the mundane.

Maybe that's why those old Beatle albums are so irritating today that just now, as I was playing *Rubber Soul* while writing this article, I took it off to type in silence, and my friend working nearby agreed that what once was ecstasy, the heart's rush of being in love for the first time, had through some curious process become a mere annoyance.

The Beatles today are out of time, out of place, out of sync with a present reality that isn't particularly grim (from this chair, anyway) but neither is it exactly amenable to certain types of artifacts.

But the real artifact, of course, is not the record. It's the mood. It's the innocence, it's the unconscious sense of intimacy and community which automatically self-destructed the instant it became self-conscious, i.e. the very day we opened up *Sgt. Pepper* and saw those four smiling mustached faces assuring us with a slightly patronizing benevolence that all was well. There was of course a kind of smugness about it all, which led to such successive artifacts as Manson and John Denver. I don't particularly feel like reading Bugliosi's *Helter Skelter*[3] either, not because I've OD'd on gore and outrage—it took the movies to do that—but *because it's in the past, it's boring, it's old hat even, I've been there and I just don't care anymore.*

What made the Beatles initially so exciting and sustained them for so long was that they seemed to carry themselves with a good-humored sense of style which was (or appeared to be) almost totally unselfconscious. They didn't seem to realize that they were in the process of becoming institutionalized, and that was refreshing. By the time they realized it the ball game was over. In this sense, *Rubber Soul* (in packaging) and *Revolver* (in content as well) can be seen as the transitional albums. They doped it up and widened their scopes through the various other tools they had access to at the time just like everybody else down to the lowliest fringe-dripping cowlicked doughboy in the Oh Wow regiment, and the result was that they saw their clear responsibility as cultural avatars in what started out as a virtual vacuum (nice and clean, though), which of course ruined them. And possibly, indirectly, us.

But it's okay. Because, while I would not indulge in the kind of ten-year-cycle Frank Sinatra–Elvis Presley–The Beatles who's-next-now's-the-time theories that have been so popular and so easy lately, I do think

[3] The L.A. prosecutor's book about the Manson Family.

that, like the assassination of JFK, the withering away of the Beatles has had its positive effects. Acidheads can (could?) be unbearable in their arrogant suppositions of omniscience, but if there's one thing good you can say about downs it's that nobody could get pretentious about them. The spell and its bonds are broken.

The death of the Beatles as a symbol or signification of anything can only be good, because like the New Frontier their LOVE nirvana was a stimulating but ridiculous, ephemeral and ultimately impracticable mass delusion in the first place. If the Beatles *stood* for anything besides the rock 'n' roll band as a communal unit suggesting the possibility of mass youth power, which proved to be a totally fatuous concept in short order, I'd like to know what I have missed by not missing the Beatles. They certainly didn't stand for peace or love or true liberation or the brotherhood of humankind, any more than John Denver stands for the preservation of our natural resources. On the other hand, like Davy Crockett hats, zoot suits, marathon dances, and bootleg alcohol, they may well have stood for an era, so well as to stand out from that era, totally exhumed from it in fact, floating, light as dandelions, to rest at last on the mantle where, neighboring your dead uncle's framed army picture, they can be dusted off at appropriate intervals, depending on the needs of Capitol's ledgers and our own inability to cope with the present.

The Real Paper, April 23, 1975
(Reprinted in June 1975 *Creem*)

Blood Feast of Reddy Kilowatt! Emerson, Lake, and Palmer Without Insulation!

Emerson, Lake and Palmer *must* be the biggest group in the world. It's not just that all their albums are chart sensations. What really makes ELP a dinosaur potentate is the sheer scale of the noise they emit. With ELP we're swatted into the new age of totally Technologized Rock. This is robot music mixmastered by human modules who deserve purple hearts for managing to keep the gadgets reined at all.

I went, I saw, I drowned. There was no choice. Arenas are arctic huge, but ELP has finally met the challenge of the arena and emerged the huger gnats. Three limos, three dressing rooms. Three egos exploding tight as a rapacious cyclotron and slick as Gorgo's dildo. Backstage the equipment crates clog the hallways like mainlined boulders. It takes the roadies five hours to set up, five more to break down later.

The sight of the massed ELP arsenal would chill the follicles of H. G. Wells. Synthesizers, donchaknow, up the bung: "keyboard wizard" Keith Emerson's has not only its requisite computer but its very own TV *set.* Carl Palmer has the world's first synthesized drum kit, which (but natch) he himself conceived with p'raps a little help from Keith's *personal* friend Rob Moog (inventor of samenamed instrument). This martial array of percussion also includes a libertine bell and two Arthurian-table sized gongs upon which a Chinese dragon cavorts leering in phosphor. As for Greg Lake, he mostly just switches tween his guitar and bass, but he's got enough amplification behind them two mantas to blow the Pentagon to Patagonia.

If there is an energy crisis, these guys amount to war criminals.

Even they don't know how much of this shit they're carting around with 'em. I tried to pry the techfax outa one of their roadies, but he mumbled so mungish that when I transcribed the tape all I could make out of the murk was: "28,000 . . . amperes . . . voltage . . . watts . . . 'ousand more as well . . . plus which . . . urrrhhhhh. . . ." Living in cybernetic caves. Elsewhere I glean totings of over 200 separate pieces of equipment, worth over a hundred grand. Including of course a brand new Moog, which is only one of the thirteen keyboards Keith packs for the road. After all, his nickname is Fingers.

You can readily comprehend the anticipation of meeting anybody who could churn it out so relentlessly. Those old stories of Keith Emerson actually *stabbing* his poor piano with a knife were enough to make you wanna shake the hand of such an impudent little devil. He flashed nary a dagger this night, but more than compensated when he vaulted off the stage waving what looked like a theremin around, nearly decapitating several coeds and a rentacop to forzak of supra-WHIIINE! Reclambering onstage, he capped even his own show by *wiping his ass with it:* WZZEEEEEE!

So you can further imagine our tragic letdown when we got back to the dressing room and learned that Keith refused to talk to us at all; something to do, it seemed, with a *Creem* review of ELProduct which Keith had apparently taken personally.

"Yeah, Keith took the review heavy, man," sighed ELP shepherd "The Big M." "He didn't wanna do photos or nothin'." Historically footnoting, the review in question was Alan Niester's assessment of *Pictures at an Exhibition,* which perhaps offended Keith by comparing the acquisition of his albums to bubblegum card collecting: "Thus, since I've been into Emerson for so long, take it from me, you heard one Emerson album, you heard 'em all . . . [But this album] shows Emerson at his best. As for these other guys, Lake and Palmer, forget 'em, they're no more important than Davison and Jackson were in the Nice. All Emerson really needs is Emerson."

Which sure shows where that piano-pounder's head is at: that review was not only favorable, but went so far as to paint said keyboarder an even loftier genius than he must conceive himself, shunting L&P off to the sidecar. Some people just don't know how to accept worship gracefully, but that's okay, because L&P are such good sports they overlooked the insult and not only consented to be interviewed but were genial as chowder to boot. Glad to see there's class *somewhere* in this band.

A beamy sod is Carl Palmer, in his charcoal black chinee pullover and matching jammerbottoms. Friendly and attentive, he looked straight at me and smiled guilelessly all the way through the interview. He's straight-A and true-puce, as is Greg Lake, who with his babyfat beamer and dutchboy bob looks like a deejay I know.

However I'm paid to be skeptical; prying at the scabs of their *real* motivations, I wondered oh-so-idly whether they thought of this dream scam they were in as more of an artform than a) a business or b) entertainment. Hell, Alvin Lee and Deep Purple both as much as admitted to me on separate yoric occasions that they were only in it for the bucks.

"It's principally entertainment, I think," said Greg Lake, shooting me down as ingenuously as I've ever been twisted. "It's not art in the same way as painting a picture." Oh. "We're very conscious of playing our performances as close to the way they were written and the record was made as possible. That's what the people come to hear."

Up the people, I say. Did Beethoven give two armpit-farts for the people? Aren't you guys supposed to be in some sense student-heirs of the Classical Tradition whatever that is? Name-droppers at court tell me Keith had ten years of music lessons when wee, which may be the only reason he didn't stay in his career as bank teller. What's more, Niester was right: the Nice were at least 80 percent pure treadle for Emersonic virtuositisms with a concretely classical cast. But they never became the popular sensation that ELP is, which maybe was why in 1970 Keith jettisoned ListDavJack, and culled Greg from King Crimson and Carl from (kak, gug) Atomic Rooster so this ostensibly super-groupic triumvirate could begin plotting their ascendance.

Carl takes up the tale: "When we first came together, we went musically for something that we thought was different at the time, which Keith had involvement with—classical music. The first piece of music we ever played together was 'Pictures at an Exhibition.' And the reason for learning that was that we could all be together on the same musical plane, to see how we got into things as a band."

Why not "Pressed Rat & Warthog?"

"It would have been foolish to pick a rock song by another band to learn, so we took a whole work, and learned about instruments and the way they're used to do different things in orchestras. And out of our band we tried to make a mini-orchestra sound."

But *why?* Everybody knows Classical-Rock (alternating with -Jazz) Fusions never really work. Perhaps what really paved the astroturf for ELP was *2001,* that dopey cozzed collegiate smoker flick: not only did it star a computer that could kick ass on Keith E.'s in a microsputum, but crafty Kubrick saw sure the soundtrack was fattened with all the glorioski Classicorn any rube could swallow. "Also Sprach Zarathustra," and Keith Emerson heard the word just like he was Joseph Smith shoveling off the tablets. By the time Kubrick got to *Clockwork Orange,* thereby installing Beethoven in the prostate projection chamber of next-up fad of trendy androhoodlum, the insidious befoulment of all that was gutter pure in rock had been accomplished. It's worse than eclecticism, it's eugenic entropy by design, and Emerson and cohorts are more than mere fellow travelers.

When most people get ready to make with the R-C Fusion they generally approach it by way of "upgrading" rock. Whereas, I said, I get the feeling that ELP are after just the opposite. And I admire the piss outa them for it! What could be *more* fun than tromping up and down Mussorgsky's spine for 45 minutes or so?

No go. Mr. Lake: "To be serious it's not necessary to be miserable. We don't sit there with long faces, but we're serious about the work we do. And you'd probably be inclined to get a more conservative vibe off a band like ours than somebody like the Who perhaps."

You guys are simply not cooperating at all. What is all this brick-walled *orthodoxy?*

"We've tried to play things like 'Pictures' in the way we play our music, more snappy and dynamic than it could have ever been conceived; Mussorgsky didn't have electronic instruments."

Better, but still hardly the stuff of legend. I'm glad you got the gonads to claim *improving* the old dead geek, yet you speak in tones of such pope-sucking *reverence.* Don't you realize that the traditional and still unchallenged viewpoint among the real Mentholatum classical fans is that the one thing which totally destroys the sensitivity and signification of any piece of classical music is loud amplification?

Greg: "That's often true. Depends, doesn't it, how well the adaptation is done. I've heard lousy orchestras, too; that's my answer to that."

Yeah, but you're doing all this stuff on your terms, on your ground. With an audience fulla ravenoid Quaalude freaks or worse. Something's gotta be compromised.

Lake holds the floor: "It depends what your criteria of judgment is. If they can enjoy 'Pictures at an Exhibition' by us, it's just as good as them enjoying 'Pictures' by Mussorgsky. In fact, a lot of people get to hear it that never would otherwise. So for the little bit you compromise, you also open the door for a lot of people." I never in my mottled career saw anybody walk the line between utter insult to established canons and incongruous regard for those same canons so ingenuously.

You must have gotten a lot of flak from purists, though. For "disrespecting" the classics, I mean. You know what I mean.

Palmer slices the guppy again: "Not really. I played the piece to a professor at the Guild Hall in London. He told me that for three people, having to deal with electronics and things, he admired it. We've had that happen other times. There was a piece called 'Toccata,' by Alberto Ginastera, he's a Brazilian composer, and his was the greatest credit we've ever had. We recorded it, and took the tape to Brazil to ask him to hear what we've done with his music before we released it, because you have to have the guy's approval. And he said: 'That's the way it should have sounded.' "

This is getting more disgusting by the second. So you got patted on the head, so what? How in the name of all that's crass can you possibly sit there and tell me that while stabbing your pianos and wiping your ass with theremins you're simultaneously on a goodytwoshoes mission to bring Good Music to the rabble?

The most insufferable snob, the most hateful patronization, is the one that's unaware, the guileless shiv. "We hope if anything we're encouraging the kids to listen to music that has more quality." Carl, if it makes a difference at this point. These guys have been android gang-brainbanged by their very axes. "We don't come along to educate them. We come along to entertain them, and if they're ready for it, they take it."

A lot of musicians, I say, (thinking I'm drowning them in irony) have a condescending attitude. Zappa, say.

"Most bands have a condescending attitude," sez Carl, "because when you're playing something you believe in anyway, you're trying to make everyone else believe in it. American musicians seem to have that attitude. Every American jazz musician I've met has been arrogant, maybe a little big-headed. It's just the nature of your country that makes you this way. I don't think jazz musicians in this country have presented their music any different in the last 30 years. They still wanta do club dates, but they wanta get across to the mass, they want people to buy their records. When you go to the Village Vanguard in New York, you see somebody like Charlie Mingus playing up there. He's got the most diabolical sound onstage, he's trying to amplify his bass by putting it through a 12-inch speaker! And then they're expecting new listeners to come in and say, 'Yeah, this cat's great.' You go to see a jazz artist and you're disappointed, it's not there. All the instruments are acoustic, they don't get a good sound, it's not a good club. . . ."

I was stunned, but I managed to mutter something about how those clubs are where most scuffling American jazzmen, lacking either the money or propensity for gimmickry necessary to channel their music through ten thousand monster amps, are forced to play—

"No, they don't have to play there, those are places they make themselves play—"

—because of the racial, social, and aesthetic conditions prevailing in this country, where quite naturally the watered-down and contrivedly "palatable" floats the marketstream better than the uncompromising—

"People like Buddy Rich manage to get out and play bigger places. I'm sure that if I were a jazz musician I would never let myself get restricted."

I'm sure that if you were a "jazz musician" you would be white and no matter how many whooping teenies you could marshal you'd still have to learn how to improvise on some level beyond the sort of hackneyed rock progressions, scales, and Hollywood-burnished cops from the most obvious classical sources, i.e. you'd have to somehow progress as a *musician* way past the level of Heaviness you've attained in your present affiliation.

Keith Emerson never played an interesting solo in his life. Hell, might as well admit it all the way, they're not even solos, they're just some guy racing all over a keyboard like Liberace trying to play Mozart behind a Dexamyl OD. To make the crucial distinction, trained fingers might as well be trained seals unless there's a mind flexing behind them.

But that's beside the point, finally. Because this success saga has nothing to do with reality. None of this ever had anything to do with music, either, and even less now than ever before, as the emphasis shifts with subtle firmness from "show" to "spectacle."

So who cares anyway? That's what I asked Lake and Palmer, referring to their incredibly elaborate stage setting even more than the histrionics that go on within it, which in fact are fairly low-profile except for Emerson. Do you, I wondered, think you're more theatrical now, and why so?

Palmer: "No, not really. That may be an elaborate set to you; to me it's very basic, it's what I need to perform the way I perform. My drums are not just a piece of engineering, they're set up medically correct for my body to function the right way behind that drum set, which is just something I have to take into consideration now."

Oh, kind of like a splint, you mean. That's cool. So where, speaking from the driver's seat, do you draw the line between music and pure effect?

"There's only one kind of effect we do that involves electronics. That's with Keith's synthesizer and the computer at the end of the show. And that effect is created by synthesizers, but music has been written around it, or rather music has been written and that effect was added, because it gave a visual thing as well as an audial thing."

Okay, your grandeur is established—but isn't there a point at which you do all this stuff merely for crowd reactions?

"No," insists Carl. "I do it because I like to be in front. In what I do. On that stage right now I've got a hand-built drumset that's engraved, and I've got the first percussion synthesizers. I don't do things for the reaction, I do them because I like to be the first, whether I believe in it 100 percent or not. If I'm doing it, someone else does."

Yeah. But don't you ever find that you reach a point where whatever emotional content the presentation might have is overrun and washed away by the technology?

Greg Lake: "Good question. No . . . no. Because we choose the places in which to express the emotions, and the places in which to express the technique, hoping one doesn't interfere with the other."

But don't you get a feeling of sterility?

Carl: "No, never. We're working much too hard for that. We've taken time off to come back with a different show. We had about four tours prior to the layoff, and we needed time to rethink what we wanted to do. We also wanted our own record label [Manticore], we wanted to get things more businesslike. All these things take time. We're really not into coming in and saturating a market and taking out the money."

Ignoring for the moment that the reply was not an answer to the question, you may have noticed that these fellers speak most cogently when they speak as businessmen. There is absolutely nothing of the desperately egocentric "artist." Their rap in this area reminded me more than anyone else of Dick Clark. So who would ever say that this band is sterile, that they're not forever forging ahead? If you can't have real quality, *why not* go for quantity on a Byzantine scale, why not be pompous if you're successful at it? Who needs to feel anything when you can move with the flow of the current? Does NASA have a soul? Does it need one? Don't you kinda admire it precisely for its sleek unfeeling lunar inhumanness? And since the only thing that really counts is the hardware, as these boys will almost admit, why bother with personalities in this story at all? Why not just publish an itemized list of the contents of their arsenal with accompanying charts and diagrams? So of course I asked 'em: How much equipment you trundling around the country on your bearers' heads? How many amps? I couldn't even count 'em, I said.

"It's got beyond my understanding as well," admits Greg. "I don't know the total capacity of it."

Oh well, no matter. It's just good to see you extending yourselves; so many rock bands are *so* lazy. I really feel for you guys. And of course I want you to know how much all of us out here appreciate the way you've borne up under all that pressure to create such enduring masterpieces as "Benny the Bouncer." But don't worry, readers: they'll be back before we know it with another mind-bolting album and sold-out tour to match. If they don't blow a circuit or drool in one of their manifold sockets.

Creem, March 1974

C'mon Sugar, Let's Go All-Nite Jukin' with Wet Willie

1

"**Wet Willie," from whence this passel o' scragglers** derived their handle, is a regionalism referring to an Alabamian practice of sucking on your finger and then shoving it up somebody's ear. It also means that dirty stuff you're thinking right now.

2

The first time I saw Wet Willie I got excited as hell. You would too if you were in Macon, Georgia, whooping it up deep Friday night down at Grant's Lounge call of the wildest bar this side of the frontier. Hambones and grease are cruising through the air like your very lobes flow deep in the marrow of the Gulf Stream, and the Hatfield Clan (THC) have just gone off, looking in their combination jock and lipstick drag like one of Captain Beefheart's old crews and sounding like a damn good skillet bar band. Every slick black honker in town has just had his turn in the night's mighty tenor battle, and now the dazed stage is took by a bunch of high hop-steppin' Suthun lads who don't play no queer-bait but they jive as good as they want. Up front's a rangy-boned cussed-callow youth who looks just enough like Jagger without overdoing it a la Aerosmith; he's a real rawhide power swaggerin' son of the soil and he commences to whoop out some of the hottest, nastiest, most needlin' to the point harp heard since early Paul Butterfield, with the rest of the band cooking like ten Rastamaniacs straight behind him all the way. He limbers up the whole damn club with a good excursive and precisely economical few minutes of this Hohnerific, and then he throws back his head and commences to shout:

You're just hangin' out
At the local bar
And you're wondering'
Who in the hell *you are!*
Are you a bum, or
Are you a star?
Keep on smilin' through the rain . . .

And you best believe it gave me chills.

Next day me and the rest of the passing freebooters pile into big daddy Phil Walden's limousine complete with Scotch and teevee in the back, and head down to Statesboro, home of Blind Mason Williams' celebrated "Statesboro Blues" (also covered by Loggins and Messina) to get the Willies live and slithering just one more time. I made short work of the Scotch, turned off the toob when they started the 14th Andy Griffith rerun of the day, entertained the car with my Lou Reed tapes till they formally and politely requested I get that faggit *crayup* off or land on my ass in a Georgia gully.

Had a guzzlin' contest with the Wet heads in the locker dressing room of the gym they're playin' at: Jack Hall, brother of aforescrawled lead holler Jimmy and the funkiest bassist this side of the Famous Flames, struts up to me with a bottle of Jack Daniel's and puts his finger on the side about an inch below the water line: "Laiester, can yew draink this down ta thair?" Shitcheah man, I grabbed that slumgullion and gozzled it whole, slammed it back in his mitt and didn't even wiggle. Everybody else in the room whooped in admiration. I was in the South, and it felt fine.

Next minute while taking a piss I got a notion, so I asked 'em if I could introduce 'em when they went onstage. They assented, so I ran out and assaulted the rabble with thunderbolts of loving invective: "Ladies and gentlemen! Boys and girls! B-b-b-*bruh*-thuhs in *s-s-siiiiis*-ters! Streakers and Ralph Meekers! I am about to show you something the like of which you have never seen before! It's gonna blow your head clean on out the door! It's gonna have you down on your knees on the floor, *baaaaiiig*in' for more! So all I wanna know is . . . *are you ready for the night train,* drivin' you insane, straight outa your brain? Ready ready readuhreadahreadyeeeeaaaah! Gone, gone gone! I got my *eyes* wide open! I give you, on Capricorn Records, *the Wet Willie Band!*"

And then they came out and did it again. They tore that joint down and smoked *awhile* Jim. (If these crackers can play like niggers and get rich at it I can damn sure talk like one and get hung.) It was here that I first noticed the way Jimmy Hall takes immediate command of the stage, stalking from one end to the other like a mudcat in heat. I also noticed even more clearly what I had first beheld in the dressing room, that his sister Donna Hall, who sings soul jones backing with Ella Avery in the Williettes, is the hottest little piece I ever saw in my long lined life. She's got skin as succulent and fresh as hell yeah Dixie peaches that adorn the space just above her cute little bellybutton, big dark eyes you could fall into, and a mouth perfected in constant moue as though blessed with the power to suck a nectarine dry by remote control. That's just for a leetle taste of euphemism so she won't think me uncouth like unto these Southland raggedymop bopboys. Unfortunately, I never copped her sweetmeat 'cause next time I saw her she was in the company of a certain internationally famous popstar with big muscles.

3

That was also the next and latest (but not last) time I saw Wet Willie, on my own turf in Detroit. They came up for a tour with Grand Funk but had to cancel out Thursday because Mel Schacher had sprained a lug nut. So we took 'em out to the house and they immediately commenced to browsing my stack of skin magazines. "Sheeyit," said Jack, "ah shore hope ah git laid whal ah'm up here." "Me too," chimed Jimmy. "Ah'm tard o' jaikin' off alla tam."

"Don't worry 'bout a thing, boys," I hoorawed them. "I'll line up some priority-primoski local talent when you come back to make the gig on Monday."

Thus did I simultaneously embark on my new career as a pimp (beats the pus outa rock writing) and discover that much as I had suspected through recent observation of other touring aggregations, the much-vaunted sexual wildebeasterity of popular rock musicians is in large part a myth. Now, I ain't saying the Willies is queer or limp or nothing, they're right fine ruttin' tuttin' down-home boys, it's just that they're a leetle *shy.* I called up Detroit City's number-one-with-a-bullet groupie the day of the gig, and quacked: "Lissen honey, there's some real hot rock action hittin' town tonite, so get your posse down to Cobo Hall and make them boys feel at home in Moblow!" "Who is it?" "Wet Willie." "Might as well, I know all those dumb azzes in Grand Funk too well. . . ."

So the great night fell and the groupies were swarming like flying poltroons, having come from far and wide to check with their very own accoutrements the efficacy of this legend I had blabbed up to them via phone. They were gathered around in packs preening and pouting away to beat the band senile, and I just kept on smiling and drinking till I got so drunk I ran wild, which is what always seems to happen to me whenever Wet Willie's around and playing. Which they did in a supertight set of old faves and new raves double-clutching out of nowhere to get an encore from a packed arena of the sickliest Detroit jades.

It was a heartwarming sight and when it was all over I went back up to the dressing room to see how the romancin' was enhancin'. Shame to my eyeballs, what do I see but a whole room fulla hot giggling tease and in the eye of the storm these five musical-type busters lookin' sorta confused though not half as hangdog as the Blue Öyster Cult whom I had seen trying with even less fervor in identical circumstances a week previous. These chicks wasn't the best in the world (fact they wuz ogly as weasels)—but then again there is an old Southern motto having to do with draping one part of the anatomy with a flag thereby to attend to another part sans distraction. But this one bitch steps into the room and looks at the table and says something about the lunchmeat laid out for sandwiches, so Jack Hall starts leering under his breath: "Yeah . . . *meat* . . . uh . . . *ah* lak meat . . . you meat . . . uh, meat . . ."

Hailfar and bustification! I could see they needed a little prodding, so I grabbed this one notbad missy and sayd: "Hey, waht's yore name girl?" (Every time I get around these wino saltines I start talking like 'em too, can't help it.) "Mary Lou." "*Mary Lou,* woo hoo!"—yanking her and Wet Willpower lead guitarist Rick Hirsch Certs-range—"Mary Lou, meet Rick Hirsch of the famed and brilliant hot fire lickin' Wet Willie Band." And then I jutted my jaw through Rick's right eyeball: "This is mah sister boah yo better take good cair of 'er you hear?" and walked away.

I turned around and looked at them. The damsel was trying to engage her temporal and wavering swain in the patter precipitating carnal envelopment, but he just stood there, like a water moccasin on a rock in the Gobi, and when they had parted in brief and minor sorrow I went up to him and shook that diz down straight: "What's the deal here? Doncha wanna get laid?"

"Sure," he admitted to me, "but I don't wanna put any effort into it. They gotta take me by the hand and lead me right into the bed or I don't even try."

Judas Priest! Did you ever? Well I never! My career as rock 'n' roll pimp came to a timely end right then and there. Now, as we all know, limeys are incapable of getting it up unless receiving head while prone on silk sheets in a hundred-dollar-a-day hotel room, but these Southern boys are asskickers and poonlikkers from way back, and the only way I can account for this generalized lapse in the humpadelic heatwaves is that they're jes' plain bone *lazy.*

But there *is* hope for this band yet in the poontang glorioski department. Dori McMartin, a young lady of Canadian extraction acquainted with the author and a dues-paying member of the Rock Writers of the World, reports that whilst sharing a joint with Willie pianist John Anthony, she inquired, "Why are all you Southern boys so shy with the girls?"

He looked deep into her guileless Ontarioan eyes with his bulging booglarizers, took her hand and swelling and drooling intoned: "*Now* do you think all Southern boys are so shy with the girls?"

I'm not able to tell you whether or not John got his willie wet in some other fine foxbox later; I know all the rest of the boys did, and hell, they didn't half try. John's a strange one anyway—in some ways the true personality of the band, his bulging eyes, almost Romanly chiseled face, gleaming skin, and general weirdness mark him such deep intrinsic Soul of Honk that he comes clean out the other end of the barrel and damn my eyes if he don't look like something straight out of Genet. Which only adds to the luster onstage, when he's standing there in his fedora and red-and-black pinstripe gangster suit whanging away at the keys like the joyride bastard son of Jerry Lee. He's a diesel cooker and an outside looker, and hell, when I slammed on my *Rock 'n' Roll Animal* tape big Lou moaning out "Heroin" in the vast asteroidal Pecos spaces of our skulls he was the only one who'd sit there with me to catch the vibe.

4

Tell you something else about John Anthony: he's smart. Because he's the only Wet Willie who won't do interviews. I tried but failed to pry a quotable out of him, and horny as he was he would only talk to Dori with the tape recorder shut off and clear in the back of the bus.

Because he contends that it's all said in the music and the rest is just froth and frosting. Zen wisdom in that boy.

Yeah and it was borne out when I sat down in the bar with the rest of these bazookas, and set about spelunkin' on *roots* and *music* and the (lordy save my ass in a sling for nuns) *meaning* of it all.

Q: "Lester, don't yew think we're the blackest white band yew ever heard?"

A: "Yeah, so what?"

Q: "Huh?"

Gotta say Wet Willie do the best white rock slash James Brown act cum Yardbirds (it's in the harp) and whatever you want since Bernie "B.B." Fieldings' Black Pearl. So get it while you can, look at Granny run run, ain't everybody home, slammin' it right there with all the fire and fuck and feed you can feel. Or filibuster.

Singin' in a honky tonk café
Nobody's hearin' what you say
They're too busy drinkin' anyway
You gotta keep on smilin'

Jimmy Hall said that. Bob Dylan didn't say nothin' this year. But then, neither did John Anthony. But then, he didn't have to.

Creem, October 1974

Bob Dylan's Dalliance with Mafia Chic: He Ain't No Delinquent, He's Misunderstood

It is automatically assumed that every Bob Dylan album is an event, and *Desire* is certainly no exception. It is not, however, the event that it might appear to be. It is not an event because of the inclusion of several drearily rambling Marty Robbins cum *Pat Garrett & Billy the Kid* sagas of outlaw's progress from cantina to cantina. This album is a landmark neither because of the back-cover slice of imitation Patti Smith poesy by (presumably) Dylan, nor because of the offensively portentous liner puffery provided by a senile Allen Ginsberg, who ironically was one of Dylan's major influences back when Ginsberg was perhaps the premiere American poet and Bob on his way to being declared that by people who didn't know any better (like me, for instance).

We can't even assign historic import to *Desire* on the basis of "Hurricane," the undeniably powerful single which, in a controlled spasm of good old rabble-rousing, spits an inflammatory account of the railroading of Rubin Carter, onetime contender for the Middleweight Boxing Championship of the World, on a mid-Sixties murder rap.

If you feel yourself responding cynically when someone relates that "Dylan's returned to protest songs" as if it's exciting news, it just may be that your instincts are in healthy working order. Look at it this way: every four years Dylan writes a "new" protest song, and it's always about a martyred nigger, and he always throws in a dirty word to make it more street-authentic. I don't use the word "nigger" for effect or to make myself look hip, but rather because just like our fathers before us that is all Jackson and Carter have been to him: another human life to exploit for his own purposes.

Dylan doesn't give a damn about Rubin Carter, and if he spent any more than ten minutes actually working on the composition of "George Jackson" then Bryan Ferry is a member of the Eagles. Dylan merely used Civil Rights and the rest of the Movement to advance himself in the first place; "The Times They Are A-Changin' " and "Blowin' in the Wind" were just as much a pose as *Nashville Skyline*. Which actually was not only kosher but a fair deal, because the exchange amounted to symbiotic exploitation—the Movement got some potent anthems, Dylan got to be a figurehead, and even if he was using his constituency art is more important than politics in the long run anyway.

But why, in 1975, should Dylan return to what, in such a year, passes for activism? Because he's having trouble coming up with meaningful subject matter closer to home, that's why: either that or whatever is going on in his personal life is so painful and fucked up he is afraid or unwilling to confront it in his art. And, again, one is not sure that one can honestly blame him. When *Blood on the Tracks* was released, I felt as ambivalent about it as it was about its subject matter, and I remained that way. After initially dismissing it on one hearing as a sprawling, absurdly pretentious mess whose key was the ridiculously spiteful "Idiot Wind," I found myself drawn back to it repeatedly by a current that I was not at all convinced was entirely wholesome; I would get drunk and throw it on, finding profound aphorisms alternating with oblique poetry, belching outbursts of muddled enthusiasm: "Goddamn, he's still got it!" Then I would sober up and it would sound, once again, dull, overlong, energyless, the aphorisms trite and obvious, the poetry a garbled parody of the old Dylan. But I persisted, there was *something* there that mattered to me, and I ultimately found out what it was. I discovered that I only really wanted to play this record whenever I had a fight with someone I was falling in love with—we would reach some painful impasse of words or wills, she would go home, and I would sit up all night with my misery and this album, playing it over and over, wallowing in Dylan's wretched reflection of my own confusion: "Women—who can figger 'em?" I imagine it was also a big hit with the recently (or soon to be) divorced.

At length I concluded that any record whose principal utility lay in such an emotional twilight zone was at worst an instrument of self-abuse, at best innocuous as a crying towel, and certainly was not going to make me a better person or teach me anything about women, myself, or anything else but how painfully confused Bob Dylan seemed to be. Which was simply not enough.

So I looked forward to *Desire*. Maybe Bob had managed to figger the critters out in some flash of revelation, or could at least provide some helpful tips for the rest of us involved in the great Struggle. Perhaps, at last, he had something honestly uplifting to say about men and women, male bonding, pet training, and all the other baffling forms of interpersonal relationships known to this planet. So if it seems like I'm hard on him now, if I seem unduly vitriolic, it's only because (a) everything I say is the truth, and (b) I myself was such a sucker I still looked to him to tell me something and now must suffer the embarrassment which is my just deserts.

Because *Desire* is a sham and a fakeout. Ignoring the "El Paso" rewrites and ersatz Kristofferson plodders like "One More Cup of Coffee" (which is easy), we come at length (and it reflects neither generosity nor inspiration that side two of this album is almost thirty minutes long) to "Sara," wherein Dylan, masks off, naming names, rhapsodizes over his wife in mawkish images ("sweet virgin angel . . . radiant jewel") cheap bathos (when in doubt, drag in the kids playing in the sand on the beach), simple groveling ("You must forgive me my unworthiness"), and, most indicatively of *Desire* as a whole, outright lies. To wit: "I'd taken the cure and I'd just gotten through/Stayin' up for days in the Chelsea Hotel/Writin' 'Sad Eyed Lady of the Lowlands' for you."

Bullshit. I have it on pretty good authority that Dylan wrote "Sad

Eyed Lady," as well as about half of the rest of *Blonde on Blonde,* wired out of his skull in the studio, just before the songs were recorded, while the sessionmen sat around waiting on him, smoking cigarettes and drinking beer. It has been suggested to me that there are better things to do with albums than try to figure out what drug the artist was on when he made them, but I think this was one case where the chemical definitely affected the content of the music. Those lyrics were a speed trip, and if he really *did* spend days on end sweating over lines like "Your streetcar visions which you place on the grass," then he is stupider than we ever gave him credit for.

Now. I know I stand at this point in possible danger of plunging quill-first into full-scale Webermanism,[4] but I do think that if you are going to assert that a piece of music is the unburdening of your soul down to the personal pronouns, then you should tell the truth. I also think that if he is capable of lying about and exploiting his own marriage to make himself look a bit more pertinent, he is certainly capable of using the newsy victims of his topical toons with even less attention to moral amenities. "Hurricane," like many Dylan songs of his distant past, purports to be a diatribe expressing abhorrence of racism, but there are many forms of inverted, benevolent prejudice known to the liberal mentality, and I find a song like "Mozambique" rather curious:

I'd like to spend some time in Mozambique . . .
All the couples dancing cheek to cheek
It's very nice to stay a week or two . . .
There's lots of pretty girls in Mozambique
And plenty time for good romance . . .
Magic in a magical land

[4] A. J. Weberman was a self-proclaimed "Dylanologist" of the era who plundered his idol/target's garbage for clues to his life and music, and developed an elaborate and, most agreed, ludicrous interpretation of key words and phrases that explained what Dylan "really meant" with his songs.

Ah yes, a beautiful, simple people, aren't they, Mr. Christian? Unfettered by the corrupting complexities of civilization, no? So primitively pure and natch'l, just fuckin' and a'dancin' barefoot there on the beach. Maybe that's what enables Rubin Carter to sit "like Buddha in a prison cell."

Which brings us to Dylan's demonology, and the biggest lie of all. Now, just like *Blood on the Tracks* was ultimately redolent of little more than mixed-up confusion as regards romantic obsessions, so a line like "All the criminals in their coats and their ties/Are free to drink martinis and watch the sun rise" is not exactly going to enlighten us as to the subtleties of social injustice today. Because the processes of oppression, however brutal, are subtle; Ralph J. Gleason was *right* when he extrapolated old Dylan lyrics into "No more us and them," and Dylan himself, in the mid-Seventies, is still playing cowboys and Indians.

I said earlier that Dylan was merely using Carter and George Jackson as fodder for the propagation of the continuing myth of his own "relevance." It's difficult to prove that from "Hurricane," in part because the performance is so drivingly persuasive, in part because Dylan does seem, at least superficially, to have his facts down: a man was framed for a crime he most likely didn't commit, and the probable reason he was framed was that he preached black liberation in an atmosphere of white supremacy. Of course, the fact that he was framed doesn't prove that he was *innocent* of the crime, either; but for once Dylan's simplistic broadsides seem to have coincided with reality, justice, and Rubin Carter being on the side of the angels.

But I have to make a confession: I don't give a damn about Rubin Carter, whether he is guilty or innocent, or about racism in New Jersey. At least for the purposes of the present inquiry, all I care about is Bob Dylan, and whether he is being straight with me or not. I don't think he is, anywhere, and I think you can find all the evidence you need in *Desire*'s longest cut, the ponderous, sloppy, numbingly boring eleven-minute ballad "Joey," about yet another folk hero/loser/martyr, mobster "Crazy Joey" Gallo, who was murdered in a gang war in Little Italy in 1972.

New York City readers may not believe this, but it's probable that most of the people, especially young ones, who buy this album across the rest of America do not know who in the hell Joey Gallo was. Since this song is hardly going to help them find out, is in fact one of the most mindlessly amoral pieces of repellent romanticist bullshit ever recorded, let me preface an examination of Dylan's most transparent dishonesty with a brief bit of history:

During the Sixties, there were five Mafia "families" dividing up the pie of various turfs and rackets in New York City, under the control of one Godfatherlike "boss of bosses." Although the modern Mafia encourages more of a "businessman" image and tries to play down the bloodletting, the families are generally fighting among themselves for greater power and influence, and one of the most successful families during the Sixties was the Profaci family, which later became the Colombo family. In intermittent but very bloody opposition to them were the Gallo family, led by the brothers Larry, Joey, and Albert "Kid Blast" Gallo, who were never quite able to attain equivalent power even though they remained the overlords of one small section of Brooklyn. According to a detailed analysis of mob warfare by Fred J. Cook in the June 4, 1972, *New York Times,* "The severe bloodletting in the Profaci-Colombo family began when the greed of the Gallo brothers set them lusting after [the former's] power. Indeed, it touched them with the kind of madness that drives a shark berserk in a blood-stained sea," and the Gallos tried every lethal ploy they could think of to muscle their way into a bigger piece of the action. In October 1957, Joey Gallo, acting on a Profaci contract, blasted the notorious Albert Anastasia, onetime lord of Murder, Inc., out of his barber's chair in a celebrated rubout, thus paving the way for Carlo Gambino to become, and remain, boss of bosses through the Sixties and early Seventies. But the Gallos never found any more favor with Gambino than they had with his predecessors, so they embarked on an all-out war with the Profacis that lasted from 1961 to 1963; though there were no real winners, the Gallos were no match either in numbers or tactically for the Profacis, and the war ended in early 1962 when Crazy Joe Gallo was sentenced to seven to fourteen years in prison for extortion, and, a few months later, Joseph Profaci died of cancer.

While Joe Gallo was in prison, he read extensively, becoming a sort of jailhouse intellectual, and when he was finally released in 1970 he began to cultivate contacts in the literary and show business worlds, who welcomed him to their parties and obviously considered him an exotic amusement indeed. Jimmy Breslin's book *The Gang That Couldn't Shoot Straight* had been inspired by the legendary ineptitude of the Gallo family in their early-Sixties bids for power, and Joey developed close contacts with Jerry Orbach, who played a character corresponding to him in the movie based on the book, and his wife Marta, with whom, in the last months of his life, Joey began collaborating on various autobiographical literary projects. Out of Radical Chic bloomed Mafia Chic; he became something of an aboveground social figure, and told columnist Earl Wilson that he was "going straight."

Apparently that was a lie, however. While Joey was in prison, his gang languishing and awaiting his return, a new figure had arisen from the Profaci ranks to bring New York mob power to a whole new, all but avant-garde level: Joe Colombo. Colombo founded the Italian-American Civil Rights League, an organization ostensibly devoted to deploring and "legitimately" opposing the "prejudice" which caused most Americans to link mob activities with citizens of Italian descent. Between 150,000 and 250,000 Italian-Americans joined the League, and the impact on politicians was considerable, which was how Nelson Rockefeller and John Lindsay ended up having their pictures taken with underworld toughs. Joey Gallo returned from prison with his power on his own turf intact, but of course completely cut out of the Colombo empire. On June 28, 1971, Joe Colombo was gunned down by a supposedly lone and uncontracted black man in front of thousands of his horrified followers at a rally in Columbus Circle. The consensus was that Crazy Joey was behind it, especially since he'd perplexed other Mafiosos by hanging out with black prisoners during his stay in the joint, and ostensibly aimed to start a black mob, under his control, when he got out. According to many inside sources, there was a contract out on Joey Gallo from the day Colombo died, and on April 7, 1972, as he celebrated his 43rd birthday in Umberto's Clam House on Mulberry Street in Little Italy, an anonymous hit man walked in off the street and shot Crazy Joey to death much as Joey had murdered Albert Anastasia. It was the end of a gang war that had lasted almost a decade and a half—a few more of their henchmen were disposed of, and the Gallo family was decimated, their power gone. Mobsters in general breathed a collective sigh of relief—the Gallos had always been hungry troublemakers—and went back to business as usual.

It is out of this fairly typical tale of mob power-jostlings that Dylan has, unaccountably, woven "Joey," which paints a picture of Joey Gallo as alienated antihero reminiscent of *West Side Story*'s "Gee, Officer Krupke" lyrics "He ain't no delinquent, he's misunderstood."

Always on the outside of whatever side there was
When they asked him why it had to be that way
Well, the answer—just because

Joey Gallo was a psychopath, as his biographer, Donald Goddard, confirms, although the analyst who examined him while he was in prison diagnosed Joey's disease as "pseudo-psychopathic schizophrenia." Joey's answer: "Fuck you. Things are not right or wrong anymore. Just smart or stupid. You don't judge an act by its nature. You judge it by its results. We're all criminals now. . . . Things exist when I feel they should exist, okay? *Me. I* am the world." Toward the end of his life, his wife routinely fed him Thorazine, which he docilely took, even though it still didn't stop him from beating the shit out of her.

Dylan then goes on to paint a romantic, sentimental picture of Joey and his brothers in the gang:

There was talk they killed their rival
But the truth was far from that
No one ever knew for sure where they were really at

Well, according to the D.A. at Joey's early-Sixties extortion trial, "In the current war taking place between the Gallo gang and established interests, there have been killings, shootings, strangling, kidnappings, and disappearances, all directly involving the Gallos. Interestingly enough, since the defendant's being remanded on November 14 in this case, there have been no known offensive actions taken by the Gallos in this dispute. This would give some credence to the belief that Joe Gallo is, in reality, the sparkplug and enforcer of the mob." But who believes D.A.s, right? Okay, try his ofttimes enormously sympathetic biographer: "Almost all the charges ever brought against him, even in the beginning, were dismissed. No witnesses. . . . Once people got to know that careless talk was liable to bring Joe Gallo around to remonstrate and maybe make his point with an ice pick, witnesses in Brooklyn became as scarce as woodpeckers. Once the story got around that Joey had gripped a defaulter's forearm by the wrist and elbow and broken it over the edge of a desk to remind him that his account was past due, the Gallos had very few cash-flow problems with their gambling, loan-sharking, and protection business."

Most interestingly of all, his wife tells the story of how she became innocently entangled for a moment with a member of Joey's gang as they drunkenly tried to pull their coats off the racks of a nightclub cloakroom. Later, in bed, Joey accused her of kissing the guy, and she responded that that was absurd because, for one thing, he was wildly unappetizing. But Joey hounded her about the matter, convinced that her confession would prove that he had seen what he had convinced himself he had seen and was therefore not insane. Finally, to prevent further harassment (to perhaps, in fact, save her own life) and reassure him as to his sanity, she "confessed." The next night, as they lay awake together in bed again, he casually remarked, "Say, listen—you remember that guy at the club? The guy you were fooling around with? He's dead. I forgot to tell you. . . . Yeah. Last night. He had a terrible accident on the bridge. His car went out of control. . . . That's a terrible thing. He was a nice guy."

Later in the song Dylan asserts that "The police department hounded him." Considering the number of rackets the Gallos were involved in, nothing could be further from the truth. Goddard: "Right from the start, relations between the Pizza Squad [NYC anti-Mafia cop team] and the Gallo gang had been imbued with a grudging professional respect, which, in certain cases, shaded into something close to affection. They played the game by the rules." Adds a cop: "They're a peculiar mob. . . . They knew what we had to do and they weren't going to question it. They treated us like gentlemen. That don't make them good guys, but they had a little more savvy [than the Colombos]. It was like 'Why stir the pot? If you're going to be down here, let's make it pleasant for both of us.' It's a game. If you get caught, you get caught."

Perhaps most curiously of all, Dylan says that "They got him on conspiracy/They were never sure who with." Funny, because everybody from Goddard to the courts and cops agree that Joey's downfall came when, early in May 1961, he tried to muscle in on a loan shark named Teddy Moss. Moss resisted, and, in the presence of undercover cops, Joey said "Well, if he needs some time to think it over, we'll put him in the hospital for four or five months, and that'll give him time."

But how can Dylan have a martyred Mafioso without an evil judge:

"What time is it?" said the judge to Joey when they met
"Five to ten," said Joey
The judge says, "That's exactly what you get."

This is what, for want of a better phrase, must be termed poetic license. The truth is that Joey's lawyer was as lame as his gang, and never made it up from Florida for his trial, and Joey refused to have anything to do with the two other lawyers appointed to represent him, choosing to stand mute while the D.A. delivered a steady stream of evidence that was pretty solid in the first place and never disputed. That Joey allowed this to happen suggests, not that he was railroaded, but merely that he was incredibly stupid. Goddard: "Readily concurring that Joey was 'a menace to the community,' Judge Sarafite chalked up the first victory in the Attorney General's [Robert Kennedy, who once branded Joey Public Enemy No. 1] assault on organized crime by handing down the maximum sentence of seven and one-quarter to fourteen and one-half years' imprisonment."

Dylan: "He did ten years at Attica/Reading Nietzsche and Wilhelm Reich." He also read Freud, Plato, Spinoza, Hume, Kant, Schopenhauer, John Dewey, Bergson, Santayana, Herbert Spencer, William James, Voltaire, Diderot, Pascal, Locke, Spengler, Wilde, Keats, Shakespeare, Goethe, Will Durant, Oliver Cromwell, Napoleon, Adenauer, de Gaulle, Lenin, Mao Tse-tung, Clarence Darrow, and Louis Nizer, as well as taking part in a homosexual gang rape about which he bragged at a cocktail party after his release: "He described how, with several other convicts, he had spotted a pretty young boy among a new batch of prisoners and laid in wait for him. Dragging him into the Jewish chapel, they ripped his pants off and were struggling to hold him down when one of them heard the rabbi talking in the next room. A knife was immediately put at their victim's throat with a whispered warning not to cry out, and the rape proceeded in an orderly fashion, each man taking his turn in order of seniority. They wanted this kid, Joey said, while his asshole was still tight."

This was most likely not, however, the reason that (according to Dylan) "his closest friends were black men." It was "Cause they seemed to understand what it's like to be in society/With a shackle on your hand." And also, as previously stated, because Joey for a while entertained dreams of launching a black Mafia when he got out. The psychoanalyst who interviewed Joey in prison voices agreement with

Dylan in more clinical terms, but adds, "Joey was a terrifically prejudiced guy . . . on a strictly, and deeply, personal level, he was a knee-jerk nigger-hater," and also allows that it was "entirely possible" that "I was conned by one of the greatest con artists of all time."

After Joey is finally sprung, Dylan has him blessing both the beasts and children: " 'Twas true that in his later years/He would not carry a gun." Of course not; no Mafia chieftain ever has, unless in unusually dire fear for his life. The cops would like nothing better than to send one of these guys up on a carrying concealed weapons rap, and anyway that's what the wall of protective muscle that accompanies them everywhere is for.

" 'I'm around too many children,' he'd say/'They should never know of one.' " Again true—mob leaders have always been scrupulous about keeping their wives and children universes removed from the everyday brutality of their work. Anybody who saw *The Godfather* knows that. But as for Joey's magical touch with children, let his daughter, Joie, speak: "He would come home and say, 'Make me some coffee.' And I would say, 'Daddy, I have homework. Can I do it later?' 'No. Now.' It was like I was refusing him, and nobody ever did that. He was the king, and I couldn't stand it. . . . He used to abuse Mommy terribly, and I resented him coming between us. He broke her ribs once. . . . I used to complain to Mommy about him and bug her to leave him. 'What a man you picked,' I'd say. 'Who'd want to live with that maniac? You've got to be crazy to put up with this.' So then I'd divorce him as my father. I'd take a piece of paper and draw a very fancy certificate that said, 'I, Joie Gallo, hereby divorce Joey Gallo as my father.' "

But who but a biographer would let a goddamn kid mouth off like that anyway? A good slap in the puss and they hie to their place. Which is where they belong when the fast bullets fly, as Dylan's vocal lurches to the denouement of his most mythic of sagas:

Yet he walked right into the clubhouse
of his lifelong deadly foe

Emptied out the register
Said "Tell them it was Crazy Joe"

One day they blew him down in a
clam bar in New York
He could see it comin' through the door
as he lifted up his fork . . .
Someday if God's in heaven
overlookin' His preserve
I know the men that shot him down
will get what they deserve.

And then, for the last time, the chorus that drones through this whole long, boring song:

Joey, Joey . . . what made them want
to come and blow you away?

There are several theories in answer to that question. The most prevalent was that, since most people took it for granted that Joey was behind the shooting of Joe Colombo almost a year before, there was an open contract out on Gallo by the Colombo family, meaning that Joey had effectively committed suicide in having Colombo rubbed out. Two other theories advanced by investigators have Gallo once again trying to muscle in on territory occupied by other, more powerful mob factions. In one case, he could have told two thugs to crack a safe for $55,000 in Ferrara's Pastry Shop in Little Italy, a landmark frequented by Vinnie Aloi, at that time a very powerful capo in the New York Mafia. This would certainly have been the straw that broke the camel's back in regards to the mob bosses' patience with Gallo's hustles, as would another incident reported in the June 4, 1972, *New York Times:* "Three weeks prior to Gallo's getting killed, he, Frank (Punchy) Illiano and John (Mooney) Cutrone went out to the San Susan nightclub in Mineola, L.I., in which John Franzese [another powerful capo in the Colombo family] is reported to have a hidden interest. Joey is reported to have grabbed the manager and said, 'This joint is mine. Get out.' In other words, he was cutting himself in. This was the first sign we had that Crazy Joe was acting up again."

In any case, any of these courses of action (and Gallo may well have undertaken all three) amounted to signing his own death warrant. An interesting sidelight is that at this time Joey was broke, practically reduced to the shame of living off his bride of three weeks; his mother had already mortgaged her house and hocked her furniture to pay for bail bonds. Meanwhile, of course, he had begun to hang out with what Goddard calls "the showbiz, table-hopping cheek-peckers' club": Jerry and Marta Orbach, the Ben Gazzaras, the Bruce J. Friedmans, Neil Simon, David Steinberg, Joan Hackett and her husband—people that, as his bride Sina warned him, "might be exploiting him for the thrill of having a real live gangster empty their ashtrays and talk about life and art." Marta Orbach told him Viking Press was interested in publishing whatever literary collaboration he could cook up with her, so they began making daily tape recordings of his reminiscences at her house. At first it was supposed to be a black comedy about prison life, but then there was talk of an outright autobiography and even a meeting with an MGM representative to discuss selling it to the movies—so there is also the remaining possibility, as a final theory, that just about anybody in the underworld, getting wind of this, might be nervous enough about possible indiscretions to want him snuffed.

The two key points here are that (a) by this time he was totally pathetic (Goddard: "He had outgrown the old life. To allow himself to be forced back into it was unthinkable—a submission to circumstance, a confession of failure. As for his new life, the prospect was hardly less humiliating. It entailed another kind of surrender—to showbiz society and public opinion. His self-esteem would depend, not on his power and sovereign will, but on how long an ex-gangster could stay in fashion. Like an ex-prizefighter, he might even be reduced someday to making yogurt commercials."), and (b) Dylan got even the very last second of Gallo's life wrong: "He could see it comin' through the door as he lifted up his fork." Gallo was shot from behind.

So all that remains is the question to Bob Dylan: Why? And since that is one I doubt he is going to answer (his new collaborator, Jacques Levy, already put in a defense to the effect that Dylan wrote about Billy the Kid, so why not Joey Gallo), the only thing remaining is to suggest antihero fodder for future Dylan compositional product: Elmer Wayne Henley, William Calley, Arthur Bremer, and that kid who tried to rob a bank at 13th Street and Sixth Avenue and ended up drunkenly requesting replays of the Grateful Dead on the radio. Certainly they all qualify as alienated victims of our sick society, every bit as much on the outside as Joey Gallo.

One does wonder, however, what Gallo would have made of Dylan's tribute to him; and one receives a possible answer in Goddard's book, where Gallo's ex-wife describes borrowing a hundred bucks from Joey's father to buy records so that the Prince of Brooklyn, always a fan of contemporary music, could catch up on what had been happening in soundsville during that decade he'd been away reading Reich in the slams: "He got especially mad over a Byrds album called 'Chestnut Mare' that I wanted him to hear. 'Listen to the lyrics,' I said. 'They're so pretty, and so well done.' 'I don't want to hear any fags singing about any fucking horse,' he says—and he's really venomous. 'It's not about a fucking horse,' I said. 'If you'll listen, it's about life.' But he doesn't want to hear about life either. . . . Next thing I know, he jumps out of the bathtub, snatches the record off the machine, stomps out in the hall stark-naked and pitches it down the incinerator.' "

The Village Voice, March 8, 1976
(Reprinted in *Creem,* April 1976)

Anne Murray: *Danny's Song*

Anne Murray is the real thing when it comes to popular music of quality and enduring significance circa 1973, a hypnotically compelling interpretrix with a voice like molten high school rings and a heavy erotic vibe. What Anne Murray is about, make no mistake, is S-E-X with a capital X. Maybe you're scoffing right now, you can't feel her vibe because you're so burnt-out and jaded and steeped in sleaze that it takes the sight of Linda Lovelace jacking off 14 braying donkeys with her nostrils while giving head to the entire class of '44 and playing pingpong on Henry Kissinger's nuts with her toes in Todd-AO just to get your attention. Well, that's your problem.

Anne keeps the heat up and brings you back again and again enraptured and slavering precisely by the scientific application of that time-honored and almost forgotten erotic technique—the holdout. She's the ultimate tease, because she gives you nothing but her vibrating *presence.* No foldout covers with Lainie Kazan cleavage, no four-page spreads in *Playboy,* not even breathy vocals a la Julie London. About all they ever show on her album covers is her head, or her body's just a silhouette shrouded in the infinite intangible beckoning mysteries of the night. Which gives you a lot to fantasize.

Even if, as *Rolling Stone* recently revealed, she does have "a large lesbian following." But don't let that worry you, that's just kismet, this katy's as straight as a yardarm except for her perfect pearly tits and roundy mound o' bush and arco droolo calves and well you know the rest. . . .

She also told aforementioned mag that "I want to quit [showbiz] when I'm 30 . . . and get married and have kids, and I really don't believe you can combine career and family." Which means we'd better get into this sweet honey jive of hers fast, starting with today when you're gonna buy *Danny's Song.* This album is her supreme recorded achievement, partially because she's just now coming into her maturity, both vocally and in her choice of material—ain't no filler here, whereas some of her earlier albums were almost as patchy as those excelsior-balls Helen Reddy keeps getting twined in. But here the title song alone is worth the price. You've heard it on the radio so you know it's a masterpiece. It's by that hippie panda Kenny Loggins, but don't pay no mind, it was his one burst of brilliance. It's all about the impending birth of his (or Annie's, or somebody's) child, like *Tupelo Honey* except better because Annie ain't running from no banshees of Irish gloom, she could well be in suburbia which is part of her triumph. Those people by the air conditioners need something to identify with, and it sure ain't the Spiders from Mars.

Other highlights of the studio first side include Randy Newman's "I'll Be Home," which ain't been done this good since Barbra Streisand, except totally diff interp because Barb's schnozzonasality gave her a Little Girl Blue poignance, whereas Annie's a mature and fulfilled woman and means it not someday in the misty rosy future after she's got herself sorted out but right now, you poor grime becaked khaki'd sap! Her throat's that open!

Danny's Song really begins to whirl on side two, which was all recorded live in Ottawa before a frenzied crowd of Annie's most pantingly ardent Canuck followers. Not a dry eye or seat in the house, and her performance is suitably feelingful and intense, though of course within the proper bounds, since half her charm and mystique is that much as Annie feels her music she never resorts to strident melodramatics a la Janis or Tina. She just ain't that kinda tushie. She's subtle. "Ease Your Pain" 's by that blustery old bozo Hoyt Axton, who used to sing about cocaine until the hard life and fast wimmen got to him and he took to writing songs about and for succor. Annie gives it to him in milky globules of pure relief, too, no mistaking that aureole pillow. Freckles even I betcha. When she gives so much so consistently, you can only wonder how much she's getting, especially when she does songs like Scott "San Francisco Flower Pate" McKenzie's "What About Me," which is the next hit single here and takes a real woman's stand: Hey, you, stop walking on me! Gimmie the real thing for a change, you big lug!

Sure thing, honey! But no. She's obviously fulfilled, she don't need you. All you gotta do is listen to that rabid mob howling for more after the raveup finale of "Put Your Hand in the Hand" at the end, and you know this honey's happy, because what more than stardom could one woman ask 'cept the love of her man. She's got stardom, and we can tell from the way she sings so nice and balanced and warm she ain't no Judy Garland "Man That Got Away" Tuinal-tainted tragedy, so she's gotta have a man somewhere (bet he's a carpenter). So she's happy as a poteet, just like all us fans and dream lovers listening to her. So buy her today.

Creem, September 1973

Helen Reddy: *Long Hard Climb*

All men are weasels. The only use they have for women is to get their rocks off, and half the time the only reason they wanna do that is to prove something. Which is why all women hold them in such utter contempt.

But everybody knows that. What everybody doesn't know is the hot pulsating goodies Helen Reddy's got to offer up. Cum here woman, do your duty; drop them drawers and gimme some pooty! But no, this is one Boopsy won't do the do—she's a holdout, she's not even a tease. Anne Murray was demure but carnal—Helen is downright *prim* at times.

But that's her genius. Clearly the world stage is now readyer'n ever for some kinda prim popstar. People who think in slow motion got Roberta Flack, fags got I forget who, drunken speedfreaks got Lou Reed, hippies and jigoros got all kindsa icons, but all the young ladies of the hands-off persuasion who are good and sick of all these big pigs leering and smacking over 'em all the time have finally got a pop force of major magnitude to speak for them. And that's no small shekels, Bashkar.

In the first place everybody's too damn *blatant* today; the dildo-brandishing comicstrip superficiality of a Wayne County is a real bore. Grace Metalious said that the real sickness (which is what pop thrives on) is in the clean places, and it's still true today. MOR[5] is more perverted than glitter ever dreamed of being because glitter is too

[5] Back in the days when rockers and grown-ups were two separate and distinct creatures, Middle of the Road (MOR), also known as Easy Listening, also known as "Happy House-wives' Music," was the record-biz designation for soft, tuneful adult pop.

upfront—it's like how s&m freaks don't really dig each other: they want somebody who's NOT DIGGING IT! They want straights! Fresh meat! And the foursquare decks of Helen Reddy with enough bendo twisto English to satiate even the most jaded mugwump.

Take for instance *Long Hard Climb*'s "The Old Fashioned Way," where Helen sings, "Just melt against my skin/And let me feel your heart"—obviously an emetically graphic depiction of Burroughs' classic scene of terminal parasitic absorption as the two Venusian organisms schlup together in a slow froth of creeping green ooze like when you put salt on a snail.

But the real masterpiece here is "Leave Me Alone." Guys have had all kindsa great hostility songs for years, from John Lee Hooker's "I'm Mad" to Lou's "Vicious," but all women had to fall back on was masochistic laments like "Will You Still Love Me Tomorrow" or at best c&w you're-cut-off sops like Loretta Lynn's "Don't Come Home a Drinkin' (With Lovin' on Your Mind)." But this is a woman's song that goes all the way in the most basic terms: "Leave me alone, aww *leave* me alone. . . ." Not since Dylan's pinnacles has there been such revivifying and totally irresistible rancor. I can see this tune being a hot number on jukeboxes in bars across the USA, as the stags smooth their shags furtively eyeing the always two babes just a few tables away ("Yours doesn't look so good," if one's really fat and ugly; "Well, which one do *you* want—makes no difference to *me*." "The blonde." "I thought you were gonna say that.") So now besides just smirking "No" at these losers, the sisters have a blare of support to blast the brummels to cowering jelly under their own tables. It's the same kind of release from sexual suffocation expressed in the lines of her hit "Peaceful": "No one bending over my shoulder/Nobody breathing in my ear!" *This* is a real woman's pop anthem, and not that queasily self-conscious sisters-unite pap set in a perfect marriage of watered-down Sousa and "Waltzing Matilda."

Even when she's toeing the line Helen manages to get the irony in. "A Bit O.K." is about connubial fructification. In the morning she tap-dances while making the coffee, at night she turns off the late show and reaches for him. Perfect joy, perfect fulfillment: "Now I'm really livin'." Now you might think that's just a bogusly suburban mythical wifey-poo copout on Helen's part, but it's not. Subtle as ever, she saves her wealth of sarcasm for the chorus: "Hey hey, it's a bit O.K. [whotta testimonial!] . . . By the way, thanks a lot for givin' me a little lovin' . . ." [you miserable clumsy inconsiderate prematurely ejaculatin' grunto lug!]

I don't blame Helen and the rest of womankind for being mad. All men but me are puds. What I'd like to see is an all-girl band that would sing lyrics like "I'll cut your nuts off, you cretins," and then jump into the audience and beat the shit out of the men there. Meanwhile, Helen's chops are up: she's no artist, she's a constant *pulsation,* 50,000 watts of Helen Reddy arcing into diffusion with a glow that touches every stucco nautilus in every housing project from here to Bobby Goldsboro's composite dream suburb. Helen is not merely heavy, Helen is not just a downy-necked sex object like Anne Murray—Helen is a beacon, the perfect Seventies incarnation of Miss Liberty herself in pantsuit and bowler crooning for America in a voice like the tenderest walls brushing together—the real velvet underground.

Creem, August 1974

Grace Jones Beats Off

Where is Betty Davis now that we really need her? In case you don't remember, this ex-wife of Miles put out some fairly kinky LPs about a half-decade ago, was dismissed by critics and public alike, and disappeared. Like Grace Jones, she had no talent, was on Island, and sold herself via her purported affinity for s&m; unlike Grace Jones, she wrote all her own lyrics and didn't have a flat-top. One of her more memorable slap-'em-ups was called "He Was a Big Freak" ("I used to beat him with a turquoise chain. . . ."). As one of her album titles stated, she was truly a nasty gal, and would fit into the present schema perfectly; maybe she could even get Miles to come out of seclusion, lay down some trumpet or organ lines, invite some of the boys over, and then we'd have some *real* DOR.[6]

On the other hand, the case could be made that Grace Jones is really performing a supremely moral public service by revealing s&m for the banal and often faked little twist it is: here is Grace, on the cover of her new *Warm Leatherette* album, looking like an overstuffed easy chair with a turniphead sticking up from the top of it. Ah, you might say, but a turniphead with such blazingly evil dominatrix eyes! Faugh, say I, because I have been auditing turnipheads for quite some time and can't be fooled: I see you in there, Gracie, do you want to come out and play?

The title song of this admittedly plucky little lady's new album almost threw me for a moment, I confess, because every time I used to hear the Normal's version all I could see was all those assholes dancing at the Mudd Club, where I first heard it, and all my hostilities would

[6] Dance-Oriented Rock (DOR) was then a music-biz marketing term.

flare like the back of a porcupine's neck. Fortunately, Grace brings it all back home via the total blandness (not anomic deadness) of her singing, revealing how utterly silly it would indeed be to watch yourself burning to death in the rearview mirror of your wrecked sportscar, your puny little badass jacket just like everybody else's melting into your poptoney flesh as the handbrake penetrates your schtuplane. Also this "Let's make love before we die" business—even assuming these people could fuck under those (and no other?) conditions, one must wonder if all of them actually can and want to come that quick.

No, it's leather schmeather all the way, as a glance at some of the other songs covered here indicates—I mean I can even see the persecution if not assassination of Smokey Robinson ("The Hunter Gets Captured by the Game," now don't shudder, you're being as silly as she is), but *Tom Petty* ("Breakdown")? Even a song title as promising as "Bullshit" fails to deliver the goods, although one must sympathize with Grace when she sings that "all those assholes" (*you* know the ones) are annoying her, and adds (chorus) "I'm gettin' tired of all this bullshit. . . . /Hey Jesus c'mon down and save us." True, she's got the creme of Jamaica's session pros behind her (the Robbie Shakespeare/Sly Dunbar contingent), but there are times when, even in the tropics, a sessionman is a sessionman is a sessionman. The real question with this total newavicization of yesterday's discolettes is, Who's left to hate and blame everything on now? Answer: New Wavelettes! Death to Fashion in any form! And no slow romantic Catholic deaths either—shoot 'em on sight. Should she escape her inevitable termination long enough to make one more album, might I suggest Grace get really desecrative (Chrissie Hynde is small potatoes) and cover Lou Reed's "Wrap Your Troubles in Dreams" off Nico's 1967 *Chelsea Girl* album, which features such lapidaries as "Excrement filters through the brain," "Filth covers the body pores," and "Pus runs through minted hair." Shit, they really knew how to party back then.

The Village Voice, June 25, 1980

Stevie Nicks: Lilith or Bimbo?

I never met anybody who didn't like *Rumours.* It got played a lot around my house in the year of "Anarchy in the U.K." and "White Riot," and I think the reason why so many people who got airsick of being in the same room with Eagles records might find songs like "Dreams" bringing them to tears was that Fleetwood Mac transcended FM Hollywood, not only by playing and singing with open-eyed passion but by articulating the painful questions of love (and the real answers that hurt). "Thunder only happens when it's raining/Players only love you when they're playing" may have been obvious, but that was its very purity: *you had been there,* and could remember all too well when you first learned you can't change anybody. The song was so honest and accurate that it *became* heartbreak instead of just being about it. It was cleansing for everyone who heard it, which was everyone period.

I guess what it comes down to is where you live, and I don't just mean Hollywood or New York. That's part of it, but it's too easy. Stevie Nicks may be a space case, a terminal mutation of the genus Superstar (her manicurist gets a liner credit), and at times emetically narcissistic—the cover, which is thoroughly repulsive from where I sit as a man or graphix fan, is the worst thing about *Bella Donna,* her successful bid for solo stardom. The best things about it are state-of-the-art production, the husky passion of her voice, and her melodies, which are so tenacious I'm still listening a full two months after I first bought this record and decided it was a bunch of shit.

The reason I think it's a bunch of shit is Stevie's emetic narcissism, and one reason I'm still listening to it is that I think emetic narcissism is funny (gotta find some way to live with it, after all). Take the cover: if you think of yourself as a witch, you can probably count yourself in Stevie's constituency, and may not even mind that she's giving you the finger on the back. Some listeners may be more unnerved by the fact that the front cover credits a different hairstylist than the back and inner sleeve, and it damn sure looks like the same haircut (demand your money back). Finally, those are the dumbest shoes since the halcyon days of Quay Lewd and the Tubes. What kind of witch wears stacked heels?

But people don't buy records for shoes, they buy them for songs, and now we're back in bunch of shit territory again. There really are still some people who believe a love song says "I love you because you are like this and thus and so," not "I love you because I am like this and that and the other thing." Somewhere they exist. Though whether even they would want to listen to former toongenre at this point is admittedly questionable. Stevie, who has been known to come out with lines as good as "When you build your house/Then call me home," compares herself here to the moon, a "highway-woman," the "kind of woman that'll haunt you," a white winged dove, and the sea. It's probably no wonder she rarely finds time on this album to feel for or write about anybody else, although in "Edge of Seventeen," the album's centerpiece of tragicomic melodrama, she does anguish over lusting like the sea and then laying a 16-year-old boy.

Yet in the end it's all forgivable, even the fact that songs like "The Highwayman" are about vermin like the Eagles. ("'They are the Errol Flynns and Tyrone Powers of our day!' she exults slyly. 'So long as I have to live with them, I try to make them into the most wonderful bunch of guys I can possibly think up!'"—*Rolling Stone*) The truth is that Stevie and her equally celebritous friends have devastating personal problems that such awestruck wretches as ye beyond the Garrards don't have to cop to. As she admits in "After the Glitter Fades," she never thought that she would make it there in Hollywood, but she's got so much money coming in the windows and doors (unless "gold" refers to muggles!) that she contracts temporary amnesia four lines later and decides that "It's the only life I've ever known." Certainly it must get confusing when there's "No speed limit . . . this is the fast lane/It's just the way that it is here." And given these harrowing trials of mind and body, it's probably a double blessing that she has aforementioned friends (who after all are equally self-referential in their own epics) along for the ride. "Leather and Lace," for instance, is dedicated to Waylon Jennings and Jessi Colter and sung with Eagle Don Henley. Stevie makes Don into a wonderful guy by putting words in his mouth: "Sometimes I cry."

Still, I must say I have no curiosity whether Stevie fucked Tom Petty and if so who may have dragged whose heart around, nor does anybody I sleep with, nor anybody else they're sleeping with, nor any of the latter's other lovers (wild, huh?) As I'm sure Stevie would be relieved to know. And I must caution her that according to the *Physicians' Desk Reference,* one of the contraindications of the belladonna alkaloids is that in high or prolonged dosage they cause temporary amnesia (!) greatly resembling senility; for treatment of this type of cellular deterioration I would probably prescribe deanol acetamidobenzoate, more popularly known as Deaner-250, to be administered orally three times daily, though whether via kissing or one's own hand is best left to the individual patient.

The Village Voice, November 25, 1981

Art Ensemble of Chicago: Rated G

I've never been much of an Art Ensemble of Chicago fan. I first caught them at the Ann Arbor Blues and Jazz Festival in '72, after which they always epitomized for me a certain school of hoodoo-hokum free playing that seemed to emphasize things like beads rattling across drumheads and painting your face, at the expense (I thought) of getting down to the real soul. Even last year's widely hailed *Nice Guys* didn't do much to convert me, and when a friend took me to see them at the Public last winter I fell asleep, though I did think Malachi Favors Maghostut's clown makeup was a nice touch. A couple of months later, somebody gave me a copy of Roscoe Mitchell's *Nonaah,* and I loved it, but for (ostensibly) all the wrong reasons—I thought it was one of the most obnoxious things I'd ever heard, and called up several musician friends to play them that part about two-thirds of the way through side one where Roscoe starts making long disgusting fartlike noises and won't stop. I told my musician friends, *On the Corner* devotees all, "This record has given me new hope for jazz!" and we laughed hysterically. But I *meant it!*

My problem with contemporary free jazz, and the reason I can hardly listen to any of it made after about 1971, is that it is now really a conservative music—every bit as much so as bebop—which has not advanced, particularly in the past few years. (Just think: free jazz is over two decades old, a span of time at least half again as long as that between the bebop revolution and Ornette-Cecil et al.) I mean, where *could* it have gone after things like *Om* and *Coltrane and Sanders Live in Seattle?* In fact, it's now more like a tradition the musicians are protecting, which is cool but totally antithetical to the pagan yawp it was born as.

When an avant-garde becomes a Preservation Society, what can it do to guard its however virtuosic woofs and tweets against creeping fuddyduddyism? Well, one court of resort is humor, as Roscoe's album made me realize immediately. It was always in there anyway (cf. any number of old pieces by Ornette and Archie Shepp too, not to mention Coltrane's pre-free but nevertheless immortal "Hey fellas, where's the beer opener?" tag for *Relaxin' with the Miles Davis Quintet*), so if I tell you that it is largely with affectionate amusement that I listen to *Full Force,* the Art Ensemble's latest waxing, I hope you will recognize it as praise, not condescension. Everybody takes all this stuff with such utter solemnity; meanwhile these guys are in the studio obviously having fun. Yeah art and all that shit, and sure they're all composers as much as Glass or Reich or anybody, but jazz was originally goodtime music and in large part that's what the Art Ensemble (when *they're* good) play. So even if it doesn't always shake you to your foundations (rarely, if ever, in fact) it's still usually fun. Even the goddamn gourds and windchimes and beads on drumheads.

What I do take issue with is the contention (reiterated in the band's current bio) that any of this is really "new music." Actually it is several types of relatively "old" musics played side by side or slowly segued together. And you pretty much have to take the jive, which is painless by now, along with the real stuff.

The first side of *Full Force* is a perfect case in point. All but 45 seconds of it is tenanted by Malachi's "Magg Zelma" (Christian Vander lives!), which opens with about four minutes of miscellaneous percussion and celeste-vibes-glockenspiel and what can only be called barnyard action (duck calls, etc.), all going nowhere leisurely. Then there's a moving prayerlike tenor solo by Joseph Jarman. And into the interior: a bass vamp, driving African percussion, chugging reeds, acerbic Lester Bowie trumpet solo, the whole falling somewhere to the right of "Tears for Johannesburg" on Max Roach's 1960 *We Insist: Freedom Now Suite* and to the left of Shorty Rogers albums from a couple of years previous to that like *Afro-Cuban Influence* and *Shorty Rogers Meets Tarzan*. "Atmospheric," as they say, but it's got some soul. After that "Magg Zelma" sorta peters out over several minutes of inconclusive jamming. But you're shocked awake by Roscoe's 45-second "Care Free," a gorgeous Latin-tinged unison statement by the horns that's the most beautiful melody on the album. That they chose not to elaborate on it seems absolutely perverse.

The other side is equally whimsical or erratic, depending on your attitude. Jarman's "Old Time Southside Street Dance" opens and closes with a shrill but invigorating ensemble theme that's highly reminiscent of Albert Ayler: the solos in between are fast and fairly directionless except for Maghostut's almost rock 'n' rolly bass twonks. The complex title cut is intermittently inspired; the highlights for me are the sustained blasts at the climax (almost ruined by rattling bells) and one section where Roscoe starts repeating something that sounds like "Hojo" through his horn over and over again, ending in a laugh and a whinny straight from the Three Stooges' Curly. Bowie's Mingus tribute is appropriately Ellingtonian, and his growling trumpet summons up the ghost of Quentin Jackson's trombone on *Black Saint and the Sinner Lady* as well as Ted Curson in "Folk Forms, No. One"—it's a heartfelt performance, but neither mournful enough to truly qualify as elegy nor explosive enough to recall the Mingus I worshipped.

No way does this music have the raw edge of Ornette's "Lonely Woman," Trane's "Alabama" or Shepp's "Hambone." No way it could, I guess. What's interesting to me is how even when the passion's not what it might be or they're really sorta jacking off, the record still makes it on another level that you might even call (with no criticism implied) commercial. It's not conservatory-austere, or fueled by Sixties rage; it's got something for everybody: blues, atonality, cartoons, psychedelia even. Anybody who can endure the likes of Stanley Clarke or Frank Zappa should have no trouble with this affable crew. What it finally comes down to, I think, is that the Art Ensemble of Chicago is just good clean family entertainment. Put 'em on the next Kristy and Jimmy McNichol special. I think America is finally ready.

The Village Voice, June 2, 1980

Ian Hunter: The Coots Are Alright

Hey you, there with the glasses. C'mere. I wanna tell you something. I've been meaning to do this for years: You're gonna die! That's right! G'wan and put on all the makeup you want, Junior, hide behind yer mama's girlfriend's wife's skirt, the fact is you ain't even *Junior* no more, you're getting older every second and all of a sudden you realize they *count!* Ha! That's right, they're adding up to an ourang on your back and from here on out it only gets worse. Which actually is better. Because honesty is always better than lies. Thank god for the baby boom and subsequent falloff, because they taught us all a very important lesson: that rock 'n' roll can be made by senior citizens. But what's more important and must be understood by all is that *old is cool.* Because kids are stupid little bastards headed nowhere really but their own not-so-distant geriatric wards. Whereas the aged have already been through all their pointless pogostickings and *know* as only those who have suffered for the stupidest of causes and lost anyway can. While not as old as I'd like to be (though I pass sometimes), I've been hep to this primacy-of-age business for years, ever since I first realized that Uncle Scrooge, Charles Bukowski, and Malcolm Muggeridge were all cooler than almost any rock star I could think of. And Ian Hunter knows it even better than I, being older (he told me once that he and Kim Fowley compared ages and came out about even) and thus, with that many more hopeless campaigns under his belt, that much closer to death.

On the other hand, his solo career has not been the liveliest affair. First collaboration with Mick Ronson was like Mott the Hoople on a half-charged battery, second a pompous embarrassment trying to be Dylan not even realizing what a pompous embarrassment *he* was becoming, third a strained blareblast which perhaps fortunately for Ian was never even released in the States. *You're Never Alone with a Schizophrenic* is better than any of those as well as topping Mott the Hoople's second, third, and last albums. While it lacks the kick of Mott at their peak, it rocks down straight and muses inconclusively on the Great Question as only Ian can. But even though he fails to say anything particularly new or particularly profound about age and imminent termination, the album reeks of decay and death, which is what gives it its undeniable power.

Ian has always been the most self-conscious and self-referential of rockers. That's part of his charm. But it also assures that he will take himself with unbending seriousness, so perhaps though we all share his plight we may be permitted to laugh occasionally at his histrionic grapplings with them. (He claims *he* does, like he says "Life After Death" is a sort of speed-comedown joke, but it doesn't show in the songs, so who cares?) In "The Outsider," he prefaces a Zimmermannered desolate-journey-through-the-desert (better done by America in "Horse With No Name," really) with "Death be my mistress/Guns be my wife." Such grimness is hysterical, or are we laughing from nervous fear? No, we're laughing *in spite of* nervous fear.

What saves Ian from his own portentousness is his honesty: that "Standin' in My Light" fades out almost in midchorus, signifying his recognition that even as he bitches at these new groups replacing him on fickle fans' pinup walls he is not afraid to recognize that he too is some kinda temporary, just a buzz. He long ago gave up on being the Nazz. But who the hell wants to be the Nazz anyway? The Nazz is an asshole. Ian, harken to thy critics (we're smarter than the muses): What you do best lyric/concept-wise is random, almost beatnik jottings on the current state of yourself and the passing melee. Meaning that even on your deathbed it'll still be "Just Another Night" and I won't be surprised if you'll be caught writing a song about it in the very moment old we-know-who comes to call. At this rate you should be able to keep up the solid senders steady 'nuff to turn out one of the grandest of our elder statesmen. Besides, hell, you were *born* old, and from the looks of things a lot of those sprouts on the pinup walls are gonna croak while you're still out boozing around.

The Village Voice, June 4, 1979

The Grooming of David Johansen

There's an important difference between "fashion" and "style"; it's like the difference between "normal" and "healthy." The norm is sick and the New York Dolls were abnormal but incredibly healthy; they had style, which is something you can only possess in and of yourself—it's originality, attitudinal distinction physicalized. Whereas fashion is just a bunch of assholes *telling* you how to dress and in fact conduct yourself in every area.

I loved David Johansen. I remember seeing him in the years between the breakup of the Dolls and his reemergence, hanging around the Bottom Line and CBGB's, always in that same little red hat and red suit, unfailingly cheerful, a wiseacre even, yet there was something touching in his unstated but manifest insistence amid the wreckage of the Dolls and the glitter albatross that he was Somebody, still a contender. Once in 1975 I asked him for his phone number, and when I unfolded the piece of paper and looked at it later he'd dotted the "i" in his name with a star, something I hadn't seen since girls in my high school with names like Trixie ran for class treasurer.

We all loved him in the Dolls because he was a palooka with irony, and we loved him last year because his comeback album had an openheartedness that made up for his hack band: there was real majesty in "Frenchette," and "Donna" was simply an all-time classic song, a heartwrencher on a par with "Wild Horses" or "Just Like a Woman."

What we especially loved about him was his naturalness. He seemed undiminished by having been through the music biz wars, still the cocky neighborhood pug who was also the nicest guy in town and man enough to show it. There was an ease about him which transcended rock 'n' roll even: maybe he was hungry, but he seemed to be riding the crest of career turbulence with a sort of Top Cat insouciance that marked him as a true entertainer. He seemed to do everything perfectly with zero strain, including being a sex symbol, and naturally the less effort you put into sex the sexier you're gonna be. Some people said he couldn't sing, but they thereby proved how little they knew about rock 'n' roll, or being an entertainer for that matter, because style and pure magnetism are talents that no music school can give you—like all the greats, he redefined the territory by breaking the rules. On *Take No Prisoners,* Lou Reed said "I've got enough attitude to kill everybody in the state of New Jersey"; David was a bad boy with enough heart to *save* everybody in the state of New Jersey, but he also managed to avoid the operatic gush and windy histrionics that're Springsteen's flaw.

You have just read a list of reasons why I hate *In Style.*

I'm not even gonna talk about his concert last week at the Palladium because I think it was an off night, and last year he gave some of the best rock 'n 'roll shows I'd ever seen, so I'm sure he's got plenty more in him (in *him;* his band, well . . . hacks dressed like the Knack). There's something starting to happen here that's fascinating to the connoisseur of career twists and cosmically saddening to anyone who loves David: he's confused fashion with style, and let himself be packaged in a way that's embarrassing if not emetic. What's truly scary is how passionate and frank he is about it, maybe because he doesn't yet see the subtle, crucial, tragic difference between wearing flash clothes to accent the blaze of your own one-in-a-billion personality and *becoming* the clothes. Here's an ad from last week's *Voice:* "The new album from David Johansen does it all with emphasis on melody, a touch of class and flash . . . but always 'In Style' . . . Rock 'n' roll dressed to kill." Come on, somebody, please *tell* me he's not selling himself so desperately it's pathetic.

Meanwhile, *In Style* itself is a perfectly pleasant album if you just wanna throw it on once in awhile. Me, I have this problem separating people's music from the stance or value system behind it, and what's behind *In Style* stinks (either that or the music's just not strong enough to make you forget, like the Stones used to).

The title cut, though it's an okay rocker, embodies the problem. Like the *Voice* ad, the song's a self-exposé, an admission that to get the riches and fame he wants, he's willing to conform, to compromise himself in the meantime: "Until there comes a day that I find me a better way/I'm doin' it all up in style"—what more damning criticism of this album could I make than that? I *know* his back's to the wall, I *know* the last album didn't get any radio play, just like I know that David likes sharp clothes with pockets full of spending loot, and that of course he always wanted his picture taken by Richard Avedon. What I didn't expect from somebody as unique as David was an album of homogenized formula rock from Stones to Springsteen (*later* for Mick Ronson!), and to see him peering through the bars of a package that veers between clichéd sexual commodity and imitation jaded cosmopolite. He used to be funky and now he may be chic though I doubt it, in fact he was always chic *because* he was funky, and now . . . he's beginning to . . . look like . . .

Trash.

Oh, but don't forget the "touch of class and flash" (yeah, the *touch!*)—this is no bowzer boy making his play, selling out. And in a way he's not selling out, because this shit, to be what J. Rotten called one of the "stupid fools who stand in line," seems to be what he really and truly desires with all his measureless heart, and there's the true tragedy and obscenity. But I'd just like to ask him: David, assuming you get the stardom you want on the terms you're settling for, just how are you gonna avoid becoming the person you were talking to in "Frenchette," who mistook the glitz for the soul, or the one you're talking about/to in "Flamingo Road?" This song is half a masterpiece—the Springsteen-out-of-Van Morrison geographic metaphor is still a little too derivative—which finally just tries too hard, complete with Springsteen pomp. This is also a song about a person who, in Little Richard parlance, got what she wanted but lost what she had: she made the big time, and now she's got "half the clothes in France" (rhymes with gratuitous "leather pants"), and it doesn't mean shit, she's freezing to death in the back of a Lincoln Continental. Well, to apply the brutal logic of the mentality he's addressing, that does seem to be what happens to people whose value systems lie in their wardrobes. When he sings "I bet your conversation takes you everywhere" it breaks your heart for an instant, and suggests what he might achieve in lieu of becoming Rick Springfield for *Vogue*—a real, clear-eyed, even somewhat wise exploration of what men and women can do to each other when all the glamour's on the floor.

There's also "Justine," a song in sight of the Grail of "Donna" which is nearly ruined by another goddamn Springsteen-mold arrangement; the single, "Melody," a romping but vocally strained Four Tops tribute (so he sings more "correctly" now, so what); the disco-influenced "Swaheto Women," which is neither sellout nor much of anything else; Stonesish blareblasts "She" and "Wreckless Crazy"; and the picture postcard of "Big City." The Dolls made the subways bang-shang-a-lang, "Donna" made me cry, and this album and his current grooming may help make David Johansen a star at last. I still hope he gets there. I hope that when and if he does he's still got something to say. And I hope he looks happier than Richard Avedon could make him.

The Village Voice, September 3, 1979

Patti Smith: *Horses*

Patti Smith will survive the media blitz and everybody's hunger for another "superstar," because she's an artist in a way that's *right* old-fashioned. *Horses* lunges with raw urgency, but her approach is very methodical. She could have done this a long time ago, and has been building steadily, paying dues and learning music fit for the reaches of her poetry so as, when the song is finally delivered, to fulfill all her promises.

What must be recognized is that she transcends bohemian cultism to be both positive and mainstream, even though her songs go past a mere flirtation with death and pathology. She just saw that it was time for literature to shake it and music to carry both some literacy and some grease that ain't jive. The combination makes her an all-American tough angel, street-bopping and snapping her fingers, yet moving with that hipshake which is so like every tease you slavered after in high school.

Her sound is as new-old as her look. You hear the Shangri-Las and other early Sixties girl groups, as well as Jim Morrison, Lotte Lenya, Anisette of Savage Rose, Velvet Underground, beatniks, and Arabs. Meanwhile, the minimalism of the band forces her sound out front along with the poetry, and that sound stands. This is not a "spoken word" album, it's a rock 'n' roll album, and even if you couldn't understand a word of English you couldn't miss the emotional force of Patti's music. And you'll love it when she makes mistakes (in this era of slick, predigested "rock" as Muzak), when her voice goes ragged (but right), like the perfect act of leaping for something precious. Who needs the other kind of perfection?

Which brings up one of the truly ballsy things about this album: she is meeting the *Mademoiselle* articles and Earl Wilson columns not with some licked up tech-mech superproduction (which John Cale is certainly capable of) but the finest garage band sound yet in the Seventies. The band cooks primarily because, with certain momentary exceptions (Richard Sohl's beautiful piano intro to "Free Money," Allen Lanier's ghostly guitar in "Elegie"), they're all used either as percussion instruments or (as in halcyon days of the Velvet Underground) for the sustenance of one fortifying drone. Lenny Kaye gets off some of the best one-note distorto guitar since the Stooges' "1969," and the general primitivism makes you realize you're a mammal again and glad for it, licking your chops.

Which is not to say that there's not musical sophistication working here; it's just that it's *gut* sophistication, unfaltering instinct rather than the clammily cerebral approach of the old "poetry and jazz" albums. *Horses* is a commanding record, as opposed to demanding—you don't have to work to "understand" or like it, but you can't ignore it either; it refuses to be background music, stops the action in the room when it's on, and leaves its effects when it's over whether the listeners like it or not.

Each song builds with an inexorable seethe, a penchant for lust and risk that shakes you and never lets you forget you're listening to real rock 'n' roll again at last. Meanwhile, every song contains *moments* that go beyond raunch into emotional realms that can give you chills. In "Birdland" it's the breathtaking "It was as if somebody had spread butter on all the fine points of the stars and they started to slip"; in "Break It Up," Patti's truly cosmic sequence of "I cried 'Help me *please*' / Ice it was shining," and suddenly through that line you can actually hear her hitting her chest metronomically with her fist, leading into "My heart it was melting . . ."

Throughout, she plays with roles and masks, combining sulky stalking cat and assertedly male aggressor in "Gloria," where she expands the Van Morrison original into a wild fantasy that's a celebration of raw lust and personal primacy over any god or law. Even though she is still learning to sing her voice is all over the place, from the horny yelp of "Gloria" 's "sweet young *thuing*" to the demonic way her tongue whips the word "locker" first time she says it in "Land" to the brief unearthly but heart-grazing wordless upper register vocal flight in the middle of "Elegie."

Horses really defines itself in "Kimberly," "Land," and "Elegie," the latter two fitting together in one shattering epic of violence, flight, death, and mourning that is ultimately purgative. "Kimberly" is the most haunting song I've heard in a long time (enough so that by the time I'd had the record 48 hours it was pulsating straight through not only my days but my dreams at night), a sort of Ronettes bolero *cum* "Waiting for the Man" celebrating the act of giving birth as cataclysm (as it is) in stunning lyrics: "Oh baby I remember when you were born/It was dawn and the storm settled in my belly/And I rolled in the grass and I spit out the gas/And I lit a match and the void went flash/And the sky split/And the planets hit. . . . And existence stopped/Little sister, the sky is falling/I don't mind. . . ."

"Land" establishes an eerily malevolent sexuality in the opening build leading to the rape scene, then the wild surge, each word an explosion, of "Suddenly/Johnny/gets a feeling/ he's being surrounded by/horses!/horses!/horses!/horses!" and then into a raw, tearing chorus of "Do you know how to pony" from the old Chris Kenner hit "Land of a Thousand Dances." After that the song takes off almost literally into space, Patti's three vocal tracks weaving in and out of phase, merging splintered images as if by magic: "He picked up the blade and then he pressed it against his . . . smooth *throat*/and let it dip in/the veins/to the sea/of possibilities/it started hardening/to the sea/in my hand/and I felt the arrows of desire. . . ." all rising in one raging floodgate of sound and image to explode in choking death chillingly envisaged, life ebbing with one decelerating drumbeat to "Elegie," a gust of pure melancholy stilled just short of whole anguish in Patti's finest vocal and the loneliest piece of music since Nico's "Elegy to Lenny Bruce."

Patti's heroes may be gone, but she is both with us and for us, so strongly that her music is something, finally, to rally around. For one thing, she has certain qualities that can make her a hero to a whole generation of young girls; Patti has done more here for woman as aggressor than all the Liberation tracts published, and has pushed to the front of the media eye that it is just as much a process (ordeal) of learning to "become" a "woman" as it is for men wrestling with all this ballyhooed "manhood" business. It's this tough chick who walks like Bo Diddley and yet is all woman like we've been waiting for so long, a badass who pulls off the feat of being simultaneously idol of women and lust object of men (and women, no doubt).

And even more than that, Patti's music in its ultimate moments touches deep wellsprings of emotion that extremely few artists in rock or anywhere else are capable of reaching. With her wealth of promise and the most incandescent flights and stillnesses of this album she joins the ranks of people like Miles Davis, Charlie Mingus, or the Dylan of "Sad Eyed Lady" and Royal Albert Hall. It's that deeply felt, and that moving; a new Romanticism built upon the universal language of rock 'n' roll, an affirmation of life so total that, even in the graphic recognition of death, it sweeps your breath away. And only born gamblers take that chance.

Creem, February 1976

Better Than the Beatles (And DNA, Too)

I have been getting whiny letters from a lot of you complaining about the general state of the art. "What is all this shit?" you ask. "We thought New Wave was supposed to be this awakening of New Avenues of Self Expression and Freedom, resulting in new musical verities and new insights into the human condition even! Instead we went out and spent all this money and all these records are *shit!*"

You're right about one thing at least: all those records are shit, and you might as well have burned all those dollar bills. (Joy Division's *Closer,* 12 bucks, haw haw haw!) But those records aren't shit for the reason that you think: those records are shit because they're all *too good!*

That's right. All those stupid bands were so stupid they plumb went out and learned to play their instruments, a process as ineluctable as the putrefaction of a corpse. Teach 'em a chord or two, then just *watch* those little bastards *practice* till they can switch off, back and forth between those two chords (then three, then four . . . never shoulda learned even *one!*) deft as Al DiMeola if he wanted to play that which he probably will soon! Damn!

Which is why the only hope for rock 'n' roll, aside from everybody playing nothing but shrieking atonal noise through Arbiter distorters, is *women.* Balls are what ruined both rock and politics in the first place, and I demand the world be turned over to the female sex immediately. Only hope. Valerie Solanas was so much greater a prophet than Warhol that I can only pray she might consent to *lead* the group I'm forming. The absolute best rock 'n' roll anywhere today is being played by women: the other night I saw God in the form of the Au Pairs, the Slits are stupendous, the Raincoats are better than *London Calling* or anything by Elvis Costello, Chrissie Hynde doesn't count, Joan Jett deserves her place in the sun if not reparations, Lydia Lunch is *the* Female Role Model for the '80s besides being one of the greatest guitarists in the world . . . the list is endless. (Patti come home!)

But credit must be given to the foremothers: the Shaggs. Way back in 1969 they recorded an album up in New England that can stand, I think, easily with *Beatles '65, Life with the Lions, Blonde on Blonde,* and *Teenage Jesus and the Jerks* as one of the landmarks of rock 'n' roll history. The Wiggins sisters (an anti-power trio) not only redefined the art but had a coherent *weltanschauung* on their very first album, *Philosophy of the World.* Basically what it comes down to is that unlike the Stones these girls are saying we love you, whether you're fat, skinny, retarded, or Norman Podhoretz even. Paul Weyrich. Don't make no difference, they embrace all because they are true one-world humanists with an eye to our social future whose only hope is a redefined communism based on the openhearted sharing of whatever you got with all sentient beings. Their and my religion is compassion, true Christianity with no guilt factors and no vested interest, perhaps a barter economy, but certainly the elimination of capitalism, rape, and special-interest group hatred. For instance, in their personal favorite number, "My Pal Foot Foot," they reveal how even a little doggie must be granted equal civil rights perhaps even extending to the voting booth. Hell, they let Nancy Reagan in! They also believe that we should jettison almost completely the high-tech society which has now perched us on the lip of global suicide, and return to third world–akin closeness with the earth, elements, nature, the seasons, as in my personal favorite on this album, "It's Halloween," which emphasizes that seasonal festivals are essential to a healthy body politic (why d'ya think all them people in California got no minds?)

Unfortunately the Wiggins' masterpiece was lost over the years—it came out on a small label, and everybody knows the record industry has its head so far up its ass it's licking its breastplate. But this guy from NRBQ had the savvy to rescue it from oblivion (in a recent issue of *Rolling Stone,* he compared their work to early Ornette Coleman, and he's right, though early Marzette Watts might be more apt), so now we got it out on the Red Rooster label, which of course is a perfect joke on all those closet-queen heavy-metal cockrockers. How do they sound? Perfect! They can't play a lick! But mainly they got the right attitude, which is all rock 'n' roll's ever been about from day one. (I mean, not being able to play is never enough.) You should hear the drum riff after the first verse and chorus of the title cut—sounding like a peg-leg stumbling through a field of bald Uniroyals, it cuts Dave Tough cold and these girls aren't even junkies (of course)! They just whang and blang away while singing in harmonies reminiscent of three Singing Nuns who've been sniffing lighter fluid and their voices are just so copacetic together (being sisters, after all) you'd almost think they were Siamese triplets. Guitar style: sorta like 14 pocket combs being run through a moose's dorsal, but very gently. Yet it rocks. Does it ever. Plus having one of the greatest album covers in history, best since *Blank Generation.* God Bless the Shaggs. Now if they will only emerge from (semi?) retirement (?) no one ever will have cause again to say "Rock 'n' roll is dead, man. . . ." Up an' at 'em, Valerie.

The Village Voice, January 28, 1981

Dead Boys Almost Count Five

You could make a case that the Dead Boys are just a little Sex Pistols for the CBGB congregation to dream on till Rotten & Co. hit these shores; lead singer Stiv Bators flays his flesh a la Iggy and manages regularly to wrench his face into a sniggeringly Rotten grimace; lead guitarist Cheetah Chrome is at least as thuggish as Vicious; and the group's relationship with their audience is love-hate at best—the last two shows I saw were interrupted when beer bottles were flung at the stage (Cheetah claims it's the same guy every time). The group has more or less bragged in interviews that violence seems to follow them around, and a source as reliable as Sire Records' bio relates harrowing tales of Bators's self-inflicted cuts, bruises, and scratches, and Jimmy Zero's fan-inflicted cigarette burns.

I suppose you're going to tell me that this obligatory punk glorying in self-mutilation and sadomasochism is revolting and gets more so all the time. When Iggy cut himself, after all, he did it because he was truly insane; with groups like the Dead Boys and the Viletones it's more offensive than terrifying. It's so transparent that they're gouging themselves not because of some dark inner compulsion but for the simple reason that, like every male jerk in any fledgling band circa 1973 who smeared makeup all over his face, they think it'll make them stars.

Yet in spite of all this patent jive I not only find the Dead Boys inoffensive, I like them. Look, you may think I'm sicker than they're pretending to be, but it really doesn't hurt very much to administer those little surface cuts, besides which they're gonna get the shit kicked out of them when they go to England so they're bound to really suffer for their art sooner or later. Not that they should suffer for their art, or pay any other kind of dues for that matter; *not* paying them is what American punk rock has always been about. Jimmy Zero told me he always thought they were a comedy act, and *Young Loud and Snotty,* their first album, is classic trashy American garage rock which you ought to take about as seriously as it takes itself. People tend to forget that groups like Count Five were able to laugh at themselves in the middle of mid-Sixties marijuana longhair politics. The Dead Boys' dopey cultivated hostility doesn't bother me any more than the fact that their album is a fucking *demo,* or that they were barred from the final mixing sessions by producer Genya "Hot Pants" Ravan. They're a hell of a lot closer to the swill I grew up on (Shadows of Knight, Standells, Chocolate Watch-band) than all those crappy English bands imitating the Ramones.

There are those who will argue that the Dead Boys' original material is sexist. What a brilliant deduction. But, as the Spokesmen spake in "Dawn of Correction," "You missed all the good in your evaluation." The good is that like most punk bands, the Dead Boys are probably too drunk to get it up anyway, are scared shitless of real s&m, and in general conceive of sex not as a matter of male supremacy but as a dirty little business. Take a song like "Caught With the Meat in Your Mouth"—where groups like Aerosmith indulge in stud-posturing, Bators asserts just what the title says, that he's got something on the crummy bitch and, implicitly, since this door swings both ways, on himself as well. Nowhere on this album does the miserable little snerd sing the words, "My dick is 10 inches long." He can't, because like the rest of the group he's Catholic (it is a fact that all of them used to be altar boys), so sex is a matter riddled with such guilt that both Stiv and Ms. Lunch[7] are

[7] Lydia Lunch was Stiv's girlfriend in those days, and later a rather polarizing, downtown New York guitarist and singer in her own right.

humiliated. Either that or the meat in her mouth is a symbolic communion wafer, in which case both parties are doubly blessed. It's getting harder than ever to tell heaven from hell these days.

The Village Voice, October 24, 1977

On the Merits of Sexual Repression

Maybe this gets down to it: the Ronettes, the Shangri-Las, the Crystals, the guy singers too, all those old classic rock 'n' roll songs were fueled by one thing: *sexual repression,* and consequent frustration. They may have been sexist, they may have been neurotic or even masochistic—sometimes I think the whole reason pop music was invented in the first place was to vent sick emotions in a deceptively lulling form. THEY WERE LITERALLY EXPLOSIVE WITH ALL THAT PENT-UP LUST AND FEAR AND GUILT AND DREAD AND HATE AND RESENTMENT AND CONFUSION. And it gave them a kind of anarchic power, which can still move us.

Listening to certain old Shangri-Las sides, you might find yourself laughing and crying at the same time. And the Spector stuff... not just the storied Wall of Sound but the *urgency* in those girls' voices spelled pure sex, distillate of every scene between a boy and girl at the drive-in, vacant lots, house when the folks were out, wherever we found to sneak off to back then to see how far we could take it this time.

All that frustration got channeled into rock, all those powerful emotions were way out front and there was plenty of meticulous detail in the productions behind them. They were like magnificent tapestries depicting the most embarrassing and ridiculous yet painful situations, and they stand to this day.

While Blondie hardly constitutes a Wall of Sound, it wouldn't be fair to hold that against them. They're not the Blondie Orchestra, they're a good little rock 'n' roll band which has been steadily evolving from the garage without ever losing sight and understanding of what was good, if not better than the rest, back there. Their songs are mostly good. Debbie's got about as good a voice by traditional "singing" standards as a lot of the people who recorded in the early Sixties. But you wouldn't dare line one of these cuts up next to a Spector or Shangri-Las production, because it'd sound downright pallid. The reason you wouldn't is that (as I keep harping on) the music seems to have no really strong emotions in it, and what emotions do surface occasionally, what obsessions and lusts, are invariably almost immediately gutted by fusillades of irony, sarcasm, camp, what have you, ending up buried.

IF THE MAIN REASON WE LISTEN TO MUSIC IN THE FIRST PLACE IS TO HEAR PASSION EXPRESSED—as I've believed all my life—THEN WHAT GOOD IS THIS MUSIC GOING TO PROVE TO BE? What does that say about us? What are we confirming in ourselves by doting on art that is emotionally neutral? And, simultaneously, what in ourselves might we be destroying or at least keeping down?

In the last few years we have seen the rise of a type of music perhaps previously unknown in human history: music designed specifically, by intent or subconscious motivation, to remove what emotions might linger in the atmosphere around us, creating a vacuum where we can breathe easier because we're not so freaked by each other even though we still don't communicate. That's your basic disco, of course. But it's not just disco music that does this. It's all kinds of music and you can talk all you want about Muzak and the wimsy weasly pre-rock popular music our parents lived and loved to, "How Much Is That Doggie in the Window," but that wasn't the same because all those songs were based upon a view of social intercourse pretty much agreed upon by everyone listening. Whereas no such thing really exists now. So there's a whole new genre of air conditioner music, climate control, antidepressant/antipsychotic music, music designed to neutralize and pacify and ultimately render stillness rather than the jungle pounding of two lovers' hearts or the Beaver Cleaver sappiness of "Doggie in the Window." Before, all music you heard was designed to put something *into* the room; this new stuff is designed to take something *out.*

Blondie has, it seems, embraced this aesthetic more or less wholeheartedly. But when you're always taking out instead of putting in . . . well, it's just like a bank account, isn't it? Pretty soon there's gonna be nothing left. And that kinda would seem to make you a musical vampire, of sorts.

Patti Smith, for all her pretensions, her wrongheadedness, her narcissism, her addled crusades, is still singing from her however mottled heart. She contributes something to the environment when she's on, she stands for something too no matter how etc., but she's real, flesh and blood comes through those grooves, which I think is one reason why she has so many fans. Or Lou Reed, for all his monotonal mutterings, there's so much pain suffused just under the monotone, so much despair and desire and human regret, that even at his most cynical you can feel him struggling with himself, fighting his demons. But Blondie . . . do they have that kind of courage?

Like Bryan Ferry in Roxy Music, they're trying to create a sort of deliberately rococo, overstuffed art rock that hides what the artist is truly feeling by dropping well-turned ironies all over the place, by coming up with synthetic soul-searchings that purport to be even more interesting than the real thing. Or they just camp it up. But Bryan Ferry was in the grips of real romantic lobster claws, and no matter how many times he transposed what he was going through before putting it out in song you always knew he was going through *something.* There was a grand passion, a vitality and even kind of poignancy about his music even at its archest and most exasperatingly evasive.

Whereas with Blondie you get no such vibe, 90 percent of the time at least. What you get instead is a pervasive coldness, and even that's not so bad, since they don't just write pop love songs. What are they driving at in most of their lyrics? Are they telling you to leave them alone? Are they kvetching about their career? Are they concocting little sagas based on everyday events that never become compelling? Or are they being deliberately mundane to the point of madness? . . . What, if anything, do these people actually *care* about?

Or if all they want to do is entertain, then why do they act so serious about what they're doing? Maybe they think they're Dorothy Parker, commenting lightly and wittily on the passing mobs without ever getting in too deep. Which is okay, too, except . . . It's impenetrable. Talk about walls of sound, THEIR MUSIC IS A WALL. It's designed that way, most likely from self-protective instincts that're not necessarily unjustified or misguided but . . . they're dealing in media that ostensibly communicate . . . then eventually the audience begins to receive an impression of some hermetic body of people, a little cabal, who've locked themselves in and are nursing a siege mentality when nobody really is out to get them.

The press ain't nice, don't play fair, you get burned once and you're more careful the next time. But you don't walk around in these giant suits of armor and exoskeletons steeling yourselves against new attacks every corner you turn. Sooner or later, you would have to say something you really mean. "Shayla" and "Union City Blue" come closest, but they're both third-person songs. When are Blondie gonna write a first-person song—aside from "Living in the Real World," which is just an awfully early case of the old familiar syndrome of rockstar self-pity—that expresses how they truly feel about themselves, each other, their friends, lovers, acquaintances, relatives, the landlord, ANYBODY, ANYTHING? Just make it definite and act like you mean it.

To maintain stardom as a function of non-empathetic distance, to keep them wanting more even as you toss the dirt of your contempt in their faces or just turn your back like Miles Davis did for most of his career . . . well, this is no easy trick to pull off. It takes an extremely complex personality and one who is also a master of shifting masks and disguises, the complete chameleon (Dylan, Bowie). Either that or the innate ability to project something menacing and dangerous, however spurious this impression may be, that keeps them at bay (Lou Reed). Most artists of any type just don't have it.

Debbie, to me, is transparently a nice girl, not insipid like some but hardly redolent of danger. Who among our celebrity/folk-heroes is redolent of danger anymore? They're all a bunch of bland-outs. That seems to be what people want. Maybe, in fact, that very craving accounts for more of Blondie's' popularity than we might have previously suspected.

Let it never be forgotten that until Patti Smith slashed through the barriers like a henbane banshee in 1975, rock was almost exclusively a male-supremacist world. Most of the early Sixties girl groups were too ethnic, too Eastern seaboard streetgang–vibed for the kind of mass crossover appeal Debbie's achieved. Janis Joplin was too pathetic, a freak for the freaks. Grace Slick prefers her vast storehouse of private jokes and has gone out of her way to be unglamorous. Patti's still too jungle for *TV Guide.* So that leaves one person, the woman whose fate it is to end up getting called the "Queen of Punk."

from the book *Blondie,* 1980

David Byrne Says "Boo!"

One day someone I love said, "You hit me with your eyes." When I hear David Byrne's lyrics, I can imagine him saying the same thing in language just oblique enough to turn the pain into percussively lapping waters.

These are mutant times, and Talking Heads are the most human of mutant groups. Byrne has mental institution eyes, but unlike Patti or R. Hell they don't broadcast danger: he just looks like some nice nut holidayed from the ward with a fresh pocket of Thorazine. He and the rest of the band seem in both their music and physical presence to combine a sinuous plantlike *sway* with a hypertense, mechanical rigidity. They're a marriage of diametrical opposites—abandon and inhibition, anxiety and ease, freedom and impingement into paralysis.

I was a little put off by *More Songs About Buildings and Food,* not only because I found the music hard to get into but because I suspected that like old Andy Warhol who kept lurking around them the Heads or Byrne might actually think that buildings and food are every bit as significant and worthy of emotional concern as mere human beings. The stance seemed deliberately evasive, modish in the worst way. Of course I missed the point. From "Love Goes to Building on Fire" out, Talking Heads are (about) humans who feel pinned by circumstance, reacting like scarecrows and windmills to the erosions of experience, registering everything precisely from a slight distance while the passion is pent, even boiling . . . *over here,* and often finds its only outlet in the rhythmic undertows. They're also about new feelings for new social structures: "No Compassion" ("Go talk to your analyst, isn't that what he's there for?"), "The Girls Want to Be With the Girls" (why not, especially since most of the guys are too uptight to play with them), "The Big Country" (finally somebody said it: there is nothing beyond Jersey; Jack Kerouac made all that shit up, he was a science-fiction writer).

Fear of Music provides Heads'/Byrne's most explicit blueprint yet for survival in the face of paranoias—real or imagined, makes no difference. It's also the best Heads album yet because the production is up to or above the quality of their second, while the songs have a flow that makes it more immediately accessible. Byrne's a kind of Every-neurotic, wandering through the world encountering ouch-producers every step and breath he takes, relaying them back to us filtered through his sense of humor, his natural musicality, and the ever sifting-shifting medium that is Brian Eno. *Fear of Music* might as well have been called *Fear of Everything.* Show me an item extant sentient or otherwise in the world we share and I'll show you a clinically certified list of reasons why proximity to said item should be considered risky if not downright lethal. Under such circumstances, you have every right to be wrong. McLuhan missed it: we're not a global village, we're a global OUT-PATIENT CLINIC, and the life force itself is most fully embodied in a frenetically twitching nerve. But even with that on your side there is one thing you must face: YOU HAVE NO FRIENDS ANYWHERE. Nothing and no one. Also, NATURE IS PERVERSE. E.g., air and new Heads tune of same title: it's not just cigarette smoke or auto exhaust or the pollutants factories chuff out—it's air *qua* air that's out for your ass. Because in this most richly diversified of all possible universes, it just might happen to be the case that AIR DOES NOT LIKE YOU.

The refusal to face or understand such facts is why we're all terminally psychotic and no doctor, pill, book, or guru holds the cure. The disease is called life and there is no cure for that including death (makes fertilizer::continuation of life-cycle::no good) so ha ha the joke's on you from cradle to crypt. David Byrne knows all these things; what's more he knows that "Some people don't know shit about the . . . AIR . . ."

That's the trouble with our society today: people take everything too damn much for granted. They think the disease is gonna shit out pills to cure itself. In this album Dr. Byrne examines various popularly proposed panaceas with dissecting knife and discards them one by one.

Socialized day-to-day living in this imminent nullkrieg is outlined in "Life During Wartime": "This ain't no party, this ain't no disco, this ain't no fooling around/This ain't no Mudd Club, or CBGB, I ain't got time for that now." When there is no firm ground, the only sensible thing to do is keep on the move, ergo finally, on their third album, this song becomes the first example of what might qualify as the Heads' version of "road" songs—the other one is "Cities"—most of which boil down to "A lot of ghosts in a lot of houses," who just like befuddled birds may "go up north and come back south/Still got no idea where in the world they are."

"Drugs" is a hilariously solemn recitation of the usual chemical comicstrips, and "Animals" puts away all those maudlin mabels like Robinson Jeffers and Euell Gibbons who belabor us with man's odiousness behaviorwise when stacked up against our noble ancestors dwelling next door in the wilds or more properly zoos. But the bottom line is that "They're setting a bad example." The truth, as Byrne points out, is that animals, besides having no intelligence beyond brute fear reflex, are a bunch of smug little bastards who are *laughing* at us just because we keep drawing diagrams across a universe they knew was chaotic in the first place.

Which brings us to David Byrne's basic philosophy of existence: To feel anxiety is to be blessed by the full wash of life in its ripest chancre—everything else is wax museums. Having rejected drugs, animal husbandry, jogging not to mention breathing itself, towns, cities, and whole continents in his search for some little nook where he can relax for even one instant, Byrne finally lays it on the line: "Heaven is a place where nothing ever happens."

Every state but zero cool emptiness, every place on the map but

Nowheresville, spells anxiety under a wide assortment of brand names. Once yanked, nerves never forget. You are going to be driven crazy by all of this, no, wait, you ARE crazy BECAUSE of all this, or maybe JUST BECAUSE PERIOD, and you always will be as long as you live. Crazy is simply your birthright, signifying citizenship in the human race. Those furshlugginer animals never go crazy. Air doesn't go crazy. Only you. And that's because, as Misterogers has been trying to tell you for years, you're a *special* person. Isn't it wonderful? Sure. So give up all those silly little totems you got clenched in your itty mitt: drugs, religions, politics, family, jobs (well, maybe them you better keep), even rock 'n' roll, because "Electric Guitar" has been bad, not only guilty of crimes against the state but deserves to be spanked and put to bed, besides which "the copy sounds better," as everyone knows.

So what's left? Nothing, and it's not heaven. "Everything seems to be up in the air at this time," says David. The implicit answer in all these songs is that, given the hopelessness of the situation, we should also recognize how hysterically funny it is. In the Middle Ages the population of Europe felt so haunted and tainted by the Devil, so hopelessly damned, that they developed a predilection, as manifested in the paintings of Bosch, for taking all this damnation and redemption stuff as a kind of huge joke, with God, Satan, and the demons as cartoon characters. The closer you get to whatever you're terrified of, the more it and your dread begin to seem like old friends, ergo terror decreases. David Byrne seems to be a sort of dowser's wand for neuroses and trauma, and as darkness looms over all of us, he strolls down its maw, placid, bemused, humming little tunes to himself. Sometimes I think *Fear of Music* is one of the best comedy albums I've ever heard. Which doesn't mean the fear isn't real. Byrne just reminds you that it's something you're going to have to live with, so you might as well get a kick out of it while you can.

The Village Voice, August 20, 1979

A Bellyful of Wire

Wire. Think about that word and what it has meant in your life, perhaps even the lives of your ancestors. Then think just how hot you'd be hoppin' to get a chance to hear a group whose sound might live up to such euphonious appellation! Wire. The Sound of the '70s. Flat. Dead. Dull. Thud. Mud. Plod. Sod. But mebbe with a whiplash on the counterstroke.

Since this is *The Village Voice,* I will now insert my obligatory cross-cultural reference in record review (cf. past works of Messrs. Wolcott, Carson, Hull, etc.): Alfred Kazin said of Louis-Ferdinand Celine that, "He writes like a lunging live wire, crackling and wayward and full of hidden danger." I don't know that strictly speaking one could say that about the first Wire album, *Pink Flag.* In the first place, Celine was a fascist, or at least a voice of appeasement, and Wire's politics from their flag on down the pole are leftoid all the way like all good little British bands these days. (Which may be easy glory but at least beats the standard New York "Politics is *boring,* man.") In the second place, the first Wire album was one of the deadest things ever recorded. It was so dead I bet if old Thomas Alva woulda heard it he mighta thought twice about twitchatangling the next century's ears up in all such hobglobular *kfwaaaaaaat.* It was so dead I was stunned to find myself putting it on my record player again and again, listening intently to those Ramonic thunderthuds 1:01 long and lyrics the likes of "Be good to your TV set." But play it I did, and to this day I'm damned if I know why. Though I remember Joe Fernbacher once wrote a review in *Creem* of

Angel's first album wherein he praised it by listing the various types of monotony extant and providing pointers as to which cuts on Angel's deeboo corresponded to which monovariant.

Chairs Missing, Wire's second album, available only on import, is, I am sorry to report, not monotonous. I still haven't figured out why I'm sorry. (Louis Lomax to A. Warhol on national TV in 1966: "Do you represent the new generation of young people who are saying that everything is nothing?" Warhol: "Uh, no, we, I think, represent the ones who think nothing is something.") They just don't sound like a wire all the time this time. Sometimes they sound like several species of small furry animals grooving with a pict, if you get my drift, if not I will come right out and say it: Syd Barrett. Early Pink Floyd, to be sure. "Outdoor Minor" is just "Arnold Layne" on a different drug besides being a HIT***HIT***HIT. Quite lilting it is, and clocks in at only 1 min 45 secs. Mind you that's after they've subjected you to 5 mins 46 secs of "Mercy," which is the aural equivalent of being a somehow still living sardine flopping helplessly on the Guyana-mounds of your buddies as the poor soul about to eat you unrolls the tin. I'd pay eight dollars to hear that, wouldn't you? Sure. It doesn't hurt at all.

"I Am the Fly" sums things up quite nicely, I think: "I can spread more disease than the fleas which nibble away at your window display." Hooray! Avis! Also, have you ever noticed how deeply all these new wavers are into dislocation of their bodily organs? I guess it all started back when Papa Lou had the unmitigated gall to crow, "But the funny part was what happened to her nose/It grew and grew till it reached all of her toes/Now when people say her feet smell they mean her nose." That's poetry, buddy—let Allen Ginsberg shove his punkpomes up his own slothful rectum. Now we got severed limbs and fingers and a ganglial spew flyin' all over the *No New York* album. Siouxsie and the Banshees as usual are getting in on the act ("Be a carcass—Be a dead pork/Be limblessly in love . . . In love with your stumps" etc. etc. etc. ad greenie-hock to the max), but it took Wire, Wire, and only Wire to bring it down to the gut level (well, actually a bit nor-east) in "Heartbeat": Sound of sperm whale taking a slow piss, then thudthudthudthudthudthud, yes it's those li'l footpats, jus' like "I Think We're Alone Now." As indeed we are, for: "I feel icy I feel cold I feel old. Is there something there behind me I'm sublime. I feel empty I feel dark I remark. I am mesmerized by my own beat like a heartbeat."

Betcha never thought you'd live to see Beckett's *How It Is* souffled up into a rockin' powwow jamboree! This cut, whose entire lyrics I quoted above, runs 3 mins 15 secs. And of course says it all. The nitty-gritty: a heartbeat. *No* suggestion of any of the romantic implications that organ's been saddled with so often. But Wire lay it on the line that aortic bivalves and nuthin else is exactly what's comin' down the lyric-as-poetometaphorical-relevance chute. Well, there is the question of solipsism, but I think that word's a bit overworked lately, don't you? Fact is, the *earth*'s a solipsist by dint of the fact we don't give much credence to anybody else being out there. So who cares if you, modurban consumer profile, wanna scuba down in your own little headphone dopepipe womb? A man's got a right to his privacy, which is why I don't even mind that half of Wire's lyrics still don't make any sense; communication was a misnomer in the first place anyway. The crucial difference is that whereas Pink Floyd wanted (pretended?) to take you to *outer* space (big deal, go watch Buck Rogers), Wire wanna isolate and dissect leucocytes. They're into the micro rather than macrocosm. If Jerry Brown is our next president and doesn't ask them to play at the inaugural ball I'm going to shoot him straight-on dat alpaca-furrowed brow. Rock critics need media attention too.

The Village Voice, April 23, 1979

Jello Biafra Is No Cretin

It is no longer enough to be a hostile ugly yowling asshole. You'll notice I left out "cretinous"; Jello Biafra is not a cretin. But seeing the Dead Kennedys at Irving Plaza Saturday night reminded me a lot of encountering Toronto's Viletones at CBGB in the summer of 1977. This guy Natzee Dog hung from the rafters, crawled all over the stage, and hurled himself on the first row till his body was one huge sore. Somebody asked me what I thought and I said, "Fine with me—in 1972 every band in the world was Grand Funk, now every band in the world is the Stooges." I didn't tell Natzee Dog that, though; I told him: "You guys were cooler with hockey haircuts."

Now, however, it is no longer enough even to cut your body to shit: you have to have a phalanx of big ugly skinhead-goons (imported from Washington, apparently the same guys Black Flag brought up for their show) to hurl themselves on the audience with brutal but monotonous regularity in suddenly institutionalized slam-dancing. And now I don't think everything is so fine musically either, because obviously every band in the world is not the Stooges—every band in the world is the Dead Kennedys. I just got back from Austin, Texas, and they got a hundred of them there if they got one. They don't get written about as much in *NME* anymore, but they still got a whole slew of them back in England, too.

Artistically, on a scale of 100, I'd rate the Dead Kennedys about a 34, I guess. Jello has very little stage presence, his singing's not too interesting (forget feelingful, that's a joke in front), the guitarist has one or two more moves than the usual run. Yet they packed the place out;

maybe it has something to do with the name (supposed to be *outrageous,* y'know . . .). I asked some kids standing next to me, one of whom was wearing a Ramones T-shirt, what they thought, and they all agreed they sucked. "Just another imitation Ramones," said the kid in the T-shirt. The question is, how many of these did we ever want or need beyond keeping certain winos out of the gutter by sticking 'em up on stages with guitars in their hands and letting them bang and yowl away to their hearts' content. I think that the true musical originality and importance of the DKs can be deduced from the conversation among four of their fans in the lobby on the way out, wherein they absolutely *could not figure out* whether the band had done one of their favorite DK anthems or not.

Then there is the matter of politics. I have listened to DK songs with titles like "Kill the Poor," "When Ya Get Drafted," and "Chemical Warfare," both live and on their album, *Fresh Fruit for Rotting Vegetables,* and my editor assures me that Jello Biafra may very well mean what he says ("Neutron bomb blah blah Big Business wants war blab blare I'm gonna turn nerve gases on country club golfers blur blear etc. etc."), however naive and condescending he is. It makes little difference, though, since aside from the catchphrases the overriding extent to which the DK's lyrics can be said to be "political" at all is the way they consistently veer towards antisocial juvee-delinquent antics like stealing people's mail, with a marked tendency to mutate, perhaps through methamphetamine logic (cf. "Drug Me"), into hateful but impotent fantasies like "Let's Lynch the Landlord" and "I Kill Children" (closest thing to a funny line: "Offer them a helping hand/Of open telephone wires"). Finally, I don't think *anybody* who consistently heaps flailing jackbooted *shtarkas* on their audience to (literally) beef up the show (even if it needs it, from somewhere) by getting some kinda altercation started can be said to have good politics. It's just like Jello Biafra introducing one song by sneering, "This song is about *dress codes* . . . in other words, *people like you* . . . it's called 'Halloween.'" Hmm, lessee, you're wearing haircut and torn T-shirt first introduced by R. Hell over five years ago, but you make sure to get the T-shirt torn off so you can then writhe your topless torso around and ultimately hurl it into the crowd just like Iggy over *ten* years ago . . .

But yes, I guess you are sincere. You do hate current American life, Jerry Brown, and Ronald Reagan. So do I. But so do Black Flag, and all the other stupid possibly proto-fascist/racist California nihilists. And somehow I didn't get the vibe off your audience I've gotten off certain other punk audiences where you would actually see things like 12-year-olds wearing "STOP WAR" graffiti. Even if you mean what you're saying about capitalism, consumerism, etc., I don't think they're listening. I think that, to the extent they can tell you apart at all, they come to you for the same reason they go to see Black Flag, and for that matter the Plasmatics; I think they come for the Goon Brutality. Fine. Sirhan Sirhan, call your office.

The Village Voice, April 29, 1981

If Oi Were a Carpenter

Hardcore and oi: two continents, two masses of disaffected youth, two musical forms so redolent of the zeitgeist! Of course, some people will tell you that they're the same thing and in fact that all practitioners of both constitute variants on the same band, but this is absolutely untrue. Hardcore sounds like rolling clods of lumpy excrement with broken bones sticking out, while oi sounds like craters of dribbly gruel with patchy tufts of straw poking up. And they said there were limits to what you could do with three simple chords!

Admittedly, these are delicate distinctions. But delicacy is what this music is all about. It's like the blues or "Why" by the Byrds, anybody can play it, but it's really hard to do it just exactly right. Some people say the best way to listen to it is in anthologies where every track is by a different band, but personally I find these catarrh-concatenations a bit disconcerting, since you've no sooner got cozy with one noxious exudate than *in less than two minutes* you have to adjust to a completely new one! No, the way to go about it is to locate a whole LP side by one band, eight songs in a row that possess only hair's breadth differences between them *yet still are not boring!* Then you can appreciate the true name of this game: TOTAL IMMERSION.

I would, however, like to call for an end to certain recent tribal wars (fat chance). This stuff sounds a whole lot like much of the heavy metal shit I grew up on, if you forget your guitar-flash Aerosmiths or maybe guitar solos altogether and dig back into some of the really vile metal stuff like early Grand Funk, Bloodrock, and Jukin' Bone, or play a Black Sabbath track at twice the speed. (Supposedly the Angry Samoans said their EP could be played at either 33 or 45 rpm, to prove exactly that point.) Plus now all the lyrics are social protest, which however retarded—in fact, *especially* if it's retarded—beats any amount of sexual rodomontade.

I have before me a list of names: Circle Jerks, Flesh Eaters, Minutemen, Germs, Exploited, DOA, Dead Kennedys, Bad Brains, Fear, Replacements, Really Red. Behind each of these names is an album and behind each of these albums is an anxiety attack. But some anxiety attacks are more equal than others. DOA's songs are too long, Bad Brains' tape has bad sound, the Flesh Eaters' lead singer Chris D. sounds parched and thin. Two groups only have given me two full sides of unalloyed satisfaction: the Circle Jerks from L.A. and the Exploited from Scotland.

Circle Jerks are a good example of why the L.A. hardcore scene isn't just a replay of English Ramonesclones ca. '76–7. They're tighter, more structured songwise (bridges), play faster, and *enunciate their words clearly* (Darby Crash notwithstanding, but that was part of his style). Limeys on the whole can't sing their own goddamn language so any civilized person can understand them, but when it comes to spitting "Where's the gun? Here's my head" in a way that communicates to the heartland, the Circle Jerks would make early Iggy proud. Their first album, *Group Sex,* is for me far superior to their newie, *Wild in the Streets,* probably because the sound is clearer and sharper (produced by *David Anderle*???) and early material like "I Just Want Some Skank" doesn't have to reach so far to be anthemic. I'm just not sure the Jerks are ready to tackle international politics yet.

Every song on the Exploited's *Punks Not Dead* is an anthem; unfortunately I still can't remember what most of them sound like, and the lyrics are a dead loss, but the titles are indicative: "Cop Cars," "Army Life (Part 2)," "Blown to Bits," "Sex and Violence," "Dole Q," "I Believe in Anarchy" ("still"). The album gets over on a combination of portly peacock-Mohawked lead singer Wattie's winsome earnestness and solid production (which helps enormously, as one listen to their mud-puddle of a live album will attest). There's even a part at the beginning of "Blown to Bits" where the Les Paul gets passed around and all the other guys in the band show lead guitarist Big John and the world how to play the song's riff ("I knew it, I knew it!" he wails). I'd have to call the Exploited charming, and within their charm and the total-immersion syndrome of the fans' listening habits there lies a larger truth about both oi and hardcore: that for all its pro forma obnoxiousness, at its real core this music is as comforting and predictable, safe and conservative (even reactionary) as the heavy metal whence it really sprang. The difference is that where heavy metal still bonds its audience together through phallic aggression, and oi is politicized football chants for unemployed louts, hardcore's three chords provide its fans with walls that shut them in and any other world out—even when they're slamming in the pit. Hardcore is the womb.

The Village Voice, April 27, 1982

\\\ ///

PANTHEON

/// \\\

I Only Get My Rocks Off When I'm Dreaming: So You Say You Missed the Stones Too? Cheer Up, We're a Majority!

They came again this year, hurtling around this land on a carom even more apocalyptic (if less bloody) than the one in '69, and *I missed 'em.*

The greatest rock and roll band in the world, *for sure,* and my heroes ever since I got my first look at Mick's leer way back in '64: the decadent badass princes we'll never put down or lose!

I saw them in 1964 on their second American tour, and in '65 twice. The second time, in December, I *cried* because I thought they'd turned away from the True Faith of Pure R&B and sold out to the crass commercialism of rock.

I'll never forget that day. My girlfriend and I took the bus all the way from our suburb into downtown San Diego, went right to the concert hall ticket window, and suddenly I said: "Fuck it! Fuck them! Who needs 'em?" And went staggering erratically in the general direction of Skid Row, dropping tears as big as cantaloupes.

Since we'd had our own troubles, my girlfriend thought I was crying over her and me. When she found out I was crying for the Stones you better believe she was pleased as puke!

"You're so immature!" she said. "Here I thought it was all because you loved me, when it's really because you're mad at the goddamned Rolling Stones."

Damn straight I was! After four fantastic albums of the purest r&b (like "Off the Hook"), they'd let me down *mucho queaso* with the release of "Get Off of My Cloud"—which even Mick Jagger later called "just a bunch of noise" (I love it now, of course, and could give a flying fuck what he thinks) and *December's Children,* their worst album to that point. It has several songs on it that sounded half-completed, as well as the insipid "As Tears Go By" (yeah, I get the hots for that piece of crap now, too, of course *D.C.* ditto). Even Andrew Loog Oldham's all-time worst liner notes.

But the day of the concert found all my blustering disdain drained to sheer distilled sorrow. A fan in mourning! Oh Stones, Stones, how could you do this to me? Andy and I walked downtown a ways, a little bitty tear letting me down every so often. Finally we stopped into a little Coney Island hotdog trough. We ordered. I glumly flipped the pages of the jukebox, put in a coin, and played "Get Off of My Cloud."

Man, those tears started pouring out like piss from an elephant! The farther the Stones got into the song, the more distraught I became. Stop *breaking* down!

Suddenly, Andy was up, resolute, yanking me out of my seat and through the door, literally tugging me back into the concert, running as fast as she could with a big imbecile in tow, blubbering and falling all over himself.

When we got there, she snatched my wallet out of my pocket, threw the money at the ticket seller, and yanked me inside. We found our seats, I wiped my eyes and cheeks on my soggy sleeve, and THOSE MOTHERFUCKERS PLAYED ONE OF THE MOST EXCITING CONCERTS I'VE EVER SEEN IN MY LIFE! Rejuvenation!

It was almost as good as the night earlier that year when I'd sat there in the same half-filled theatre, shrieking in harmony with all those wet-pantied little boppers. I was a groupie! Still am, in a way. Every time I've seen the Stones, or missed them, every time they've come over here or released a new album or even made a bit of news like pissing on gas stations or going to jail for dope, it's made waves in my own life.

Exile on Main Street came out just three months ago, and I practically gave myself an ulcer and hemorrhoids, too, trying to find some way to like it. Finally I just gave up, wrote a review that was almost a total pan, and tried to forget about the whole thing. A couple weeks later, I went back to California, got a copy just to see if it might've gotten better, and it knocked me out of my chair. Now I think it's possibly the best Stones album ever.

Meanwhile, what with traveling and general sloth, I somehow missed seeing any of their concerts this tour, and for some reason even the full bloom of my love for the album couldn't make me care that much.

What was responsible for my dramatic turnaround on the album? I don't think it matters much. Why don't I care that much whether I get to see the Stones live this time? That's another story altogether. It's directly related, I think, to the difference that you find in the album if you listen, and what you couldn't help but see operating on this tour.

The Stones still have the strength to make you feel that both we and they are hemmed in and torn by similar walls, frustrations, and tragedies. That's the breakthrough of *Exile on Main Street.*

Exile is dense enough to be compulsive: hard to hear, at first, the precision and fury behind the murk ensure that you'll come back, hearing more with each playing. What you hear sooner or later is two things: an intuition for nonstop getdown perhaps unmatched since the *Rolling Stones Now!,* and a strange kind of humility and love emerging from a dazed frenzy. If, as they assert, they're soul survivors, they certainly know what you can lose by surviving. As they and we see friends falling all around us, only the Stones have cut the callousness of '72 to say with something beyond narcissistic sentiment what words remain for those slipping away.

Exile is about casualties, and partying in the face of them. The party is obvious. The casualties are inevitable.

Sticky Fingers was the flashy, dishonest picture of a multitude of slow deaths. But it's the search for alternatives, something to *do* (something worthwhile, even) that unites us with the Stones, continuously.

They are the masters without peer at rendering the boredom and desperation of living comfortably in this society. If you recognized yourself watching the last TV station sign off at 3 A.M. in "What To Do," chances are you reveled in the rich, sick ennui of "Dead Flowers" and you saw your own partial fragmentation between the sonic iceflows of "Sway."

Most of us didn't get the real words, because at their most vulnerably crucial moments they were slurred and buried in the tides of sound. Jagger *had* to sing it that way, in "Sway" and again in much of *Exile,* because that is the way his pride works. Besides, anything else would make it all too concise and clear—like putting the lyrics on an album cover, which is the most impersonal thing any rock 'n' roll artist can possibly do.

Exile on Main Street is the great step forward, an amplification of the tough insights of "Gimmie Shelter" and "You Can't Always Get What You Want." A brilliant projection of the nerve-torn nights that follow all the arrogant celebrations of self-demolition, a work of love and fear and humanity. Even such a piece of seeming filler as "Casino Boogie" reveals itself, once the words come through, to be a picture of life at the terminal.

"Rocks Off" and "Shine a Light" present the essential picture, the latter song addressing the half-phased-out but still desperately alive person who speaks in the first. This music has a capacity to chill where "Dead Flowers" and "Sway" tended to come off as shallow, facile nihilism:

I always hear those voices
on the street
I want to shout
but I can hardly speak

I was makin' love this time
To a dancer friend of mine.
I can't seem to stay in step . . .

And I only get my rocks off
when I'm dreamin'

Headin' for the overload
Stranded on a dirty road
Kick me like you kicked before
I can't even feel the pain no more.

The sense of helplessness and impotence is not particularly pleasant, but this is the way it is today for too many. Such withering personal honesty is certainly a departure for the Stones.

"Kick me like you kicked before. . . .": the Stones talking to their audience, the audience talking back. Old lovers who may have missed the bourgeois traps of "Sittin' on a Fence" but got waylaid anyway by various disjuncture; they certainly don't yearn like saps to get back to where they "once belonged" but they do recognize the loss of all sense of wonder, the absence of love, the staleness and sometimes frightening inhumanity of this "new" culture. The need for new priorities.

When so many are working so hard at solipsism, the Stones define the unhealthy state, cop to how far *they* are mired in it, and rail at the breakdown with the weapons at their disposal: noise, anger, utter frankness. It's what we've always loved them for. And it took a lot more guts to cut this than "Street Fightin' Man," say, even though the impulse is similar: an intense yearning to merge coupled with the realization that to truly merge may be only to submerge once more. A recognition that joining together with the band is merely massing solitudes.

The end of the line and depths of the despair are reached in "Shine a Light," a visit to one or every one of the friends you finally know is not gonna pull through. A love song of a far different kind:

When you're drunk in the alley baby
With your clothes all torn

And when your late night friends
all leave you
In the cold grey dawn
Oh, the Scene threw
so many flies on you
I just can't brush 'em off . . .

When Mick says he can't brush off the flies, it's not some bit of macho misogyny, but a simple admission that applies to himself as well. The sense of entropy, of eclipse, is as total and engulfing as the sorrow. "Soul Survivor" follows immediately, of necessity, carrying the album out strong and fierce because the Rolling Stones are about nothing if not struggle. They have finally met the Seventies totally.

What *Exile on Main Street* is about, past the party roar, is absorption. Inclusion. Or rather, the recognition of exclusion coupled with the yearning for inclusion: "Let me in! I wanna drink/from your lovin' cup." When I saw them for the first time in 1964, a friend turned to me and said, "The great thing about the Stones is that the Beatles are so distant and perfect that you feel like they're from another planet. But with the Stones, you feel like you're at home." And it is still true, except in a much more profound way.

If *Exile on Main Street* is about the need for inclusion, the latest Stones tour is about the tactics of exclusion. If the album cries out for the reciprocal resolution of tension, the tour runs on crackling rails of tension, frustration, disappointment, and envy. It may not have been planned that way, but that's how it works out.

The entire project looks to a moderately jaundiced eye (what other kind is there with the Stones?) like an exercise in manipulation at the highest level. If "Rocks Off" asks for a recharge from the street, this tour has been designed to leave you stranded on a dirt road.

Consider the fact that the Stones consciously and carefully chose to do their 32-stop tour in a series of concert houses generally smaller than those of 1969, with audiences systematically limited. At every stop, only a certain percentage of those who want to will be able to see the Stones. Never enough tickets; they're always gone in no time. Standing in the sun for hours until the man finally comes out and announces that this one's sold out, too. Tough luck kid. But, if you're rich, maybe you can find a scalper.

These conditions, combined with the police and security measures which have been fantastically (and understandably) elaborate, have not set well with the underground press or the hip community at large—one paper after another has run denunciations of the Stones as mercenary pigs, usually alongside a piece of equivalent length rhapsodizing over the show and music themselves, as well as overloads of photos. Some of the accusations have validity, and some are freelance paranoia, but certain facts must be considered and certain questions asked.

Why did the Stones and their organization choose to limit so severely the audience at every show on the tour?

Possible answers:

1. Afraid of another Altamont, they wanted to prevent tragedy, as well as reduce the likelihood of personal harm to themselves. The Rolling Stones have a lot of enemies in America, whose faces they have never seen: in the New Left, women's liberation, people who still nurse real or imagined grievances over the last tour (including bikers, who felt that they had been roundly shafted on Altamont) as well as various cranks, ODS, Bremers[8], etc. Just say the Stones never quite understood everything involved in the Altamont flashpoint, and went out of their way to ensure that on this tour nothing but a good time would be had by all lucky enough to get inside.

[8] Arthur Bremer was the misfit who nearly succeeded in assassinating Alabama governor George Wallace during his surprisingly strong run for the Presidency in 1972, and for a while thus stood as a symbol for crackpots of all stripes.

2. The Stones recognized that neither audience nor band gets off properly in vast arenas due to the impersonality, as well as hugely erratic acoustics; so they sacrificed the really big money in favor of relatively small environments where a certain intimacy could cook between audience and band, resulting in better music, more satisfied customers, increased relaxation, better vibes all around.

3. The Stones knew that if they consistently limited the number of people who could see them, a huge tension would be set up which would add to the excitement, the sense of a momentous historic occasion. The external hysteria in each city might, by this stratagem, be simultaneously stroked and tethered short of total chaos. The Stones could barnstorm the colonies, make a certain percentage of their fans happy, capture the attention of a drooling press resulting in cover stories everywhere, sell out every house, make history, stay in the news, keep everybody in America in a state of anxiety till they left, enjoy a manageable apocalypse with no bummers or miscarriages, come off as simultaneously the last word in outrage (like *Life* magazine clucking over the illegitimate children in their collective wake) and good, professional guys (nobody died).

The first two answers make pragmatic sense but the last sounds so much like Mick Jagger it's all but irresistible. Most likely, it was a combination of all three. Even the third does not seem a total act of manipulation. The distance between intentions and effects is often so vast in matters of this kind that you could *almost* (but not quite) easy-ride with a creep like Jerry Garcia babbling about how there are no bad people, only victims.

Take Altamont. It was great! I was really glad I went—no question of preferring that experience to Woodstock, which I missed. But, I remember thinking all day, "If I was waiting to see anybody but the Stones, I'd leave this fucking shitheap right now." I remember the naked sobbing girl who came stumbling down past us, shoved by some irate redded-out boyfriend up the hill, everyone ogling her and snickering, and her attempts to cover herself as she dazedly picked her way back to her friends, stumbling as she stepped uncertainly through the tribal circles of beatified freaks who dug it all laughing and grabbing. And I remember the freaked-out kid shrieking "Kill! Kill! Kill!" I remember the Angels vamping on him, too, and then seeing him passed in a twitching gel over the heads in the first few rows and then dumped on the ground to snivel at the feet of total strangers who would ignore him, because the Stones were coming on in a minute which would be two hours. But nobody wanted to take their eyes off the stage for fear of missing them.

I don't think the Stones saw much of this. If they did, what could they do? Call it off? Call out their bodyguards? Call the police? But the Stones are not innocents. As successful as the tour just ended was in avoiding Altamont II, it's not all instant party. It doesn't even stop at money, power, and ego, as Ralph J. Gleason wrote, although that's a third of it. Another third is rock 'n' roll.

The other third is law 'n' order.

The incredible degree to which security was enforced on this year's tour was justified—mostly—by the facts of life circa 1972. But there are always casualties, not to mention simple injustices. In San Diego, for instance, some hip con made up several hundred fake tickets and sold them. As a result several hundred people with legitimate ones found themselves stranded outside the arena. With no recourse but to, quite appropriately, rip the joint to rubble. Wouldn't you? Or wish you could, if you didn't have the guts? Where does "drive myself right over the wall" stop? Should it? I don't know.

The most interesting form of security on this tour, though, was that phalanx of mostly nonuniformed bodies which kept the Stones permanently insulated: a phalanx of concentric circles. Right. Just like Dante, if a trifle more sleazy and less important. The Stones are a target for every parasite alive. So they and the parasites end up, starting at the smallest and innermost circle and moving outward, with:

- The Stones. Eye of the hurricane.
- Their entourage. Family friends, occasional acolytes, and *musicians not in the Stones.* You don't think Bobby Keys rates with Charlie Watts, do you?
- Roadies, technicians, businessmen, PR people. They get to hobnob with the Stones, though perhaps not so much as the inner circle.
- Members of the press traveling with the Stones. These people get to see a lot of the band—sometimes more than the friends, sometimes less than the drones. Anyway, they garner plenty of anecdotes and style notes, even though most of their articles are elegant press releases.
- One nighters. Media people in each city with backstage passes, who get to interview or photograph the Stones or just stand around.
- Media people and assorted rock scene hustlers who got in free, courtesy of PR, but with no backstage passes. They get to sit out front, which is reasonable. There's always too many people backstage.
- Next, of course, the paying audience. Used to be that included everybody who gave a shit in the first place. On the first few tours, nobody was excluded, because the Stones didn't fill the house that often. By 1969, everybody knew; part of the excitement was that the next day or in the wee hours after the concert you'd reconnoiter with your friends to bask in the memories. It may seem petty, but it was important: "Geez, weren't they fabulous!"

If you can say that now, you're a member of an elite. Chances are two out of three Stones fans missed 'em in '72, which puts you outside the eighth circle, in the real circle with no boundaries:

EVERYBODY ELSE

There is no way this cannot sound like sour grapes, but it really isn't. A tour of this size is an undertaking on a scale with building the pyramids. One could even say that it's not all champagne and rockin' glory for the Stones either. A friend who traveled with them told me that they were consistently surrounded by people of an extremely low caliber. Low in many ways, he said: mean, unhealthy, alternately hostile or sycophantic (depending on who they were dealing with), burnt out, tattered, unpleasant to look at and be around. The Stones' patience with them, he added, was unbelievable.

Then again, I don't see many rock 'n' roll bands at gigs with people around them that I could admire or care to exchange two words with. Burnt-out cycle. The Stones are professional artists and businessmen, doing a job, giving something for all they receive.

But it's also true that this tour probably made as many people unhappy as it made happy. There's a line in "Torn and Frayed" about "impressive rooms filled with parasites." While it's true that almost nobody gets to hobnob with the Stones that the Stones don't want to look at, it's also true that when you're in the kind of elevated position they're in, people keep relating to you in the most peculiar ways. Nobody wants to look too eager. Meanwhile, you're traveling fast over enormous distances, losing track of day and town and when you last slept. I imagine it must get kind of hard after a while to bring most of the hangers-on into focus. If you did, who knows but what they might turn out to be a pain in the ass.

I guess I just feel that circumstances effectively disrupted that certain aura of spiritual intimacy represented by the comment of my friend at the '64 concert, and even by meeting friends after the '69 shows. The Stones were with us even after we went home.

I don't feel snubbed because Mick Jagger didn't call me up the minute he hit America, to thank me for my *Exile* review. It's just that even though I don't exactly have any illusions to be destroyed anymore—even illusions about the Stones being inhuman manipulators with evil ends—I'm happy with what illusions I do have. You probably are, too.

So this piece is dedicated to all the people who didn't see the Stones this time, from one who excluded himself for no particular reason, but wouldn't worry too much about being excluded anyway.

Creem, January 1973

1973 Nervous Breakdown: The Ol' Fey Outlaws Ain't What They Used to Be—Are You?

Those poor bastards.

I'm talking about the Stones, of course. They've got problems aplenty these days, and it's really not their fault, so we should pat 'em on the back and give 'em a helping hand, maybe with a tablet of speed in it to get their next album or at least their current spirits out of the doldrums.

You may think I'm being condescending, but I'm not. The Stones are popstars, light years from where you and I sit in stucco puzzling out whether *Goat's Head Soup* is their latest triumph or the epitaph of old men or just . . . the Stones can still put us through those kinds of changes, like when so many people gave months to the challenge of *Exile on Main Street,* and came up winners because it paid off so monolithically.

The only question remaining in this cozy situation, then, is:

Q: What if the Stones *no longer pay off?*

A #1: You desert 'em. After all, they're justa buncha old men.

A #2: What kind of friend are you? You grew up with these cats! Christ, are there no values left in this lousy culchuh?

What's wrong with the Stones, you say? Oh, honey. This really can't be the end, more like one of those situations where the whole enterprise, in spite of all nostalgic emotionalism, just seems to be unreeling out into space somewhere like a kite lost in spring. And we're powerless to stop it.

The Stones are getting flaky; that much is obvious to anyone who's listened to their last couple of albums or observed them recently. How much you may like their recent music is irrelevant—it's the mood and the manifest state of the nerve that counts.

Summer before last the Stones did their biggest U.S. tour ever. Unlike '69, everything was tightly arranged with no room for Altamonts or anything beyond minor antler-buttings. But there was something about it. You just had to look at the pictures in *Life* magazine or anywhere else to know that the Stones were getting a little dazed.

Mick's dancing was as urgent as ever—maybe more so, because these days the live Stones seem to carry a last-ditch mood of amped-up desperation that they saved for pure effect in looser times. In 1969, *Rolling Stone* captioned a tour shot with something like: "You could see the evidence of years in Mick's face."

Yeah, coy minco dervish in Uncle Sam hat. He was more cute than dangerous, and the Stones didn't seem particularly concerned about anything but a good time until those grinding too-late moments at Altamont, where Mick's utter impotence in the face of the forces he'd unleashed—it was all too obvious: "*Broo*thers and *siis*ters," he pleaded in a voice as shrill and thin as Chip 'n' Dale, "let's all *pleeeeuhze* just *cool* out. . . ."

Like Betty Boop trying to quell a race riot. What the hell was this guy talking about? As soon as they pounded into "Carol" you felt like somebody'd jolted your mainvein with a hot shot overload of pure methamphetamine, and snuff was just another rimshot whizzing by. Hell's Angels were smashing kids' faces to pulp with pool cues, and even Marty Balin got decked. Verily it's no wonder that when the Dead arrived and somebody gave them a report—"They're even beatin' up musicians!"—Bob Weir observed: "Just doesn't seem right, somehow."

Nope. It wasn't just Altamont or the Stones, the *whole peace brat society* was wrongo to the liver. The Stones had expressed it in "Gimmie Shelter," but they were even less prepared to deal with it than we were. And if you can even believe that was four years ago, you gotta ask yourself if you're any *better* equipped to deal with this mess now. Because you really don't wanna ask if the Stones are.

Death of Innocence in Woodstock Nation my ass, Altamont was the *facing up.* And the Stones were stuck in the middle of all of it, partly at fault, partly the confused patsies from out of town who'd tried in their own mallethanded way to do something nice for a group of people toward whom, nevertheless, they almost certainly felt more contempt than anything else. The Stones never bought all that brothers and sisters crap, but they were just beginning to be distanced in a truly uncomfortable way which they certainly brought on themselves. When Jagger raised his delicate arm in the power fist that tour he just looked silly, but when he tried to reverse the manipulative thrust of his presence at Altamont he made himself suddenly and completely pathetic for the very first time because he was a total failure. All he could do was incite, the collegiate insurrectionist with half his act down and nowhere to take it but self-immolation.

The Angels looked at him with obvious contempt on their faces: little fag. It took Keith Richards, the phased-out ghost of last summer, to exert the necessary mojo, seething forward and jerking the mike: "Look! Either you guys stop that shit, or you get *no more music,* do you understand? You, out there, I saw you doing that, and you better *knock it off,* man!"

It was the first time all day that anyone in a position of authority had directly and angrily demanded that the *Angels* cool out. Grace Slick had set the tone that morning when Balin got slugged: "People, let's not be laying our bodies on each other unless we intend love. . . ." Or, as I muttered when David Crosby was onstage: "Screw you, you asshole. You're not my brother." It would stand to reason that among those here only the Stones would have the guts and perception to adopt that kind of position and stick with it. Keith was pissed and moving. Jagger was sad to look at. The others were impassive. As always. Would Bill Wyman move a facial muscle while staring at a ritual disembowelment? Whee, everybody gets numb. But from that moment on you never saw Jagger quite the same again. First vivid experience of the dimension of Stones weakness, and it stayed in the mind.

The latest U.S. tour was all precaution, no major skirmishes, just a slow cancer. Great tour, socko, *Clockwork Orange* pix in the press showing where it all came from, but, but . . . but Keith was hardly even there, even in the pictures he was just an earthbound shadow following music down a windy street, any street, while Mick Taylor played the solos. Mick Jagger was working harder than ever before, but that was just it: you could *see* he was working. The whole tour carried a mood that left you with the feeling that the artificial hysteria had finally tumbled past the overload, and strained nerves were not just visible but twitching all around. *Exile on Main Street* grew and the new songs were great, the press gushed, but people were beginning to get irritated—The World's Greatest? Who was to say these guys weren't dying?

Not Keith. Who was suddenly beginning to seem the crucial one, as Jagger flopped around in his jumpsuit and just looked more like a society creep every new picture. But Keith, Keith was obviously one of those people (like Bob Dylan circa '66) who look the absolute best of their entire lives when they're clearly on the verge of death. It seemed to lend him a whole new profundity and eloquence, *even though he was barely playing at all!* But then again, who else was there to concentrate on now?

He looked like everything dark and tragic that the Stones trip had ever threatened: soul flattened, skin sallow, bone scraped, and behind the reflector-shaded eyes the suggestion of a diseased intelligence too cancerous to spit imprecations anymore. Fucked up. It was beautiful. Junk bust in France, passport miasma, more rumors: disciplined self-erosion, on for six months, then abrupt shutoff for six months, then back. Lovers succumbed; they didn't have that much control. Neither did Charlie Parker. They all die sooner or later, and it's always sooner.

You can say that all this text amounts to is a romanticization of the ugliest sort of unsupported myths. But that was always what the Stones were supremely good for. And maybe it won't matter for any of us out here who just live for a record, a tour. Because the legal-governmental-immigration-chemical tangle grinds on, and if he sticks around Keith may not be able to leave his own block without running headfirst into the sort of authority which has made sporadic and often amusing attempts to close in on the Stones while waiting for something like this for years. Only too glad to shut you down, jive boy. Stay in your room and run the distillate of your not aborted but rather overfulfilled, exploded potentials for the rest of your life . . . so if he can't tour, and Ron Wood is in . . . maybe he doesn't play much guitar onstage anymore, and sure Ron Wood's a great chunky chording boyo from the pubs, but Ron Wood is not Keith Richards, nor are the Stones anything but disintegrating shards of past glory without Keith standing there. I don't even care whether he's awake or not. Prop him up. But don't muddy the line up any more than it's been already.

On the other hand, it has also been suggested that the reason the Stones are touring so extensively now is that they're planning to break up soon, soon as they can get out after wringing a few more big bills from it. They would never say that, but they emphatically deny Keith's departure: "It wouldn't be the Rolling Stones without Keith Richards." Which everybody knows. That's why the atmosphere is getting so grim.

The others, good as they play, look more like sessionmen all the time. Even ugliness only goes so far.

They went home then, in the fall, and you read the stories in every magazine, and they were all terrible. The stuff filtering back through the fields of rusted wire was much better. Like Keith at the Jamaica *Goat's Head Soup* sessions: according to a friend, wiped so far off the map that he picked up a bass and began trying to play a lead guitar line through it for a take. And was so gone, supposedly, that he kept on for 13 minutes before he realized he had the wrong instrument.

It was funny, and it was hearsay, and the rumor mills and professional scenemakers banter over lives: an English trade held a music biz poll asking who would be the next rock person to die. Keith came in first. Lou Reed was second. Eric Clapton placed. Mick missed out. Too bad. I think I might like him better now if he was in trouble. He seems too smug, or perhaps it's just the rational indifference of a realist, and I don't like his wife. Rumors of rock couples in elegant swaps didn't help the quease. You always knew, really, that the predilections of certain of your heroes were exactly what you didn't want to think they were when you were in school. "Memo from Turner" was cool, anyway—it appealed to your vicarious need for dips into sleaze, as well as (on a slightly different level) to the defensively twisted and even more amoral desire to kick the cat's face in even as you baited him into his groveling rodent hardon. Great macho nihilism.

But now Jagger was overstepping the tolerance of even us television sleazoids. Not by his preferences in flesh, but the flesh merchant he hooked up with. David Bowie, that chickenhearted straw man of suck rock you love to hate. Can you come to terms with a genuinely deviant sensibility, after all the goodtime burlesque acts, or would you rather just shoot the worthless pretentious motherfucker dead and put a stop to all this utter fraudulent bullshit about what a superstar he is? Especially since the entire thing is a ruse from his musical empire to his sexual self-hype: usual disreputable sources have it that his favorite quail is prepubescent girls. But whoever he humps makes no difference, he's still scum. Yeah, says the dazed reactionary fan, let's kill faggots and get rid of all this arch Broadway/music hall shit. There's a sense of utter despair in the atmosphere and if our heroes are gonna turn to pure crap we might as well blame somebody. Especially since it's happened before.

Lou Reed. Done in. And brought it on himself to a large extent. Although you begin to wonder about those theories, prevalent that summer of '72 when the Stones were on tour while Lou was in London trying to make a comeback through advanced stages of combination toxicity. The theories said that Bowie's whole tactic was to eliminate the competition by buying them up. Either that or fucking them. Same thing. A friend went to London on Bowie junket, observed the Bowie/

Reed phenomenon at fairly close hand, came back accusing Bowie of outright vampirism. I laughed.

But what is it, really, that's so infuriating about these stories? Not an attack of defensive conservatism in the face of the homo peril. Naw, it's the incest angle that rankles. Somebody oughta make a law that no popstars are allowed to have romantic or sexual entanglements with each other on pain of death. For movie stars it's okay, but where's the rock 'n' roll equivalent of Liz and Dick? Rock people are too self-conscious to do it with any grace. Somehow it blows all the Jagger charisma to see him and Bowie dancing and lolling on each other's laps at David's "retirement" party while their wives made out with quiet dignity in the glare of the paparrazzi . . . great pictures from that party: Bowie staring intensely at nothing, looking best; Jagger looking tattered, old, used-up, unelegant, plain bad, definitively flaky, head bent as he stares into his wineglass and purses his lips as if about to spit a rancid sip back; Lou Reed pudgy faced, matted shock of hair, nervously glancing to the side, beginning to resemble Porky Pig . . . as good as the famed Iggy-David-Lou pic in its way, because this time everybody really looked like garbage . . . and other pix of Mick dancing, incredibly stiffly, with that bitch he supposedly immortalized in song on his new album. This is rock aristocracy? Do we need aristocracy? Bad companions. But maybe he's found his level, between these creeps and Bianca's social contacts. And the capping irony is that there is really nothing on *Goat's Head Soup* as strong and Stoneslike as "Watch That Man" on *Aladdin Sane*. Eliminating the competition . . .

A fan's notes: Mr. Nice Guy's Mick's rep, after all that devil crapola, but somehow it's just impossible to care much anymore. Last year he was singing about what he looks like this year. It sounded better than it looks. Just like Jagger on the *Goat's Head Soup* album cover, the filmy scarf or whatever it is making him look sorta like Judy Garland in *Meet Me in St. Louis* . . . don't like that smile, it's just vacant . . . who is this guy, anyway . . . and inside Charlie and Bill no longer likeable, but not even interestingly unpleasant . . . the whole thing is just pretentious,

Mick Taylor is a big asshole obviously trying to look bad, amoral, like early Lou Reed or something: four years and he's finally pushing toward what he sees as consonance with the Stones image. But that's not their image anymore, Mick. What is? Nothing. Nondescript fabulousness. A fade in general. The only one that looks human is Keith, and that's only because he really looks like he's on the edge this time, his eyes are so out of sync they don't look like they belong to the same face. Oozing from deathly preserved charisma to bloblike distaste.

So what I say is fuck 'em. On September 28th of this year, Jagger sang "Angie" in heavy makeup and leather boy drag on the ABC-TV/ Don Kirshner *Midnight Special.* The night before, Mickey Rooney and Milton Berle sang some old musical comedy flytrap about what a hunk o' man Flo Ziegfeld was, and it was far more transsexually elaborate. Berle's been doing this *schtick* for twenty years and Mick (in spite of the "Have You See Your Mother" jacket foreplay, which was more of a joke than a move) had to wait for Alice Cooper and Bowie to make it all right. The Stones had class once, why are they trying so hard now to retain a tooth-hold of their outrageousness by doing things they don't need to do at all? When what really counts, the music, is finally beginning to turn bland.

There's no point in blaming them, though. They're helpless. In the past ten years the Rolling Stones created an enormous situation in which they're just a factor now. They're ironic victims of the endless new world which it was their triumph to create, because their efforts helped make it possible for hordes of other hopefuls to move into a relatively vacant atmosphere of electricity, expectation, and money. Flooding the market. Which is where both we and the Stones stand right now; up to our asses in brackish water.

When it gets like that, you've got to maintain a standard of surpassing brilliance just to keep up with yourself, even if the balance of your past work wasn't that brilliant. Because by the cumulative eminence of your enormous pile of past accomplishments and the mere fact that you have managed to sustain, you have set an impossible standard which you've gotta struggle constantly to meet if only to keep yourself from being drowned in all the scunge passing through. Like the New York Dolls—new Stones album's gotta be a classic or all the so-called arbiters of taste will jump on it and proclaim the Stones senile has-beens and the Dolls the new true mania. Not that that matters at all, but these little clamors mount up, and every one drains a little bit of energy and momentum from the Stones.

Another danger is that no matter how excellent you continue to be, people will just get bored with you. Not anybody's fault particularly. But the Rolling Stones, my god, how many different ways can you recycle Chuck Berry riffs? How many different phrases can you use to talk about balling before you have to resort to outright grossness? And when you reach that point (which means you have begun to lose the battle), how long do you think you will last trying to come up with new variations in grossness and obscenity until it becomes merely depressing? There's only so much mung to go around, and most artists do their best work in a very compressed period of three to five years or at most ten years. The Rolling Stones lasting twenty, thirty years—what a stupid idea that would be. Nobody lasts that long—very few novelists; the greatest directors don't turn out classic movies over a forty-year period. So as the ideas peter down the general body of personal and artistic interest in the creators has gotta wane.

In other words, why don't you guys go fertilize a forest?

Q: What can you say now that hasn't been said yet about the Rolling Stones?

A: Turn on the radio. Where you'll hear a rather raggedly sung ballad that grows on you, and is certifiably the best song on *Goat's Head Soup.*

Q: Still, why jump right on a ballad for the first time in history?

A: Because none of the fast songs are hit singles. They're not much of anything, in fact, except unlistenable on a nice, forgettably nonoffensive label.

There is a sadness about the Stones now, because they amount to such an enormous "So what?" The sadness comes when you measure not just one album, but the whole sense they're putting across now against what they once meant.

They were suppliers of context: a friend once said when I played the Yardbirds for him that, "It sounds like they just sat down and said, 'Okay, you mothas, here's what you're going to be doing for the next five years!' "

The Stones were saying the same thing in "Honky Tonk Women," and "Brown Sugar," and "Sympathy for the Devil." They provided a full arsenal for lesser bands to loot at will: riffs, melodies, attitudes, approaches to lyrics, concepts in packaging and even clothes and haircuts. So in a sense they held the entire music industry together, because without at least one band charting out the new territory there's no place for the hype to go.

Somebody's gotta tell people what they're gonna do tomorrow, or they may not even get out of bed. It's unfortunate, but that's the way it is. Every day a new album comes out by a new band from England or L.A. or anywhere and the first song's a direct "Honky Tonk Women" steal, with Allman Brothers or Winwood or some other vocal style overlaid. Second song's a steal of Lou Reed's "Sweet Jane," combined with Stones guitar moves. Etc.

These records keep piling up, and most of them are garbage, but the point is that somebody's gonna have to start providing all these brainless ditzels with some new ideas pretty soon or the whole thing's gonna break down! How many times can you recycle "Honky Tonk Women"? Just because the Stones have abdicated their responsibilities is no reason we have to sit still for this shit!

Because there is just literally nothing new happening. Bowie is a style collector with almost no ideas of his own, Reed's basically just reworking his old Velvets ideas, people like Elton John are reaching back into nostalgia but that's a blind alley, and everybody else is playing the blues.

So unless we get the Rolling Stones off their asses IT'S THE END OF ROCK 'N' ROLL! I'd like to just flip 'em the bird, because I'm mad at 'em, but unfortunately I'm not in a position to do that and neither are you. We are in a position to do absolutely nothing but go get these saggin' junked-up jerks and punch 'em up straight again or not only will there be no more Rolling Stones records, there won't be any New York Dolls or Lynyrd Skynyrd records to flush all those hot Stones ideas away. There won't be nuttin'!

So I hereby issue the Rolling Stones a challenge on behalf of myself, *Creem* magazine, and yourself if you so desire. I challenge those lazy, sniveling, winded mothermissers to PRODUCE or mark off the days till their next American tour 'cause we're gonna bounce 'em off the walls of every arena in the Western Hemisphere!

Creem, December 1973

It's Only the Rolling Stones

The rut to which we have all been habituated: we've been sitting around half a year muttering and we know it's time for that Stones single and album that'll save our airwaves and our summer and our souls and our faltering faith. And yet we wait each year less tenterhooked because we're only pragmatic, colluding with the inevitability of erosion. So when the single comes out it falls way short of the heroism that was ever only intermittently there, and satisfies our fidgety compulsion to write 'em off once and for all. Born to lose and hell Brian didn't even have the sense to die on the highway.

Yep, here they are again, cinemarketing their dubious magic more shamelessly than Mad Dogs & Englishmen, and what do we snap on the dial but this crunchy little number which sounds at first like something Leon Russell might have concocted for T. Rex. Jagger's voice is more strained and thin and mannered than ever, Keith (hope for some reason) is upchucking his usuals with scant fervor, and the whole mess drones on twice too long but becomes a hit anyway because there's nothing else on the radio. And since there's nothing else in the LP racks but Aerosmith plodders like Bad Company, we buy the single. Home, headphones, and second playing we begin to catch a familiar, belabored yet somehow still-moving last-gasp:

If I could stick a knife in my heart
Commit suicide right on the stage
Would it be enough for your teenage lust

Would it help to ease the pain
Ease your brain

Pretty good, an MC5 reference and Iggy prophecy in the same stanza. Meanwhile you pin him in white pantaloons schmucking around backstage at Eric Clapton concerts. Clearly this old boy's got credibility problems.

/// \\\

If you think I am going to review the new *It's Only Rock N Roll* album right now, you are crazy. But I am going to swim in it.

/// \\\

If they don't come through you're lucky, because you got yourself to fall back on, so don't worry, but meanwhile you gotta tear those pictures down from your wall and paste up some new icons which probably don't even exist.

Ain't it American to think Mick Jagger is as dopey as you and me, wandering from bistro to backstage as if he didn't have something better to do like sitting at home reading the new Joseph Heller book (both of which are where the real terror is), preserving his mystique, but no the guy wants to look regular just like Dylan before him except he also wants in like Lennon wanted in when he married Yoko and compromised himself in the process. Just a misunderstood adolescent who needs love so kick him in the head while the time is right. I remember when the Stones meant something but it's banal to say that by now and we will have to work harder. Hours slogged working for the luxury of enjoying the Rolling Stones. Which is not the way it should be at all, right? Right?

We don't care, we eat product as cynically as they dish it, too bad.

After all, the Stones have a lot to stand for. After all, so do we. Tedium is relative, right? So they're asking us simpleton questions: Did you ever wonder what would happen if we set rock in space and forgot about it? Did you ever wanna kill what weaned you? Well, don't try too hard. The next generation will not live for no burnout myth and then how will we all look clinging to and rationalizing this shit? Eight-year-olds are gonna demand that somebody say something pretty soon. This album will not endure, but neither will *Blonde on Blonde*. They will never surf again. So maybe we should appreciate the noise they make drowning, friends.

/// \\\

Dear Mick,

You always play ignorant. Why?
You've been projecting yourself on me all along.
You remind me of an apathetic antibody. But that's all right.
There is a certain resignation about you. But you're not stagnant.
You hate pretension in all its forms, so you overcompensate.
You like things for the wrong reasons. Always.
If you ever got sick I would never be around you. I would never see you. Why take chances?
We haven't known each other that long.
The best things are the ones that start slow, uncertainly, and build.
I don't love you. I just like being around you.

/// \\\

The Stones have become oblique in their old age, which is just another word for perverse except that perverse is the corniest concept extant as they realized at inception which is more than you can say for Lou Reed who had to go solo to figure it out. A load of laffs is what you won't get from any new Stones album and more's the pity. It's like they believed that Hollywood slit in *Star* magazine who said Mick was just an old buzzard and are determined to prove themselves while we lose interest, spattered mutterings that surface here and there, like that bass whomp that Charlie gives the opening of that damn latest single which like the bricks smashing together in the second chorus of "Hip Shake" proves he's still the greatest drummer in rock because the most subtle. He hits you when you least expect it while doing a job, and that's where the true story is. You've all gotta get straight and discover your alienation which is why do ya think kid the Stones work so hard touring year in and out just like Bill Wyman told me in an interview I never transcribed because he was such a cipher: "We're too busy to be decadent." Right, right, so is my mother, why don't you wait tables for a while, take a vacation, or at least commit suicide for real? Sense of struggle in the merest filler which maybe is funny ultimately. *Exile* was like a sheathed nerve that surfaced in weeks. *Soup* was friendly and safe. I want the edge and this album doesn't reassure me that I'll get it, what a curious situation to be stuck in, but maybe that's the beauty of the Stones, hah, hah, kid? This album is false. Numb. But it cuts like a dull blade. Are they doing the cutting, or are we? What do we want to kill? It's already died, enjoy the Rolling Stones while they move like waxen athletes through our community stating their perfect pall and putting it all into place for one moment since time don't wait and rock 'n' roll is only a moment while we wait for the next presence to assert itself. And honey, I ain't talkin' about no stars.

The Village Voice, October 31, 1974

State of the Art: Bland on Bland

There are two things to be said about this new Stones album before closing time: one is that they are still perfectly in tune with the times (a.k.a., sometimes, trendies) and the other is that the heat's off, because it's all over, they really don't matter anymore or stand up for anything, which is certainly lucky for both them and us: I mean, it was a heavy weight to carry for all concerned. This is the first *meaningless* Stones album, and thank god. No rationalizations—they can now go out there and compete with Aerosmith, or more precisely, since just like the last two before it this album's strongest moments are Jagger singing ballads, the "adult pop" market. Barry Manilow, even.

I don't even hate *Black & Blue* like the new Led Zep, which admittedly is unworthy of hatred from anybody except a true patriot who expected more than what you knew you were going to get—what you get here is sweet flow Muzak dentist office conversation piece bright eyes shining in the face of nothing at all which they will not even confront and more power to 'em. Yeah, I watched him die. Shit, don't even feel like a voyeur, 'twas all done in the name of art or the roto swagger or something, sokay Mick, I still like you like an old dull friend who you keep around for purely compassionate (empathetic?) reasons and because you remember when. Like whoever it was that started the Velvets. You're stuck in a retread, stomp on it, no, not good enough, I hear you growling but you can't barge in, especially since you insist on invoking Jamaica/reggae which you mighta been there but on the recorded evidence you know nothing about or at least can't translate as you used to godamighty do so well.

So you're a washout. That's why I like you now. I identify with the wretched of the earth, like any self-respecting liberal, beyond that all my vicarious fantasies are numb null-nodes, and damn if you haven't qualified for some time now so welcome to the museum, jump and shout work it on out goo goo wah wah pedaling backwards. All the uptempo "numbers" on this album with the exception of the of course by now obligatory "reggae" numbah and the disco chant which is not so droll nor offensive as plain palatable like okay you wanna reduce yourself to the level of the most banal music around because you've always tried to keep up, fine, but all the other rockers sound like water-logged "Brown Sugar" and even that's okay because what the hell you know I mean they're good guys even if they did fuck up Ron Wood apparently because even last tour last summer he played such monstro chunka wailout guitar with the Faces (in such contrast to how blithely he blended into the general lifeless woodwork of the Stones tour), whom he apparently hated (nobody with sensibilities intact could like Rod at this point anyway) and maybe that was why he was so good therein at least at the end, but now he's slapping palms foreheads synapses collapsed with his idol Keith (which makes him Nick Kent) and the result is that, going strictly by this album, Ron Wood is no longer a raucket guitar hero. He's succeeded in becoming as dead and anonymous as Keith. Take a gander at the cover and realize they're even coaching him in the art of looking grim, I mean you cannot be a true-blues badass Rolling Stone and SMILE, which is further loggings of toobad toolate blues, because Ron Wood has proven himself one of the great smilers of all time. It's like he's in Keith school, and at this point the smartest move missah Richards could possibly make would be to start a mail correspondence course sent off matchbooks to look sexily defunct.

Because Keith is just a dumb shit who never figured out that there was anything good to be said on guitar after Chuck Berry, the worst kind of oldies-fetishist, fuck his image, you could look like that if you were a rich junkie too, outlaw my ass, he's boring, a word I seldom invoke because there's too many good books to read to ever get bored and too many fine fine records to listen to but this ain't one of them.

I won't even comment on the lyrics because they don't mean shit. They're stupid and deserve to be. Not even "Memory Motel," which I could get a cheap shot off by saying the line "You're just a memory, that used to mean so much to me" applies to the Stones, but I don't believe that, I just love 'em for getting wasted, as they are, and slowly dying with such immaculate sense of timing, I mean they still can do no wrong, except if you really are dumb enough to expect a Statement, well, NO STATEMENTS HERE. They even copped out on the s&m cover packaging originally envisioned, for which actually I am glad, gladder than about any of the music herein, because there is plenty enough too much ersatz plethora of s&m culture around as it is, and even s&m freaks probably gotta resent the Stones for not really contributing to it but always *playing* at the most chichi trendy formulaic cuffs of bondage. When really they were always in bondage to some stupid idea of themselves. I mean, Jagger and Townshend—*who cares if they're 30 years old?* Even a single reader of this magazine? No. Nobody gives a shit about their hang-up about that but Jagger and Townshend. Patti Smith is 30, the author of this piece is 27 and still stands upon his head on occasion cartwheels for the party, Charlie Mingus is 54 and still breathing fire in his stance if not his most recent music. He learned the obvious lesson that old can mean Duke Ellington mellow, not the garbage heap, but the Stones want to be on the garbage heap, where else you gonna pitch outlaws, but sorry, I can't take it for anything but product, a year and a half in the making too, ha, what a joke, what a great laugh, what a band what a group what a charge what a rock 'n' roll band what a band what a band what a band, goodbye.

P.S. (of course)

But and then at that time also, I recall with my old bud Mick, swam out scenes a good drifter cannabisalt off the boardwalk entirely, and we listened a tune a time or two, and to conclusion we did come, most specifically that this here makes hay jump and spindly-leg jeckyl hustle because it's funny and good as gone can be—"Hot Stuuff"—when Mick comes on with that jive Rasta growly blab and actually nerves up to "Allayoupeapalinnyaksitay, I know yall goin' broke, to everybody in Jamaica, livin' workin' in the sun, yer hot stuff," yeah, hot hicks wack on down, let those Jaymochan rude boys get their mitts on your gullet dad, they'll squeeze till you forget about tryina be anybody's badass, but slopfingered wimp as you are you're all right. Because for one thing we figured out that Bianca is smarter than you and it blew your mind that such a phenomenon could exist so you write all these mushy love ballads your last alpees while she fucks off with Ryan O'Neal. "Hey honey would you like to get something to eat . . . ?" Chick sal san on rye, quick or slow don't make no, gone bleared kid you are in the age you have declaimed yourself, hand of fate sureshot horseshit, you still could if you would but you won't but that's okay because we love you for what you are. Less than nothing, because you were something once. So thank you for not aspiring: you are an inspiration to the blank generation whole.

Creem, July 1976

Kind of Grim: Unraveling the Miles Perplex

I have been wrestling with this Miles Davis thing for what has amounted to years now, and even though I still haven't gotten it figured out, perhaps an expository dissection of my confusion can be instructive to you, if you care. Certainly Miles has been leading quite a few of us along by the nose, tying our tympanics and our standards up in knots (especially reviewers) as we try to figure out whether the relative nonimpact of all this shit boils down to us or him. Here, then, is the problem, with a roster of alternative solutions (take your pick, if you pick):

Ever since *Jack Johnson,* which came out in 1971 and was his last incontrovertibly masterful album, Miles has become something whose antithesis he had been for the previous 20-odd years of his career: erratic. Critics particularly had trouble deciding whether albums like *Miles Davis in Concert* were difficult, dense masterworks or plain old dogshit: it wasn't even as simple as the fact that Miles is a figure traditionally deemed above criticism, but rather that nobody wants to be caught sitting on yesterday's curb wacking their doodle to old blowing sessions when Miles is sculpting new thruways and monorails. Briefly, he laid on us such bones of great contention (although not very many people wanted to say so in public) as *Miles at Fillmore, On the Corner, Big Fun,* and *Get Up with It.*

Now. For anyone who has been following Miles' career farther back than *Bitches Brew* there were at least parts of each of these that were a bit difficult to swallow. At least if your listener's integrity extended to yourself (fuck the public: anybody that buys Stanley Clarke albums deserves whatever they get). *Miles at Fillmore,* way back in '70–71, was the first one I remember being a bit thrown by: it was obvious that he was extending the *In a Silent Way/Bitches Brew* approach (which Joe Zawinul has never gotten nearly enough credit for, and may have been almost wholesale ripped off when you get down to it, despite the avant/MOR row of pap he's been plowing with Weather Report), no, rather he was *reiterating* the leaps of those albums in a way that not only added nothing, but was literally not up to Miles' traditionally Mandarin-impeccable standards.

I dismissed it as an off-note unaccountably put on record, but then he followed the brilliance of *Jack Johnson* and the relative comeback of *Live Evil* with *On the Corner,* which still reigns supreme as the absolute worst album this man ever put out. On this experiment in percussion and electronics, what little actual trumpet you could pick out of the buzz-whiz and chockablocka was so distorted as to be almost beyond recognition. And this from the man who made a good deal of his rep on the devastating, transcendent depths of pure human emotion he could find in his soul and axe. It seemed almost to amount to a form of suicide, or at least an artistically perverse act of the highest order.

There were, of course, the Faithful who declared foursquare like Jann Wenner of John and Yoko's *Wedding Album* that Miles Knows What He's Doing Even If I Don't—Ralph J. Gleason, a man whose penchant for glib preachments and name-dropping could be eternally excused by his boundless passion for musical art, devoted a lead tandem review in *Rolling Stone* to *On the Corner* and the then-current Santana album. They were, he said, a new genre of "street music" with heavy Third World (or at least American Ethno-Cultural Minority Group) ramifications, directed to audiences of same with the review's obvious though unstated implication being that if we the (presumably) white jass-buffs couldn't get with it maybe it was only meant for the bros.

I have in my time heard similar claims made, in more stridently specific terms for mediocre-to-ghastly albums by people like Archie

Shepp, Joseph Jarman & The Art Ensemble of Chicago, and Sun Ra, and they were every bit as big a platter of horseshit in those instances as with Miles. Gleason once told me that Shepp was working in an area where it was very difficult indeed to tell "good" playing from "bad" and that therefore *Three for a Quarter, One for a Dime* was one of those then-proliferating albums which were simply immune to critical arbitration. I mean, if "free" playing's tenets are adhered to to the letter then we really have no business telling Archie Shepp, for instance, that he has been exploiting the ethnocentricity and oppression-bred anger of his own people for about half a decade now, do we? Who are we, a bunch of white boys who have never felt Mr. Charley's boot, to say that *Three for a Quarter* is nothing more or less than a crappy album of jackoff squacksquawk tenor blowing slung out by an artist who doesn't seem to have very much respect for his audience?

No, we must admit that we, or our forefathers, or somebody, stands guilty of 400 years of YOU KNOW WHAT. But I will also go on record as saying that I have been listening to all kinds of jazz including more "free" rambles than most sane people (I used to listen to Coltrane's *Ascension* and Albert Ayler's *Spiritual Unity* while eating breakfast), and even though I don't know the first thing about the technical aspects of music, I can tell good jazz, free, or otherwise, from bad, and Archie Shepp has put out a whole lot of albums that are either gibberish (*Three for a Quarter*) or blaxploitation bullshit (*Attica Blues*). Ask just about any musician and he'll tell you that with certain minor exceptions, isolated tracks and such, Pharoah Sanders has been totally uninspired and unforgivably gimmicky since Trane died: and I had the laff riot of seeing Sun Ra live in Berkeley a few years back, the old wack-dome himself along with a full troupe of dancers, percussionists, etc., two sax players chasing each other through the audience staging a mock cockfight with their horns SQUEEKASWANKASQUOOONKRRRRRONKARGGHHH etc. much to the delight of the 99.999 percent white audience.

The Connection between all this and Miles' ouevre is a connection, precisely. Even though he still doesn't move as many units as the prodigal Stanley Clarke or blear-orbs McLaughlin, it's safe to assume that in 1976 at least a couple of double-disc meistersplats of murk-mung elektro-Miles are as essential a component of the cokespoon swinger's pad as the proper brand of aromatic candles. So Miles is not just background music but an essential part of the conspicuous consumption mores of a certain current subculture, and perhaps should not be criticized as music at all, but rather in accordance with their rise or fall on the barometer of college student and pimp-chic Hip. So maybe Tom Wolfe should start reviewing his records instead of me.

On the other hand, Miles has meant a lot to me ever since I first heard *Birth of the Cool* when I was too young to understand it, and while I still think I can tell good Miles from bad (the latter being something never experienced on wax, at least, till this decade), I'm still not ready to write him off as so many others have done whether they pay lip service or not. This in spite of the fact that the one time I finally got a chance to see him live, in 1973, he was such an asshole that his cooking (and, of course, unidentified) backup band put him to shame, while the titan himself settled for stalking sullenly around the stage, pausing his premature curmudgeon's sulk every few minutes to lift his horn and blow three to six random careless and totally irrelevant notes, or to find himself wandering behind an electric organ on which he randomly essayed two-finger off-notes more suitable to in-store demonstration than what was going on around him. The highlight of the concert was when some smart-aleck in the audience threw a Frisbee, it hit him in his black badass dog-mean s&m choker, which fell off. His entire performance, from music to personal bearing, was a giant fuck-you to everybody present (including his fellow musicians?) and I hated his guts. If you wanted to rationalize this shit academically you could see it as the logical extension of his legendary proclivity for turning his back on his audiences, except that when he used to do that he was playing music that could snap your soul in two at the same time, besides which it's a matter of simple convenience (after all, why should we extend him any courtesy?) to reject all such notions which can only encourage more infantilism, and merely write the guy off as an asshole. And quite possibly a burnt-out one at that.

But here I sit, nearly three years later, and this man and his music refuse to ease their stranglehold on my tastes, more, my emotions. I am obsessed with him because he once released *Sketches of Spain,* which contains an *adagio* passage in Rodrigo's 'Concierto De Aranjuen' which may hold more distilled sorrow than any other single solo by anyone I have ever heard; I am obsessed with him because *Kind of Blue,* like *Birth of the Cool* a decade previous, defined an era and produced some of the most beautiful, spacious, expansively inspired music it was to know; I'm obsessed because *In a Silent Way* came close to changing my life, reinstilling a respect for the truly spiritual aspects of music when I was otherwise intent on wallowing in grits and metal; I'm obsessed, simply because he is Miles, one of the greatest musicians who ever lived, and when a giant gets cancer of the soul you have to weep or at least ask for a medical inquiry.

Which is why I have been studying Miles' work for the past year or so, trying to figure out where (if?) he went wrong. Think about the fact that his guy has been making "jazz" records since the late Forties, and that many of them, way more than any single musician's share, have become (to borrow the title of one) milestones. The man has defined at least three eras in American music—can Dylan say the same? Never mind that when *In a Silent Way* came out it had the same effect as Charlie Parker's renaissance and influence on his followers—i.e., it ruined a whole generation of musicians who were so swept by its brilliant departure that they could do nothing but slavishly imitate so every goddamn album you heard dribbled the same watered-down-kitsch-copy of Miles' electric cathedral—it remains that now, seven years later, *In a Silent Way* not only has not dated but stands with *Sketches of Spain* and a few other Miles albums as one of the sonic monuments of our time. And that's neither hype nor hyperbole.

But since then, the years, private problems, celebrityhood, hipper-than-thous—*something, whatever,* has taken its toll. *On the Corner* was garbage. So was, with the possible exception of one bit I have been told about but am unable to find in its four unbanded 30-minute sides, *Miles Davis in Concert. Big Fun* and *Get Up with It* were largely leftovers, with predictably erratic results. The former's "Go Ahead John" was a cooker, but too much of the rest was something never previously expected of Miles: simple ideas repeated for whole sides, up to a half hour each, in an electronicized repetitiveness and distortion-for-its-own-sake that may have been intended as hypnotic but ended up merely static. What was perhaps even more disturbing was that once you got past the predictability and disappointment and analyzed the actual content of the music, it took Miles past his traditional (and traditionally heart-wrenching) penchant for sustained moods of deep sadness into a new area redolent more of a by turns muzzy and metallic unhappiness. He should have called one of these albums *Kind of Grim.* And mere unhappiness, elaborated at whatever electro-technocratic prolixity, is not nearly the same as anguish.

Much of Miles' finest music, from *Blue Moods* to "Prayer" on *Porgy and Bess* to *Sketches* to *My Funny Valentine,* has been about inner pain translated into a deep mourning poetry so intense and distilled that there have been times when I (and others have reported similar reactions) have been almost literally unable to take it. I have always been offended when people ask me to take off any jazz record because they find it "depressing," but secretly I always knew what they meant. Because there were times when I found Miles' anguish not purgative but depressing, when I had to yank *Jack Johnson* out of the 8-track deck because I could not drive to the laundromat with such a weight in my heart; but I also knew the reason why I (and, if I may be so presumptuous, the nebulous anti-jazz people I just mentioned) was depressed: *because at that moment there was something wrong with me,* of a severity that could reach by degrees from my consciousness to my heart to my soul; because I was sweeping some deep latent anguish under the emotional carpet, or not confronting myself on some primal level—*and Miles cut through to that level.* His music was that powerful: it exposed me to myself, to my own falsity, to my own cowardice in the face of dread or staved-off pain. Because make no mistake, Miles understands pain—and he will pry it out of your soul's very core when he hits his supreme note and you happen, coincidentally, to be a bit of an open emotional wound at that moment yourself. It is this gift for open-heart surgery that makes him the supreme artist that he is. So, obviously, I am damned if I am going to shrug him off at this point. I am going to tear these fucking records apart and find out what the source of the cancer running through them is, praying for cure.

There are various theories being bantered about the grapevine concerning Miles' present state, many of them having to do with his personal problems (health, personal relationships, etc.), and they are undoubtedly a major contributing factor in his decline, but to write a fade of this magnitude off to gossip fodder would be cheap, and since he hasn't incorporated his personal problems into his hype/legend like certain other artists, they remain nobody else's business. It's too easy to concoct chemical or sexual demonologies. What emerges from *Big Fun* and *Get Up with It* is a sense of depression so deep and unconsolable as to be cold as the floor of a morgue. When you think of the cokespoon set that buys these albums because it's *Miles,* man, because of some stupid image, it's impossible to imagine them actually sitting there and listening to the entire half hour of "He Loved Him Madly," *Get Up*'s opener and one of the most truly bereaved pieces of music ever put on record. It didn't sound like the recently deceased Duke Ellington, to whom it was ostensibly dedicated, at all; but it sure did sound like death. Like a grief beyond all wails, darkness, darkness and loneliness that became positively clammy, like a lifetime prison sentence in a diving bell in the blackest depths on the bottom of the ocean. How many people could even *take* music like that, especially at such length?

Of course, the rest of the album was the usual hodgepodge, tossing together unreconstituted dreck, an old outtake with the "superstar" band he led in the early '70s, one fine side-long Spanish-tinged slipstream, and one terse, fiendishly humorous exercise juxtaposing standard funky blues harp with some of Miles' most biting trumpet work in ages. What it all added up to was a good bit more than the standard eccentric-avant-garde artist schtick ("I'm Miles, I can put out anything")—clearly this music was indicating that something was wrong with the progenitor, that he was not indulging himself or tapped out or merely confused. That he was sick of soul.

Which of course, providing you believe it, still doesn't solve the problem: IS THIS GOOD MUSIC OR NOT? And, ARE NOT SOME COURAGEOUS ACTS BETTER LEFT IN PRIVATE?

Agharta, his latest, offers few clues; it's recorded live in Japan, Miles lets his sidemen solo at respectable but probably disproportionate length, and his own outings are what we have come to expect save for one brief moment of openhearted breath-caught-in-the-throat Old Miles in the middle of "Theme from Jack Johnson," which incidentally sounds very little like its namesake if that matters. So I am going to further complicate the Miles conundrum by answering all the questions raised above with some more:

1. Is this music good or bad?
2. If it's bad, does Miles know it?
3. If it's bad and he knows it, is he
    (a) just telling his audience to get fucked;
    (b) fulfilling contractual obligations;
    (c) groping for something he is at present incapable of fulfilling;
    (d) putting out product because like Dylan, John Lennon, etc. he simply has nothing better to do and can't admit he's washed up?
4. If this music is good, does that mean that Miles is trying to tell us something we may not want to know (cf. latent anguish theory)?

5. If this music is good, is it also good for us?
6. If it's good and the effect of that goodness is to depress us, should we keep listening?
7. If it's bad, are reviews like this not the worst possible medicine for Miles' afflictions? Should we tell him he's jiving himself, and effect a boycott until he relocates himself?
8. If it's bad, why am I so much more fascinated with Miles in a state of decay than I was when he was making one fine, solid, mainstream album after another?

I won't pretend to have the answers to any of those questions, but I will say this: the very fact that they had to be posed makes this music more interesting and provocative than nine-tenths of everything else being released today. For Milesophiles, I'd suggest that you go back to two early albums for the precedent to his current dilemma: to *Miles in the Sky* for a preview of the spaciness that made *Bitches Brew* almost too airy and some of its followers almost invisible; and to an album that has been called at various times *Jazz Track, Frenzy* and *Elevator to the Scaffold*[9]. That was the soundtrack to a French thriller that Miles laid down with some European nobodies way back in 1958, it was completely different than anything else he was doing at the time, and in its deep-night sense of terminally disconsolate moodiness has remained a classic over the years that prophesied the artist's recent psychic plunge.

As for all this new Miles music, I sit here at the end of *Agharta* with a rubbery weight at the bottom of my heart. I'm no masochist, and nobody could ever call Miles maudlin, but I'm not sorry. I have finally learned to think of Miles' most recent music and what he has done to his art as taking a jewel, a perfectly faceted diamond as big as the earth shining brighter than ten thousand suns, suppose you took that jewel and with implacable, superhuman, malevolent hands *crushed it* in on

[9] Available currently as *Ascenseur Pour L'Echafaud (Lift to the Scaffold): Original Soundtrack* (Verve).

itself, compressed by a force beyond comprehension until it was half its original size, black all over and a cold and unbreakable lump. I think of that diamond as the emotional capacities of Miles' music, as Miles' heart; my theory re the musical personality of Miles Davis is that he has committed upon himself, his heart, just exactly what was done to that diamond, for reasons having to do with great, perhaps unbearable suffering. In Patti Smith's words, his music now to me is "a branch of cold flame," and I think that, crushed as that heart is, the soul beyond it has not been and cannot ever be destroyed. Like Graham Greene's "burnt-out case" (and he was not referring to drugs), perhaps that is all that is left. But in a curious way that almost glows uniquely brighter in its own dark coldness; and that, that which is all that is left, is merely the universe.

Phonograph Record, June 1976
(Reprinted in *New Musical Express,* April 30, 1983)

Miles Davis: Music for the Living Dead

Miles, you worthless wretch! Here we wait all these years—Okay! It's hip for every no-ears trendy in the world to like *On the Corner* now! *Satisfied?*—and you hand us this Death of the Cool plate of half-thawed cryogenic *Bitches Brew* doodles! And that *vocal!* Good lord man, in terms of self-service via groveling acolytes, James Chance was cooler than this when he had that girl warble "He's almost black. . . ." while he gurgled out one of his hideous sax solos, almost as hideous as those squishy little noises you're making under that sub-EWF simpering! Miles, you should have died!

Now that the dust has settled, the most appropriate word for Miles Davis' "comeback" album, *The Man with the Horn,* and his concurrent series of live gigs would probably be "tentative." Stanley Crouch wrote in *The Village Voice* of the Avery Fisher Hall concert I attended: "Miles Davis' performance struck me as a con job in its obvious manipulation of the audience's eagerness to like whatever he did . . . but his home-made post-bebop sound is still more moving than anything I've heard on trumpet since Clifford Brown." The *Boston Phoenix*'s Bob Blumenthal quoted a friend asking, "What Miles Davis song title captures what's been going on here?" Blumenthal settled for "Great Expectations," somebody else said "So What," and I'd settle for either "Stuff" or "Paraphernalia." Then he wrote: "It now seems silly that anyone expected Davis to return with either another radical departure or a reconsideration of his pre-electric music. We should have known that he would pick up where he left off, with open-ended, vamp-driven, funky electric jamming."

Yeah, except this ain't where he left off. He left off with *Agharta* and *Pangaea,* two concerts recorded on the same day in Japan. The former, an afternoon concert, was the last "new" Davis LP released in this country (in 1976) before *The Man with the Horn,* while *Pangaea,* the evening show, is only recently available here on import. And there was a fury completely absent from either *Man* or the recent gigs in that music, especially in *Pangaea,* whose first side's violent, headlong assault had led me more than once to call it "the first jazz of the Eighties."

The truth is that the jazz of the Eighties, if there's going to be any that matters, probably began in 1972 with *On the Corner.* God knows few enough people had any use for it in the Seventies, including me, who had followed and loved everything Miles did from *Birth of the Cool* on out, and couldn't even *hear* it, much less feel its cold flame and realize its intentions, for five years after it was released.

I think one reason so many of us had trouble with that most radically abrupt of Miles' departures was what we perceived in the album as an absence of exactly that emotional quality Crouch spoke of. It's always been axiomatic that even if others had greater technique, or he seemed in the Sixties to have been "passed up" by his alumni like Coltrane, or even that he seems to many ears to have been playing the same blues solo in different settings for decades, still, *Miles has more soul.* If *On the Corner* could hardly be accused of being that same solo, it also could be (was) accused of having no discernible emotion in it.

The two keys we missed were rhythm and attitude. For the first time a Miles Davis album was conceived not as a setting for the type of deeply emotive trumpet playing on LPs like *Sketches of Spain* and *My Funny Valentine,* but as a world and a world-view fully realized in which all parts were equivalently integral to the whole. It was like a big painting of a whole city laid out as if on a map come wrigglingly alive. It was like a hive. Those who still don't "get it" might be best advised to put it on cassette and listen to it while walking around downtown Detroit, New York's 14th Street, or any really busy, crowded urban area. (Though interestingly enough I first really heard it when I was in

Jamaica, where it was suddenly almost obscenely, frighteningly alive, and its sense of menace unmistakable.) As an old girlfriend said once when we drove through ghetto Detroit with it on the box, "I get it; this is an *environment* record." But that environment doesn't have to be funky; what was initially perceived as emotionless in the music turned out actually to be an alienation so extreme that we could only grow into it and the album as time caught up with us and we caught up with Miles. In fact, the music seems to change with and comment on different environments: in more low-rent areas, on the (real) corner, it not only catches the rhythms of human movement, but each instrument, and each little melodic or rhythmic figure (what once seemed like doodles, squiggles) that appears briefly, disappears, and reappears again several minutes later, is like a different one of the characters you see regularly passing through your local interzone, blending at first but eventually becoming the cast of an urban drama without beginning or end in which they are all hanging out. Play it in Macy's or midtown Manhattan or at the shopping mall and it grows discernibly colder, the wriggling entities more sinister.

It is, in fact, pretty cold everywhere, but it is a coldness of rage at the very heart's death. If Miles seemed to be losing his capacity to feel, he only predicted what would soon begin to happen to all of us. Ever feel emotionally impacted? That's what *On the Corner* and almost all Miles' subsequent (pre-*Man*) music is all about. Take the most expansive heart in the world and subject it to unknown force with almost unimaginable pressure, compress and crush it relentlessly until it is one small cold hard ball of anthracite black hate. Then watch it begin to turn in the void, spitting occasional needles of light. That's what I hear in this music, that and the perception of being constantly surrounded by alien entities, insectival and reptilian, swarming all around you *On the Corner.* In later works the sense of menace grows—"Rated X" on *Get Up with It* is so relentlessly malevolent it's like being eaten alive by giant insects—as does the sense of claustrophobia and depression ("He Loved Him Madly" might well be the most depressed piece of music of the Seventies, which is saying something), till finally it all explodes on the first side of *Pangaea* into a tangled scream for freedom (which tried only semisuccessfully to tear itself loose from depression and blind-alley, closed-circuit rage in *Agharta*).

Now, allowing for the facts that all the material on these albums (*On the Corner, Miles Davis in Concert, Big Fun, Get Up with It, Agharta, Pangaea*) was not released in the exact order it was recorded—things get especially dodgy in *Big Fun* and *Get Up with It*—and that some of it was "assembled" from tapes by Teo Macero, it still cannot be denied that there is a perception of society, or say one's place in the scheme of things and how one feels about it, at work here. Some alienated critics and fans have written this music off as failed experiments that should have been left in the can, or even sweepings from the recording studio floor that are revelatory only of the creator's failing chops, but that's only because most of them can't hear it, and to the extent they can, do not like what they hear. After all, who wants to be told YOU ARE DEAD for 30 minutes or an hour at a time? Nobody, so of course it gets translated down into things like the jazz drummer who once told me, "Even most of the musicians who say they like Miles' *On the Corner* stuff are really just trying to be hip."

Which may be true too, but still doesn't (cannot) negate the truth, more manifest every day I'd say, that this music is about something, and what it is about is what we are becoming: post-human and, concomitantly, technology-obsessed. This is the poison whirring through the wiring of a supersociety which has become a cage, what Max Weber prophesied when he wrote before the First World War of a populace "embracing . . . mechanized petrifaction, embellishing a sort of convulsive self-importance. For of that stage of this cultural development it might truly be said, 'Specialists without spirit, sensualists without heart; this nullity imagines that it has attained a level of civilization never before achieved.'"

By now you probably think I've stretched a subjective impression way too far. Okay then, look around you. Do those look like people?

Hell, they ain't even good enough to be animals. Androids is more like it, mutants at best. They have become the machines they worship, successfully post-human. Now go look in the mirror. Like what you see? Think you're pretty cool, eh? Well, reflect on the fact that *they all think the same thing when they look in their mirrors.* And you look just as grotesque to them as they do to you. Now go put on, say, Side Two of *On the Corner.* Feel more at home now?

Look, I don't expect Miles Davis to stand up and say, "Yes, all my mid-Seventies music was intended to reflect a society in which narcissism is giving way to solipsism," or even, "You say I stopped playing with soul, but it's you that've lost your souls." And I may well be wrong about all this, but I do think I hear him saying, musically in pieces like "Rated X" and "Mtume," "You think *this* is oppressive? Well, this is what you look like to me." And I do know that this music has a certain strange power and pertinence that even in an album as second-rate as *Miles Davis in Concert* (which sounds, as a friend put it, like it was recorded on a day when everybody in the band had bad hangovers) makes it matter in a way that's at least *different* from the way things like *E.S.P.* and *Nefertiti* mattered. Yes, it means more to me personally than they did (though not more than *Sketches of Spain* or *Kind of Blue*), though maybe that's because I am so emotionally impacted that I have successfully used the second and fourth sides of *Get Up with It* to pull me out of deep depressions on more than one occasion. No lie; friends report similar results with "He Loved Him Madly." It seems somehow that the coldness of emotional death in that music touches the emotional repressions inside us which have culminated in such gulfs of seemingly pointless unhappiness, that Miles' heart, even as it is dying if it is dying, somehow touches ours and makes them live again in a way that even something like "My Funny Valentine" or "Concierto de Aranjuez" might not be able to just now. Because even at their most meditative those were expansive musics, and before we can feel them again something has to light up the parameters of the cage. Or, as somebody else once said, "Nothing in my dreams, just some ugly memories."

In the meantime, there is *The Man with the Horn,* obviously a set-up media event, pleasant enough but at best Miles (who, it must be said, looked at the concert like a man who had been gravely ill) just getting a toe back in the water. It sent me back to *Bitches Brew,* which (except for the crappy powerchording guitar) is pretty much where it noodles, and made that album sound positively *heavy* instead of a little too airy as always before. But look at it this way: how would you feel if you were Miles Davis and opened *Billboard* and Chuck Mangione had the Number Three album in the country while CBS was deleting some of your recent catalog? You would go through a period of black-on-black bitterness and then you would begin to strategize. It's not so much the fact of a vocal (how about Bob Dorough singing "Nothing Like You" on *Sorcerer,* or that track from the *Birth of the Cool* sessions?) as the *nature* and *lyrics* of the vocal that're bad, but if it gets Miles radio play, sells the album along with all the other tinselly hype and gets that Chuck Mangione audience to go for his next release as well, then my most cherished hope could only be that he would hit 'em with a 30-minute "Rated X." They won't like it, but maybe by then, only 10 years after *On the Corner,* they'll at least have some idea what's hitting them. And why.

Music and Sound Output, December 1981

Captain Beefheart's Far Cry: He's Alive, But So Is Paint. Are You?

Don Van Vliet is a 39-year-old man who lives with his wife in a trailer in the Mojave Desert. They have very little money, so it must be pretty hard on them sometimes, but I've never heard them complain. Don Van Vliet is better known as Captain Beefheart, a legend worldwide whom the better part of a generation of New Wave rock 'n' roll bands have cited as one of their most important spiritual and musical forefathers: John Lydon/Rotten, Joe Strummer of the Clash, Devo, Pere Ubu, and many others have attested to growing up on copies of Van Vliet's 1969 album *Trout Mask Replica,* playing its four sides of discordant yet juicy swampbrine jambalaya roogalator over and over again until they knew whole bits—routines out of his lyrics, which are a wild and totally original form of free-associational poetry.

There are some of us who think he is one of the giants of 20th-century music, certainly of the postwar era. He has never been to music school, and taught himself to play about half a dozen instruments including soprano sax, bass clarinet, harmonica, guitar, piano, and most recently mellotron. He sings in seven and a half octaves, and his style has been compared to Howlin' Wolf and several species of primordial beasts. His music, which he composes for ensemble and then literally teaches his bands how to play, is often atonal but always swings in a way that very little rock ever has. His rhythmic concept is unique. I hear Delta blues, free jazz, field hollers, rock 'n' roll, and lately something new that I can't put my finger on but relates somehow to what they call "serious" music. You'll probably hear several other things.

This is going to be a profile partially occasioned by the release of his twelfth (and best since 1972's *Clear Spot*) album, *Doc at the Radar Station.* This is also going to be, and I hesitate mightily to say this because I hate those articles where the writer brays how buddybuddy he is with the rock stars, about someone I have long considered a friend and am still only beginning to feel I understand after eleven years. Which is perhaps not so long a time to take to be able to say that you have learned anything about anyone.

/// \\\

Meanwhile, back in the Mojave Desert, Don Van Vliet is enjoying a highly urbane, slyly witty (anecdotes and repartee litter the lunar sands like sequins 'n' confetti on the floor of a Halloween disco), and endlessly absorbing conversation with a gila monster. "GRAAU-UWWWKKK!" says the big slumbrous reptile, peering out its laser-green lidless bulging eyes and missing nothing. "Brickbats fly my fireplace," answers Van Vliet. "Upside down I see them in the fire. They squeak and roast there. Wings leap across the floor." "KRAAUUAU-UWWWKKK!" advises heat-resistant gila. Van Vliet the Captain nods and ponders the efficacy of such a course. They've both just washed down the last of the scalding chili fulla bigeyed-beans from Venus what glare atcha accusingly as ya poppem doomward inya mouf. The Captain, Van Vliet, call him which you choose, has chosen to live out here, squatflat wampum on this blazoned barren ground for many a year. Don't see too much o' the hoomin side o' the varmint family out here, but that's fine with Cap Vliet, "Doc" as he's called by the crusty prospectors hung on lak chiggers from times before his emigration to this spot.

/// \\\

Have you ever had somebody you idolized or looked up to as an artist?

Can't think of anybody, other than the fact that I thought van Gogh was excellent.

How about in music?

Never in music, I never have. A hero in music. No, fortunately.

So you didn't listen to like Delta blues and free jazz and stuff before you started to—

Not really . . . I met Eric Dolphy. He was a nice guy, but it was real limited to me, like *bliddle-liddle-diddlenopdedit-bop,* "I came a long way from St. Louie," like Ornette, you know. It didn't move me.

Dolphy didn't MOVE you?

Well, he moved me, but he didn't move me as much as a goose, say. Now that could be a hero, a gander goose could definitely be a hero, the way they blow their heart out for nothing like that.

Is that because you think that people generally do it for purposes of ego?

Um, yeah, which I think is good because it gets your shoes tied. You know what I mean, it doesn't scare old ladies, you get dressed. So I think that's nice.

You don't think it's possible to create art that's egoless, that just flows through you?

That's possible, I'm tryin' to do that, on this last album definitely.

Well, one thing I find is that the more I know the less I know.

Me too. I don't know anything about music.

/// \\\

As reviews over the years have proved, it's always difficult to write anything that really says something about Don Van Vliet. Perhaps (though he may hate this comparison) this is because, like Brian Eno, he approaches music with the instincts of a painter, in Beefheart's case those of a sculptor as well. (When I was trying to pin him down about something on his new album over the phone the other day, he said: "Have you seen Franz Kline lately? You should go over to the Guggenheim and see his 'Number Seven,' they have it in such a good place. He's probably closer to my music than any of the painters, because it's just totally speed and emotion that comes out of what he does.") When he's directing the musicians in his Magic Band he often draws the songs as diagrams and shapes. Before that he plays the compositions onto a tape himself, "usually on a piano or a moog synthesizer. Then I can shape it to be exactly the way I want it, after I get it down there. It's almost like sculpture, that's actually what I'm doing, I think. . . . 'Cause I sure as hell can't afford marble, as if there was any."

Much of what results, by any "normal" laws of music, cannot be done. As for lyrics, again like Eno, he often works them up from a sort of childlike delight at the very nature of the sounds themselves, of certain words, so if, to pull an example out of the air, "anthrax," or "love" for that matter appears in a line, it doesn't necessarily mean what you'll find in the dictionary if you look it up. Then again, it might. Contrary to *Rolling Stone,* "Ashtray Heart" on the new album has nothing to do with Beefheart's reaction to punk rockers beyond one repeated aside that might as well be a red herring. ("Let's open up another case of the punks" is the line reflecting his rather dim view of the New Wavers who are proud to admit to being influenced by him. "I don't ever listen to 'em, you see, which is not very nice of me but . . . then again, why should I look through my own vomit? I think they're overlooking the fact—they're putting it back into rock and roll: bomp, bomp, bomp, that's what I was tryin' to get away from, that mama heartbeat stuff. I guess they have to make a living, though.") He laughs about the misinterpretation, but since the song is pretty clearly about betrayal, I asked: "What was it about the person in the song that could make you care enough to be that hurt?"

He says: "Humanity. The fact that people don't hear it the way you really mean it. Probably for a similar reason that van Gogh gave that girl a piece of his flesh, because she was too stupid to comprehend what he was doing. I always thought that he gave her that as a physical thing to hold onto because she didn't accept the aesthetic value of what he was saying."

"We don't have to suffer, we're the best batch yet." Would you care to comment on what that lyric might mean?

Yeah, what I was doing there was having these cardboard ball sculptures, fake pearls, real cheap cardboard constructed circles, you know what I mean, floating through that music. Actually, I was afraid to sing on that track. I liked the music so much, it was perfect without me on it. And so I put these words on there, you know, they're just cheap cardboard constructions of balls of simulated pearls floating through, and it's an overwhelming technique that makes them look like pearls. "We don't have to suffer, we're the best batch yet" were these pearls talking to themselves.

As opposed to the other ones. What does it mean when you say, "White flesh waves to black"?

God, I don't know what that means. It means, it's just a, uh, it's merely just a painting, you see, that's poetic license.

I thought you were talking about racism.

Oh, no. I don't know what to do about racial or political things. It was just a poem to me. A poem for poem's sake.

I was also thinking of when you walk around looking at people who have turned themselves into commodities.

Yeah, we're the best batch yet! We're the newest best that has been put out. Well, that has to do with that, too. You know, I'm, uh, ahm, whaddaya call it, it isn't schizophrenic but it is, uh, what people in the West think of people in the East, you see, meaning that in some instances they think that people are crazy who think multifaceted, that there's many ways of interpreting something. I mean 'em all. I can't say I don't know what my lyrics mean, but I can say that, uh, yeah I know what they mean, but if you call it you stop the flow.

/// \\\

Van Morrison has said that he doesn't know what a lot of his own lyrics mean, and even if Beefheart does, or they mean something different for each of us, I think, as with Morrison, occasionally you feel that the voice of some Other just might be speaking through this singer at this particular time, as if he were an instrument picking up messages from . . . Doc at the Radar Station? (About the various voices he switches off between, often in the same song: "I'll tell you the truth, some of those guys really scare me, that come out at me when I do some things, like 'Sheriff of Hong Kong,' I never met him before. Or she, I dunno . . . it's like different, uh, uh . . . you see, I don't think I do music. I think I do spells.")

Wherever Don Van Vliet gets his rules and messages from, it's rarely the external, so-called rational, I think psychotic "civilized" society we've known and lived in. He chooses to live *out* of it, mentally and physically, and began trying to escape from it at a very early age: "I never went to school. I wet my pants and my mother came and got me as I was running and I told her that I couldn't go to school because I was sculpting at that time a hell of a lot. That was kindergarten, I think. I tried to jump into the La Brea Tar Pits when I was three, whatever that means. They caught me just in time. I was so intrigued by those bubbles going *bmp bmp.* I thought I would find a dinosaur down there. I told my mother when I was three years old—she showed it to me not too long ago, in this baby book in that horrible Palmer Penmanship method of writing that she used, you know that fantastic curlicues type stuff that had everything to do with everything other than what it said, on this old yellow piece of paper it's written out, that if she would stay on one side of the room and I would stay on the other, that we would be friends the rest of our life. I used to lock myself in a room and sculpt when I was like three, five, six."

What sorts of things did you sculpt?

Oh God, things that I would try to have moved kinetically, try to move these things around. These were my friends, these little animals that I would make, like dinosaurs and . . . I wasn't very much in reality, actually.

Do you feel bad about that?

No, I feel good. I was right. The way people treat animals, I don't like it. One of my horrible memories is the great Auk, the fact that it was extinct before I was born. What a beautiful bird.

What were your parents like?

Pretty banal. They moved me to Mojave, that's where they kept the Japanese-Americans during World War II. They moved me up there to keep me out of a scholarship to Europe for sculpture. They wanted to get me away from all the "queer" artists. Isn't that awful? Periscopes in the tub, right?

/// \\\

In this sense, he's still not very much in "reality." His problems with record companies over the years are legendary. Yet he has, somehow, kept on making those amazing albums; just when you've almost given up hope, somebody else comes along and offers him a contract, and he does another one, and it doesn't sell. Jon Landau told me in 1970, when he was my record reviews editor at *Rolling Stone:* "Grand Funk will be more important to the history of rock 'n' roll than Captain Beefheart. And you can quote me on that." But there *are other occasions,* like the time I met a young woman in a bar who was not a scenemaker or into avant-rock, and when I asked her what kind of music she liked she said: "This guy I heard named Captain Beefheart. There was just something kind of real sensual and musky about it. I dunno . . . it was different, but I loved it."

Beefheart himself thinks women tend to understand his music better than men, so, especially since he can be so elliptically, obscurantistly difficult to pin down in interview and describing his music in prose is kind of like trying to catch the prism of a dragonfly wing and hold it intact in the palm of your hand, I'll talk about his wife. Jan is a young woman of such radiance and wholehearted sincerity that it can be a little stunning at first meeting. Phrases like "earth mother" are too quaint, dreary, way off the mark. She is as active an artist as he and the complexities of her mind are fully up to his moodswings, which can give you jet lag. Which doesn't mean she's the archetypal Great Artist's Nursemaid either—she won't take his shit, and he can be a tyrannical baby at times. Like a lot of us.

Jan helps mightily at broaching some kind of rapprochement communications-wise between this man and the world at large. In other words, she translates. In both directions. You'd see the same thing at the UN. And if Don is not exactly intoning "Klaatu baraada niktu," he does at times seem almost like a visitor from another planet, or more precisely someone still stunned by his first sight of this one, as I suspect he always will be. Perhaps he just doesn't have those filtering mechanisms which enable most of us to cope with "reality" by blocking out at least eighty percent of it.

According to his set of filters, inanimate objects are alive, and plants and animals share with them the capacity to think as well as feel. Don sees perspicacity in a mesquite, an old broom handle even. If his lyrics are about anything absolutely, they are about ecology.

/// \\\

You're a painter. In "Run Paint Run Run" are you saying that the paint itself is a conscious entity with a will of its own?

Yeah! Definitely! Hey, you got it. Yes, it does have a will of its own.

Do you generally feel that about the things around you, inanimate objects?

Um hm. Yeah, I really do. I think they're all alive. Don't you?

I don't know.

Come on, you do too . . .

So how do you and the paint get along?

Pretty damn good, I'll tell ya. I'm just looking forward to getting enough money to be able to really paint big. I don't wanna paint any littler than five by five. But I'd like to paint twenty by twenty.

Do you and the paint ever have fights?

Yeah, definitely.

Do you feel the same way about the electric guitar, that when you plug it into the wall it's this battle of wills sort of?

I think so. It'll spit out atcha anything that's out there.

Was that what you were talking about in "Electricity"?

Yeah, that had a hell of a lot to do with it. . . . It always seems to come out the way it wants to, y'know.

/// \\\

I think that partially Don anthropomorphizes animals and objects as a defense against humans, who empirical observation has told him are by and large incomprehensible to themselves as well as him, that's when they're not also out to getcha. He's like an Androcles that would chat a spell with Leo but see fangs and claws on a delivery boy. Lacking aforesaid filters, he has devised an elaborate system of checkpoint charlies to keep most of humankind's snoots at bay. This can sometimes be frustrating. His favorite device in the past was to always say some bigtime gonzo Dada non sequitur ("All roads lead to Coca-Cola" was the first one I ever heard), then look you straight in the eye and insistently enquire: "Do you know what I mean?"

"Yeah, sure, Don, sure!" *everybody* (except Jan) would always huffn-puff. He is a very charismatic person, a guru, of sorts. He knows how to charm, and has a way of flattering you by asking you all kinds of questions suggesting real concern. He really means it, too, his basic philosophy has always been summed up in the open invitation to share his suddenly brighter sunshine in *Trout Mask Replica*'s "Frownland." But see, that's just it: it was always *his sunshine,* on another level all these things were and are distancing devices (though he's not nearly as egocentrically defensive as he used to be) and it can be extremely frustrating because no matter how intimate you get with somebody if *all they ever say* practically is stuff that sounds like it came out of their lingo-tango lyrics (another technique is to ask you to elaborate when you ask a question and then just agree with you) you go home with a tape recorder full of words that mean nothing in particular and the sad hunch that there was something a bit impersonal about this whole affair. I've been told that with Don the best countertactic is to try and pin him down: *"Just exactly what do you mean?"* But somehow I've never been able to draw that hard a line. The man is too magical. Literally. Once in Detroit I walked into a theatre through the back door while he was onstage performing. At the precise moment I stepped to the edge of the curtains on stage right, where I could see him haranguing the audience, he said, very clearly, "Lester!" His back was to me at the time. Later he asked me if I had noticed it. I was a little shaken.

The years of what career-oriented folks would file as "failure" have ripened and mellowed Don; like most of us, he's grown up some, albeit perhaps against his will. Once I listened to him rant drunk and bitter all night; now I ask him: "Do you think the music business will ever find you 'commercial,' and do you care?"

"I don't think they ever will," he laughs, "and I don't care. I'm just thankful that an audience is listening to me."

He just lets it turn with the earth, though he was particularly angry in the past when a band he literally taught to play cut some sides under his name without even telling him. There are also many of us who think Frank Zappa, with whom he grew up, wouldn't be hock in a spittoon, much less a "composer" (anybody says that certifies themselves a moron) if there had never been a Don Van Vliet on this earth. When Zappa established his Straight Records in 1968, he invited Don to join a carny sideshow which also included the GTO's, Alice Cooper, and Wild Man Fischer, producing, or so he was credited, *Trout Mask Replica.* That record was four sides, 28 songs cut in two days of the most unparalleled ruckus in the annals of recorded sound. In it, after relatively unfocused albums for Buddah (with whom he even scored a minor hit in '66, "Diddy Wah Diddy") and Blue Thumb, Beefheart and his unearthly looking cabal of spazmo henchmen seemed effortlessly to cook up the so-far still definitive statement on the possibilities for some common ground ("fusion," I believe they called some bathwater quickbuckaroos bearing scant relation a few years later) on which raunch rock, slide-slinging Delta blues, and post-Coltrane/Shepp/Ayler free jazz might consecrate a shakedown together.

Like almost all of Beefheart's recorded work, it was not even "ahead" of its time in 1969. Then and now, it stands outside time, trends, fads, hypes, the rise and fall of whole genres eclectic as walking Christmas trees, constituting a genre unto itself: truly, a musical Monolith if ever there was one. On it, Beefheart, behind a truly scarifying gallery of separate voices, becomes at various times a sagebrush prospector, Jews screaming in the ovens at Auschwitz, greased-back East L.A. pachuco, a breakable pig, an automobile, "Ant Man Bee" (title of one song), a little girl and her brinechawed seafarin' aged father (in the same song), a Pa Kettle–mischievous "Old Fart at Play," and several species of floral, piscatorial, and amphibious life. The band, under his tutelage, thereon reinvented from the ground up rhythm, melody, harmonics, perhaps what our common narrow parameters have defined as "music" itself.

Since then he has released seven albums of varying quality. The immediate followup, *Lick My Decals Off, Baby,* was brilliant though a little abrasive even for my ears at the time it was released. 1971's *The Spotlight Kid* was more commercial, though hardly compromised, and many people regard 1972's *Clear Spot,* a minor masterpiece of sorts, as a dance album in disguise. Two later records on Mercury, *Unconditionally Guaranteed* and *Blue Jeans and Moonbeams,* were baldfaced attempts at sellout. *Shiny Beast (Bat Chain Puller),* a charming but relatively minor work, was released by Warner Brothers in 1978. None of these albums has thus far sold more than 50 or 60 thousand, and that's over a long period of time; only *Trout Mask Replica* and *Shiny Beast,* in fact, remain in the catalogues.

Perhaps it is the "success" ("triumph?") of the New Wave that has emboldened Warner Brothers. In any case, *Doc at the Radar Station* is one of the most brilliant achievements by any artist in any year. And in

1980 it seems like a miracle. It certainly is not compromised, and I doubt that it will get any radio play in this country at least, but then I said the Clash didn't have a prayer. While some of his self-acknowledged acolytes have gone on to stardom, megabucks, pop-out lunchboxes, etc., the progenitor remains in his Mojave trailer, where he barely has room for an indoor easel. (So if any neo-Florentine patron is reading this, I will make a plea that Don would never make or ask anyone else to make for him: support a real artist.) I'm not sawing violins in half—Don certainly doesn't feel sorry for himself, and in late 1977 when he reappeared at the Bottom Line with a new band and *Shiny Beast* in the wings, he had the distinct air of a, well, I don't even feel "survivor" is the word. A patriarch, perhaps, a high priest, born again from Ancient Egypt smiling like the spuming headwaters of the Nile, long weathered body holding just that many mysteries, arcane secrets from half-apocryphal texts of hoodoo mojo Coptic canebreak healings of the kind Ishmael Reed likes to dream up.

Next to him, Dr. John looked like Gary Glitter: all soot, no zoot. He could go fifteen rounds brainwave-to-brainwave with Screamin' Jay Hawkins and judges who know nothin' anyway call it a draw. Might be the white Leadbelly. Too much in love with living to be Robert Johnson. In the late Sixties, some hotshit young hitpicker got famous by proclaiming that Don Van Vliet, if he wanted to, could be "the greatest white blues singer in the world." That would have been as dumb as settling for a moosehead over the fireplace when you've lassoed the Loch Ness Monster and taken it to dinner, highballs, and dancing. Like van Gogh doing pasteup for Bloomingdale's. Make no mistake, Captain Beefheart is an absolutely authentic chunk of taproot Americana on a Mark Twain level with Paul Bunyan stature.

But today an artist is expected to market him or herself as a commodity to be generally recognized. So in that sense it's no wonder Don retreated to the Mojave Outback. On the other hand, the old garret routine doesn't exactly work anymore either. And Don has pretty much been through his phase of living out the Artist-as-Genius/Idiot-

Savant cliché. On the phone the other day I mentioned Andy Warhol, and Don said, "He soups things up. But isn't it nice, being able to say that we're not like him?" At the time I thought this was a shopworn verbal popper combined with an absolutely childlike attitude: "Isn't it nice, being able to say that we're not like him?" Well, yes, it is, and Mr. Rogers will be here at 3:30. This plus the fact that artists know how much they can get away with, how much we in fact *expect* of them, can lead to truly sick situations, disastrous for all concerned: "Isn't it nice, being somebody's pet?" I feel like even the word "genius" should be put in quotation marks because the very concept has a way of getting out of hand, like an unruly child. Artists often end up conspiring with their adoring audiences to insure their own isolation. Once, a very long time ago, I saw Don go sweeping imperiously in and out of hotels until he found one that met his aesthetic specifications, entourage (including me) trailing embarrassedly behind while he wore a cape and doodled on a pad the whole time.

Still, there *is* something ingenuously natural about him. I don't think, for instance, that he necessarily "tries" to "create" these things, they just sort of . . . happen to (through?) him. In the course of this process, he has managed to practically reinvent both music and the English language. And if you think that's a thorny thicket of defenses to try and hack through so as to get to the actual *person* back there, you're right. He embarrasses you with his effusiveness, he feels misunderstood and craves desperately to talk with anyone who, he's satisfied, understands what he's trying to do. I don't know why he thinks I understand it. I only understand a little part of it. A lot of it is Sanskrit to me too. But you'll never miss the feeling however obtuse the structure, because this man is almost 100 percent feeling, can be feverish with it, leads with every open nerve end till sometimes you wonder if he has a mind at all, or just threw the one he had away one day because every pore in the body is a knowing little eye fiercely darting at experience.

Now, there is no reason on earth why such a creature should be articulate. Except that he is. But on his terms, most of the time. And this is what has always bothered me. What good is being an artist, creating all these beautiful things, if you can't just throw down your defenses *sometimes* and share things on the common level of other people? Without that, it's barren and ultimately pathetic. Ultimately, without some measure of that, it can never matter as art. 'Cause art's of the heart. And I'm talking about the heart that flies between two or more humans, not to the ghost of the great Auk, or a glob of paint, or any of his other little friends. All this week, one song off *Trout Mask Replica* kept playing in my head: "Orange Claw Hammer," an unaccompanied field holler-like poem about a man who's been away at sea for years and catches first sight of his daughter since she was in swaddling. He grasps her hand and offers to "Take you down to the foamin' brine 'n' water, and show you the wooden tits on the goddess with the pole out full-sail that tempted away your pegleg father. I was shanghaied by a highhat beaver-moustache man and his pirate friend. I woke up in vomit and beer in a banana bin, and a soft lass with brown skin bore me seven babies with snappin' black eyes and beautiful ebony skin, and here it is I'm with you my daughter. Thirty years away can make a seaman's eyes, a roundhouse man's eyes flow out with water, salt water."

Now if that isn't pure true American folklore then you can throw everything from Washington Irving to Carl Sandburg and beyond in the garbage. I'm saying Don Van Vliet, "Captain Beefheart," is on that level. But what I realized this morning, the reason why it was this song stuck out from 26 others: because it's not about the "Neon Meate Dream of a Octafish," but something that happened between people.

/// \\\

Why do you almost always talk elliptically?

Due to the fact that probably it's very difficult for me to explain myself except in music or paint.

But don't you think talking that way all the time is kind of impersonal, a distancing effect?

It probably comes out very personal in the music. That's where I'm truthful and honest. I don't know how it happens exactly, but my mind *becomes* the piano or guitar.

What about when you're alone with Jan?

We don't talk too much. Because we trust each other, and we don't have that much faith in the spoken word. I guess it's true that I do talk selfishly, as a conversationalist.

Well, don't you think you're missing something you might get from other people, by being that way?

Sure, but they usually won't accept me anyway. I'm comfortable talking to you. Not many people seem to have things in common with me. I guess what intrigues me the most is something like seeing somebody wash my windows—that's like a symphony. But if you and I are friends, and you trust me, we should be able to have a reciprocal conversation.

We're talking without talking. I mean that in a good sense. We're saying things that can't be put into the tongue. It's like good music.

/// \\\

In the end I'm not sure which of us is right. I am probably unfair in wanting everything so explicitly defined from *everybody,* demanding the rest of the human race (perhaps especially ironic in the case of artists and musicians) be as verbal or verbose as I am. I can't say that he's wrong in choosing to live out of society, because this society itself doesn't seem to have much of a future, and doesn't seem to care either. A goat and a corporation exec, or most rising young affluent career people around this town for that matter, come up about even conversationwise, and the goat smells better and is fun to pet so there you are. As for art that deals with human situations, almost none of the art being produced from *within* the society these days does that, so why pick on Beefheart because he'd rather commune with paints and bats in the fireplace? Certainly he illuminates more about the human heart, and the human groin for that matter, than all these dry dead literati and "minimalist" artists and juiceless composers. As for Don Van Vliet the man, each passing year seems to bring him farther out of defensive obscurantism, measurably more open and trusting, which is really wild in itself because the world around is careening in exactly the opposite direction.

Besides which on another level it's none of my business anyway, except insofar as he chose to make it so. If he is somewhat in retreat, it can be justified on all the levels above and several more I'm sure, besides which who isn't in retreat these days? His kind takes a lot more courage than most, and as an artist he is so far removed from any kind of burnout that he can't even be called, like I said earlier and like all the Neil Youngs and Lou Reeds who made it from the late Sixties to this point relatively intact, a survivor. More like a natural resource. The difference, finally, is that, to use an example by one of his favorite writers, he'll never give us his version of *Macbeth*. He would rather be the Grand Canyon.

The Village Voice, October 1, 1980

Deaf-Mute in a Telephone Booth: A Perfect Day with Lou Reed

You walk into the dining room of the Holiday Inn filled with expectation at finally getting to meet one of the musical and psychological frontiersmen of our time, Lou Reed, who with his group the Velvet Underground was singing about drag queens and heroin at least five years before such obsessions reached the mass level. Who began a comeback as a solo artist last summer in England, and under the wing of David Bowie produced *Transformer,* a classic of mondo bendo rock. Who then, having come out of the closet at last, returned to his New York home and ushered in 1973 by getting married to an actress cum cocktail waitress named Betty (stage name Krista) Kronstadt.

On top of all that, both *Transformer* and the single from it are enormous hits. Lou Reed is not only a legend: he's a star. In one of the interviews he did last summer, Lou said: "I can create a vibe without saying anything, just by being in the room."

He was right. You sit yourself down, and sure enough you become aware pretty fast that there's this vaguely unpleasant fat man sitting over there with a table full of people including his blonde bride. Pretty soon he comes over to join you and the tic becomes focused too sharply for comfort. It's not just that Lou Reed doesn't look like a rock 'n' roll star anymore. His face has a nursing home pallor, and the fat girdles his sides. He drinks double Johnny Walker Blacks all afternoon, his hands shake constantly and when he lifts his glass to drink he has to bend his head as though he couldn't possibly get it to his mouth otherwise. As he gets drunker, his left eyeball begins to slide out of sync.

In spite of all this, however, he manages to live up to his reputation for making interviewers uncomfortable. He fixes you with that rusty bugeye, he creaks and croaks and lies in your face and you're helpless. He lies about his music and his album covers ("That was me in drag on the back of *Transformer.*"). Most of all, he lies about himself. But he qualifies it by saying, "I don't especially tell the truth most of the time anyway."

He's pretty cool about most of it, though, so you can't really get too mad at him about that. Like Nick Kent, who is there for the *New Musical Express,* is right in the middle of asking him a question, when Lou interrupts: "Aren't you hot with that scarf on?"

"No," wheezes Nick nonplussedly, "I've got a cold."

"Try Vicks VapoRub," Mad Ave libs Lou. "I came down with a very bad cold in Boston, and it works. You've gotta lie there for two or three days with that gop on your chest and a towel or something, and every once in a while somebody has to have the nerve to reach into the bowl of that shit and rub it in. Like I remember," he free-associates, "when everybody was taking acid and we discovered Dippity-Do, and everybody said, 'It's just like a cunt, it's fantastic!' And we all ran into the bathroom and started fingering the Dippity-Do jar."

Everything is yoks to this bibulous bozo; he really makes a point of havin' some fun! Although it does disturb his friends and fans to see him in such failing health. But he can find a joke even there. At one point I asked him when he intended to die.

"I would like to live to a ripe old age and raise watermelons in Wyoming." Then he takes another glug and machos: "I'm outdrinking you two to one, you know."

"Are you proud of yourself?"

"Yeah. No, not actually; it's just that a single shot of Scotch is so small that you've gotta nurse it like it's a child or something. I drink constantly."

"How does it treat your nervous system?" I probed.

"It destroys it," he beamed.

"Then how do you intend to raise your watermelons?"

"Well, my time will come. By now I'm getting tired of liquor because there's just nothing strong enough. Now if we were drinking 150 proof sake, or something like that, *then* I could get *drunk*. . . ."

He is equally frank on the subject of drugs: "I take drugs just because in the 20th Century in a technological age living in the city there are certain drugs you have to take just to keep yourself normal like a caveman. Just to bring yourself up or down, but to attain equilibrium you need to take certain drugs. They don't getcha high even, they just getcha normal."

Normal Lou Reed reached for a Marlboro. As he fumbled to tear a match out of the book and strike it, his hands trembled so fiercely that you wondered if he was going to be able to get that butt lit.

This interview was turning out so fabulous I knew it was now time to get our hooks right down to the nitty gritty, and talk about sex. What *about* the relationship of what you're doing artistically to the gay scene in general and specific?

Wax eloquent, for once and finally, he did. Listen, kids, you may think you've got your identity crises and sexual lateral squeeze plays touchdown cold just because you came out in rouge 'n' glitter for Dave Bowie's latest show, but listen to your Papa Lou. He's gotta nother think for you punk knowitalls:

"The makeup thing is just a style thing now, like platform shoes. If people have homosexuality in them, it won't necessarily involve makeup in the first place. You can't fake being gay, because being gay means you're going to have to suck cock, or get fucked. I think there's a very basic thing in a guy if he's straight where he's just going to say no: 'I'll act gay, I'll do this and I'll do that, but I can't do *that*.' Just like a gay person if they wanted to act straight and everything, but if you said, 'Okay, go ahead, go to bed with a girl,' they're going to have to get an erection first, and they can't do that.

"The notion that everybody's bisexual is a very popular line right now, but I think its validity is limited. I could say something like if in any way my album helps people decide who or what they are, then I will feel I have accomplished something in my life. But I don't feel that way at all. I don't think an album's gonna do anything. You can't listen to a record and say, 'Oh that really turned me onto gay life, I'm gonna be gay.' A lot of people will have one or two experiences, and that'll be it. Things may not change one iota. It's beyond the control of a straight person to turn gay at the age he'll probably be listening to any of this stuff or reading about it; he'll already be determined psychologically. It's like Franco said: 'Give me a child until he's seven and he's mine.' By the time a kid reaches puberty they've been determined. Guys walking around in makeup is just fun. Why shouldn't men be able to put on makeup and have fun like women have?"

Lou Reed just may have a better perspective on this supposed upheaval in sexual roles than any of these Gore Vidals and Jill Johnstons. Dudes comin' outa the closet in droves and finding out they're homosexual! Ha! Only trouble is that Lou's thinking also makes him a product of the rigidly dualistic era when he grew up, a hell of a Fifties cat for somebody who helped usher in the Seventies. He thinks you're either some blissfully "normal" heterosuburbanite weekender on your own, or otherwise you gotta be some mungstreaked depravo wretch skulking through the gutter on all fours. Listening to him talk, you can't help wondering how much of Lou Reed's songs are about people he makes up, as he claims, and how much of them are about himself. In which case—if, say, "Perfect Day" is autobiographical—he must be the most guilt-ridden person on the face of the earth. Which would make it hard for anybody to live up to their own legend.

If Lou Reed seems like rock's ultimate closet queen by virtue of the fact that he came out of the closet *and then went back in,* it must be also observed that lots of people, especially lots of gay people, think Lou Reed's just a heterosexual onlooker, exploiting gay culture for his own ends. And who knows but that they may be right. When I asked him about his plans for his next album, he said: "I may come out with a hardhat album. Come out with an antigay song, saying 'Get back in your closets, you fuckin' queers!' That'll really do it!"

But let's just suppose that Lou Reed is gay. If he is, can you imagine what kind of homosexual would say something like that? Maybe that's what makes him such a master of pop song—he's got such a great sense of *shame.* Either that or the ultimate proof of his absolute normality is the total offensive triteness of his bannered Abnormality. Like there's no trip cornier'n s&m, every move is plotted in advance from a rigid rulebook centuries old, so every libertine ends up yawning his balls off. Just like Lou said earlier that day: "There's really no interesting information to hold back. Everybody insists that there's a story here, and there really isn't. It's like a clamshell that's been eaten."

/// \\\

The concert was okay. Reports on this tour have varied dramatically—depending on expectations and how Lou happens to be feeling, I guess—and his band, a bunch of high school kids assembled by Steve Katz, is more than adequate.

But there's probably more going on here than meets the eye. Katz must have had plenty of musicians to choose from—he could conceivably have assembled a high-charged ensemble a la Elephant's Memory, he could certainly have gotten a crew of faceless high-tech sessionmen if they didn't want anybody to detract from Lou. But what he got was a bunch of competent high school kids off anybody's block, *who also happen to be some of the ugliest cretins ever assembled on one stage!* These guys are the absolute apotheosis of the Flushing NY or Hoboken NJ schlub. They're so *nada* that they become *not* faceless, you can't ignore 'em because they contrast so sharply with Lou Reed's leather trip.

For somebody who has based so much of his career on sex, Lou Reed has certainly surrounded himself with an asexual band. It would be easy to conclude that this is simply because he didn't want anybody else stealing the show (in which case it backfired—his bassist is the ugliest person I have ever seen) or that he's so dunced out he didn't make such considerations (unlikely). So you end up with the possibility that Lou may have an *intentionally* asexual band as a reaction to glam-rock and his own image. Which, if you follow that logic to the terminal, reeks of self-destructive guilt. Just imagine if Lou Reed did to his lead guitarist what Bowie does to Mick Ronson—pretending to blow him—he'd look like the archetypal homosexual criminal. It would be the most repulsive (in a sense never dreamed of by people like Alice Cooper) spectacle in the history of rock.

The audiences, however, usually love the show, and it's gratifying to see them flood down to the stage at last, giving Lou Reed the adulation he's deserved for so long. It's only because when you start to think about the basic lameness of his band, the dirgelike tempo at which he sings most of the songs, the generally funereal atmosphere, and the speculations that all this leads you into, that you begin to get bugged. Because Lou Reed's finally got a chance at real sustained stardom, and he is *blowing* it. He's still riding on the legend now, but people are going to get tired damn fast of a legend who slunks out with a bunch of blobs behind him, sings his songs as if he's falling asleep, forgets the words half the time, stands as still as if he's embalmed except for remembering every five minutes or so to wiggle his ass or wave his hand whether it's really the time to do it or not. His whole career at this point is like welching out on a bet.

My personal payoff with Lou came when we got back to the hotel after the gig. About a dozen people sat around a shadowy suite while the Original Phantom Purveyor of the New Rock got drunk on his ass and rambled on to the point of babble. I got totally blasted myself, my disappointment came through, and I started baiting him:

"Hey Lou, doncha think Judy Garland was a piece of shit and better off dead?"

"No! She was a great lady! A wonderfully wise and witty lady . . ."

"Hey Lou, then doncha think David Bowie's a no-talent asshole?"

"No! He's a genius! He's brilliant!"

(It makes sense that Lou would say that, since he allegedly made an ass of himself by falling in love with Bowie when he went to England last summer.)

"Ahh, c'mon, what about all that outer 'Space Oddity' shit? That's just Paul Kantner garbage!"

"It is *not!* It's a brilliant masterpiece! Oh, you are so full of *shit!*"

"It was dogshit. Why don't you get off all this crap and just try being *banal* for a change? Why doncha write a song like 'Sugar, Sugar'? *That'd* be something worthwhile!"

"I don't know how. I would if I could . . . I wish I'd written it. . . ." Jeez, the poor bastard was getting so pathetic even his overweening maudlin streak was beginning to get to me! Like all the last year, every time his name comes up all you hear is "Poor Lou!" Poor Lou, poor Lou, poor poor poor Lou Reed! You wouldn't wanna be in his shoes! The tortured artist! The poor hamstrung sensibility! But I was too drunk for brakes, so I got even more personal and abusive: "Hey Lou, why doncha start shooting speed again? Then you could come up with something good!"

"I still do shoot it. . . . My doctor gives it to me. . . . Well, no actually they're just shots of meth mixed with vitamins . . . well, no actually they're just vitamin C . . . injections."

It went on like that for a while; finally, the whole thing sort of flaked into silence, and a girl from his organization had to come and carry him off to his room. But I'll always carry that last picture of him, plopped in his chair like a sack of spuds, sucking on his eternal Scotch with his head hanging off into shadow, looking like a deaf-mute in a telephone booth. (He's still pretty cool though; I stole that last phrase from him.)

If all this makes you feel sorry for him, then you can compliment yourself on being a real Lou Reed fan. Because that's exactly what he wants.

/// \\\

Then again, maybe time is still on Lou Reed's side. A few days later I was sitting in my room when the door flew back and in barged Josh, nine-year-old son of one of the people I live with. He's one of these typical little prepube smartasses with long hair and a big mouth, and he immediately demanded: "Where'd dja get alla records?"

"Cute kid," thinks I, "maybe I'll give him a copy of *The Electric Company* soundtrack."

"Hey!" he poots. "Yagotenny *Vaaaan* Morrison or *Leeon* Russell?"

Awright you little popsicle pecker, I'm getting tired of all this blatant trashing of respect for elders. So I drag out a copy of *Transformer:* "Wanna hear *this?*"

"Naaah," he snorts. "I awready got a copy."

"Oh yeah. What's your favorite song on it?"

" 'New York Telephone Conversation.' But my brother likes the one that goes 'shaved 'er legs an' then he was a she.' " His brother is eight.

"Well, then, whattaya think of it?" I was a broken man.

"I think it's great! We play it all the time."

So there you are. A bit later I tried to put on an America album and the brat called me a "health food eater." He's obviously a prodigal snot, but you can't ignore the evidence: Lou Reed may be leagues from the peak of his creative powers, he may be a deteriorating silhouette of a star . . .

But give him a child from the time he's nine.

Creem, July 1973

Monolith or Monotone? Lou Reed's *Metal Machine Music*

I have a few theories concerning this new Lou Reed album:

1. In general, Lou is not excessively fond of other members of the human race, so this album is, or wants to be, some kind of ultimate antisocial act. When the MC5 debuted, John Sinclair said that they and their music would "make you feel it, or leave the room." Lou wants to make music that'll make you feel it *and* leave the room. That way he can be happy: alone, with his machines. Has he succeeded? No. Everybody stayed put when it came on. They chuckled at it, and went back to their chores. (If Lou really wants to get into irritation scientifically, he should study the work of somebody like Sparks.) He has succeeded in taking a hissing Muzak whiz. Perhaps I should also mention that I like this record. Why? Because I am an Insect Death buff.

2. Just because it's only an A-head playing around with electronics and tape recorders doesn't mean it isn't valid. There is a rising line of aggression running through "European Son," "I Heard Her Call My Name," "Sister Ray" and the Stooges' *Fun House* album which finally achieves psychosis in *Metal Machine Music,* and Lou plays amplifier as well as he plays guitar.

3. You know when you get so tense and anxiety-ridden that all the nerves at the back of your neck snarl up into one burning ball? Well, if that gland could make music, it would sound like this album.

4. This is what it sounds like in Lou's circulatory system.

5. Most of the people who buy *Metal Machine Music* are going to be pretty mad at Lou, but it's an even bigger joke on RCA, and the ultimate fall guy is the artist himself. Because what we are witnessing here is commercial suicide. *Sally Can't Dance* was the first, and probably only, Lou Reed album to go Top Ten. The collection of outtakes from *Rock 'n' Roll Animal* he marketed last spring was proficient but too ballady for a live album and generally inferior to its predecessor. Even hardcore fans like your reporter, who is something more in the realm of a fanatic, found themselves playing it a couple of times and filing it. *Animal* was a real sleeper on the charts, helping to break Lou on radio in many areas previously hostile to "glam rock" like the South, but *Live,* after resting at a hardly awe-inspiring 62 for a couple of weeks, died fast. Now he's put out this migraine, which will get zero radio play and bomb so bad it'll make *Berlin* look like an Elton John album. All of which will insure that the buyers will stay away in droves when he releases his next set of "songs," *Coney Island Baby,* in September. It's refreshing that the guy's not content to merely grind out one album a year, but do you suppose that all this frenzied pseudo-activity is Lou's terrified reaction to having, just once in his life, climbed far enough from his "street punk" roots (pretensions) to make Top Ten? In any case, a death wish is being fulfilled before our eyes, *corporately.*

6. Anybody who doesn't jack off at least three times a day is a queer.

Creem, September 1975

Your Shadow Is Scared of You: An Attempt Not to Be Frightened by Nico*

In the autumn of 1968, an album came out which changed my life. It is still changing my life, and apparently has had similar impact on others, because the editor of this magazine not only asked me to write this article, but has been calling, cajoling, nearly threatening in her attempts to have me get it in. This from the editor of a national, commercial magazine, over a ten-year-old, out-of-print record which most people haven't heard and wouldn't want to if they knew what was in it.

So I guess my editor and I are smitten. But the quality of the smiting is more than just peculiar; this article was assigned and written for fear as much as love, or the love of fear. In *Stargazer,* his poetically definitive book on the Andy Warhol universe of the 1960s, Stephen Koch tried to come to some understanding for himself as much as his readers of Warhol by resorting to a quote from Baudelaire: "Half in love with easeful death." Then, just to drive home the point he was making about the intimacy between narcissism and Warholvian deathly otherness, he wrote: "*Half* in love. Exactly."

*"This article was originally written in 1978, for Diana Clapton's brief-lived but much-missed *New Wave Rock* magazine. It was laid out and ready to go, then aced out at the last second by coverage of the Nancy Spungen murder, after which the magazine folded. Although it may seem a bit dated in places, I think the piece holds up, especially inasmuch as A) the album is timeless, and B) it is now available again, as an import item. I would like to thank Diana again for having the editorial soul to make such an assignment in the first place."—Lester's preface was added when he gave this piece to *What Goes On.*

Anyone more than half in love with death would have to be a monster, of course. Perhaps a Gilles de Rais, Idi Amin, Adolf Hitler. But there are some who would inflict the rarefied atrocities of Gilles de Rais, Idi Amin's bludgeoning nullification of all humanity, and the howling yet systemized totalitarian lockstep of Hitler—all upon themselves and no other. Sometimes, for performing such stupefying acts against their own persons, such basically pathetic people become culture heroes. In such a climate, the relationship between the artist (for that is what the people who I'm talking about are, though there are plenty of private citizens torturing and snuffing themselves in the same way) and his or her audience must be exceedingly odd.

Lou Reed went on the radio here in New York the other night to play some of his favorite records by other people and take calls from listeners. One kid called in and said, "That girl who died in 'Street Hassle,' was that someone you knew?" "Why?" said Lou. "Well," said the kid, "I mean did that really happen, did somebody really die in real life?"

"Would that make it a better song?" asked Lou Reed.

Now it's very easy to just write that kid off as an asshole, until you start to ask yourself just why you would want to listen, all the time, to a song about someone dying from an overdose of heroin. You might then begin to wonder if you are not the junkie, a junkie for the glimpses of the pit, half in love with easeful death at best—at worst, vicariously getting off on other people's pain and calling it cute decadence.

The only trouble is that there is so much beauty mixed in with the ugliness. So what we have is a simultaneously transcendent and twisted work of art by a creative force whose vision has been itself twisted by circumstance, but because of that, and because the intertwining of beauty and horror runs so deep, the creator perversely keeps pursuing an admixture of his basest and purest elements. And if you are the type of person who likes being around such art as a regular thing then you are going to end up a little twisted too, if you weren't in the first place.

In which case you will have a minor problem which you will never be able to share with most people. A minor problem and a minor jewel. A jewel with facets of disease running all through it. You can turn it any way you like, look at it in any light or from any angle, but you can only escape being . . . sullied? by the grace of what amounts to the soft hand of death by turning your back entirely.

And that too would be unfair, in a sense, to both yourself and the artist. Because in raising the base or crippled or tormented or mutilated to such a level, the artist has it seems done something at once noble and rather evil. In loving it you too become culpable, and then will try to seduce others, secretly hoping the whole world might one day come to wear your stigmata. Hence this article about *The Marble Index*, an LP by a German woman who calls herself Nico, with arrangements by John Cale. Like Lou Reed, both of them used to be in the Velvet Underground, though neither has ever attained anything close to his media attention and record-rack popularity. There are reasons for that, of course: whether he's creating good art like *Street Hassle,* or crap like *Rock and Roll Heart,* Lou Reed seems to be an idea of the negative which most people can accept, or even find funny.

I think *The Marble Index* is the greatest piece of "avant-garde classical" "serious" music of the last half of the 20th Century so far. The other night I played it for my new girlfriend, and she pronounced it "depressing." That doesn't particularly alienate me from her, because it's not like the only alternative for her was Peter Frampton, but more especially because her reaction was perfectly reasonable and even, in being negative, perhaps ultimately correct. Great art has always confirmed human values, but what are we to do when the most that our greatest works of art can affirm is that the creator fears he or she may be slowly, but surely, losing humanity entirely, along with the rest of mankind?

I don't know if I would classify it as oppressive or depressing, but I do know that *The Marble Index* scares the shit out of me. But what scares me even more is what most people seem to want instead. Every time I see some kid with concentration-camp-cropped hair maybe tinted green with maybe a garbage bag over his or her genuinely pathetic belittled frame, I want to puke and maybe even cry a little at the same time. Because so much of this punk rubbish is based on the stupidest apprehension and declamation of how proud one can be that "We don't *feel!*" when they don't even realize the horror and irony Johnny Rotten spat into that particular phrase. When *The Marble Index* was released a lot of record buyers wanted some vainglorious apocalypse and now most of them want either to be mommied Frampton-style and told that everything is okay snookums, or they want to be bludgeoned into a kind of terminal insensibility that they mistake for freedom from the contradictions in their lives and surroundings which are eating them alive, or they want to be told that it's all just a bunch of shit and the best is as good as the worst. But it just ain't so, and they know it in their guts, so they resort in desperation to something like Elvis Costello, who, when he last played a big hall in New York and mouthed that cheap line about how he doesn't wanna be your lover/"I just wanna be your victim," the audience actually fucking *cheered,* as if there never was anything alive between the hand-in-glove poles of happyhappy and what is finally merely banally disgusting mean-spiritedness.

Maybe this would make more sense to you if I told you that I want to run so far from presuming to define or even describe this record because I love it so passionately that I'm terrified of what that might say about me. There are no cheap thrills on *The Marble Index,* no commercials for sadomasochism, bisexuality, or hard drugs dashed off for a ravenous but vicarious audience—rather, it stares for a relatively short time that might just seem eternity to you into the heart of darkness, eyes wide-open, unflinching, and gives its own heart to what it finds there, and then tells you how that feels, letting you draw your own value judgments.

I played *The Marble Index* for a woman I loved about a year ago. She had never heard about Nico, never heard of John Cale, never really heard the Velvet Underground except in the context of this whole humorous but basically jive media game I set up with Lou Reed for a while. She listened to the whole thing in a state of mesmerism bordering on shock, then said of Cale, "He built a cathedral for a woman in hell, didn't he?" I called her up again today when I was fucked up about this article and she said, having still only heard it that one time, that she thought Nico was lost in her own blackness. I said, "But there's a pearl in there." I could hear her shudder over the phone, and suddenly she started talking very fast, and this is what she said as I madly pecked at my typewriter struggling to keep up: "Her whole body can glisten, she's just like a seed, the original seed of intercourse, her whole body can shine like the sun hits the water with sprays of light, and yet she's chosen to *de*-create from the surface to de-create again and again until the only message is 'I'm the life force itself, I'm the will to live,' a human embryo without hope of maturity, just sending signals. SHE'S IN THE WOMB, and what you call the pearl is just the pearl inside Mama's belly, the pulsebeat. She's accomplished de-creation: 'Let me be behind everything human, oh god, the fact to catch a star in your eye or touch another human being, to feel another human being, to touch another universe is nothing, is just a frozen borderline'—that there is no nexus, just retreat, until the frozen borderline, until all you feel is the white light of survival and the abyss is the ocean around her. It's one teeny star, one microstar in the macrocosm of her body, and it's all she's chosen to have, she's obliterated them all, stamped them out. She is a black hole in space with one point left. And then this is what she says: 'It's empty, it's black, it's alone, it's a whirlpool, an eddy, it's nothing,' but it's not nothing, it's her that's nothing. And that's why she could mutilate an insect, because that little wasp or grasshopper had more life than she ever could at all. She wants to mutilate it too because it's another act of negation, because it snuffs more light out of her star. She's like Beckett's play *Breath,* she's trying to find the last breath so she can negate breath, love, anything. A soft look would kill her."

She's quite a rock critic, that old girlfriend of mine—sometimes she scares me even more than Nico. But then, I'm scared of everybody—I'm scared of *you.* My girlfriend's eloquence was one reason I loved her almost from first sight, but not why I had to get halfway to the other side of the geographical world to be able to write a song that said how much I loved her. It was because of something obviously awry in me, perhaps healing, at least now confronting itself, which is one way to perhaps not rot. There's a ghost born every second, and if you let the ghosts take your guts by sheer force of numbers you haven't got a chance though probably no one has a right to judge you either. (Besides which, the ghosts are probably as scared of you as you are of them.) Nico is so possessed by ghosts she seems like one, but there is rather the clear confrontation of the knowledge that she had to get that awfully far away from human socialization to be able to write so nakedly of her love for damn near anyone, and simultaneously and so crucially the impossibility of that love ever bearing fruit, not because we were born sterile but directly the opposite, that we come and grow ever fiercer into such pain that we could sooner eat the shards of a smashed cathedral than risk one more possibility of the physical, psychic, and emotional annihilations that love between two humans can cause, not even just cause but generate totally as a logical act of nature in its ripest bloom. Strange fruit, as it were. But only strange to those who would deny the true nature of their own flesh and spirit out of fear, which reminds me somehow that if you seek this album out you should know that this is a Catholic girl singing these songs, and perhaps her ultimate message to me was that the most paralyzing fear is not sin, not even the flight from the feared object/event/confrontation/*who cares what*—that the only sin is denial, you who would not only turn your eyes away from what you fear as I sometimes must turn my ears away from this album, but would then add injury to what may or may not be insult by asserting that it does not exist.

But is she only asking us to let the full perception of the fear flood our hearts, or leading us on to embrace the death she seeks? I don't know. What I do know is that when I first set out to write this article I got very high—I was so stupid I thought I'd just let the drugs ease my way into Nico's domain of ghosts, then trot back and write down what I'd found there. But when I went and picked up the album, her face on the cover, in a picture I've seen a thousand times, seemed to be staring directly at, *into* me with a malevolence so calm it was inhuman. It was like holding a snake in your hands and having it look you right in the eye. I put the album down and walked away, but when I looked back I saw those two eyes, following me around the room. Let me add that drugs have not ordinarily affected me in this way, at least since the Sixties. I finally got up the nerve to put the album on after that experience, but found it almost unbearable to listen to. Not that it wasn't beautiful, rapturous in fact, but that its beauty was so deathly and its rapture out of such agony. It's putting lead weights in my heart because I don't want to listen to it right now (and of course the lead weights are not *The Marble Index* but its reflection into me of my unknown fears and pangs), but I have to gather some notes and lyrics to finish this article now, so while I do that you all be sure to run right out and buy it, okay kids? Except you can't, because it's not even available anymore. I can just imagine the demonstration demanding its reissue: everyone in black robes and hoods, carrying torches with cold fire and a casket containing the wax effigy of a giant insect. But enough evasion; I'm going to go subject myself to this damn thing once more. And I certainly hope you bastards appreciate the passion behind this pointless self-torture.

/// \\\

You get two songs. In each case I'll quote from the lyrics, with a minimum of interpretation, and then tell what Cale's music sounds like. Not that they are two such separate entities, however: this was a marriage made in purgatory.

"Frozen Warnings"

Into numberless reflections
Rises a smile from your eyes
Into mine
Frozen warnings close to mine
Close to the frozen borderline

Through a pale morning's arctic sunlight glinting dimly off the snow, a bank of violas emits one endless shrill note which eventually becomes electronically distorted by points of ice panning back and forth through the space between your ears, descending and then impossibly ascending in volume and ineluctable intensity until they're almost unbearable though infinitely graceful in their beauty; at length they wind off into the skies trailing away like wisps of fading beams.

"Evening of Light"

Midnight winds are
landing at the end of time
The story is telling air to lie
Mandolins are ringing
to his fires singing
Conscience sink into a
slumber till the end of time
. . . the doorbells hum
unto the undead end of time
In the morning of my winter
When my eyes are still asleep
A dragonfly lay in the cold
dark snows I'd sent to kiss your
heart for me.

(Nico's concept of love: While she lies interred in the endless wastes of the arctic night, she has sent an *insect* to the object of her affections, to kiss his heart yet. But even the insect must die before it can reach him, the soft rustling of its gentle wings stilled under drifts that eventually preserve its frozen corpse for eternity under a snowbank that becomes an ice mountain, the insect and Nico having become one in endless sleep, for they were the real lovers in the first place after all.)

The children are jumping
in the evening of light
The tears and sins are heavy
in the evening of light
Midnight winds are landing
at the end of time

A trickle of harpsichords out of the sky which drop gently at first and gradually increase in volume and presence in the mix until they seem to almost lacerate, punctuated occasionally by the shiftings and groanings of bowed basses like famished carnivores in some deep bog from which they ascend with the by-now violent intensity of the harpsichords, now accompanied by some electronic gnashing noise which sounds like someone's nerves are being roasted on a spit. All of this gets more and more intense until the violas return to arch up in a series of twisted pterodactyl shrieks, the harpsichords pounding down like murderous hailstones, the basses sounding militant air-raid, two-note alarums before crashing to their own death, the whole sucked away by a series of hissing, clicking, buzzing electronic processors, simply more dead information being disposed of.

What Goes On, January 1983

Jim Morrison: Bozo Dionysus a Decade Later

We seem to be in the midst of a full-scale Doors Revival. It had been picking up steam for a while, but when Jerry Hopkins' and Daniel Sugerman's biography of Jim Morrison, *No One Here Gets Out Alive,* became a Number One best-seller last year, all the Doors' LP product began to move in a big way again. Now there is the inevitable talk of a movie of Morrison's life, with (shudder) perhaps equally inevitable hints that John Travolta might have the starring role. The first question that would occur to anyone might be that asked by the first person I told I was doing the article: "Yeah, just why *is* there this big Doors fanaticism all over again, anyway?" The answer to that is not so hard to find, though in the end it may be questionable just how much it really has to do with the Doors. I'm reminded of the younger brother of an old girlfriend—he recently graduated from high school, and still lives with their parents in Detroit, and when she told me he was playing in a rock band and I asked her who his favorite artists were, she said: "His three favorite groups are the Yardbirds, Cream, and the Doors."

Think about that for a minute. That kid is now entering college. The Doors broke up ten years ago this July—well, okay, Morrison died then, and if you want to call the trio that went on after his death the Doors you can, but nobody else did—and Cream and the Yardbirds have been dead since '68–'69. Sure all three of them were great groups, but were they all that epochal that somebody who was in elementary school when they scored their greatest triumphs should look back to them like this, to be holding on to them after that many years? Yeah, the Beatles were one thing, but *Cream?*

Perhaps a more apposite question, though, might be can you imagine being a teenager in the 1980s and having absolutely no culture you could call your own? Because that's what it finally comes down to, that and the further point which might as well be admitted, that you can deny it all you want but almost none of the groups that have been offered to the public in the past few years begin to compare with the best from the Sixties. And this is not just Sixties nostalgia—it's a simple matter of listening to them side by side and noting the relative lack of passion, expansiveness, and commitment in even the best of today's groups. There is a halfheartedness, a tentativeness, and perhaps worst of all a tendency to hide behind irony that is after all perfectly reflective of the time, but doesn't do much to endear these pretenders to the throne. Sure, given the economic climate alone as well as all the other factors it was a hell of a lot easier to go all-out berserk, yet hold on to whatever principles you had in the Sixties—today's bands are so eager to get bought up and groomed and sold by the pound it often seems as if even the most popular and colorful barely even exist, let alone stand for anything.

So what did the Doors stand for? Well, if I remember correctly, back in 1968 when I was living in a hippie crash pad in San Diego, California, all my roommates used to have earnest bull sessions far into the night about the "Death Trip" the Doors were supposedly on. Recall this one guy used to sit there all day and night toking on his doob and intoning things like *"Genius* . . . is *very close* to . . . madness . . ." instead of doing his homework, and he had a high appreciation of the Doors' early work. Me, I always kind of wanted Morrison to be better than he actually was, like I wished all his songs could have had the understated power of, say "People Are Strange" (*Faces look ugly when you're alone/ Women seem wicked when you're unwanted* . . .) and, like many, it was only after being disappointed that I could learn to take the true poetry and terror whenever it could be found and develop an ever-increasing appreciation for most of the rest of Morrison's work as prime Bozo action.

As for the Poet himself, Hopkins' and Sugerman's book is primarily interesting for what it apparently inadvertently reveals. In the foreword, on the very first page of the book, Sugerman lets go two sentences which have stopped more than one person of my acquaintance from reading any further: "I just wanted to say I think Jim Morrison was a modern-day god. Oh hell, at least a lord."

It is never revealed whether Hopkins shares this assessment, but the authors then go on for almost four hundred pages, amassing mountains of evidence almost all of which can for most readers point to only one conclusion: that Jim Morrison was apparently a nigh compleat asshole from the instant he popped out of the womb until he died in the bathtub in Paris (*if* he did indeed die there, they rather gamely leave us with). The first scene in the book takes place in 1955, when Jim was twelve years old, and finds him tobogganing with his younger brother and sister in the snowcapped mountains outside Albuquerque, New Mexico. According to Hopkins and Sugerman, Jim packed his two moppet siblings afront him in the toboggan so they couldn't move, got up a frightening head of downhill steam and aimed the three of them straight for the broad side of a log cabin:

> *The toboggan was less than twenty yards from the side of the cabin on a certain, horrifying collision course. Anne stared dead ahead, the features of her face numbed by terror. Andy was whimpering.*
>
> *The toboggan swept under a hitching rail and five feet from the cabin was stopped by the children's father. As the children tumbled out of the sled, Anne babbled hysterically about how Jim had pushed them forward and wouldn't let them escape. Andy continued to cry. Steve and Clara Morrison tried to reassure the younger children.*

Jim stood nearby looking pleased. "We were just havin' a good time," he said.

Surely an auspicious episode with which to begin recounting the life of a god. But it is only the beginning. Later we will see Jim's little brother breathing heavily at night due to chronic tonsillitis and the future Lizard King sealing his mouth with cellophane tape and laughing at his near-suffocation. Or ridiculing a paraplegic. Or, at the age of seventeen, rubbing dogshit in his little brother's face.

What the book makes clear is that this sort of thing was no different in kind from later Doors-era antics like covering an entire recording studio (when they first went in to cut "The End") in chemical fire extinguisher foam, or dragging a cab full of people up to Elektra Records president Jac Holzman's apartment in the middle of the night, where Jim ripped out massive amounts of carpet and vomited all over the lobby. Yet this was the sort of thing that not only the authors but his friends and fans from the Sixties seemed to admire, even encourage. On one level it's just another case of a culture hero who you may not by now be so surprised to learn you would never have wanted to be around. On another, though, it's just more Sixties berserkitude of the kind that piddles down to pathetic sights like Iggy Pop walking through a song called "Dog Food" on the *Tomorrow* show in 1981 and then telling Tom Snyder that he represents the "Dionysian" as opposed to "Apollonian" type o' performer. But there was a time that was true for both Iggy and Jim, though one must wonder just what the creepily conservative teenagers of these supremely Apollonian times might see in this kind of behavior which if anybody they knew was imitating would probably cause them to immediately call the cops. These kids would feel threatened by any performer who came out today and started acting like Morrison did, so is it only the remove of a decade that allows them to feel safe enjoying his antics? Or is it that, just like they could conceivably march happily off to get shot to pieces in El Salvador or Afghanistan to the tune of "The Unknown Soldier" without perceiving any irony, so they can take the life and death of Jim Morrison as just one more TV show with a great soundtrack? And could it be that they are right? If Jim Morrison cared so little about his life, was so willing to make it amount to one huge alcoholic exhibitionistic joke, why should they or we or anybody finally care, except insofar as the seamy details provide trashy entertainent? Or do they, like Danny Sugerman, take exactly these rantings and pukings as evidence he was a "god" or at least a "lord?"

Similarly, in the legendary Miami "cock-flashing" incident, the book reveals that likely all that really happened was he made a fool out of himself, moving entertainingly if not smoothly from "Ain't nobody gonna love my ass?" to "You're all a bunch of fuckin' idiots," surely an appropriate *homage* to the Living Theatre's *Paradise Now.* When you're reading all of this stuff, one emotion you may well feel is *envy,* like I *too* would like to be able to have a fullblown temper tantrum whenever I pleased, and not only get catered to by everybody around me but called a genius and an artist for letting myself act out this way. Or actually, any of us who aren't catered to in this way can count ourselves lucky, because it's supremely unhealthy. In a way, Jim Morrison's life and death could be written off as simply one of the more pathetic episodes in the history of the star system, or that offensive myth we all persist in believing which holds that artists are somehow a race apart and thus entitled to piss on my wife, throw you out the window, smash up the joint, and generally do whatever they want. I've seen a lot of this over the years, and what's most ironic is that it always goes under the assumption that to deny them these outbursts would somehow be curbing their creativity, when the reality, as far as I can see, is that it's exactly such insane *tolerance* of another insanity that also contributes to them drying up as artists. Because how can you finally create anything real or beautiful when you have absolutely zero input from the real world, because everyone around you is catering to and sheltering you? You can't, and this system is I'd submit why we've seen almost all our rock 'n' roll heroes who, unlike Morrison, did manage to survive the

Sixties, end up having nothing to say. Just imagine if he was still around today, 37 years old; no way he could still be singing about chaos and revolution. There are some people who think that everything he'd been through had finally wrought a kind of hard-won wisdom in him that, had he lived, would have allowed him to mellow into perhaps less of a cultural icon and a better poet. Though there is another school of thought which holds that he'd said it all by the first Doors album, and everything from there on led downhill.

My response is somewhere in between. I never took Morrison seriously as the Lizard King, but I'm a Doors fan today as I was in 1967; what it came down to fairly early on for me, actually, was accepting the Doors' limitations and that Morrison would never be so much Baudelaire, Rimbaud, and Villon as he was a Bozo Prince. Surely he was one father of New Wave, as transmitted through Iggy and Patti Smith, but they have proven to be in greater or lesser degree Bozos themselves. One thing that can never be denied Morrison is that at his best (as well as perhaps his worst or some of it at any rate) he had style, and as he was at his best as a poet of dread, desire, and psychic dislocation, so he was also at his best as a clown. So it's no wonder our responses got, and remain, a little confused.

Certainly there are great Bozo moments scattered through the Doors' records: the mock-portentousness of the "Do you remember when we were in Africa?" coda to "Wild Child," the drunken yowling sermon *Yew CAN-**NOT** pe-TISH-SHON the lo-WARD with PRAY-yer* at the beginning of "The Soft Parade"; the whole idea of songs like "Five to One" and "Land Ho," extending to the rhythmic bounce of the latter. Hopkins and Sugerman point out the line *I see the bathroom is clear* in "Hyacinth House," and of course there are many here among us who always thought "The End" was but a joke, not to mention the scream of the butterfly. I recall sitting in another hippie pad, in Berkeley during the Summer of Love, when one night in our dope-smoking circle on the floor we were not at all nonplussed to hear the FM deejay take off "The End" halfway through and bury it with snide comments before returning to his fave rave Frisco group; admittedly there was probably some Frisco vs. L.A. chauvinism at work there, but we laughed right along with him at this "masterpiece." Finally, the Bozo Classic to end 'em all was probably *Absolutely Live,* which included such high points as Morrison stopping "When the Music's Over" to scream at the audience to shut up; the way he said *Pritty neat, pritty neat, pritty good, pritty good* before "Build Me a Woman," which begins with the line, *I got the poontang blues;* the intro to "Close to You": *Ladies and gentlemen . . . I don't know if you realize it, but tonight you're in for a special treat*—crowd cheers wildly—*No, no, not that, not that . . . last time it happened grown men were weeping, policemen were turning in their badges . . . ;* and, best of all, the (almost certainly improvised) sung intro to "Break on Through #2": *Dead cat in a top hat suckin' on a young man's blood/wishin' that he could come . . . thinks he can kill and slaughter/thinks he can shoot my daughter . . . dead cats/dead rat/thinks he's an aristocrat/that's crap . . .* —true street poetry indeed. Plus the bonus of a brief reprise of the *Petition the Lord with Prayer* bit, in which this time he sounds like no one so much as Lenny Bruce doing Oral Roberts in his "Religions, Inc." routine—listen to 'em and compare.

In the end, perhaps all the moments like these are his real legacy to us, how he took all the dread and fear and even explosions into seeming freedom of the Sixties and made them first seem even more bizarre, dangerous, and apocalyptic than we already thought they were, then turned everything we were taking so seriously into a big joke midstream. Of course, there are still the other songs too, which will always be starkly poetic in the evocations of one *gazing on a city under television skies,* perhaps the best conjurings of the L.A. myth in popular song: "End of the Night," "Moonlight Drive," "People Are Strange," "My Eyes Have Seen You," "Cars Hiss by My Window," "L.A. Woman," "Riders on the Storm." But even in these there are lines, all the "Mr. Mojo Risings," that give away his own sense of humor about, if not his talents as a poet, certainly his own persona and even the very real way in which he let his pop stardom lead him unto a betrayal of his poetic gifts. And perhaps what we finally conclude is that it's not really necessary to separate the clown from the poet, that they were in fact inextricably linked, and that even as we were lucky not to have been around any more than our fair share of "Dionysian" infants, so we were lucky to get all the great music on these albums, which is going to set rock 'n' roll standards for a long time to come.

Musician, August 1981

Bring Your Mother to the Gas Chamber!

Part One: Are Black Sabbath really the new Shamans?

I need someone to show me
The things in life that I can find
I can't see the things
that make true happiness
I must be blind.

—Black Sabbath, "Paranoid"

The world's comin' to an end.

—British bobby, interviewed on
network news in the first
bloom of Beatlemania

We have met dark days; the catalog of present horrors and dire morrows is so familiar there's not even any point in running through it again. It may be a copout, but people will do almost anything now to escape from the pall. The (first) Age of Anxiety gave way to the clammy retreat of the Fifties, when every citizen kept a tight bomb shelter, then to the sense of massive change in the Sixties, but the passing of that agitated decade has brought a new Age of Implosion, yesterday's iconoclastic war babies siphoned off *en masse,* stumbling and puking over each other at the festivals which were celebrations such a short time ago. Tying off their potentials and shooting them into the void in bleak rooms.

It's a desperate time, in a "desperate land" as Jim Morrison said just when things seemed brightest. If the terminal dramas of the Doors and Velvet Underground were prophetic, their "sordid" plots have now become the banal stuff of everyday life, which certainly doesn't lessen the pervasive dread, but does imply the need for a new music, a music which deals with the breakdowns and psychic smog on another level and, hopefully, points toward some positive resolution.

We have seen the Stooges take on the night ferociously and go tumbling into its maw, and Alice Cooper is currently exploiting it for all it's worth, turning it into a circus. But there is only one band that has dealt with it honestly in terms meaningful to vast portions of the audience, not only grappling with it in a mythic structure that's both personal and universal, but actually managing to prosper as well. That band is Black Sabbath.

The band's first album made the Top 20 in England, their second went to Number One, the single of its title song made number three on the British charts, and by the time they came to America their record company was ready with a hype fronted by "LOUDER THAN LED ZEPPELIN" banners, though, as lead singer Ozzy Osbourne says, "They had to drop that fairly soon because we just told them not to fuck around." The company has never really known what it has in the group or how to handle them. But it really didn't matter at all, because Black Sabbath wasted no time in repeating their English triumph in this country; all three of their albums were on the charts at the same time for months on end.

The audience, searching endlessly both for bone-rattling sound and someone to put the present social and psychic traumas in perspective, found both in Black Sabbath. They *were* loud, perhaps, with Grand Funk, louder than anything previously heard in human history; they possessed a dark vision of society and the human soul borrowed from black magic and Christian myth; they cut straight to the teen heart of darkness with obsessive, crushing blocks of sound and "words that go right to your sorrow, words that go 'Ain't no tomorrow,' " as Ozzy sang in "Warning" on their first album.

The critics and others who just couldn't hear it, whether they were so far from it as to find their spokesman in a James Taylor or merely felt that the riff's essence had already been done much better by the Stooges or MC5, responded almost as one by damning it as "downer music." Since much of it did lack the unquenchable adrenaline imperatives of its precedents and one look around a rock concert hall was enough to tell you where the Psychedelic Revolution had led, the charge seemed worth considering.

Lots of Black Sabbath fans take downs, but there are certainly many that don't and just as many barbiturate and heroin casualties that have no truck at all with the group, including many of those devotees of the mellow acoustic sound who are supposedly into healthier lifestyles than the minions of the music of desperation. But somehow it's easier to picture the kid down the block, as fucked-up as we've watched him become, slumped in his bedroom gorged on Tuinal, listening to Black Sabbath prate of the devil and nuclear war and what a cruel kitchen the world is, nodding to himself as he nods along anyway and finding justification for his cancerous apathy.

That's the public myth. But it's not exactly Black Sabbath's myth, not really, and a consideration of the true vision inherent in their downer rock reveals that phrase for exactly what it is.

/// \\\

You that never done nothin'
But build to destroy
You play with my world
Like it's your little toy
You put a gun in my hand
And you hide from my eyes
Then you turn and run farther
when the fast bullets fly.

—Bob Dylan, "Masters of War"

Now in darkness world stops turning
Ashes where the bodies burning
No more war pigs of the power
And as God has struck the hour
Day of judgment, God is calling
On their knees the war pigs crawling
Begging mercies for their sins
Satan laughing spreads his wings.

—Black Sabbath, "War Pigs"

Listen to my last words anywhere. Listen to my last words any world. Listen all you boards syndicates and governments of the earth. And you powers behind what filth deals consummated in what lavatory to take what is not yours. To sell the ground from unborn feet forever. . . . And what does my program of total resistance and total austerity offer you? *I offer you nothing. I am not a politician. These are conditions of total emergency. And these are my instructions for total emergency that if carried out* now *could avert the total disaster* now *on tracks:* Peoples of the earth, you have all been poisoned . . . *any minute now fifty million adolescent gooks will hit the street with switch blades, bicycle chains and cobblestones . . .*

—William S. Burroughs,
"Last Words [of Hassan i Sabbah]," *Nova Express*

Despite the blitzkrieg nature of their sound, Black Sabbath are moralists—like Bob Dylan, like William Burroughs, like most artists trying to deal with a serious situation in an honest way. They are not on the same level of profundity, perhaps; they are certainly much less articulate, subject to the ephemerality of rock, but they are a band with a conscience who have looked around and taken it upon themselves to reflect the chaos in a way that they see as positive. By now they've taken some tentative steps toward offering alternatives.

In his book *The Making of a Counter Culture,* Theodore Roszak suggested that given the current paucity of social leaders worth investing even a passing hope in, the coalition made up of the young and the free-form wing of the Left should turn to the ancient notion of the *shaman,* the holy madman whose prescriptions derived not from logic or think tanks or even words sometimes, but from an extraordinarily acute perception of the flux of the universe. Well, we've reaped Roszak's script in spades by now, there's a shaman slouching on every corner and tinhorn messiahs are a dime a dozen. Some are "political" and some are "mystical" and some are building their kingdoms on a "cosmic" stew of both, and each seems to have his little cadre of glaze-orbed acid casualties proselytizing for him.

Then there are also the cultural shamans, Dylan being the supreme artifact: Biblical, rooted in the soil and tradition and his own Old Testament brand of conscience. Burroughs too, of course, and his "Hassan i Sabbah" is nothing more than a particularly malevolent form of shaman, while the "Nova Police" are the benevolent regulation agency out to save the universe from addiction and control. Burroughs has been one of the foremost moralists in American literature; his work amounts to a demonology for our times, portraying the forces currently threatening our planet's survival as evil gods operating from without.

Where Black Sabbath fits into this seeming digression is that they unite a demonology not far from Burroughs' (if far more obvious) with a Biblical moralism that makes Dylan's look positively bland, although they can be every bit as vindictive as Dylan with the Jehovan judgments.

They are probably the first truly Catholic rock group, or the first group to completely immerse themselves in the Fall and Redemption: the traditional Christian dualism which asserts that if you don't walk in the light of the Lord then Satan is certainly pulling your strings, and a bad end can be expected, is even imminent.

They may deny all this; Ozzy Osbourne responded to a question about how the band's concept came about with a vague "I don't know. I met the guys, we got together and rehearsed for about two years, starved, bummed around hoping for a break and it just happened. You relate to me that it's about doom or something, but I can't relate it to you because I'm in the middle of it."

It really doesn't make any difference how conscious they may be of what they're saying, though. The message is there for anyone with ears, and it's unmistakable. The themes are perdition, destruction, and redemption, and their basic search for justice and harmony in a night-world becomes more explicitly social all the time. On their first album that quality only appears in one song, "Wicked World." But the prevailing mood is a medieval sense of supernatural powers moving in to snatch the unwary soul and cast it into eternal bondage.

The band was named after an above-average British horror flick from Hammer Studios, starring Boris Karloff, and their namesake song actually opens with rain sound effects and a tolling bell that's echoed in the slow, dolorous fuzz guitar that will set the pace for opening cuts of future albums and do much to lend credence to the "downer rock" stigma. Satan appears in their material in this song for the first time, leering and licking his lips as he tots up the fresh-caught souls.

Since the band's name is what it is and the thematic content of this album, as well as its packaging, leaned so far toward this sort of thing, it's easy to see why people should stereotype the group as either exploiting for profit or living and promulgating the form of pop black magic which finds high school girls intently reading books on how to become a witch and trying out spells on prospective boyfriends (and a sharpie like Anton LaVey[10] cleaning up) even as dead (literally)-serious organizations such as the Process carry out their grim rites in Los

[10] A media Satanist, author *(The Satanic Bible),* and High Priest of the Church of Satan in hippie-era San Francisco.

Angeles, Mexico, New York, and elsewhere, promoting total nihilism and the end of the world, engaging in incredible machinations to, yes, get people in their power (obtaining zombies fit for any job they don't want to soil their own hands with) even committing murder in some instances with the ritualistic precision of absolute psychopathy. There are scheming salamanders like Manson everywhere, finding fantastic utility in this phase when it comes to their own less bizarrely "religious" ends. What black magic is about is absolute control; since rock 'n' roll is power music with strange effects on people, with undercurrent themes of almost fascist dominance and subjection running from the earliest blues through the Stones to Alice Cooper, there were bound to be some psychic and subcultural connections made. No doubt there are Black Sabbath fans who like the group because it seems to reflect their own preoccupation with hocus-pocus and supernatural manipulation, just as people once used the Velvet Underground as soundtracks for the hard-drug movies they're living to the stone hilt.

But the band themselves will have no part of any of this, according to Ozzy: "We never have been into black magic. But one time, just to get a break, we decided to do a thing because it'd never been done before—the crosses and all that, the black mass on the stage, but we didn't intend it to be a thing where you go onstage in a pair of horns, and yet even now people come up and think we're going to put a fucking curse on them. Or if they're not afraid they think we're heavy, heavy heads. After the show once we went back to the hotel, and I could hear a lot of feet walking up and down the hall outside, so I went and opened the fucking door and there's all these weird people with black candles walking up and down and writing crosses on the doors and things, and they fucking frightened me, I tell ya. We all blew the candles out and sang 'Happy Birthday,'" he laughs. "They didn't like that at all."

When you begin to listen to their music with open ears, it quickly becomes apparent that rock 'n' roll sorcery is only a handle devised to make Black Sabbath into a concept more immediately graspable. As much as Satan, the righteously vindictive Old Testament God and spiritual-supernatural agonies recur in their music, they are almost invariably used to make a moral point.

The Black Sabbath vision of life on earth and the machinery of civilization becomes concrete on their second LP, *Paranoid,* whose very first song ("War Pigs") takes the epithet applied so indiscriminately for the past half-decade to anyone the speaker happens to be in disagreement with, and carries it to its ultimate gross characterization in a vignette reminiscent in verbal content and unbridled bitterness both of Dylan's "Masters of War" and the firebrand rhetoric of agitprop pamphlets of the Socialist Workers and other parties farther left dating back to the First World War. I remember seeing old books with vitriolic cartoons of Capitalist Pigs (literally) strolling along in top hats and waistcoats with buttons ready to pop from the accretions of fat, lighting giant Havana stogies with $100 bills. Possibly the only difference between that and this or Dylan's song is that those cartoons were conscious, inflammatory propaganda and this is (you can accept this to whatever degree you choose—I tend to take it all the way) true folk culture, where the hatred is more organic and sensate, churning straight up from the bowels in catharses of rage as apocalyptic as the End they visualize in this song and "Electric Funeral," probably the two most vicious statements we're ever going to hear from this band. Even Dylan, after finding it in himself to write "I hope that you die," realized that there was nothing more he could say on the tip of that particular limb.

"War Pigs" ends up a fantasy of Judgment Day, the sword of the Archangel cleaving the necks of those who have chosen to serve Lucifer and now must follow him into Gehenna. You can laugh, but Black Sabbath are something like the John Milton of rock 'n' roll: "You turned to me with all your worldly greed and pride/But will you turn to me when it's your turn to die?" The Christianity running consistently throughout their songs is cruel and bloodthirsty in the way that only Christianity can be (which is to say, lopping off heads with feverish pleasure, clad all the while in the raiment of righteousness and moral rectitude). "Electric Funeral" is their picture of atomic war as the Second Coming.

And the vengeance motif ain't just limited to Biblical referents, because "Iron Man," one of their greatest songs, is a piece of almost pure program music utilizing lugubrious drums clomping like the falls of golem feet and a guitar riff that swoops recklessly like a Hulk arm demolishing buildings, to depict a miscreant, much reminiscent of the Karloff Frankenstein's monster who really only wanted to play with the other children, who finds himself ostracized as a total freak because of his size and lumbering lack of grace (maybe Iron Man is really a symbol and fantasy for every adolescent ever tortured by awkwardness and "difference") and responds with understandable rage and a havoc-wreaking rampage. People are strange, when you're a stranger. "Iron Man" is a melodrama of alienation, just as "Paranoid" is a terse, chillingly accurate description of the real thing, when you suddenly find that you've somehow skidded just a fraction out of the world as you have and others still do perceive it. "Paranoid" renders perfectly the clammy feeling of knowing that at this point there is absolutely no one on the planet to whom you can make yourself understood or be helped by. All alone, like a real rolling stone; it's no wonder in such circumstances that the imagination might get a little hairy, and turn to dreams of science-fiction revenge. I've felt the arctic wedge of disjuncture myself at one time and another, stuck in the painful place where you can only send frozen warnings cross the borderline and those inevitably get distorted. Because they've captured it so well Black Sabbath means a lot to me and a lot of my friends for "Paranoid" alone. With the experience so common these years is it any wonder that this group has conquered the world (so to speak)?

And now that they have conquered it by detailing several of our most prevalent forms of malaise, what have they got to offer as curative? Well, this is where their moralism begins to break down, for many of us at least, because what else would an Old Testament group be offering but Jehovah? Or, to slip across a few centuries into the Greek Scriptures, Jesus. It's not that they're acting as sycophants for the virulent proliferation of hippie fundamentalist sects. *Master of Reality* conveys the impression that with the cloud of gloom hanging over their persona, and the "downer-rock" label, they felt obliged to carry their moralism into outright proselytism, suggested by "Lord of This World" and clinched in "After Forever," which follows a paean to the joys of cannabis (see, kids, we don't take those horrible pills, we use and advocate this healthy stuff . . .) called "Sweet Leaf" with:

Well I have seen the truth
Yes I have seen the light
and I've changed my ways.
And I'll be prepared
when you're lonely and
scared
at the end of your days.

The song goes on to assert that, "God . . . is the only one who can save you now from all this sin and hate" and even includes a line that goes, "Would you like to see the Pope on the end of a rope—do you think he's a fool?" Well, yes, and yes, as a matter of fact, because the Pope is a War Pig if ever there was one, or at least an evil angel. Maybe I'm making a fool of myself but I see this band making an attempt to provide direction for a generation busy immolating itself as quickly as possible. Since nobody else around that I can see seems to have any better advice for them than Black Sabbath, it pains me perhaps unduly to see them suggesting the hoariest copout conceived in 2,000 years. I mean, what's the difference between a vegetable babbling about how much crank he can hold and stay alive, and one locked into repeating a zealot litany with mindless persistence to every stranger coming down the street?

But then, I suppose I shouldn't expect Black Sabbath's answers to be sophisticated. *Master of Reality* has more than one alternative to suggest anyway. "Into the Void" is a fantasy of escape from the dire mess in this orbit via "Rocket engines burning fuel so fast/Up into the night sky they blast . . ." *al la* the reedy Starship recently promoted by the Marin County Cocaine Casualty Musical Auxiliary. This version of the fantasy at least has the advantage of some solid, pulverizing music behind it.

A much more interesting solution is drawn in "Children of the Grave," a deep, gutty, driving piece that's one of the highlights of their current live show. It couches the expectable hints of looming catastrophe ("Must the world live in the shadow of atomic fear?") in a romanticized picture of the children born in a megaton shadow standing their ground, insistent on the salvation of the planet, with an uncharacteristic happy ending: "They'll fight the world/Until they've won/And love comes flowing through."

Which is fine with me. The song's cloudy romanticism removes it from the limitations of any one faction's Utopia, even if it does bear about as much dialectical meat as Grand Funk singing "People Let's Stop the War."

Part Two: Black Sabbath and the Straight Dope on Blood-Lust Orgies

When it comes to politics rock 'n' roll bands usually have more to say in or more that can be read into (which amounts to the same thing) their music than when they actually talk about it. Ozzy Osbourne is basically about as politicized as your average musician, and while he responded to a comment from the other end of the room to the effect that Nixon should be shot with a wave of the hand—"They're all bad as fucking one another, politicians"—he saw the songs themselves in quite literal terms as graphic depictions of the state of things today: "The day of writing bullshit songs is over, as far as I'm concerned. I like to think that if people listen to the words they'll get the truth of the song, like the lyrics to 'Children of the Grave.' It's about the kids of today. In America the revolution that's in people's minds is ridiculous, because if they believe in it strongly enough and it's for good and they wanna get something out of it, then by all means revolt. You're gonna hurt something on both sides whether you let it stay the way it is and just ride it out or do something different. You couldn't get it into a worse state than it is now, and you could get something much better."

He is at least sincere, and if his positions seem a little naive, they still can be taken not only with a grain of salt but with the music itself as indication of a genuine concern, leading even to the conclusion that for all the ugliness and hatred in their music, for all the specters of wicked enemies crawling on their knees through brimstone toward the base of a white-hot mushroom cloud, the ultimate thrust of what Black Sabbath is saying or trying to say is an uncommonly humanist impulse. And because they do care, and because they hit the nerve square-on as often as they do, and because even their phantasmagorias of malediction and punishment are so vivid, and because they are better at all of this (musically and thematically) than Grand Funk and just about any other working Third Generation band with the possible exception of Alice Cooper, and because Alice Cooper doesn't really mean it and Black Sabbath does, it's mighty difficult to overstate how much we've needed them and still do.

So let the "downer-rock" slander stand, because at this point it's hard to imagine anything that could really drag Black Sabbath down. They have a pretty good idea where they stand in the mythic arena behind the public eye, and take the drug culture and the staples connecting them with it the only way they can, with equanimity: "We get knocked by a thousand people saying it's downer rock," observes Ozzy. "If we weren't here, they'd still be taking the downers. People are gonna take dope whether they go see James Taylor or Englebert Humperdinck. I really can't see that we've enticed it at all. I mean, since you've heard our music, you haven't started taking dope. . . ."

"Not since."

"If you take dope," he continues, ignoring the preeningly hip wisecrack, "you take dope because you like to get high. You don't take it because four guys are making loads of money saying 'You must take dope.' If they want to use us as an excuse, go ahead."

The trouble with that position, though it's perfectly correct, is that people pick up on things in the ghastliest, most uncalled-for ways. Black Sabbath has a drug song called "Hand of Doom" that, aside from having an arrangement with incredible dynamics including upwards of half a dozen breaks, is one of the strongest, starkest statements yet on the chemical plague to come out of pop music. It's almost as good as Lou Reed's "Heroin," and positively demolishes such false sentiments as Neil Young's "The Needle and the Damage Done" or John Prine's "Sam Stone," because it doesn't romanticize too much (the element is inescapable) and doesn't turn the subject into grist for a soap opera. Instead, in grim, straightforward language, it describes a person dying slowly by their own hand, and points out the insanity of it firmly.

But there are people who will come along and take a song like this and automatically pick out some of the harshest lines with peculiar logic, taking them as an affirmation of that self-destructive cycle. They think Ozzy is saying, "*Take* the acid! *Stick* the needle in! Don't stop to think about the consequences, because we could all be minute specks of radioactive excreta in just four seconds now. Among other good reasons." I must admit that, having lived that syndrome to some small degree myself, *I* sort of get that out of it, perceiving it as tangible thrill to hear a rock star backed up by a driving rhythm section spit out the most nihilistic, amoral injunctions possible; I often felt this way listening to the early Velvet Underground, and Mick Jagger communicates the same sensation in some of his more decadent moments. That's exactly what it is, a sensation, like the feeling you get at the movies when you see a shotgun blast somebody's guts through their back in slow motion, a rusty kick turned to when *schticks* more moral have begun to pass your jaded palate with scarcely a glint of recognition, and you just want to come as close as you can to the blood-lust orgies, death, or utter degradation without actually having to experience them firsthand. It's the last honorable form of vicarious entertainment, not to mention being the essence of cowardice. But that's the way it seems to be today.

Ozzy expects such reactions, and manages to be philosophical about them: "The weird thing about audiences is that they'll get a song and fuck it around to the way they want to think. The lyrics to 'Hand of Doom' are the goriest, most filthy lyrics you could find for drug addicts. . . . It's like, when I was a kid I'd see a Western film and say, 'Wow, the Range Rider just shot Dick West in the 'ead, and it's really ridiculous seeing this guy do this dramatic death.' But now it's gotten more realistic, where you can see them shoot somebody and it actually just blows them to pieces. And that's the way it really is. When somebody puts a gun to your head and pulls the trigger you're fucked, and it's like somebody puts a gun to your arm and shoots you dead when you do dope this way. After one concert in America, I don't remember where it was, on the floor, there was about a thousand fucking syringes; I was amazed, I felt sick, I really felt ill to think I had just performed to people that were that one step closer to the hole. I can understand why people want to take dope; it's pressure, basically, and fear. This country is frightening for the younger generation because it's at war."

If his words at times seem like something lifted directly from one of the band's songs, that's only because the songs are so reflective of the general attitudes of young people in this country and Europe today. Ozzy Osbourne is somebody you could have gone to high school with. But I can't totally swallow that the war in Vietnam and the specter of the draft are heavy enough to be an absolute factor in so many people trashing their lives with drugs; there's got to be something else. So I said that when I went to rock concerts I often had the impression that people were sitting in trenches almost as degraded and unpleasant in their own way, and asked him if he thought that they were doing all that they are doing to themselves to keep from sitting in a trench Over There, if people were actually killing themselves as a response to the possibility of having to kill someone else.

He thought a minute, straightened the towel wrapped around his hair (freshly washed for the evening's show). "I can't really say. I think it's having to live in the city, because all cities are like a big garbage can. My hometown Birmingham is just like this place [Detroit], violence and such, and I've been through it all. I've been in fucking prison, I've bummed around, but it's only the city that makes you do things. I'm lucky—I could portray the way I was reared and brought up, I went through a lot of the stories your people are going through right now, violence, getting cut to ribbons and stabbed and everything . . . so a lot of this naturally comes out in our music. I don't know if we're always as close to the edge as people seem to think our music is, I would think not, but sometimes we feel pissed off, so we write that kind of song. Other times it just comes out, like 'Paranoid' just happened, we wrote that and recorded it in half an hour."

Despite all their phosphorescent imagery, one of the distinctive things about Black Sabbath is that they do tend to think quite literally, and the ratio of artifice and contrivance, not to mention plain attitudinal dishonesty toward the audience, in their music is unusually small. Just compare them with someone like Alice Cooper, who is a great rock 'n' roller and true original and fine singer in the Freddy Cannon tradition and all that, but wraps himself in more tissues off the rotting haunches of P. T. Barnum every tour, who doesn't really mean anything he says as far as I can see, and regards the whole thing with cynical good humor and high-energy professionalism as simple Show Business. Alice Cooper is selling a product; so are Black Sabbath, I guess, but they don't exactly know it, or at least are far more concerned with sharing their understanding of the world than with being the flashiest, hardest-workin' band in show business. And, raw as the product sometimes gets, this quality demands our respect. They say what they must and mean what they say, even if the collisions between their perception of the hurricane whose eye they ride in and the audience's reality can sometimes be jarring.

Ozzy remembers, "We did a gig once, and they were all sitting down at the front shaking their fists and scowling at us . . . gettin' off on our downer music." He laughs, but not too heartily. "I was holding the mike stand tight, shaking, and the first five rows all have fucking bottles in their hands. I had visions of somebody blowing me head off. I like to see people getting up, grooving around, dancing and having a good time. But sometimes I think to myself when people are really going nuts, are they aware of what they're dancing to, are they aware of the lyrics and the concept of the song? I mainly just want to go onstage and give people a good time, but I still wonder exactly where they're at sometimes."

I'd heard tales of Black Sabbath concerts that would make a fragile soul blanch; Sandy Pearlman told me that at the last one he attended, nobody in the audience could even stand up, barely managed to applaud, and bodies were sprawled everywhere. But the Black Sabbath show I attended not long after the interview with Ozzy was, contrary to legend, pretty much like any other rock concert, no excess of ODs or obnoxious incidents obtaining from too many people at one time in one place being so fucked-up they hadn't the slightest idea what they were doing or why.

On the other hand, Sabbath's opening act on the current tour is Yes. This double bill sold out Cobo Hall, the biggest pleasure palace in these parts, where they have hockey games and Big Time Wrestling on weeknights, and which only the very biggest draws in rock can fill. Even aside from the general draftiness of such a place, where any amount of volume can get lost in the moldy corridors and spacious obscurities, the audience was at least 60 percent a Yes turnout. Yes has just begun to come into their own superstardom via "Roundabout" and their *Fragile* album, and, as you might expect when the act puts titles like that on its creations, the fans tend to be a slightly different breed of mutt. Pushing the mean age up toward college level, I would think.

In fact, I was amazed at how well-behaved and in what good condition the crowd seemed to be. Wandering among them, you just noticed faces and bodies and clothes in the most normal way that you sometimes all but forget, this being one time you couldn't routinely read somebody's psychic centigrade on their face like some strange barometer. If more than a minority were flying blind, they were putting up an awfully good front.

Since this story was originally going to be a graphic tragic survey of the littered battlefield of the contemporary concert, with pitiful panoramas of passed-out pubes and other alliterative gimmicks, most of us from *Creem* prepared ourselves for the harrowing experience by consuming a down or two ourselves. Now there we were, practically (or so it seemed to me) the only barbiturate reprobates in sight for miles. Ever alert for lurid detail, *Creem*er Jaan Uhelszki reported to me that someone tried to sell her a pill called Carbotrol in the bathroom, and that at one point she saw a girl puking. One miserable fucking puke!

Also, marijuana was legal in Michigan now and for about the next three weeks, due to a high state court ruling that since the possession law was about to convert to a misdemeanor the old one would be unenforceable in the meantime, so everybody can smoke themselves silly wherever they want with no fears greater than emphysema. Journalistic dynamite! I expected people to be walking around casual as dons puffing languidly on joints just like they was cigarettes, never even removing the things from their mouths, or maybe indulging in mass orgiastic smoke-frenzies such as prophesied by John Sinclair and Jerry Rubin, but damned if I didn't see nary a public toke all evening. Everybody just sitting there in their seats with their hands folded listening to the music. It was positively spooky.

Yes played a slick, flashy set of Formica art-rock that wowed 'em to the rafters. They got an incredible standing ovation encore, where Sabbath, the headliners, didn't even come back or get asked to; at the exact instant that "Paranoid," the last song of their set, died away and they started off, the audience began to flow down into the aisles as if cued. And I thought encores had become an unbreakable social custom!

Of course, they didn't play a particularly mind-bending set that night; the chemistry between an audience and an act is always a more delicate thing than some people realize. On top of that Sabbath, to my utter amazement and again confounding the legend, played a set at a volume level roughly average for a scuffling non-sequitur band with one album out second-billed at the Eastown Ballroom, a trashy dive of local repute. After all the slush in the press about Warner Brothers executives packing special earplugs at all times in the event of having to attend a Black Sabbath show in the line of duty, I couldn't believe this spate of whispery feedback and conversational vocals—I was pissed!

It must also be remarked that they don't have the stage show of the century—Geezer Butler gets in some nice hunchover-and-rearback english on bass, Bill Ward is about average for drummer histrionics, but Tony Iommi plays guitar in a fixed stance with eyes glued to the frets, as if he were concentrating so deeply on what he was doing that he could be home in his Birmingham parlor and the audience a solitary titmouse. Ozzy has fun onstage, more than you might expect with material of the type they specialize in, confirming his earlier remark that "Our music to an extent relieves the tension which builds up in people. When I get onstage and start looning around, I feel a big relief, I know that something's getting released."

Yeah, me too, whether I'm listening to your records stomping off a bad day with a bottle of wine in my own parlor, or watching your stage hop, which is pretty nifty kid. You ain't no Mick Jagger, but you ain't pretentious when it comes to wigglin' either. In fact, your bouncy enthusiasm, confessing the same sense of ingenuousness that your manner and conversation do in person, is infectious, and I really wanted to have a good time even if my big Teenage Wasteland exposè piece was shot and even if the volume was on vacation and even though my back and feet hurt and I was tired and cold and basically bored. I wanted to have a good time not only because I like Black Sabbath but because you *made* me want to, and I guess that's why I'm pissed off, because except for a few minutes of churning and growling roar-along with "Children of the Grave" and the much-too-short "Paranoid," I just killed time that set, I just sat and waited half-hearing like I usually do at these things, and it wasn't really anybody's fault, not even my own. I almost wonder if I *don't* prefer it when everybody's drugged and obnoxious.

When you took off your shirt it didn't have quite the James Brown drama of Mark Farner's symbolic Unveiling of the Plowboy Rock Prince biceps, but it was a nice gesture anyway and one of the two crazy teenage girls behind me who squealed for you all night yelled, "Take it all off, Ozzy!" They were wearing dark-velvet suits with swirling Edwardian capes and black wooden crosses hanging on leather thongs around their necks (even though I noticed that of the band only Geezer was still sporting his lucky crucifix), and at some point early in the set one of them actually yelled, "You devils!"

When the human sea surged down the center aisle in a massive jam just as your set was beginning, I began to get my hopes up, especially when a dozen or so harried ushers and rentacops came scurrying from the open spaces at the sides of the stage and began to make a series of futile attempts to break up the bobbing Black Sabbath congregation by hand and accusing flashlight. The faithful stayed put, though (most of them couldn't have moved anyway), and pretty soon a large crucifix made out of two boards wrapped in tinfoil and nailed together, which some dizzy zealot must have actually lugged down to this gig from Pontiac or somewhere, was hauled aloft near the rear of the congregation and passed from hand to hand, slowly and cumbersomely without doubt, up to the front until somebody was actually holding this big silver elephant of an icon right in front of your face as you sang, obscuring the view of people behind them and becoming a bit absurd in the urgency to do something that might provoke a sign of affirmative recognition from their heroes. Even if it's only because they think that you're strange (but don't change . . .) and must be at least incredibly eccentric and at most unspeakably depraved and they hope to catch a glimpse of some telling gesture that will hint at the lives you must lead.

Which gives you a lot to live up to, maybe. From the interview:

"People say, 'Fuck, man, do you realize how big you are?,' and I'm gettin' on a plane, gettin' off a plane, and goin' home. . . . Everybody thinks a tour is just one big rockin' dope sex orgy, and you do meet some incredible chicks on tour, and they'll do anything to get at you. Like one morning I'm sleeping and the phone rings: 'Hello.' And this very breathy voice on the other end: 'Hellooo.' 'Who are you?' 'I'm the Blow Job Queen.' Now, really! So when she said, 'And who are yooo?,' I said Geezer and gave her his room number. Next thing I know he's calling me up saying she's in his room and he can't get her out. So we all go over and say, 'Please leave,' and she says, 'No! Why? I give the best blow jobs in the West. Don't you believe me?' We don't want to hurt her, we don't know fucking what to say or do, so finally we all threaten to piss on her if she doesn't leave, and she does.

"People really go weird, man, it's fuckin' funny at times, like 'Touch my hand!' and you go 'What?' and they go 'He's touched my hand!' and run off in the crowd." He laughs. "They tend to think of you as a fucking miracle man or something. A great person I met once was Peter Green of Fleetwood Mac. And I asked him why he quit the band and he told that he'd been slogging around for about ten years or so, and when it did eventually happen he said he started completely to lose his identity. And that's what I don't want to do. I don't wanta be 'OZZY OSBOURNE,' I just wanta be me, like you are you, and live an ordinary life. Now I'm a bit financially secure, I've bought my own house, I've got my own wife and two kids and that's all I want. I mean, I'm just an ordinary guy making music. I'm very depressed, personally. I'm a fucking neurotic. But people tend to think that we live Black Sabbath. Well, I love the band, I've worked through all the stages with it, but I love my home and my family a thousand times more. Because *that's* reality, that's what I live for. People tend to fucking think that I go home and whip my wife to shreds, you know . . . I'm not saying I don't," he laughs again, "but they think my mother was a vampire bat, and my father was a fucking graverobber. People think that that sort of thing, that and violence, is exciting. Kim Fowley told me, 'I tell you what you wanna do next man, you oughta go to Mexico and buy a corpse, and take it onstage and stab it.' And it's getting to that point. We intend to be around for a while, but we don't nurse any illusions either. Black Sabbath was just a successful thing that happened, you can't predict how or why, it's just one of those freaky things in life that happens. I can't go doing this forever. Sooner or later it's going to fizzle out, when fucking Adolf Hitler and the Gestapo start coming after us or something. And then there'll be a new thing called Gas Chamber Rock: 'Bring your mother to the gas chamber!' "

Creem, June–July 1972

Eno Sings with the Fishes

I've never seen anybody make it harder on himself than Brian Eno. He keeps making these beautiful, brilliant records by processes so arcane that discussion of his music often results in the conclusion that he's some flipped-out technological whiz kid or art-school dilettante.

That's how droves are driven away from same beautiful, brilliant albums, a clear case of methodology getting in the way of desired results, i.e. (supposedly), mass communication. But since explication of said methodology is essential to adequate description though *not simple enjoyment* of the music, I'll attempt a brief translation: this cat thinks if you know where you're going to end up, you might as well not get moving in the first place, so he's devised all sorts of little diversionary tactics (Oblique Strategies, he calls them, and has marketed them as playing cards; "Honor thy error *as a hidden intention*" is the first one) to ensure that whenever you set out in pursuit of a work of art you'll get hopelessly lost and thus end up with a masterpiece.

Of course, artists in all media have been dicking around with variants of this approach for years, and no matter how assiduously Eno applies it through endless retakes (*Before and After Science,* his new album of *songs,* took two years and 120 tracks to complete) it still seems to bespeak a certain yearning for passivity, a desire to let some nameless Other take creative control and dictate the resultant piece through its own mysterious processes.

I'm not putting Eno's methods down, though. They're boring as shit to talk about at much length and probably unnecessarily complicated, but they've given us some of the most amazing albums of the decade: *Here Come the Warm Jets'* "Baby's On Fire" alone surpasses anything by Roxy Music in conceptual audacity and feral force, and his second sonic collage, *Taking Tiger Mountain (By Strategy)* was endlessly intricate, teeming with so many unheard-of inspirations that it may be another 10 years before the rest of rock catches up. (And the last time I made so fulsome with the superlatives I was reviewing Miles Davis' *In a Silent Way,* so listen before you laugh!)

Another Green World—his first solo experiment with what he called "unengaging" music—certainly had its fans, though I found much of it a bit too, well, "Becalmed," as one of its precisely programmatic titles declared. Those little pools of sound on the outskirts of silence seemed to me the logical consequence of letting the processes and technology share your conceptual burden—twilight music perfectly suited to the passivity Eno's approach cultivates. It's certainly relaxing—I even know people who do yoga to it—and at its extremes it produces lovely sonic wallpaper, like the two Fripp and Eno albums, the lulling *Discreet Music,* or the new German import, *Cluster and Eno,* an ECMical instrumental meditation with two German keyboardists who make music so placid you realize how much heavy-metal edge Fripp's feedback pastorales had all along.

Me, I'm a modern guy, but not so modern I don't still like music with real heavily defined *content* that you can actively *listen* to in the *foreground.* That's why I'm pleased to say that, while I still don't think it matches *Taking Tiger Mountain, Before and After Science* is an inspired and inspiring album. And, as usual, Eno says his mouthful about which way his muses are blowing; he claims that this album is "ocean music," as opposed to the "sky music" of *Another Green World.* Shamelessly, he even employs the kind of effects—bells, synthesizers, etc.—that a good movie soundtrack composer would use to suggest the slow-motion world of undersea, and nautical references keep cropping up in the lyrics.

Side two seems to drift on currents with a logic of their own which, interestingly enough, lead his melodies very close to the spawning ground of lullabies (maybe that's where flirtation with the Other leads: regression). I bet small children wouldn't need any involved techni-conceptual explanations to relate to this music. They might even be able to explain the lyrics of "Here He Comes," a song about a boy whose "sad blue eyes . . . fill the deep blue sky," better than I ever could. Eno says he gets lyrics purely by association and is not particularly interested in what they might actually mean, which leaves the listener to impose his own scenarios on even the most specific songs. "Julie with . . ." could be a murderer's ruminations, or simply a lovers' retreat . . . or Julie could be three years old. Anyway, in this song, which contains not a wasted note or word, a perfect little world is realized. Like all the songs on *Before and After Science* and its predecessors, it's program music but, as always, the listener is ultimately left to complete the picture himself.

On the other side of the album a variety of musicians permutated from track to track cook in a way that makes you forget all about Eno's theorems, and suggests that this may be the real lost chord in rock-jazz-experimental fusion music. "No One Receiving" has a discoish rhythm that seems to arc off into space with haunting vocal "in these metal ways/in these metal days," "Kurt's Rejoinder" is a whirlpool of plucked strings, percussion, and synthesized voice, and "King's Lead Hat," emphasizing Eno's affinities with New Wave in its rushed mechanical rhythms and clacking dissonances, has more of the dense Velvet Undergroundish charge and churn of *Tiger Mountain*'s "Third Uncle." All of it is music that you can almost literally *see,* as befits Eno's current interest in movie soundtracks. In fact, the album is being marketed in conjunction with four offset prints from watercolors by artist Peter Schmidt, paintings that parallel the music in portraying very little—usually interior worlds, lonely and haunted, where often the only human presence seems to be the passive eye of the beholder.

The Village Voice, April 3, 1978

John Lydon
Across the Border

Corrective comedy doesn't always work.

If the jewel which everyone desired to possess lay far out on a frozen lake where the ice was very thin . . . while, closer in, the ice was perfectly safe, then in a passionate age the crowds would applaud the courage of the man who ventured out. . . . But in an age without passion . . . people would think each other clever in agreeing that it was unreasonable . . . to venture so far out . . . the eyes of connoisseurs would appraise the accomplished skater who could skate almost to the very edge (i.e., as far as the ice was safe and the danger had not yet begun) and then turn back. . . . And then, stimulated by a gush of admiration, they all comfortably agreed that they might as well admire themselves.

—Kierkegaard, *The Present Age*

Kill someone
Be someone
Kill yourself!

—Sex Pistols, "Belsen Was a Gas"

With that furious shriek the (real) Sex Pistols' recorded career stops. There is a moment of silence and then the San Francisco crowd goes wild. It's one of the most frightening things I've ever heard, but it also makes clear why the Pistols had to break up. Because there are only so many times you can tell somebody something in plain English till you realize they don't get the irony even in that; they don't hear the words. All they see is a reflection of a spurious notion of the self and a spurious passion too, so you stop attempting to communicate. If people want to think Belsen was a cheap joke, that's their problem.

Maybe you just realize that you cannot kick intentional cripples awake, so you tell everybody what not to expect (first Public Image Ltd. album) and then give 'em what you really want to do (second) and if they don't like it, fine. Because you are left alone to make music, which is finally more important than fucking with the media.

Second Edition née *The Metal Box* (the latter perhaps the greatest packaging concept in history, and I don't give a damn about the price, I've bought two copies already and how much else is there that's worth any money at all?) is one of the best records I've heard since, oh, say, maybe *White Light/White Heat.* It's assured. It's no joke unless you want it to be, in which case you're welcome to all the Gary Numans. This is a real ensemble making passionate music out of noise and sonic scraps. Quote me: "the first music of the Eighties." It's not entirely new; there's Spanish guitar in "Memories," and the ending of "Swan Lake" harkens back to the Velvets' "Loop" and the ending of the original "White Light/White Heat." "Radio Four" even sounds a little bit like Eno, but all those hours in the studio and remixes (there are between three and five—I'm not entirely sure which—mixes of "Swan Lake" a.k.a. "Death Disco" on various records) paid off. It's not arty, either—what it is is bitter and variform, an hour well-spent. It hasn't a commercial chance in hell and wasn't even necessarily designed that way, nor is it particularly obscure—you can't get much more blatant than the group's name itself.

John Lydon, on this album, sheds an image he wishes desperately the rest of the world would let him forget ("Albatross," 12 easy minutes of loping almost-funk that prove with the rest of the LP that this group is dubwise way beyond any slavish imitations, in fact has a concept of bass like nobody else in white music history), and battles the whole Eng./Mod.-American/*Happy Days* culture of ultimately entropic nostalgia or cannibalism as we used to call it ("Memories," in which the mix shifts gears in a truly startling way); then there's "Train Round the Bend" for Hammer Studios film freaks combined with more anti-pop-slop bile ("Poptones"—with this imagery, this guy shoulda been writing E.C. comics). "Careering" is ineluctably ominous complete with what sound like cawing crows and pistol shots, and may or may not be about what's happening in Ireland; either way, the sheer velocity of a line like "A face is raining across the border" is enough to wing you. "And No Birds Can Sing" paints lifeless manors with perfectly sculpted lawns in Britain or Beverly Hills (makes no difference), built on a riff ascending forever like the mewlings of all the aborted fetuses piled at the city dump, while "The Suit" describes a social climber who is what he wears, so his clothes and even his skin are no better than the last rusty safety pin in Babylon. "Swan Lake" is about the living dead *sans* romanticism ("Words could never say the way/I see it in your eyes"). "Graveyard" is all the guitar solos taken out of these songs and melded into one purposive mass, while "Socialist" is the best keyboard instrumental since Dave "Baby" Cortez's "The Happy Organ" and sounds like brain lobes being extracted and wriggling on the table while the cymbals grieve as best and fast as they can. The rest of the album consists of a statement of purpose which, near as I can decipher, works out "Pop-Rock-Fear-Hate" over and over while Lydon lays it on the line after some equally uncompromising guitar work: "Voice moaning in a speaker/Never really getting too close."

For all Lydon's protestations, *Second Edition* is as close as you can get right now. The reason for the protestations, the group's name, the unglamorous photos, the box itself is that he doesn't want to be a pop-star anymore. And who can blame him? You *can épater les bourgeoise* till you're dead, but you really don't have to prove anything to anybody and they're not gonna listen anyway. My only criticism is that sometimes he comes off a little self-righteous ("You never listened to a word that I said" or "You make me feel ashamed"—who the fuck does he think he is?), but this album makes it clear that he, Keith Levine, Jah Wobble, and whoever else comes or goes in Public Image are gonna be around for a while. Personally speaking, I don't mind a bit if they'd rather spend all their time in the studio and come up with something as fine as this instead of touring. You did it, you snide little bastard. Now do another one. Keep to yourself. We don't want to meet you anyway.

The Village Voice, March 24, 1980

\\\ ///

TRAVELOGUES

/// \\\

Killer Frogs in Transatlantic Blitz: A Franco-American Chronologue Starring Les Variations

Allen Park, Michigan, USA–April 1974—A bunch of us are in the Allen Park Hockey Rink, supreme arena of this bratwurst burg, watching BTO break on thru to Cobo Hall while the sweat off the pubes condenses in the air, when out comes this bunch of funnynosed dark-complected guys outfitted in spangles crossbreed Arabian Nights and hey-mofo-I'm-a-rockstar. They set up and begin to play this odd swirling churn which sounds like "Jumpin' Jack Flash" with Joujouka stirred in, so being the steely lobed old cynics we are we retire to BTO's dressing room to drink up all those Mormons' beer.

Which is where, later, I first meet Les Variations, the world's first French-Moroccan hard rock band. They return from their set bouncy with distinctly anti-Gallic cheer, and assert themselves most ingenuously: "Allo, Lestair, I am Alain Tobaly, zees eez my brothair Marc who plays lead guitar, that's our drummer Jacky Bitton and Jo Leb who zings, we *love* America and rock 'n' roll, 'ey man, you like Vats Domeeno?" Meanwhile the frosting on the cake is this semiportly guy about 40 years old standing in the corner in black trenchcoat and maitre'd's pencil 'stache; that's Maurice Meiman, and he's the main chef d'rhythm 'n' druse in this band, i.e. his oud (a traditional Moroccan instrument somewhat like a gutsier lute, first popularized here by Ahmed Abdul-Malik) and violin serve up the real swirling Arabic drone which is principally what they're referring to in calling their first album *Moroccan Roll* and what gives them promise of being the first group to take the wedding of eastern music to rock one modal noodle farther than the Velvets did with "Black Angel's Death Song."

They're a motley clutch of frogs and excited as hell to be playing this third-level sweatpit, and the star of the hour is bassist Jacques "Petit Pois" Grande. Jacques has been pulling yuks right and left trying to talk in a Michigan accent, which from his French gullet comes out something like a catarrhed Mexican trying to imitate Donald Duck. But now he is preoccupied not unnaturally with things carnal, importuning me, practically shaking me by the shoulders: "Ze *groopeez,* Lestair, wair are ze *groopeez?*"

"Look man," I diplomacize, "I don't have to hassle with that shit, I got my old lady with me." Who then gives me a look that could wither a barracuda, as I steer Jacques in the general direction of the poon pool. There is indeed a whole row of them up 'gainst yonder's wall, poised on high school cafeteria scratched-iron chairs with their legs crossed smoking cigarettes, casting appraising glances every whichaway like iguanas' tongues uncurling in a rain forest. But en route poor Jacques' eyes get snagged by one of the *Creem* girls, who is a classical looker but also happens to be accompanied: "Ah, Lezlee Brown, ze beeyootivul Lezlee, I love you but you are wiz zee uddair buoy, oh, what can I do?" Wailing his heart out, jeez, now I understand Charles Aznavour as well as why they lost the war, but I try to set him straight, pulling him aside and epitheting him upside the ear: "Look, you bimbo, they're *right over there,* now get to it while you've got the chance!" "Oh no, I love *Lezlee,* but zhe doz not love mee, oh . . ." Meanwhile Leslie is giggling, the rest of the room is in an uproar, and I'm getting to like these guys.

/// \\\

New York City—May '74—I'm in New York for Mott the Hoople's opening at the Uris Theatre on Broadway, when who do I spy in the lobby milling amongst the general scenemakers and rock critics who have fled Queen's set but Les Variations. First up is manager Alain to greet me so effusively it's almost embarrassing: "Lestair, my good friend, how 'ave you been, you look magnifique!" meanwhile hugging me and pinching my cheeks, practically kissing me in a typical display of warmth that has the prominent homos in attendance just standing around and laughing. And the thing about it is that it isn't hype, he's genuinely glad to see me, as are they all, like a pack of frogified Will Rogerses they are so full of openhearted excitement and affection simply at being in America that the poor sweet fools just go around hugging everybody in delight. Now if you've ever been to New York City you can imagine what an incongruous spectacle their ingenuousness makes, and further how they manage to charm the hell out of the rock press and most of the other people they met here. I run into Jacques and even though he had a moderately classy groupie on each arm the first words out of his mouth are: "Eez Lezlee Brown here?"

/// \\\

Paris, France—July '74—I'm sitting drunk on absinthe in the George V, one of the classiest hotels in the burg, having made my way clear across the pond to catch Les Variations, who have by now become my fast friends even though I still haven't seen 'em live and don't much like their album, on their home turf. Paris would be a great city if you'd get rid of all the people, who are the deadest, coldest, glummest, most maudlin clot of sad sacks I have ever witnessed in one place in my life. I had heard of their legendary hostility and anti-Americanism, and was hoping at least for a wine bottle upside the head and "Vietnam war pig!," but no such luck. Instead we visit all the old and legendary avant-garde watering holes, La Coupole, Café Flore, and they're full of drab and beaten souls who're whiling away the days with sullenly intense discussions of the comparative merits of Samuel Beckett and Robbe-Grillet. We're at Café Flore and I ask Alain, "How come everybody here is so *gloomy?*"

"It's a gay bar," he says.

I see, that makes sense, that all the old avant-garde watering holes would turn into places where old faggots hang out, except that it's more than that, it's the French sense of clammily melodramatic gloom and defeat which comes from, among other excuses, taking it up the ass in two successive world wars. So I start trying to get 'em riled, yelling "We're surrounded by *beatniks!*" and "Is there an Existentialist in the house?" But it did no good, they just kept sitting there dying. I was beginning to wonder about this apparent contradiction between the open-endedly buoyant spirits of everybody in Les Variations and the suffocating, pretentious, *ostentatious* misery all around us, but the answer may lie in the fact that Les Variations are mongrels, nomads, gypsies even. Yowza dey done come up de Mediterranean from their native Morocco, and they were the first rock group ever in France to break that country's pop charts out of the stranglehold of traditionally bathetic ballads and third-rate Elvis imitations like Johnny Hallyday.

Almost literally an overnight sensation, they have given French kids something to rally around besides whatever scrapings of America they can get their mitts on. And believe me, those kids are hot for what we got. For instance, did you know that in France there is a Robot A. Hull[11] Fan Club? That's right, and I even dredge myself up from the absinthe to take in a record store where they sell such things as bootleg disques of the Flamin' Groovies (major cult over there), Lou Reed (depicted with fangs on the cover), and a godawful jam between Jimi Hendrix, Johnny Winter, and Jim Morrison, who did not sing but played the drums (cover of this one a classic: skull a la Grateful Dead except with Hendrix 'fro and do-rag, and down in the lower left hand corner is *an actual blood stain smeared on each copy of the album jacket*). This same store also carries large stacks of dog-eared back issues of *Creem*, going at undoubtedly astronomical prices, and the clientele of this establishment and numerous others like it, I learn, consists of a teenage French underground who call themselves Les Punques and

[11] At that time, a *Creem* writer.

do such things as wear black leather jackets, listen to old MC5 records, and read *Creem.*

It is out of this miasma of miscegenation that Les Variations have arisen like some brash beacon, first flashes of national pride as a stake in the rock dream, and it's in Paree's storied sleaze palace the Olympia that I finally get to see them strut their stuff. I'm up for it and more than ready to see a little bloodletting, being hep to the legendary hooliganism of Parisian audiences, who may like rock 'n' roll but only incidental to coming to break the hall to pieces. Les Variations are somewhat alienated by all this, being partisans of the pure *musique* as they are. Marc says: "I love the audience in America, because they can understand the music much more than in France. Here when you play they don't understand shit, they just come here to boogie, but not to boogie in the right way, just to break some beer cans on the head of each other. When you just give them the rhythm it's okay, but you can't play anything soft or like that, but in America you can make them understand because they're more cultured in the music."

So Les Variations gives them the rhythm, Jo Leb shouting something that sounded like "Je suis un singer dans un rock 'n' roll band," running to the apron of the stage and edging back. Marc studiously avoids anything soft, tearing out riffs that reminded me most of the sorts of exchanges Fred Smith and Wayne Kramer used to get in in the old MC5. Maurice just stands there, dignified and characteristically somewhat distant as befitting his seniority, sawing away at his violin in wriggling bellydancer soundtrack that somehow fits the rest of the band's basic Stones moves in the same way that Roxy Music's own churn managed to mate the Velvet Underground's gutter slide with Euroclassical sonorities without emerging the idiot bastard son of Van Der Graaf Generator. And the kids scream and storm precisely as per script.

In the several months since then Les Variations has produced a new album, a sort of concept number (a concept album, explains Jacques, is one where "all the songs run together . . . no break . . . a little *Tommy*") which Marc calls "our autobiography, about our youth in Morocco, and then when we grow up in France, and we go to Amereeca and rock and roll." There have also been changes in the lineup, with the addition of keyboard player Jim Morris, and Jo Leb (who said to me last year, "I don't want to be the star, I'm just a singer. In France people will try to take the singer and say 'You're stupid, I can make you star in six months if you stop to be in that band,' and I say fuck off, I don't wanna be on your system.") leaving to make a solo album and a movie with Catherine Deneuve. He is being replaced by Robert Fitoussi, who may be hard for you to spell but's a music biz name in France, was born in North Africa like the rest of the group, and sang on Yes keyboardist Vangelis Papathanassiou's solo album *Earth,* as well as pulling off a string of hits worldwide under his own name including the number-one-in-Brazil "Superman Superman." But in the end it's not personalities, or musical gimmicks (concept albums, heavily hyped Casbah-vibes) which will endear them to Yankee brats; it's the same kind of unforced excitement which got to the critics, which a band such as Bachman-Turner Overdrive also has; it is perhaps their very ingenuousness which will make them stand out in any crowd at all.

Creem, February 1975

Innocents in Babylon: A Search for Jamaica Featuring Bob Marley and a Cast of Thousands

The first thing that should be established is that I was only in Jamaica for a week, and there is no way to compress Jamaica or its music scene into one week, or one article. So what you are about to get is just the surface, the shell. But I hope that if you look beneath this surface you may begin, as I am, to figure out a lot of what is going on in Jamaican music, and a little of the turmoil currently besetting Jamaican society.

I can't say that this piece is really representative of that society, even from an outsider's viewpoint, because I never got out of Kingston, a bullet-pocked industrial metropolis not dissimilar to Detroit. Even though Jamaica is a country where 2 percent of the population has 80 percent of the money and the rest suffer some of the worst poverty in the world, it's also true that in Jamaica at its least urban the poor can live more comfortably than most other places in the world: build a simple house in the country, start a garden, grow food and herb, pick fruit off the trees, or go to the ocean and catch fish. The trouble begins when country people come into Kingston, lured by promises of a better life in the big city. They end up in slums like Trenchtown and Jones Town, living in shacks and incredible squalor. The result, of course, is crime and violence both "random" and "political."

Out of all this, however, like oppressed black people in other places before them, they have created a vital indigenous musical form called reggae. Reggae has been intimately linked with the growing awareness on the part of western Caucasians of Rastafarianism, a primitive mystical-religious sect which has been around Jamaica for several decades now. The Rastafarians believe that Marcus Garvey, father of the Back to Africa movement, was a prophet who foresaw the coming of Jah, the Savior also promised in the Bible, a Savior who would lead all oppressed black people to their Promised Land. Garvey said the Savior was coming in 1927, and in 1930 Haile Selassie was crowned Emperor of Ethiopia, becoming the first black head of a 20th Century African state. Ergo, the Rastas believe that Selassie, who was born Ras Tafari and ruled Ethiopia till his death in the Seventies, was (is) Jah; and that soon he will return to bring the Rastas, who believe themselves to be the lost tribe of Israel, home to Ethiopia a.k.a. Zion. In the meantime, while they await Armageddon as prophesied in the Bibles they read daily, they'll have nothing to do with Babylon, the present system of things—they do not vote, instead espousing pacifism, anti-materialism, growing their hair out in long, wild, bushy patches called dreadlocks, and the smoking of lots of herb a.k.a. ganja a.k.a. weed/tokes/dope to us, which they believe to be a mystical sacrament of Jah. Soon, through the combined forces of Jah and higher herb consciousness, Armageddon will come in the form of a mystical revolution which will topple Babylon and set all Jah's children free to return to Paradise.

In other words, kind of a Third World cross between John Sinclair and Jehovah's Witnesses.

Out of all this has risen one major musical figure, who represents to Jamaicans approximately what Bob Dylan represented to white American college students ten years ago: Bob Marley. Marley and his group the Wailers have thus far released four albums (plus two earlier ones in England and several more in Jamaica) which have made him a star among white youth in England, but is just beginning to break through in America, where reggae is still regarded as a bit of a curiosity by most white listeners and outright disdained by blacks. Which is why I, along with a raft of other white journalists and photographers, was flown down by Island Records for a sort of Cook's Tour of Jamaican music and the somewhat obligatory interview with Bob Marley.

/// \\\

I am on the phone with an L.A. rep for Island, who shall henceforth be referred to as Wooly, because of the cap this white lad wore, in imitation of the Rastas, throughout his stay in Jamaica. I tell him that, even through I love reggae with a passion that is threatening to cost me some friends, I have always considered Bob Marley's records rather cold and he is in fact my least favorite reggae artist.

He laughs. "Shhh—you're not supposed to *say* things like that!"

"Okay, then, where's this guy Marley at?"

"Well, Bob's philosophy can be summed up in one word: 'righteous.' "

"Do you mean like righteous weed, or the righteous wrath of Jehovah, or righteous brothers and sisters living off the land . . . ?"

"Well, kind of a combination of all three."

"I see—he's a hippie."

"Right."

/// \\\

Jamaica is still undergoing what might be termed a colonial hangover. It has no real indigenous population, not even a few scattered enclaves like the American Indians, because the original Jamaicans, the Arawaks, were all slaughtered by Christopher Columbus and the Spaniards. The island was for centuries but one protectorate in the British Empire, and in fact only gained its independence in 1962. Since then it has made very little progress toward autonomy, and there is a lack of motivation among most of the people that can be ascribed to more than the tropical climate. All the most negative connotations of "laid back" can be found in Kingston—people are slow, lackadaisical, facts get lost in the haze of ganja and time barely exists. "I'll be back in 45 minutes" can mean three to six hours, "We'll get it together this afternoon" may mean tomorrow night or never at all. One writer on this trip claimed that every horoscope in the *Daily Gleaner* counseled "patience," and there is an expression that you hear constantly which perfectly sums up the lazy, whenever-we-get-around-to-it tempo of Jamaican life: "Soon come." I think the discernible lack of motivation on the part of many Jamaicans can be ascribed to a rather complex combination of ganja, lack of education, and having little to no idea what to do with themselves as a people in the absence of colonialism. A lot of people (especially Americans) feel that legalization of herb would be the answer to the island's economic problems; I think that the situation in Jamaica is the most persuasive argument I've ever seen for its *non*-legalization, and the fact that everybody smokes it anyway does nothing to contradict that. Of course, the argument could be raised that the people resort so extensively to this dope, which is not nearly as strong as legend would have it and has the most tranquilizing effect of any I've ever smoked, to blot out their feeling of helplessness in the face of such realities as that Michael Manley, the current Prime Minister who came in on a liberal reform ticket, is now taking on some of the earmarks of a dictator. As for the Rastas, it makes sense that they should dream of a pilgrimage back to the cradle of Ethiopia since all black people in Jamaica are descended from people originally brought here as slaves, except for one hitch: the current government of Ethiopia is almost virulently anti-Selassie, and would hardly welcome an influx of Jah knows how many thousand dreadlocked dopers with almost no skills or education. I seriously doubt most of the Rastas know this, just as I doubt that most Jamaicans would know or care that their "freedom" has made the island perhaps more wide-open than ever for colonialist carpetbaggers.

What all this has to do with reggae is that for most reggae connoisseurs the old-time Jamaican music scene is rabble-rousingly epitomized in *The Harder They Come,* the Perry Henzell film about a youth who records a song he wrote himself for an unscrupulous (and archetypal) producer who pays him twenty bucks and tells him to scram. He is forced to resort to selling herb for money, the producer rips him off for all royalties, his dealings lead him to a shoot-out, and the great twist upon which this intentionally amateurish film hangs is that the kid is Public Enemy Number One and has the Number One hit single at the same time: a Bob Dylan wet dream.

Understandably, this film is banned in Jamaica. But conventional wisdom has it that the music-biz situation depicted in it has been rendered a thing of the past, principally by the founder-president of Island Records, Chris Blackwell. When reggae first became a popular export, in England in the late Sixties and early Seventies, the big English reggae label was Trojan, where boxes of tapes with nothing but artists' names and song titles printed by hand used to arrive to be be waxed and sold with the artists in most cases receiving no royalties at all. It must be remembered that most of the people making this music come from poverty and illiteracy so extreme that they can have little to no idea of the amounts of money to be made from it; undoubtedly many have been satisfied merely to have a record released with their name on the label and voice in the grooves. In such a situation many vital performers and groups, such as the Pioneers and even Desmond Dekker (who had a U.S. hit in '69 with "Israelites") were allowed to die on the vine, and Chris Blackwell is the first exception to this—the first person to try to build the careers of individual reggae artists and an international market for them.

Many people, however, feel that conditions for Jamaican musicians are much the same today as in *The Harder They Come,* even if most don't actually resort to picking up the gun. The content of the records being released has become increasingly geared to visions of Rasta revolution of the mind and heart, although it is difficult to see how Babylon could fall and leave the record companies standing, a paradox that your average Rasta musician is cosmically adroit at skirting. With all their talk of "Jah will provide," the Rastafarians may yet prove the first people in history to actively (if innocently) collaborate in their own exploitation by the music industry. Robert Johnson got ripped off too, but I doubt that it was a tenet of his religion. Then again, it may be that the Rastas are merely the logical extension of the sad lethargy, punctuated by random blasts of berserk gunfire, which permeates Jamaica like the smog steadily building over Kingston.

/// \\\

Then again, that lethargy may be as illusory as many other things in Jamaica. The rude boys (Jamaican street punks of the early Sixties) were not lethargic, Marley has sung that "a hungry mob is an angry mob," and there is certainly no lethargy in a white person going to a black country, or shouldn't be if he values his skin. There is something almost obscenely ironic in the need to find exotic strokes in folks so far removed from you, who are not, at all, exotic to themselves; in the way white longs to lose itself in black.

Monday. Flying over Cuba, I first realized that I was heading for the celebrated Third World. All that means for us is poor people, poorer than you or I could probably ever conceive. There's no way they're not gonna hate our guts, there's no way you're not gonna be slumming no matter who you are—I had been told that they hate our black Americans as well as white (a certain odd comfort in that), and when I got there I was to discover that the hatred you feel emanating from many Jamaicans has far more to do with class and economic status than race, and that many of them would display a genuine warmth that had nothing to do with fawning with seething guts for bwana's silver. So you might as well enjoy yourself, rubberneck, and try not to get killed. It ain't no tropical paradise to the natives; seem to remember a guy singing a song about tables turning, begin to see what it means.

Flying from Montego Bay to Kingston, impressions of California; green hillsides dotted with elegant swimming pool split-levels below, but the music reverberating in my head bespoke only Trenchtown and was at such variance with what I saw down there that I could only wonder how long till they tear this place apart, burning and looting nonmetaphorically with no metaphysical ganja above-it-all possible. You wonder if you'll be able to visit this country at all in a few years, and your wonder increases during your stay as you read in the daily papers how Manley is chumming up with Castro, supposedly all because of a cane thresher developed by the Cubans whose blueprints could revolutionize the sugarcane business in Jamaica (where it's still cut by hand) and thereby perhaps save the economy. Meanwhile, the only people more violently anti-Communist than Cuban refugees are seemingly the people of Jamaica on all class levels; you wonder at times who they must hate more—the mindlessly patronizing American and Canadian tourists, or the Communists. In any case, there's something in the air that you can breathe and taste like emotional cinders, and it isn't love. When you get off the plane in Montego Bay and walk in to get your health card stamped, Disney World calypso natives in straw hats serenade you with backdrop of Holiday Inn sign, poster advertising the beaches of Negril (where all the white hippies go), and latrine-green plaque warning in two languages that smoking, possession, or sale of ganja ("marijuana," they add in parentheses for naïve hiplets) is a crime punishable by imprisonment. From the plane window, I look down and see a red lake, which I will later discover has been turned that hue and into a quicksand bog by bauxite mining on the part of the Alcoa corporation.

The first sound I heard on arriving in the Kingston airport was the Muzak blasting a Jamaican imitation Otis Redding version of "Hey Jude," which I thought was funny enough until I discovered that Jamaican AM radio almost never plays reggae. After a week of very little beyond Helen Reddy and Neil Diamond, I would be anxious to get the hell out of this place and back home just so I could hear some Toots and the Maytals.

Kingston is very little more than a vast slum surrounding the ominous towers of babel in an enormous plastic palm Sheraton hotel, from which tourists seldom venture and around the swimming pool of which a great deal of Island Records' business is conducted. This place has a Marcus Garvey Room (I peeked in the door; it looked like one of the rooms where I used to give speeches to Rotarian banquets in high school), but that is no reason why, upon arriving or anytime else, you should buy dope, "gold" bracelets or anything from the guys hanging around the parking lot. My colleague from *Rolling Stone,* arriving a virtual rube with no one to warn him, purchased a rather small quantity of not very good herb from one of these characters for the outrageous sum of $25. I have decided that it is a truth, if not a right, that in Kingston you are going to get burned, regardless of race, creed, or color, even if you never go out in the sun at all.

/// \\\

Tuesday. Another writer, the man from *Swank,* comes to my room and turns me on to the legendary herb. It's good, all right, but nowhere near the rep. It didn't move my attention to unexpected places, inflate trivial ideas into fascinating discursions, or even get me deeper into the music like American dope. It did, however, get me stoned.

Later we went with Wooly on a ride through Kingston. It reminded me of a drab melding of California and Detroit, with slums so bad they made the latter's look like the Sheraton. Wooly takes us to the studio of Lee "Scratch" Perry, one of the most prolific Jamaican producers. True to form, Perry is not home. The man from *Time,* who had stayed up all night when he got here finishing his last story and is on a tight schedule, is visibly hassled, and in the car Mr. Swank begins to complain about the fact that everybody is waiting around for Marley to be ready to be interviewed. This writer had apparently been promised an audience with Bob yesterday, and is annoyed to learn that he will not be getting one today either.

Wooly patiently explains that no one can get a really good story on Jamaica without getting into the tempo of Jamaican life, and that everybody will take back from Jamaica whatever they bring there. Wooly is, obviously, very much taken with the tempo and lifestyle himself, even if he is staying in the Sheraton.

We go shopping at Aquarius Records, where I first experience the peculiar Jamaican syndrome of walking into one record store after another and asking for top hit singles or albums like *Best of the Maytals*, and being told again and again that they don't have them. I had a long list of records I wanted to buy, and was only able to obtain a few during my stay on the island. I discovered eventually that this was because the music business here (cf. *The Harder They Come*) was almost totally controlled by the producers, most of whom had their own record stores, where you pretty much had to go to obtain the records they had produced. And the records are not cheap, either—most albums are $6.00, one dub album was quoted at ten bucks to Wooly by a guy in Aquarius, and singles are a dollar. I wondered how a country as poor as Jamaica could support the highest per capita singles issue (thirty released a week) in the world, and was told that Jamaicans almost never bought albums—apparently pressed mainly for export and reggae-loving American tourists—but would at times actually go hungry to have money for a single they wanted.

I was also impressed to learn that Jamaica is the only place I've been where people actually like to play music louder than I do. When you go in the record shops it blares at a volume perilously close to the pain threshold, as the clerk plays deejay, switching off between two turntables and two speakers, one in the shop and one on the street. So your head gets rattled back and forth like a pinball between two raucous tracks and one speaker in the distance and another right on top of you. It's jarring, and emphasizes the violence underlying the laid-back "gentle" character of reggae. Many of these records may be little more than a rhythm with a guitar chopping out two or three chords, no solos except a guy hollering things you can barely understand over the whole thing; but that rhythm is rock steady, the guitars chop to kill, and the singer is, often as not, describing class oppression or street war. There is also a sense of listener-as-artist that is one of the most beautifully developed I have ever encountered. In the first place, all the singles have an instrumental version of the hit on the B side, so the deejays can flip them over and improvise their own spaced-out harangues over the rhythm tracks. Since Jamaican radio plays so little reggae, most of these deejays come off the streets, where until recently you could find, periodically, roots discos set up. Out of these emerged deejays-stars like Big Youth and I Roy, and along with producers like Lee Perry and Augustus "King Tubby" Pablo they have pioneered a fascinating form of technologized folk art called dub. An album by I Roy can thank six different producers on the back "for the use of their rhythms." Don't ask me where the publishing rights go. Don't ask anybody, in fact. And, don't ask how musicians might feel who play on one session for a flat rate, only to find it turn up on one or more other hit records. The key with dub is spontaneity, the enormously creative sculpting and grafting of whole new counterpoints on records already in existence. And this sense of the guy who plays the record as performer extends down into the record shops, where the clerks shift speakers, tracks, and volume levels with deft magicianly fingers as part of a highly intricate dance, creating sonic riot in the store and new productions of their own in their minds: *I control the dials.*

/// \\\

Wednesday. Waiting around the Sheraton pool for Marley. There is a mood of exasperation with the celebrated Jamaican tempo, which many business-minded visitors seem to view with disgust so extreme it turns to amusement. An English musician, here to do sessions, laughed when I asked him if the state of the Jamaican music industry had undergone any significant alteration since *The Harder They Come*. "Things haven't really changed that much. Before Chris Blackwell set up Island, musicians got six dollars a session. Blackwell revolutionized things by giving them *twelve* dollars a session, and I think by now it's up to fifteen. But I'll say this—Blackwell may be the only person I've ever met in the music business, especially in Jamaica, with *any* integrity at all. I mean, all these guys like I Roy, making these hits—do you think any of them have any money?" He laughs again. "Maybe got nice car, mon. Of course we're all still involved in fucking colonialism and exploitation of the people here, with all these record companies. It's inevitable, there's no way around it. But I supposed there's a certain price we pay too, you see. I hate this fucking place, and can't wait to get out, because I can barely get a session started, much less done, because everybody's so fucking laid back you can't depend on anyone to be at a certain place at a certain time or get any work done. Drives me fuckin' crazy. It's all 'Soon come, mon. Soon come.' "

I also have a revealing conversation with a New York music biz veteran who used to manage Mountain. Now he manages one of the top reggae acts in the world, one with records out in the USA, and he is down here trying to sign Peter Tosh, one of Bob Marley's ex-Wailers and writer-singer of the currently big, banned Jamaican hit "Legalize It (And I'll Advertise It)." My New York vet laughs and says: "This is the only fuckin' place I know where the rooster crows while I'm eating lunch. It's the only place I've been where you can buy a 14-karat gold bracelet for ten bucks off a guy in the hotel parking lot, and when you look inside 'karat' is misspelled. I've been here a fuckin' week, waitin' for one tape from Peter Tosh."

"Why didn't you just go get it from him?"

"He never got around to making a copy yet."

"You mean he has it? Then why don't you borrow it from him and make a copy yourself?"

"Well, you see, when you go to the studios, the engineers may or may not be there, and if they are there they may or may not get around to doing this or that. . . . Also Tosh wouldn't talk to the guy from *Time* magazine who wanted to interview him. Too establishment." He laughs again. (I later found out that Tosh did, eventually, speak to the *Time* writer.) As the subject turns to the reggae artist my friend already manages, he says that his charge "can't write very well. When he has to sign his name, he does it so slowly that it's embarrassing."

"Why don't you just tell him to get a rubber stamp?"

"I thought of that. He just tries to avoid having to sign autographs. As far as all the business stuff, of course, it's totally left to me."

"That must be quite a responsibility."

"You're not kidding. He can't sign a contract, but I imagine he gets around to signing the royalty checks when they come."

I believe I just saw, in the tropics yet, the tip of an iceberg.

/// \\\

Dusk. Swank and Stephen Davis, a journalist who is doing a book on Jamaica, are finally getting their interview with Marley, and have asked me to come along. I would just as soon get it out of the way. There is very much the feel that it is an audience, and everyone is anticipating a difficult time with some cat who might well figure himself the Lion of Judah. Wooly drives us there, and we wait by the car as he goes in Bob's house to check out the vibes. The house itself is a rambling ramshackle affair, a sturdy and capacious abode particularly by Jamaican standards yet looking curiously as if someone began a remodeling job three years ago and never got around to finishing it: pieces of the roof are literally falling out, and there are stacks of wood in back that serve no discernible purpose.

When Bob finally does appear, there is a sense of immediate relief: a slim, barefoot, medium-short, intense-countenanced man, he nevertheless projects an amiability that contradicts his reputation. As well he should: this guy is being billed, implicitly, as some sort of Noble Savage, a Jamaican cosmic revolutionary, and yet the truth is that while he was born in Jamaica he spent two years of his life in Wilmington, Delaware, where his mother still lives, and his father was a white lieutenant in the British armed services. Even though it is getting dark now, there is some feeling in the air that it would be uncool to do the interview(s) inside Bob's house, so first he leads us out to a corner of his front yard by the fence. I explain to him that this is no good, because the fence is by the street, and the noise of the passing cars will obscure our voices on the tapes. Which will be complicated already by the fact that like most Jamaicans and all Rastas, Bob talks in the indigenous patois that is so thick that *The Harder They Come* may well have been the first English-language movie in history to require subtitles in the United States. Of course, he could moderate the sometimes nigh-impenetrable patois enough to facilitate greater understanding, as many other Jamaicans that I met during my stay, from record producers to cab drivers, did—but then he would not be so apparently the most prominent media front man for the Rasta Revolution. So what he does instead is speak more slowly than your average Rasta, and pause occasionally to ask us if we understand. I don't remember any of us ever saying no, even though we all agreed later that there were parts of Bob's spiel that went right by us.

We took a short trek across the lawn into Bob's backyard, where he perched on the hood of his blue BMW, leaned back against the windscreen spliff in hand, and answered all our questions between laying down the gospel of Rastafari. Often there would be spaces between his statements, grand cumulous cannabinol ellipses, but all was cool. We three journalists massed our tape recorders together on the hood in front of Bob, and stood in a semicircle by the bumper, there being no place for us to sit, all of which helped to emphasize the sensation of gently ironic ethnocollision. Bob laughed often, dodged sticky questions like an old media hand, and in general maintained himself admirably for somebody who was probably stoned out of his fucking mind, as various other Rastas wandered out to lean on the car and listen in the gathering dark.

Stephen Davis began on mildly shaky ground, asking Bob if he felt any pressure since a lot of Jamaican musicians were waiting for his success to pave the way for reggae to make it big in the outside world. Bob laughed. "I never feel the pressure that much. But theah dat, is dat the reason for? . . . I never knoow . . ." He laughed again, and began to expound upon what he did know most intimately: "I have a message and I wan' to get it across . . . tha' message is . . . to live . . . y'know . . . like evrabody believe in life an' death . . . anyone can live . . . as a *Rasta*-man . . . so . . . dat is all . . . I come as a *Rasta*-man now . . . so my message call da worl' Rastafari . . ."

"Would you like to see white kids in the U.S. with dreadlocks?" I asked.

"Yeahmon!" He laughed. "Sure! . . . y'see . . . righteousness shall cover d'earth like da water cover d'sea . . . y'unnarstan . . . so . . . as far as we can go . . . we gonna live right . . . we're all jus' children on d'earth . . . but all mind—wiggy-woggy . . ."

"What do the Rastas think is going to happen in Jamaica?"

"Yehmon . . . yehmon, whoever over here has come, Rasta man mus' go over to Africa . . ."

"Will Rasta man settle for making Jamaica more like Africa and staying here?"

"No, no one settle for Jamaica . . . we like Jamaica, y'know, but—Jamaica spoiled . . . in a sense a Rasta man is concerned a history of Jamaica it has prophesy you know is something no one can change. Jus' like if you have an egg an' break, no one can put it together again—Jamaica is like dat. Something a must happen in creation, dat we from da wes', go back to da eas' . . . Jamaica canna fix I&I, Rasta man. The only way Jamaica can be fix is we bow to the colonial type a thing what dem 'bout . . ."

"Are you as disappointed," wondered Stephen Davis, not quite getting the point yet, "with the current government as a lot of other Rastas seem to be in discussions I've had with them?"

"*Well!* The present government—past, present—only one government me love: the government of Rastafari. Ca'I know it, we don' live in dem guys' a-things, y'know, we live outside it. Come like a bird—we gon' check out certain things, because we know what is going on, we know dat the rule don' come down from uptown, some a those guys a kick up hell mon, a nothing a goin' on . . ."

"Are you concerned with changing government here in Jamaica, if Rastas don't vote?" asked Swank.

"This thing'll never change, mon. Y'see da beauty 'bout it, 'bout Jamaica, is dat we come from Africa, and none of the leaders they want to accept dat. All 'em wan' call it Jamaicans, and we not Jamaicans. They all live a thing, you mus' say an die here." Will the last person leaving Jamaica please turn out the lights.

"How many people do you think would go back to Africa if they gave them what they wanted?" nervously pressed Swank.

"Well, watch me. Today is not the day, mon, but 144,000, plus a multitude followed."

"What will be the Rasta reaction if there's a lot of violence?"

"Dem guys not dealing with twelve tribes of Israel. We not talking about govanment now, govanment wrong, we talking 'bout de twelve tribes of Israel. We wan' the unity and the only unity we can get is troo Rasta. And the only way we can get the message troo right now is troo reggae."

Swank tried to bring it down to business: "Since Chris Blackwell has come down with Island Records, he seems to be someone who can communicate very well with you . . . and uh the rest of the people making the music. But CBS records, the big companies in America are catching wind of reggae and starting to come down, what do you see happening in that situation, big people from Babylon coming to exploit the music?"

"It happen faster. Jus' make the people, help to realize what is happnin', quickah. Canna stop it. Because it's not for the money, yoknow, and da big company, and a money, it's soon ovah. Because if weah brothahs da money is nothing between us." Right, and all Bob Dylan started out wanting was some couches and motorcycles. Marley did, however, have some advice for fledgling reggae musicians: "You have to be careful, ca you can get tricked, out deah. People have rob me, y'know, but once you can see dat dis is what happen, I know or I see dat dis happnin', den dat trick don' go on, y'know." He laughed. "You make record an' sell it, don' get no royalties in Jamaica for long time . . . Lak Trojan Records rob me, mon! All Trojans robbers, mon, all dem English companies jus' take Wes' Indian music."

Stephen Davis observed that it seemed that you never heard reggae on the radio in Jamaica. "Because," testified Bob, "da music is da type o' thing would show up the situation in Jamaica dat some people don' like to hear the real trut', y'know. So dem not sayin' what really happnin' down heah. But when dem don' play it on da radio, man, de people 'ave it in dem house. Goin' dance an' hear it. Radio is important, but once de music come out and dem don' wan' play on d'radio, den big promotion is dat once it's banned evrabody wants ta hear it!" He laughed again.

"But," insisted Swank, "didn't Manley promise that he wasn't gonna ban songs?"

Bob just smiled. "I dunno abouat, mon . . . Manley can' stop prophesy . . . prophesy well 'ave its coorse . . ." Someone questioned him about the Rastas' reputation for nonviolence, and Bob surprised us all with, "No, Rastas physical. Y'know whai mean, we don' come lak no sheep to da slaughta . . ."

"Like wan time," added a Rasta who had been leaning over the hood of the car, listening. It had gotten so dark that I could barely see Marley's face, and this other guy's dreadlocks looked like a tarantula crawling down his forehead.

"Like wan time," said Bob. "We don' ovalook war."

"With the situation in Kingston now, do you ever fear for your personal safety?" asked Davis.

"Nossah," said Bob. "No mon, me no fraid for them. I mean, if can avoid dem, will avoid dem, goin' down street, see a roadblock, and dere is a street for me to turn off before I reach da roadblock, you bet I'm gon' to turn off! It's no good I ever get searched."

"Ever been in jail?" I wondered. It was a stock question, actually.

"Yeh, wan time."

"For what?"

He took a long toke. "Drivin' witout license." And laughed. So did we all, but then Swank took the offensive once more. "Do you feel that this car represents Babylon?"

Bob seemed genuinely surprised. "The car? *System* represent Babylon, system represent death, we livin' in da system—"

"I was just wondering how you could feel you could have this, while—"

"Is no have dis, mon," replied Bob simply, and knocked on the hood of the car. We had been told the day before by Wooly that Bob had said the BMW stood for Bob Marley & the Wailers, so Swank offered this out somewhat sarcastically, and Bob came back, good natured as ever, with an even worse joke: "British Made . . . Warcar . . ."

I tried to smooth things over, in my own bumbling liberal way. "So then this car belongs to all your brothers and sisters as well as you?"

"Belongs road, mon!"

Davis asked Bob what he thought about people coming down to ask all these questions. "Well," said Bob, "as long as dem get da right understanding of da answers and write it . . . because plenty time, plenty guys just write for kicks, y'know, like jus' turn in a joke ting is goin' on, an is serious ting . . ."

Marley was not amused by a certain recent interview in which a writer from New York asked him such question as "Where did you get your jeans?" and "When you were in New York, did you go shopping at Bloomingdale's?"

Still, he did not seem such a solemn fellow when all was said and done, so I asked him, referring to an old Jamaican motor sport, whether he had ever rammed a goat in this car. There was much laughter all around, after which he explained, "No no no, don' think dat, man, people need live good purpose man . . . when you see a goat, you are supposed to stop, communicate to de goat, and make de goat knows de outcome . . . a goat's smart, y'know . . . when you hit a goat, man, you sad!"

"Yes, Rasta," interjected the Rasta on the other side of the hood with the tarantula on his brow. Bob then explained that ramming a goat was considered unlucky. By now most of us were packing up our tape recorders, readying ourselves for the trek back to the Sheraton, but Swank struck for one more shot at social relevance: "This is an election year, isn't it, coming up?"

Bob took a long hit on his spliff. "Yeah? Dat so?"

The Rasta with the tarantula clarified: "You can't serve two masters wan time, y'know." Another, feistier member of the brethren behind him decided to take Swank on: "Do you know about da twelve tribes of Israel?"

This, for Swank, was the last straw. "Of course I do—I'm Jewish!"

"Oh yah? What tribe you belong?"

"Well, uh, I'm not exactly sure—"

"Yah? Then how you know you member twelve tribes?"

"Because my *father* told me!"

"Your father???!!!" The Rasta thought, apparently, that Swank was referring to his Father in Heaven.

"Yeah, my father and my mother!"

"Oh, you *parents!*"

"Yeah!"

"You read tha 'Oly Bible?"

"Of *course!*"

"All da way troo?" This guy was obviously not going to be easily convinced; from the beginning, several of those in attendance had been observably suspicious of the motives of these white foreigners with tape recorders. Marley just sat back smoking and laughing. Swank, who in his life had been known to take amphetamines for his weight and est for his personality, was getting frazzled, finally allowing himself to get truly combative after having to wait on Marley and suffer evasive answers. "Yeah, I read it all the way through!"

"How long it take you?" demanded the Rasta.

"Whattaya mean, how long—it was a long time ago!"

Triumph: "You read wan chapter a day, you can read da whole Bible in tree an' a half years!"

Swank backed off enough to see the discretion of not countering with a "So what?" In fact, he didn't have much of anything to say at all, just now, and the Rasta leaped into the breach, accusing him of not really being a member of the twelve tribes of Israel, since he didn't even know which one he belonged to. They argued a bit, and Swank eventually allowed as how it was quite probable that he belonged to the tribe of Levi. I think at that moment he would have practically sworn an affidavit to that effect. So now he could slip out of further wranglings, Bob could go in his house for supper, and the Second and Third Worlds could, for this one evening at least, part gracefully and with a nice buzz on.

/// \\\

Thursday. I am in a cab with John Martyn, bombing through the streets of Kingston on the way to Strawberry Hill. John is an English songwriter who is planning to record part of his next album in Jamaica, but right now we are on our way to a Burning Spear recording session where he is going to do some guitar overdubs. First, however, we have to drive up to Strawberry Hill to pick up the guitar at Chris Blackwell's hilltop estate. The road is long, narrow and whip-winding, with perilous curves and steep drops off the shoulder, but the country around it is beautiful, lavish with brilliant green and yellow. It's a welcome respite, and the only time I will see anything close to still-existing primal Jamaica during my stay. On the way up Martyn points out to me the palatial estate of Blackwell's parents, who made millions of dollars in decades of colonial enterprise in Jamaica. On the way back down we meet, pedaling uphill on a rusty bicycle as if floating, a friend of Martyn's named Country Man. Country Man is a Rasta with university education, gifted, articulate, and imbued with enough of the unimpeachably mystical that even a cynic like Martyn (who beats your reporter) believes the accounts of him levitating on occasion. Country Man lives by swimming or rowing far off the coast into the Caribbean, holding onto a rock among the Keys with one arm, and grabbing fish as they swim by. The best story about Country Man is that his wife complained once because he would go off on such expeditions for three days at a time leaving her alone; she wanted, she said, a radio for company. So Country Man sold their house, used the money to buy her a radio, and built a new house the same day.

When we arrive at the Spear session we discover, naturally enough, that we are the first people to show up even though we are over an hour late. So we take a walk around the corner, a risky proposition for whites in downtown Kingston at any time of the day, and have a couple of drinks in a black bar where sullen youth are playing billiards. I feel only minor drafts. An old man comes up and asks me where I come from, and expresses a sentiment I would hear from a few other, mostly older Jamaicans during my stay: "Many people say bad things about Jamaica, that is violence, bad place to live. This is not true. You know, there's an old saying: believe only half of what you see—"

"And none of what you hear." I finished.

He nodded and smiled. "Right."

We go back to the session, which is taking place in Randy's Studio, which naturally enough is right over Randy's Record Shop, which may be the best store in Jamaica and is the first place you should go if you have a shopping list—Randy stocks records by everybody, not just the output of his studio and star producer, Jack Ruby, who is himself a bit of a legend. Ruby, who has also worked as a hotel waiter, started producing two and a half years ago and his biggest success to date has been with Burning Spear, a vocal trio straight out of the hills whose U.S.-released album, *Marcus Garvey*, epitomizes the more purely African wing of reggae. There is something almost aboriginal about Burning Spear—Winston Rodney walks up to the mike and begins to sing a new song about living in the hills, Rupert Willington and Delroy Hines harmonizing behind him, and there is a haunting plaintiveness in his voice as he sings of his brother going to the river to get the water for his family. As he tells this seemingly simple story, the dozen or so black youths milling about in the control room, friends of the producer and band, laugh and comment to each other approvingly. The reason they are doing this is that many of them have probably experienced what Rodney is singing about—spending a whole day going back and forth to the nearest river, which may be a distance of miles, with a bucket on your head, until the drum or barrel which is the family's only water supply is full. In the middle of the song Rodney sings "These are the sounds of the hills," and begins making bird calls and animal sounds. Martin Denny it isn't. Later Martyn, who has been warming up with some obviously overbusy Eric Clapton runs, will add a few spare, sustained-note and wah wah lines which fill out the track perfectly, especially when he plays an intentionally "wrong" note which in its strange offness somehow is exactly right for Burning Spear, whose sound always remains primal no matter how arranged.

Perhaps most fascinating is that all this goes on with seemingly little direction from producer Ruby. He watches Spear sing awhile, then, *in the middle of a take,* leaves the control board to chat with the visitors and other musicians hanging around the studio, lounging later across the board to read a copy of *Newsweek* I'd brought; then, intermittently, he would unexpectedly snap up from reading or conversation, shout "Spear!" stop the take and bolt into the studio to tell them to bring this up, take that down, change the thing around till the sound is right and tight. All this is in such contrast to conditions in American studios, where not a pin can drop in the control room during a take and there is a red light outside the door barring visitors (who come and go freely in Randy's) when the tape is rolling, that it is mind-blowing. In the midst of such seeming casualness, people talking, joking and rolling endless spliffs everywhere, there is enormous interior discipline; Ruby, while reading *Newsweek* with seeming indifference, is listening intently and in iron control all the way. I mentioned this to him, and he replied "Of course. I always know the sound I want, and I always get it." He also got two completed takes in one afternoon, which racks up pretty well against the output of any New York producer or studio, for all their comparative uptightness.

Toward the end of the session, the writer and photographer from *Time* arrive to interview Ruby, and later Martyn and I catch a ride back to the Sheraton with them. By now it is nine o'clock at night, not at all a safe time for whites, even in numbers, to be on the streets of Kingston. It is *never* safe for whites to go into Trenchtown. But now the *Time* photog is pointing at the myriad small, brightly lit black rum bars we pass, saying "C'mon, what the fuck, man, I could use a beer, let's just go in." Martyn and I cower in the back, laughing but praying these guys will not stop. Meanwhile, *Time*'s scribe is saying, "I've *got* to figure out a way to get into Trenchtown . . ." I tell him to forget it, and he replies that he's been thinking maybe around five in the morning would be a safe time.

We arrive back at the hotel in a driving rain, running past the poolside bar where under the roof Canadian tourists are singing "Granada" to organ music almost as loud as the speakers in the record stores.

I could use a little bit of cross-cultural relaxation myself. I retire to my room where I watch *Hawaii Five-O* and an old Universal Grade D musical about singing soldiers from the late Thirties, on the TV I had to order when I first checked in. Jamaican TV is weird—there's only one TV network, JBC, which turns up on several channels with things like "An Evening with the Jay-Teens," an hour of young black girls doing folk dances from various cultures against a blank backdrop. (There was no announcer, they looked like a high school dance recital, and moved as stiffly as one through all the corny choreography except when it came time to do African dances, which they performed, of course, fantastically.) The first thing I saw when I turned on my TV on Tuesday morning was a woman demonstrating the use of a steam iron with stilted delivery: "This we use to wash and iron clothes, to keep ourselves clean and our people healthy. . . ." Commercials for condoms and birth control pills also run regularly. Every afternoon the station goes off for several hours, leaving a test pattern and radio station playing the usual American pap. The rest of the programming is equally weird and scattered, featuring things like *Bachelor Father, The Six Million Dollar Man* (8:45 on Friday night—some shows come on at times like 6:02, right after headline news) and *Sesame Street,* which seems to be a big favorite. I got to watch, since there was nothing else, the singing-soldiers movies for two nights in a row, leading me into dark speculations about propaganda which were probably paranoid.

/// \\\

Friday. After breakfast I go for a walk around the block immediately adjacent to the hotel, and look into faces radiating undisguised hatred. When I stop a youth and ask him for directions to a local record store, he answers grudgingly in a patois I can't understand anyway. I have not stopped being uptight in the almost four days I have been here, and feel a strong yearning to get the hell out of the fucking place.

Back at the hotel, I run into Chris Blackwell by the pool, and he invites me to visit a couple of recording studios with him. Blackwell himself exudes an air at once sanguine and blasé—he came from money, now he's making more money, and everything about him indicates that the good life agrees with him. Sandy hair, brilliant tan that reminded me of many I'd seen in Hollywood, the kind of person who looks so healthy it's almost obscene, *too* healthy. Or maybe it is merely endemic to record industry people, this air of bland hedonism. In any case, Blackwell always looks as if he is either on his way to or from a tennis court. Now we are in a limousine, riding out to the home studios of Lee Perry and King Tubby, who live in relatively affluent sections of Kingston; these guys are two of the biggest producers on the island. Their houses look like American working-class homes circa 1954. At Tubby's I watch an engineer mastering a dub, and get to meet

Vivian "Yabby" Jackson, leader (& producer) of a group called the Prophets, whose album, *Conquering Lion,* was recorded at Harry J.'s studio across town and mixed here; I have just bought a copy of the album at Micron Records (not coincidentally, the store and label bear the same name) for five bucks, and show it to him. Then I lean over and shout in his ear over the booming dub beat: "How much money did you get for making this?"

"Nothing yet," he says.

Out in Tubby's back yard, I meet U Roy, who is not I Roy, and whose album, *Dread in a Babylon,* has just been picked up by Virgin Records in the U.K. We shake hands, and I tell him how much I like his record. I do not tell him that I thought on the first cut, "Runaway Girl," his vocal sounded much like Mick Jagger circa *Aftermath.* It is interesting to note that on the album cover he looks like some ragged shaman, squatting on the ground almost hidden behind a giant cloud of ganja smoke, dreadlocks spearing out in every direction. Now, in person, he is dressed in a beret, red sweater, and brown slacks. He puts a record on a turntable and the unmistakable, cannonade-in-a-cavern sound of dub thunders from two giant speakers set up in the dirt in Tubby's backyard. A little kid dances in front of one of the speakers, on which "Tubby" is spelled in Chinese-style lettering, pressing his ass against the speaker cloth, getting off on the vibrations, looking at me and laughing. The record playing consists of a deep rumble of Echoplexed drums, out of which, every so often an Echoplexed and perhaps reverbed male voice (which I will later discover belongs to Big Youth, one of the most venerable dub artists) hollers, "What the world needs now, is love, sweet love . . ." I blink. Blackwell laughs: "I wonder what Burt Bacharach would think of this." I suggest that Blackwell bring him down here and show it to him. One thing seems certain—old Burt is not going to get any royalties on this one. Not that he needs them. I think for a moment that perhaps there is a certain democracy in the ripoffs permeating Jamaican music, dismiss that as a dangerous notion, and start babbling to Blackwell about "folk technology." We agree that dub is fascinating, but neither of us has any idea what to do with it. Which is perhaps as it should be. The young blacks sitting around smoking spliffs and listening to this record at the customary earsplitting volume ignore us, except for one who, later in the studio, introduces himself as Clinton Williams and beckons me outside, where he hands me a piece of paper, which looks like a blank invoice, upon which is printed "The Golden-Age Furnishing Co.," along with a phone number. Williams has written his name on one of the lines, and this serves as his card. He tells me he is doing some independent producing in Kingston, has in fact produced five records, and has been a contender for the amateur lightweight boxing championship of Jamaica. I ask him how he finds time both to box and produce records, not bothering to mention that the number he has asked me to call him at seems to be that of a furniture store. He tells me that he wants to become a big-time producer, that the competition is fierce, and that established figures like Tubby and Scratch Perry pretty much have a monopoly on the scene, making it extremely difficult for a young cat to break in. Which sounds a lot like the States, actually. I press him on boxing vs. production; I mean, which is the sideline? He finally laughs. "Boxing." I ask him if he can give me a percentage breakdown on record profits as split between artists, producers and record store owners. Sure, he says. "Usually, about sixty percent goes to the store, thirty percent to the producer, and ten percent to the singer. But sometimes the producers and stores get forty-five percent each."

Back in the limousine and over to Lee Perry's. Perry is a big man in the island's music scene; he produced Bob Marley's early (and superior) sides, and his current star artist is Max Romeo, with "War in a Babylon" by Max Romeo and the Upsetters a hot item in both Jamaica and England. "The Upsetter" is one of Perry's aliases, and it is a measure of what stars producers are in Jamaica that the clerk in Aquarius had showed me an album called *King Tubby Vs. The Upsetter*, a kind of dueling-control-boards, mock-championship-match soundtrack consisting entirely of instrumental dub violence fit to shatter your eardrums. In Perry's studio, behind his house, he is a little potentate, mixing and playing back his tapes for a steady stream of admirers who stand in herb awe as he dances around his control board, changing levels and flicking switches or whirling dials with a flourish and a knowing smile of infinite humor. I can't say exactly how or why, but merely to meet and watch him work for a few minutes is to be irrevocably impressed, to know you are in the presence of genius. The décor of his studio is also instructive: blacklight posters and big color pictures of Bruce Lee (who is a big hero on the island, because guns are banned and he fights with his fists) over walls and ceiling fitted out with an interplay of bright red and green carpeting, which I found out later are, with gold, the colors in the flag of Ethiopia.

But this guy was no Rasta, no matter what he or anybody else says. This was an uptown cat. A hipster. With his hair slicked straight back, his graying beard, strutting around cocky and amused, a diminutive lion in his kingdom, he at length danced over to the corner where I was trying to be inconspicuous, squeezed past me, grabbed a bottle and, straightening up, stopped a second to look me in the eyes close as the air, smiling knowingly, and I smiled back. A few minutes later he walked up to me and said, "You wine man," and handed me a plastic cup and a bottle of something called Winecarnes, which is a local wine fortified with meat extracts that he seemingly drinks all day without ever losing his stride.

Now, dear reader, I know that this—one drunk recognizing another—is not the most profound or miraculous occurrence in the world, but here, in the middle of Herb Heaven, with every righteous Rasta and American hiplet in sight belittling the rum culture like it was 1967 all over again, it qualified as outright mind reading.

As we were leaving Perry's, walking down the driveway to the limousine, I heard a familiar sound and peeked for a moment inside the open door to the living room of his house. There, on the couch, his kids were watching a Road Runner cartoon on TV.

Back at the hotel, I made arrangements to meet Blackwell for dinner. By the pool I met my colleague from *Rolling Stone,* and over drinks Blackwell asked him what angle he was going to approach his story from. "Oh, I dunno, man," he replied, with no idea who he was talking to, "I'm just gonna use the gonzo approach for this one pretty much. I intend to do my whole story from the poolside bar and go out of the hotel as little as possible. I mean, who gives a fuck, y'know? I'm just in this for the free drinks and to see if I can get laid."

Blackwell looked a little green around the eyeballs, but went on to ask Gonzo what he thought of reggae.

"I can't remember ever hearing any. The last album I really got into was *The Allman Brothers Live at Fillmore East.* Hell, man, I don't even have a record player!"

Blackwell's jaw dropped.

Later at dinner, Blackwell is still staring sourly at Gonzo, who is raving at Michael Butler, a receding face behind a gray Van Dyke who was the producer of *Hair* and is down here getting ready to put together a reggae *Hair* with the projected title of *Babylon.* Don Taylor, Marley's manager, a thin, light-skinned black man in a Toots and the Maytals cap, is telling me and the man from *Melody Maker* that many American blacks resent Jamaican immigrants because, he says, the latter tend to hustle harder and achieve more. He cites his mother, who he says worked at menial jobs but wound up owning her own apartment house, then: "It's just like Bob. He is very dedicated to his music, but when it comes to his money, he is not going to let anyone cheat him out of any portion of his equal share."

Right. No good businessman would. A phrase often used by Rastas and heard in many reggae songs is "I and I." It can mean me, you, we, etc., all balled up in one great big cosmic loving mulch; the old "I am he as you are me as you are we as we are all together" routine. But when push comes to shove . . . well, as John Martyn laughingly put it, "I and I means me so fuck you!" Which may not be exactly what Burning Spear meant when they sang "Give me what is mine," but what the hell—I mean, we're all 20th Century folk here, right?

/// \\\

Saturday. Gonzo and I spend the day getting drunk and smoking dope in his room, reading *Rolling Stone* and *The Village Voice* and listening to the reggae which, for some unaccountable reason, is coming out of the radio. Wooly calls up to see how we're doing, and we tell him we've become Rastas and ask to borrow his cassette recorder so we can listen to Iggy tapes.

That night we are down at the bar when the photog from *Time* shows up and asks us if we want to go to some discos with him. I say sure; Gonzo stays at the bar. This shutterbug and I then drive up to Beverly Hills, the rich folks' ghetto of Kingston, to pick up Clive, son of Randy, who is going to show us where the kids dance in this town. We pass blocks of beautiful houses with sculpted lawns, and the one where the owner of Randy's Records lives is no different from the rest. Clive tells us, in fact, that their next-door neighbor is the French ambassador to Jamaica. A comparison of this picture with Perry's and Tubby's homes seems to confirm Clinton Williams' figures, and I begin to wonder what Burning Spear's house looks like. As for the discos, they look just like American discos: the floor lights up, couples dance to American soul records. The photographer keeps saying he wants more *roots,* and Clive just shrugs, so I translate: "What we're looking for is one of these places with a deejay sitting up there playing dub records and hollering into the microphone while all the guys in the crowd stand around smoking herb and vibrating."

"Oh, those," says Clive. "Not so easy to find now. They never held those like, you know, regular thing. And every time they did, seem like a gunman would show up and start firing. So now they are not allowed."

So much for discos. I suddenly notice that Clive has been taking swigs out of a half-pint bottle of his own. "What's that?" I ask him.

"Roots." He hands it to me, emphasizing that it does not contain what the label says: no rum culture here. I take a swig—liquid cannabis root extract, mixed with something else unmistakable. "There's *wine* in here!"

He smiles slightly. "Yes. A little." And takes the bottle back and pours himself another drink.

After the *Time* man and I take him home, we are driving down a street in a residential district when suddenly we hear a sound like firecrackers; it's pistol shots, and we see people running out of a bar ahead of us on the left, scattering in every direction. The *Time* guy slows down, and I begin to freak. "C'mon, man, let's get the fuck *out* of here! C'mon, turn that corner!" He had almost stopped. I guess he hoped to get an exclusive shot of authentic Jamaican street violence, which I guess is good journalistic instincts. Me, I was more interested in my own skin.

Then again, it may be that the streets of Kingston are, actually, comparatively safe for a honky next to those of Harlem or inner-city Detroit. When we stopped a few minutes later at a MacDonald's (no relation to the American chain) for some curried goat, the steering wheel on my friend's car locked and he couldn't get it started for about 20 minutes. Nobody hassled us; all we got were some black people in a minibus next to us who asked what was wrong and tried to help us get going again. Then again, the bus did say "UNICEF" on the driver's door.

/// \\\

Sunday. This is supposed to be a big day, because we have been told that there is going to be a Grounation, which I can only interpret from the rather vague explanations as some kind of Rasta raveup, which we have been invited to observe. It seems dubious to me that the Rastas would want a bunch of white folk from the United States and Britain sitting in the bleachers gawking at their annual convention, but I am anxious to check this out nevertheless. We are told that it will run from early in the evening until about 1 A.M., and I am already wondering how we can gracefully excuse ourselves around, say, 9:30 if it gets boring. I mean, I'm all for Lowell Thomas, but seven or eight straight hours of the gospel of Rastafari, which the guys in Marley's backyard had already proved every Rasta is ready to testify upon vehemently and at length with little or no provocation, did seem a bit much. Gonzo and I spend the afternoon drinking Bloody Marys by the pool; we have decided to start the booze wing of Rasta and spread the truths of that to the unenlightened, hoping for an eventual migration of all the enlightened back to Seagram's distillery in Waterloo, Ontario. Wooly and photographer Peter Simon, brother of Carly ("I'm Peter Simon, Carly's brother," was how he shook hands with Gonzo) just keep staring at us and shaking their heads as we tell them that the wisdom-inducing properties of Hops are at least equivalent to those of Herb. One thing is for sure: there will not be a bar at the Grounation.

Of course, in Jamaica not even Grounations can come off on time—it's my guess they might be sacrilegious if they did, so we wait well into the evening by the pool with Tom Hayes, an Island employee who, I have been told, is responsible for much of the label's business dealings with artists. So I ask him: "How much does a group like Burning Spear get from Island as an advance?"

"You should ask them that," he replied. "I don't think it would be ethical for me to tell you." He pointed at Gonzo. "That would be like me asking him how much you make; don't you see the unfairness of that?" Then, turning to Gonzo: "Ready for another Heineken's?" And gets up and splits for the bar to buy us a round of drinks.

Later, we're finally ready to go to the Grounation, and when the Rastas are ready for us it seems we've momentarily lost Gonzo, who is flying in the face of experience (namely his burn upon arrival) by trying again to cop dope, I mean herb, from the guy in the hotel parking lot. When he gets in the car, I ask him, "What the fuck is the matter with you? We're going to a *Grounation,* a *festival* of Rastafarians, don't you realize there's going to be more dope there than you could smoke in three lifetimes?"

"I know," he says, "but I gotta have some for later when we get back to the hotel and to get me through my flight back to New York tomorrow. I'm addicted to the shit!"

A few minutes later, Wooly and I somehow get onto the subject of Rasta sexuality. "The Rastas are not a particularly sexual people," he says, adding that "I've never seen one come on to a chick."

"Oh, really? What do you think would be the factors in that?" I had noticed that Jamaican men did seem to believe in keeping the woman home tending to the babies—you seldom saw them in record shops, for instance—although it is well known that the Rasta men do a lot of cooking and will not let the women prepare the food when they are menstruating. In fact, Jamaican men seem to have a whole fixation on the subject of the menstruation cycle—the most popular swear words are "bloodclot" and "bummaclot pussyclot," which are the worst things you can call somebody.

"I think it goes back," answers Wooly, "to the thing you see in lots of primitive societies: the belief that women are polluted, somehow identified with the forces of darkness, like witches. . . ."

"I bet I know why they don't care if they fuck or not," interjects Gonzo. "Because they're too *stoned* all the time! Hell, man, I've smoked so much dope before I didn't give a fuck about pussy."

Wooly begins to get defensive—Jesus, man, don't call the Rastas *eunuchs*—and brings up Marley's four wives and numerous children before dropping the subject like a set of barbells even though I want to pursue it further.

The seven of us—Wooly, Gonzo, Peter Simon, his collaborator Stephen Davis, Tom Hayes, me and a Rasta named Killy who is taking us—ride to the Grounation in two cars. I jump in the Volkswagen Killy is driving and begin asking him if he doesn't think this white media influx might dilute the purity of Rasta ritual. He has long thin dreadlocks running streamers past his shoulders, and is wearing a T-shirt I had seen on Wooly and others this week that says "ROOTS" with picture of same on the front and commemorates Burning Spear's recent gig at the Chela Bay hotel just outside Ocho Rios on the back. I have already been told by Wooly that Killy is not being paid by Island for services like this, so I wonder what his motivation must be. He gives me the standard Rasta sermon, adds that the Rastas want to spread their truths and rights to all the world and this is one way to do it, then gets into something about how "money is energy." Meanwhile, we have stopped off on a side street in a rundown neighborhood that is still middle-class by Kingston standards, where Killy cops some dope for Gonzo, who makes the mistake of not asking for it immediately.

Then we drive off the main boulevards into an area of rusty pothole streets winding around a lot of shacks in the classic mold—corrugated tin, clay, scrap wood and metal, cardboard, windows that cannot be closed and doors with ragged curtains for privacy, into the heart of Poverty Row. And this isn't even Trenchtown, is in fact far better—this is a section called Olympic Gardens, but it doesn't look like any garden. It looks like a slum, because that is what it is, and I doubt if sharecropper shacks in the American South a hundred years ago had much on the housing here. We finally stopped along one lane, got out of the cars and walked up to a small building out of which the least commercialized form of reggae was blasting. Black people were standing all around the outside, and the inside seemed to be jammed, but I peered over neighbors leaning against the wall into a window and saw a stage small enough to fit inside one end of a building about as big as the average middle-class American child's bedroom. On the stage there was a table, and on the table a white cloth, burning candle, pot of red flowers, Bible, and smaller, tattered book which I presumed was a hymnal. Forming a half circle around and behind the table were a group called Ras Michael and the Sons of Negus, who have two albums out in Jamaica: a Chinese-looking organist and drummer, a bassist in the corner by the back door, lead guitarist, primitive amps, and in the middle Ras Michael, a tall thin man in wool cap and striped sweater singing with ecclesiastical intensity into a microphone. In front of him was another half-circle of musicians sitting in chairs and on the edge of the stage, eight pairs of hands beating on congas and drums more primitive. In front of them about a half dozen rows of benches which seemed mainly to be filled with little children, though there were women and older people there too. Directly across from the window where I stood I saw, in another window with his back to the street, the mild stringy-bearded face of Peter Simon, bouncing slightly and smiling as if bedazzled. It looked like a good way to get a knife in the ribs.

In a few minutes a space was found for us inside and we were led around to the front of this seeming chapel, through a door and down to the very front, where Gonzo and I were seated amongst a bevy of little black kids who stared at us with a mixture of shyness, fear, and laughter. I made a face at one staring at me and she dissolved in giggles. I was not so sure that the same thing would be a wise course of action for me to take, so whenever Gonzo said something funny to me I would stifle my laughter, which naturally had the effect of stifling laughter at the dinner table when you are a child—all those repressed chuckles just kept bubbling ferociously inside, burning to get out in howls while I kept translating them into stoned, beatific smiles as I swayed to the music. It was not that there was anything funny about the situation; I was merely nervous. Or rather, *these* people and this music was not funny—*we* were funny, our presence here was funny, or was something else more easily accepted as funny, and by the time Gonzo got around to screaming in my ear that "This is better than Thelonious Monk at the Five Spot! I see the light, Lester, I've got religion! And don't ever forget that we could lose our lives at any minute!" I just had to laugh out loud.

Luckily, it was swallowed by the music, which was amazing, or seemed so under the circumstances. Ras Michael sang songs like

"None a Jah Jah Children No Cry," "In Zion," and "Glory Dawn," alternating cooking reggae with gospel chants as the drummers smoked spliff after spliff, some of them sitting there in total trance never removing the things from their mouths, sucking the smoke like air, cooking up an enormously complex rhythm conversation which was pure Africa. Killy had sat down at one of the congas, lit up two spliffs, and handed them to me and Gonzo. I smoked and tried to lose myself in the rhythm, as Ras Michael sang of flying away home to Zion and Gonzo screamed in my ear "Right! Right! Fly away home tomorrow!" One particularly driving chantlike number (number?) which sounded like a basal link between African reggae roots and Elvin Jones caught the whole room up and in that moment alone, perhaps, we all were united, flying through the rhythm. The end of each song was signalled by Ras Michael, who would intone loudly into the mike "Jah Rastafari!" to which the little children, women and men present would shout back "Rastafari!" I remember particularly one tot behind me, screaming "Migh-ty God!" It was like a cross between a Wednesday Night Prayer Meeting and a very local garage gig by a band which was itself the link between the tribal fires of prehistory, American black Revivalist Christianity, and rock 'n' roll electricity. The guitarist would get into riffs that occasionally suggested that he had been listening to Keith Richards, Duane Allman, maybe even Jerry Garcia, but this was a religious service and nobody clapped. Except Peter Simon, who kept leaning over and cooing in my ear, "Isn't this *great?* I just *love* it, don't you?" He had begun dancing in a manner that I can only compare to Joan Baez doing the Funky Chicken at the Big Sur Folk Festival, and little kids in front of him, shifting out of awesomely intricate boogaloos of their own, began laughingly to imitate him. He thought they were all getting together in One World brotherhood, laughed back and did what he was doing with more fervor; what he didn't see was that they were having a laugh over his performance with other children behind him. At the end of the set (set?) I saw him in the center aisle, palms together and head bowed in prayerful attitude. Meanwhile, the grass was wearing off, the bench was hard, and, as at many concerts, I was ready to go home before the music was over.

I don't mean to sound jaded. It had been intense, both musically and situationally; it was a capital-E experience, and, as Gonzo said, "Take a good look, Lester—this is as close as we're ever gonna get to Africa." But there was a pervasive irony to the Experience which could not be escaped. It was in seeing Peter Simon, after Ras Michael and the band had left the room as the hand-drummers and congregation kept shouting and chanting, mount the stage and stand there behind the table with the Bible and candle, smiling and clapping his hands as if leading the faithful.

And there was irony a few minutes later, as we were led out of the chapel into a space behind the house next door, where we were given herb soup ("As an offering," I was informed) and tokes off the chalice, a ceremonial, elaborately carved pipe. Ras Michael stood outside; I shook hands with him and told him, "I really dig your music, and I'm going to buy your album tomorrow." We both laughed, there may have been a moment of mutual recognition, and then he launched into the gospel of Rastafari, quoting extensively from the Bible and prophesying Armageddon. It was boring, and after a few minutes I edged politely away, after which it seemed each of our party took his turn at the same course, until Ras Michael got to Peter Simon, whose name he delighted in transposing into Simon Peter, laughing and shaking Simon's hand vigorously. (Upon this rock I will build my church in . . . *Martha's Vineyard?*) We all laughed at this, and a few minutes later I saw Peter Simon inside the house where the Rastas stood smoking herb and testifying to Jah. I could see him, through the smoke, first in the main room, then later coming out of another room in the back. I assumed at the time that that was the john and he had to use it, later realized that was ridiculous since it was almost certain that the only toilet anywhere around here was the ground. The rest of us stood around just inside the door of the house; it was a while before I realized that behind me, in the darkness, all the Rasta women were sitting in chairs or hammocks along the fence, silently watching as their children hopped around them and the men declaimed inside. The only woman I saw inside the house was one young brown-skinned girl about 20, sitting in a chair in a corner with a spliff in her hand upon which she occasionally took another hit; she was beautiful, as yet unbrutalized at least to the eye, but as she stared vacantly into space all the herb in the world could not have been cosmetic for the utter desolation that, in her silence, in her stillness, was radiated by her very youth and beauty.

Older Rastas from the neighborhood came wandering up to the house, some of them ragged, and I looked at them and then at Tom Hayes, who was wearing a pair of pants that probably cost $50, a Billy Preston T-shirt (I was in my Grand Funk) and a razor cut, and the irony turned to an absurdity so extreme it became a kind of obscenity. It was, at the very least, embarrassing, for me and for these people, and I seriously doubt if for all the talk of brotherhood of Rastafari there is anything beyond that embarrassment which they and I will ever be able to share. What I mean to say is I've been on lots of press junkets before, but this was the first one into Darkest Africa. What I meant to say is that a whole bunch of people were flown, all expenses paid, to Jamaica, so that we could look at these people, and go back and write stories which would help sell albums to white middle-class American kids who think it's romantic to be black and dirt-poor and hungry and illiterate and sick with things you can't name because you've never been to a doctor and sit around all day smoking ganja and beating on bongo drums because you have no other options in life. I know, because I am one of those kids, caught in the contradiction—hell, man, my current favorite group is Burning Spear. But I wouldn't want to organize a press party in that village they come from in those hills they sing about. And not because I don't want to pollute the "purity" of their culture with Babylon, either—because there is something intrinsically insulting about it.

At length we were able to leave. Gonzo had been edgily hunching around the doorway of the house, prodding Wooly and Tom Hayes, who as an upright drinking Englishman was much more amenable, to "get the fuck back to the hotel before the bar closes, man!" We trooped out into the street, and some of the Rastas followed us. A curious thing happened then: they had smoked only herb inside, but as soon as we hit the lane where the cars were parked they started asking for cigarettes, which we of course gave them. As Gonzo put it later: "I felt like we should have had Hershey Bars to distribute." They told us that in the middle of the band's performance (which was not in fact a Grounation at all but rather a religious concert for children—they would never let us come to the adults' affair) the police and soldiers had driven up to the place, looked in the door, and then split. I told them that the same thing happened when a rock 'n' roll band tried to practice in my neighborhood, but somehow it didn't ring quite the same. (Kingston police, I have been told, are not averse to such practices as walking into a house unannounced and for no reason in the middle of the night, interrupting a couple while they are fucking, pulling the man out of bed and hauling him in for interrogation and other sports that can be easily imagined.) I looked up and saw, at the top of a pole on the corner, two strips of black, battered metal, upon which had been crudely written in white paint instructions to go to certain addresses in the neighborhood for the mending of clothes, or to buy fish. "Look," I said to Gonzo and Tom Hayes, "advertisements." The three of us stared up, just stared, and said nothing.

The Rastas stood around or sat on the back bumper of Killy's Volks, polite and friendly conversation was made; they invited us to come back and see them sometime. Right. Eventually, without any true goodbyes, there was kind of a mutual semi-embarrassed separation, as they went back inside and we prepared to get in our cars. It was at this point that we discovered one of our party was missing. Peter Simon was still in the house. Nobody seemed particularly inclined to go in after him, so we just sort of stood around until some of them brought him out, stoned and beaming and holding hands with them like a brother to the world. Killy then told us that he had to take some members of the band home in his car, and we would all have to ride back in Stephen Davis' Toyota, plus we could drive home Chinna, the lead guitarist. Killy also said that he needed gas, produced a hose, and siphoned an indeterminate quantity out of the Toyota and into the Volks. He left us with instructions on how to get out of this neighborhood, said that in any case we had Chinna to guide us, and drove off. Now we had to squeeze seven people into the Toyota—Gonzo, Hayes, Wooly, and myself, three of whom are around six feet tall and in other respects large, into the backseat; in the front seat Stephen Davis driving, Peter Simon straddling the two front seats with his arm around the back of the seat where Chinna rode shotgun. No one spoke to Chinna; in fact, once out on a main road several of us began laughing like maniacs, and I still wonder what he must have been thinking. But some sort of pressure was off, and also the only way four of us could fit in the backseat was for one of Wooly's legs to hang out the window. Stephen Davis almost ran off the road the first time he saw a human foot bobbing up by his window. We drove for miles, followed Chinna's instructions until we arrived at what looked like a suburban 1950s American tract home, except that there were fields around it. It wasn't bad for Jamaica. As Chinna took his guitar through the front door, Gonzo cracked: "I'll bet he's saying, 'Hi, honey, I'm home!'" We wondered if Ras Michael and the rest had left in Killy's Volks for equally middle-class abodes, and Gonzo also revealed that Killy had burned him for the four dollars worth of dope he'd copped for him on the way to the Grounation. He had rolled part of it up into about four joints which he'd passed to us while the band was playing, but when Gonzo asked him for the rest of it at the end he said that we (I and I, Ethiopians and ofays) had smoked it all up. Proving, declared Gonzo, that the Rastas were not Righteous, after all.

Back at the hotel, Tom Hayes, Gonzo and I closed the bar. I had Courvoisier with Heineken chasers. Gonzo said, "Yes, tonight we have been where few white men have dared venture!" Hayes remarked that Peter Simon did not know how lucky he was to be alive.

/// \\\

Stephen Davis, Peter Simon, Wooly, and I are driving to Harry J.'s studio. Harry (Johnson) is another prolific island (and Island) producer; Marley has recorded at his studio a lot, and in fact when we get there Wooly sees a car that looks like Marley's BMW and for some reason gets nervous. It seems implicit that if Bob is there visiting Harry J. for any reason, we will have to turn around and go back to the hotel, and it occurs to me that it's a wonder Marley keeps any perspective at all with everybody treating him like this. But it's not his car, after all; we go inside.

In the car all morning Wooly has been saying "Jah Rastafari" and singing Ras Michael's "None a Jah Jah Children No Cry"; the night before, as we stood beside the door, I had asked him if Island was thinking of signing Ras Michael, and he had said no, but that after what we had just seen it might be a good idea. Now he has offered to make me a copy (a dub!) of his tape of Ras Michael's performance, and I tell him I've gotta have a cassette, and that if he can't make one easily not to go through the hassle, because I feel that Ras Michael's show is one of those things where you just would have had to have been there, and I probably won't play it much, especially if it's on reel-to-reel which I don't have equipment for. He insists, though: "Don't you want a tape to play for your friends and turn 'em on?"

It seems to me that the next logical step is home movies. Why didn't somebody give Peter Simon a Portapak?

Inside Harry J.'s studio, Wooly gives him the English edition, on the Island label, of his Jamaican hit with the Heptones, "Mama Say." Harry explodes. "What kinda crap is this? I produced this fucking record, and on this label it credit Danny Holloway [an English producer]. All he did was mix it! This's a fucking bummaclot." I ask him if this kind of thing happens often. "Never before with Chris Blackwell. Always I've trusted him." Something else occurs to me, very belatedly in fact, something so basic I had missed it all through my stay on the island: I ask him if very many Jamaican artists have managers. He looks at me as if I were the most pathetic ignoramous alive. "Not many," he says.

When we get back to the hotel, who do we run into in the lobby but Chris Blackwell himself. He has been in England over the weekend, and is just returning. Wooly is very agitated about Harry's complaint, and tells Blackwell the story. Chris is not perturbed at all. "It's a very simple problem, really. Harry J. has a big ego and so does Danny Holloway." He smiles. "And between the two of them, the Heptones haven't got a chance."

/// \\\

Two hours later. I've checked out of the Sheraton, and am in a cab on my way to the airport. I ask the driver to go by way of the Gun Court, an island attraction I'd heard about and wanted to see before I ever got here, a legend that preceded my tourism. The Gun Court was set up by the Manley regime as a way of dealing with all the berserk pistoleros and violent political agitators. What it means is that anybody caught by the police with even a bullet, even a shell casing, or any type of explosives in his possession, is whisked before a tribunal which asks him why he has these illegal and dangerous items. If he doesn't have the right answer, he is thrown in the stockade behind the Gun Court for life. Sic. 99.9 percent of Jamaicans who appear before the Gun Court have the wrong answer. And now here it is: high fences with enormous rolls of barbed wire at the top, guard towers, a yard where you can see young blacks milling around. The front of the place painted a garish red. It looks like a concentration camp, and that's what it is. I ask the cab driver what he thinks of it.

"I don' mind Gun Court so much," he says. "Other things bother me much more. On this island there is little real freedom, and now Manley is dealing with the Cubans, and we fear Jamaica will become like Cuba, where there is no freedom. No freedom under Communism, and already I don't feel free here anymore." He pointed to a pile of giant rocks left at some roadside excavation site. "You see those rocks, that's how we feel in Jamaica, like being crushed down by all those, underneath them. Manley is a dictator, of course. Under him today, the people are unhappy, and sometimes driving in the cab I don't say what I think if the rider asks me a question about politics, because I don't know who he is. He might go and tell the police, and I might not be here later. The Rastas are something else—they don' matter at all. I want to always live in Jamaica, but now I am not so sure. All I want now is my freedom."

Creem, June–July 1976

Death May Be Your Santa Claus: An Exclusive, Up-to-Date Interview with Jimi Hendrix

*(**Needless to say,** it took a lot of legwork, both on and off the astroturf, to track Jimi down; he's been a pretty reclusive dude for about five years now. But finally, using every means and pulling every string at my disposal, I managed not only to locate Jimi, but rap with him for several light-years. What follows is a direct, verbatim transcription of a very spacey rap, recorded in his plush and exceedingly far-out lair, with one of the titans of modern rock—the immortal Jimi Hendrix.)*

/// \\\

Jimi, you used to sing a lot about astral planes, the cosmos, and such when you were on earth. Now that you're out here, how does it stack up against what you originally envisioned?

Well, I'll tell ya, it's not like the advertisements. [*Laughs*] But then, neither was I. Because see, a lot of people got the wrong idea about me.

Like who?

Me, for starters. I didn't know what the fuck I was doing, except I dug r&b and Dylan, and found out howta get all these weird sounds outa my axe. That's where things got confused, just a little bit. Like I'm jammin' my ass off one night onstage at the Fillmore, playin' some kinda dirt-bike ride round the rings of Saturn, and I look out at the crowd and they're like one big pinball machine I'm lighting up, making 'em go buzz and tilt by playing "See See Rider" backwards or something I didn't know because my fingers were turning into celery stalks and I'm afraid to look at *that,* so I shut my eyes a second but there was some kinda Marvel Comic s&m Thor's Mistress flashing this whip and snorting at me in *there* so I open 'em up again fast as I can and now everybody in the audience is Bob Denver.

What? What do you mean?

I mean that every face out there looked identical, like Bob Denver on *Gilligan's Island,* with the little hat and the ratty shirt and everything, and they were all staring up at me with that goofy Gilligan look like "What're we supposed to do now?" so I screamed out right in the middle of a chorus of another song I'd forgot anyway, *"I'm the Skipper and I want you to go get Mary Ann and bring her here to me! I want that bitch on her KNEES!"* It seemed to make sense in the context of the lyrics at the time.

Well, it was a time of great experimentation and innovation, after all.

I know I changed some things, not nearly as much as some people seem to give me credit for, but I coulda really CHANGED things, I think, if I knew then what I know now. But at the time the alternative was so irresistibly tempting, and I ended up takin' the easy way out with jive and shit. So like on the night I was tellin' ya about, screamin' my lungs out at Gilligan, I had no idea in hell what the fuck Noel and Mitch were doing, they coulda been on a Greyhound to Tucson, Arizona, for all I knew or cared. So I just tore up into a long high note, held it, tore it off, and decided to get the hell out of there.

Now, no sooner do I get off the stage than who do I practically slam foreheads with but Bill Graham. Asshole's been standin' there on the side of the stage watchin' me this whole time. Now he just blocks my way, grabs my arm, stares deep into my eyes, and says: "Jimi. Why do you go out and play shit like that, when we both know you're capable of some of the best blues I've ever heard in my life, man."

Well, I hate to say it, but I just niggered out, played even more spaced than I was, because I didn't wanna hassle with the cat, I just wanted outa there. But if I'd been physically and psychologically capable of staying, man, I woulda said: "Because there are times when I strongly suspect, deep down inside, that *I hate the fuckin' blues.* Every broke-down nigger behind a mule he don't own can sing the blues. I only do blues because it's fun and easy to get into once in a while, and because I know all them ofays don't think a music show by a black person is their money's worth unless they get to hear some."

Yeah, but what about cuts like "Red House" and "Voodoo Chile?" They were incredible songs, fantastically played!

They weren't exactly what you would call original compositions. They were good takes, especially the second "Voodoo Chile." The long version had a nice feel, but it was there to fill out a double album, and Winwood played the same damn solo he played in "Pearly Queen" and every other damn session he did for about three years. I played good blues on "Red House," but it got way more attention than it deserved, probably because it was so hard to get in America for a long time. I mean, "I Don't Live Today" is *real* blues, modern blues—it's what happens when you drop a hydrogen bomb on the blues, which is what it deserves.

Listen. The blues is white music, and so was most "free jazz." All the musicians know it, everybody in the ghetto knows it because they be boppin' to James Brown and Stanley Turrentine, don't own Muddy Waters albums much less Robert Johnson, and 98 percent of them never even *heard* of Albert Ayler. My music was at least 70 percent white, if I'd played what black people wanted to hear at that time I'da been spectacularly unsuccessful in the hip rock superstar world, and if I'd gone down to the Apollo Theater and played what I played at the Fillmore I probably woulda been laughed off the stage. And knowing that has dogged my ass all the way to this moment. That and the fact that to a certain extent and in the interests of image, I had to shuck and jive because you know niggers is just sposed to be *bad* and fuck good wid big dicks an' be finger-poppin' all de time. I just added a little acid and feedback. And hell, for all of that I didn't even get laid that much either, or not as much as I should. I mean, you would think with me bein' JIMI HENDRIX and all the big deal that was made out of it, I'd be gettin' more pussy than Haile Selassie's whole harem and better quality than, I dunno, who's the hottest cunt you can think of?

Uhmmmm . . . Wilma Flintstone.

Thanks a lot. Like I coulda dug gettin' into some a that Julie Christie, you know, or maybe some a that Ursula Andress, you know *movie stars,* continental flash class clits. Instead I get all these dopey bitches wanna read my Tarot and always gotta *I Ching* in the Bantam edition in their back jeans pocket ready to spring on you at any second and tell you just the exact state of the gobbledegook. Well, I got more gobbledegook than I know what to do with already, as even a passing listen at my songs will tell you. You think I wrote all them fuckin' cosmic lyrics because I had the Universal Mind on tap? Hunh. I liked *Star Trek,* but I ain't Paul Kantner. I got more *out* of it than Paul Kantner, who shoulda profited by my bad example. I just dropped this and snorted that, and pretty soon a lotta shit was swirling about my head. Same shit as hit everybody else, really, especially Dylan, who was as inspiring and as bad an influence on me as anybody. I started out sincere, but half the time I couldn't fuckin' think straight, so stuff I *knew* was sloppy-ass jive-time mumbo jumbo came tumblin' out, and people jump up like whores for a blow of coke: "Oh wow, Jimi, far out . . ." And maybe that's where things started to really go wrong, when I saw that folks'd buy that jive as *profound,* well, I just spaced it all away.

Are you saying you were a suicide?

I ain't saying nothing, man. Except maybe that no dead niggers are suicides. But it's got nothing to do with me now. 'Cause there ain't no race bullshit Out Here. Ain't no races—"Just us angels up heah, boss!" Maybe I'll come back—just once—and do a three-night stint of *God's Trombones* as a rock opera, with Gil Scott-Heron and Stevie too. 'Cause I wanna lay some shit on Stevie—that cat is off and I don't care if he's blind, I don't care if his mama sent him to seven churches for each day of the week, he is *flat wrong,* period. I mean, nobody should know this

"Heaven" shit better'n me. I allow myself as something of an expert on the subject. It's been nothing but blow jobs 'n' soma since I bailed out back in '70. Don't *ever* go ta Heaven, man, it's the *shits.* Only reason not to split is Hell is worse, we went down there one weekend on a binge and it's the dregs. Heaven is like total stardom with a constant-touring clause, nothin' but arenas and hotels, but Hell is like Baltimore. The whole Afterlife trip is rigged to the rimjobs, and like New York cabaret cards it's one system you can't beat.

Your rap is . . . well . . . I honestly can't think of another question right now.

That's okay, I'm on speed, I'll fill in. [*Lights a cigarette, with compulsive urgency but steady hands.*]

I get a feeling you're pretty critical of your fellow musicians, dead and living.

Yeah, but it's cool, see, because there's nobody I'm more ruthlessly critical of than myself. I was a good guitar player, no Django but I did manage to come up with a few new riffs and a few new ideas about how to finger or get some weird noises outa the thing. But there ain't much percentage in ego-tripping when you're dead, so I gotta cop that that was about *it.* The songs I wrote that had actual melodies, that you could hum or have a real zinger cover, can be counted on the fingers of one hand. "Angel" I'm still proud of, as a *composition,* and a couple others. But the rest is mostly just metal riffs, with mostly jive lyrics that I talked instead of sang. I got a lotta credit for introducing "advanced technology" or whatever they're callin' it these days to rock, but the thing that almost everybody missed was that once the distortion and technology became a "required" part of the whole style and, like, institutionalized, then it was all over. Because technology is cold—so's technique, for that matter—and humans are hot. Or at least they should be. Because the emotion behind the distortion is the whole thing. And what we didn't realize was that all of us cultivating distortion so much was just digging our graves, emotionally speaking. And literally too, I guess, in some cases.

Because as time went by I began to realize that what people craved was just *noise.* Now, I took a lotta care with my own albums, the first three anyway—they were very carefully produced, all that shit. They were tight. But I was beginning to really, really wonder. Because when I listen to *Are You Experienced?,* at least half of what I hear and remember is just this really crazy pissed-offness that can't make no sense out of nothing. It's there in the lyrics and in the music too. Because that was where I was at the time. When I said, "Ain't no life *nowhere,*" I *meant* it! Meanwhile I'm thinking Do they expect me to bring the can of lighter fluid in my pocket onstage every night? Obviously something is wrong somewhere.

Well, what was it about distortion that started bothering you so much?

Well, like Graham wants blues, so do the fans, but Graham don't want distortion and they do. He thinks that's shit, and blues is "real." Well, I don't know *what* the fuck is "real." I never exactly did. Like, do I play two chords or three or just fuck around with tremolo and feedback and make funny noises and burn my guitar and swallow the strings and cannibalize my sidemen and then stand there alone on the stage with the buttons poppin' off my shirt like Brock Peters singing "John Henry" and "Cotton Fields" and a selection of work songs personally recorded on Parchman Farm by Alan Lomax? See, it seems to me when I look back that there was something larger that I always really, really wanted to do, but I could never quite get a firm grip on it.

On one level I'm really glad I got out when I did. Because it's like Kennedy, see, a legend—everybody can sit around saying, "Well, gee, nothin' happenin', but if *Jimi* was around now, *he'd* show us where it was all goin' next!" But they're wrong. I wouldn't have a fuckin' *clue* what to do now, if I was so unfortunate as to be "around." I'd probably be just like the rest of 'em, repeating my same shit over and over until everybody is as bored as I am and we mutually agree to call it quits and I'll go sit in the islands and listen to reggae or something. Or maybe, what would be even worse, I'd be one o' the ones that keeps grinding out the same old shit and *doesn't know it:* "Yeah, Jimi, your new album *Toe Jam*

Asteroid is the absolute *best* thing you've ever done!" "Yeah, like, dig, I'm hip, pops . . . just be cool." Yeah, that's how I'd cop out, come on as a real jive throwback spade wearing shades all the time, a little hat and cigarette smoke, the old Lonely Unapproachable Jazz Musician routine, sitting around in smoky clubs, sidewalk cafes, talk nothin' but bebop jive shit. "Yeah, cool, ah, that was a wiggy scene. Later." [*He breaks up laughing.*] The Thelonious Monk of the wah wah. Either that or just go hide and do session work. Become like Louie Shelton. Because I know I couldn't do what I started out to do and make it really cook.

And it ain't that I don't still got my chops. I do. Everybody's too fucking hung up on chops, though. I think the only studio album I really burned all the way was my first one. And that's after practicing night and day, year after year, trying to learn it all and do it better, coming up hard and fast and paying dues and busting your chops and out to whip ass on everybody, when suddenly one day I discovered somehow that I could be fuckin' Segovia and if that *some other weird component* is missing, then I might as well be Louie Shelton.

What is that component?

I wish I knew. I know I lost it somewhere. I take consolation in the fact that just about everybody else came up same time as I did too. Maybe we all just got too high.

How do you feel about people like Eric Burdon and Buddy Miles, whom some observers have accused of cashing in on your name or their association with you, after your death?

Listen, once you kick out you tend to let a *lotta* bad shit just go under the bridge. Fuck it, I hope they copped a few extra bucks. Besides, nobody lives forever, and I'm gonna have to sit down and have a serious talk with old Eric whenever he gets up here, in lieu of busting his face open. It's actually amusing, and besides, he really didn't know any better. Buddy Miles is a different case—I'd be afraid of getting *my* ass kicked, but anybody racks up as many bad records as that cat's probably gonna end up in the first coal cart to Hell anyway, so hopefully I'll never chance to see his fat face again.

Ever see any of the others who kicked off close to the time you did, hanging around up here?

Nah. I *hear* about them once in awhile, but I don't hang out with 'em. You wouldn't either. Morrison—I heard all about him, although I didn't see it. He put up such a big stink how he wanted into Hell and wasn't gonna accept anything else and how if they put him Here instead he was gonna make 'em all wish he'd never died, and on and on. . . .

I identify with him on a certain level—we both came along at the right-wrong time, right to become figureheads, wrong in terms of longevity. We were like the test models for crap like Alice Cooper and David Bowie. We both got suckered, but I like to think he got suckered far worse than I did. He, like, had more *complicity* in his own destruction. I like to think I just got more confused, and basically confused musically as much as in life, until it was all too much of a mess and there was no way out. I let too damn many people intimidate me, for one thing, because I knew I was off but I never had the simple street smarts to figure just maybe *they* were off too, maybe ten thousand times worse than me, so I just kind of ended up laying myself in everybody's hands. I mean, I was really an innocent, man. It's embarrassing in retrospect, and it wasn't comfortable then.

What about Janis?

I was hoping you weren't going to ask me that. Jeez, you fuckin' journalists, always after the next lurid headline. Well . . . she was pathetic there and she's pathetic here. It's not her fault, but she doesn't do anything, particularly, to try to improve it, either. That's all I got to say about that.

How do you feel about being a hot chart artist still, and record companies overdubbing other accompanists on your old tapes?

My records still selling is just like Jefferson Starship being more popular than Jefferson Airplane—quality has nothing to do with it, it's just people hanging onto things they know were good and represented something *once,* instead of taking a chance on a dubious unknown artist.

As far as the overdubbing goes, I feel almost as much indifference there. It sounds weird and egotistical for a dead guy to crow about how he was actually a one-man show, especially since his old sidemen really have no means of retorting, so obviously the smart position for me to have is no position. Why don't you go ask John Coltrane the same question, and see if connubial fidelity extends beyond the grave.

You seem pretty negative about all the people who've followed you musically on earth, though.

Yeah. I am. Because they're cold. I may have played real dogshit some gigs, and cut some tracks that were too smooth for my taste. But I was loose. There was something bigger than me sweeping me along and it killed me in the end, but some pretty incredible music came out of it at times, too. My only regret is that I wonder how much of it, under the circumstances, was really *my* music, when you get right down to it. If a fucking lightning bolt strikes you, and out of it you get a masterpiece, well, is it you or the lightning bolt? And if in the final analysis it's just no contest. You know you lost control, you let the music and the life play you, and that's why you went under. But it really happened, it was real fire and real dues, and nothing can erase that. It should be pretty obvious by now that I consider my life and my art a failure, but it was an honest failure.

What bugs me is these cats now—no bolt. And no them either! I don't mind people copping my riffs, but they're like a buncha fuckin' college students! Most of my riffs *I* copped off somebody else, but then I went on and played and forgot about it. I didn't sit around with seven candles burning in a shrine to Chuck Berry. So who even cares if cats like this Trower or that guy in Canada succeed or fail, what's the fucking difference? There is more happening in any bar on Friday night when the dance floor's full, than in all those cats' albums and concerts put together.

What's even worse is that they missed the biggest lick of all, the thing that was so discouraging to me—that I saw the end of it coming. I don't mean rock 'n' roll or popular music or even heavy metal—just the end of the particular experimental, technological branch we riffed out on and sawed through. There's got to be something else. Because one thing I learned while killing myself was that a hell of a lot of that shit was just sound and fury kicked up to disguise the fact that we were losing our emotions, or at least the ability to convey them. Most of *Electric Ladyland* and the second album sound real cold to me now. I don't know what it sounded like to me then, because I was too spaced out to make any accurate judgment except that it had all the ingredients, I got some rocks off especially in things like "Voodoo Child (Slight Return)," the albums were relatively slick and I knew they would sell.

I guess that's what I was trying to get at before when I talked about the missing component. I just forgot how to feel unless I was getting electric shocks or something—and after a while even electric shocks began to feel all the same. And even saying it like that doesn't really explain it. It's really THE great mystery, for everybody Out Here. And nobody's come up with any solid answers yet. So when you get back, when you publish this, if anybody comes up after that and tells you they got some kind of a line on it, I don't care how thin it is, well, you'd be doing me the biggest favor of my death if you'd pass it on back. I'd like that more than anything in the . . . cosmos.

[*He laughed again, briefly, then stared through us into some sort of distance. It was obviously time to go.*]

Creem, April 1976

Reprinted in *New Musical Express,* May 1, 1976

from Notes on Austin

A**ustin, laid-back and somewhat indulgent** as it is, might be a terrible place for a New Yorker or anyone who wants to move and shake culture or corporations but it's an undeniably great place to start a band, as I recently learned. No paranoia, no career hang-ups, no star trips (well, not usually), no heroin, no your drummer informing you at Thursday's rehearsal that he's just gotta play with this "Smoke on the Water" copy band Friday night instead of with you at CBGB's because he says he desperately needs the money even though he lives with his parents in Westchester. None of that kind of stuff. I met this band called the Delinquents, we said, "Okay, let's do it," I took my lyrics and guitar down there and we wrote three songs the first rehearsal and a record FIVE the second. Took me *months* to get a decent set of songs written with the last buncha assholes I worked with in New York, and longer to actually make it onto the stage with our oh-so-elaborate "show" all worked out. Six weeks here, from first rehearsal to Duke's opening where we wowed 'em unto St. Vitus in the aisles. It's almost *too* easy to make music in this town. The Delinquents have their own thing as well as working with me (in fact they sound completely different in the two contexts), and their thing is surf punks. Dick Dale and "Telstar" and alien beach parties and rantin' 'n' ravin' about whoever double-crossed you this time while the guitars flare free. Of course they're great (I think), why else would I work with them? No, they suck. They act real mad when they sing sometimes, which is cute. Do I sound supercilious? Well I don't mean to. It's just that this I feel is the essence of punk. When all is said and done. They also have yet another subgroup within the group, called Pelvic Thrust, which takes them over more towards RFE/Joy Division territory. Pelvic Thrust's most famous number is one I forget the title of all about various friends the composer had who OD'd and croaked on this, that, or whatall. It sounds exactly like "I Wanna be Your Dog" with Joy Division overdubbing, except the singer has more life than Joy Division's. Too bad. We played a frat party on Halloween where all the frats dressed up as punks and even decorated a whole room in black with torn STB posters, strips and straps hanging off the wall, everything spray painted jet black, giant smoke machines in all four corners belching out attars of mystery in which our feet did disappear, while up at the front of the room they'd built a whole little stage enclosed so come to think of it we kinda looked like we were in a big TV set playing. Maybe they figured it'd be more security precautioned for their girlfriends that way. Meanwhile, Becky is hoping no high hep whiskey'd frat takes a notion to go cop some pooz offa one o' them free-livin' punk chicks. Becky plays rhythm Stratocaster. But anyway them frat boys sure do have lots of extra moolah to throw around. I never was able to dude a party up to this extreme. We got to be little stars for a nite. We were cute, I'm sure. For instance, I was cute when I OD'd on nasal inhalers, cough medicine, Chlor-Trimeton, and malt liquor to the point that when they finally did call me up onstage to start singing my songs I of course was in no condition but through some transference of memory and association was seeing a traumatic room of my childhood and came on or at least felt like this tragic stricken gloomy poetic young soul who obviously was just too sensitive to live. I slurred through about a verse and a half and half-swept, half-tumbled off the stage. The whole Byronic romantic-agony schtick, with palpable overlay of skid row. Cute, eh? The frats didn't care. They loved it. They loved everything we did: Byron, Pelvic Thrust, atonal feedback raveups, surf toons—it was all gravy to them. Musta had a wild old time that night. Before the set I walked into a room across the lower forty of the frat house where we were supposed to be able to just tap right up all the beer we could drink, gratis. Of course there was no beer. Somebody pointed me to a

30-gallon brand-new garbage can in the middle of the room filled with some red liquid substance almost brimming over yet still no one would say what it was. "Try some," they smiled strokingly. What nice folks. Southern hospitality. You really can't beat it. I looked at this tub of what for all I knew might have been the blood of aborted fetuses mixed with chemical waste from bauxite ecologic rape and a generous quantity of Mello Yello treated with red food coloring. Then on the other hand it could turn out to be a consummate blend, importunate yet magisterial, of several of the finer chateaux in Europe's most cobweb-dusty vintage stock. You just never can tell. Momentarily sargasso'd by indecision, I cast back in my mind for some roughly analogous incident, back to my high school days and all those horrid yet great fun beer blasts we had where everybody tried to cop a few free feels off their or somebody else's girlfriend really made no difference before puking all over our tennis shoes. What ever happened to those good old times? Apparently they were back again for these young citizens and scores, nay, *armies* like them 'cross the nation, who perhaps were more fortunate than even we (who were there and repress traumatic memories) realize in having never endured the first go-round of those wonderful old days, which of course was why they were all hopping on it now. Right on 'n' more power to 'em, I say, quaffing another hearty Viking stein of brew, 'cause as ever power's to the people and these are one kind of people just as worthy as any other of their day in the sun, just folks and not the first in human history to lob a rotten egg or two your way. But gazing fondly backwards I came upon something which I'd all but forgotten, the noxious memory of which was still enough to jolt me from my reverie. I looked at the big can full of red fluids. "Ah, no thanks anyway," I said. "Uh, say, that wouldn't just happen to be one of these things you hear about sometimes, where they take about fifty fifths of all of 'em different kinds of booze and empty 'em together in one big vat . . ." They leered at me. I hightailed it back to our own special little dressing room off stage left. Here's what our gentle cultured hosts were so kind as to provide our little dressing room with: (1) chair, folding; (2) a broken card table partially propped on some stacked cardboard boxes; (3) great and historic paddles that'd warmed umpteen generations of pledges' butts, hung upon the wall in precise symmetrical formation all the way around the room, which wasn't all that far since it only really had two walls in the first place; (4) best of all, our very own BEER MACHINE! Yes, that's correct: a soft drink dispenser just like by any gas station, except ours had cans of Coors and Miller and Lite in it. Of course, you had to pay. But the beers were reasonable at 50 cents per. Like many magical devices, this beer dispenser contained a surprise within. The surprise was that when you put in your quarters and pressed down on the handle, no can of Coors came rolling out. But do listen, this is unusually cute. What you had to do, see, was get down on your knees, then stick your hand and then your whole arm almost up to the shoulder in, up, around, back, over, under, and through this monster until you've almost broken your arm and worn out the knees on your pants, and only then, just then, did your numb embarrassed fingertips suddenly run smack up against a cool plump little can of beer just waiting there all for you. So you'd wrench it out, around, down, etc., after which you were free to drink. Now, I don't think it was just my chemical state that made this operation seem more than a little bit like sticking your right arm up a great robot cunt from Stanley Kubrick's dreams, there to wrench off perhaps a fallopian tube. Freud: whatta guy. What I'm really *still* pondering, actually, is the possibility that just maybe this was not in fact a defective machine awaiting repair at all. Just *maybe* this was a deliberate sabotage, maintained this way all the time, in the cause of ribald party winky fun 'n' noisome hijinx. What better way to prove your manhood before the whole house than to risk one's only strong right limb away aloft in the maw of a vibrating corporate clammy cunt complete with rubber around the opening? Frigidity jokes. Comparisons with recent dates. Why, the possibilities were endless. Which led me to a further line of speculation: did they reserve this little manual safari for pledges and unsuspecting but good-natured (hey, I can take a joke; what the hell, guys!) strangers like us, or did they see to it that all of them had to go through these post-penetration exertions and contortions every single time they needed a fresh can?!?! Go on, *tell* me it's out of the question! One never really does know precisely how far these lads are into s&m, after all. For which one is thankful. But whatever the state of each housebrother's private relationship with the beer machine, they loved us, and why shouldn't they? We were the geek show! The whole band except me had on all kinds of makeup, glitter, masks, beards, weird shit to the max. Add on top of that everybody being stoned and drunk and you had a Halloween surely to be remembered even if you forgot all the exact details. I was so fucked up that at one point, wandering out into the smog of the dance floor, I saw Andy's girlfriend, and thought we were now in some kinda local New Wave club fulla more or less relatively normal people, and further that the band had been playing for at least eight hours, that it was 6 A.M., I could see dawn breaking cerulean and pink through the ceiling, and I thought Jee-ZUZ do they work these bands hard in these places. Man, I thought, I could never be a rock 'n' roll star, I haven't got the fortitude. I thought the band looked terrible onstage, five poor wasted haggard manikins on a numb treadmill killing themselves in liege to dreams of a train to nowhere, oh I was bathetic, except of course nobody else knew even though I thought they all could see 'cause it was all happening inside just like always with psychedelics. To everybody else I'm sure now that I just looked like some old drunk stumbling around the place: "What's that old wino doing hanging around with that band?" "Shit, I dunno, maybe he's one of 'em's uncle or something. You know how these musicians are." "I think probably we should just throw him the hell outa the house." "Nah, fuck it, he's about half passed out anyway. He's probably just their mascot or grampa or something." So I lurched back around to the dressing room, where I'd managed last time I'd been there to plop myself down on the card table, knocking it off the boxes and spilling beer all over the place four times in four minutes. Now my *New York Rocker* was all soggy and I was in no condition to read it anyway.

Life was hopeless. I snored beneath a monolithic wave of existential despair. Sartre was right in *Le Nausee:* I was now on that rack at the precipice's edge where one may shudder with horror to actually find oneself unable to pick up a simple glass of beer. Then again, one may not. The Pacific Ocean broke through the ceiling and froze, backing up on itself. Actually I made that up. I was too stupefied for hallucinations. The band called me back up at some point and I must have sang something though I can't imagine what, then I remember coming to again to find myself standing in the middle of the stage with my guitar strapped on and plugged in, playing sparse fills that actually fit. What a pro! Then I blacked out again, came to 20 or 30 minutes later just in time to be called up to sing "Louie, Louie," which ever since *Animal House* has been appropriated and crowned the Frats' Official International Anthem in Perpetuity; it brings a tear to the pudgy shelf of cheek as the notes and those perhaps a bit sentimental but always stirring lyrics conjure up sad remembrances of beerbusts past: The night they gang-raped the ugly girl nobody liked in Gamma Delta Phu. The memory of making one puking little pledge eat a bloody Kotex and smack his lips after each swallow squealing "YUM YUM, FINGERLICKIN' GOOD!!!" The night they homosexually molested, physically abused, and then sodomized collectively those creepy little pledges they didn't wanna let in anyway 'cause they dressed Robert Hall's and came from some crummy little town in Pennsylvania where they talked funny and were Amish or something. Something different anyway. Something no good. And how after that they told the sniveling little cunts that they better not tell anybody or they, the frat honchos, would see to it that word was spread all over school these new enrollees were nothing but Queers. Come on, who would believe it of US? No one. A joke. But hell, that's all it was in the first place, was just a damn good joke. Well I got on up and commenced to sing "Louie, Louie." At first I was just gonna slur my way through it, but then as I gradually realized that not only was I conscious but even relatively sober and lucid and finally reclaimant of my faculties, I began to apply myself, to care, to work at the phrasing, thinking about what to stress or underplay and where and why. I mean, after all, it's something of a challenge to daub in the shadings on lyrics like "On the ship I dreamed she there/Smelled aroma (the roses? Romilar? Rope burns?) down in her hair." It's not exactly "Miss Otis Regrets," but it'll do. I began to play with the rhythm, holding notes or parts of phrases, trying to make them soar out, then biting them back viciously. No doubt I sucked. Nobody cares. In fact they were in ecstasy. So who knows, maybe I didn't suck. Which just might be the essence of Frat Existence and Philosophy: Hey, you, World—*I DON'T SUCK GODDAMMIT*!!!!! Right, fine, you don't, me neither. Hell, for all *I* or the rest of the band or the *whole entire room* knew, I could very well be singing the greatest version of "Louie, Louie" of all time! Shit, and nobody there to record it! Though actually the Delinquents did happen to have their tape deck on, told me next rehearsal that it'd sounded great and offered to play it for me. I demurred. But I guess that means I really did sing it better than anybody else ever. Why should they lie to me? The only fly in the ointment, and I wonder if I am the only one that knows it, is that I also know that whether I sang it the best version of all time or the absolute mange-ridden worst in a long slumgullion of stinkeroos, it makes absolutely no difference whatsoe'er. What a song. It's like the weather. Indestructible, yet still mysterious, inscrutable as Madame Nhu's death mask. We finally finished up and got off—well actually I'd been finished and off for quite some time—and after packing up we walked around the house a bit, mingled with the natives. We'd mingled with 'em before the set too. Still didn't get acquainted with anybody. Since then I have had occasion to converse (somewhat under duress, I should probably also state) with certain denizens of this particular subculture, at which time I learned that they are quite literally impossible to talk to or with, and for that matter even when they're not around there's not a hell of a lot to say about 'em. They're kinda like, anthropods, or something. Marginally extant. As I trundled from room to room in their palace, I could overhear scraps of bypassed conversations. "—called Johnny

Rotten and the other one named himself Sid Vicious. They stab themselves with pins to protest society!" "Sounds *sick* to me." "Well, of course I wouldn't actually go so far as to just lay down and *buy* one o' their records, y'know, but still you gotta admit they're pretty funny." "—puts out like a generator! Go on, call her! Here, I've got the—" "—ive thousand a *month* plus dividends, premiums, bonuses, perks, the works! Plus they're gonna show me how to fix—" "If you puke in the sink again we're gonna throw you on the floor and piss all over you." "—and so then the fag that's dressed as Frankenstein says to the girl Mad Doctor—" "I just *don't!* I just *don't,* that's all!" Well it was all fairly fascinating even though there was a whole lot I didn't understand. It's always broadening to the character to delve into new and unknown social milieus, and then, perhaps even . . . *go native!* Outside on the sidewalks all of us in the band gathered to discuss the evening's events. It seemed that most of them felt that some new and perhaps meaningful rapprochement had been forged, certainly encouraging, one short but significant step on the road to eventual utopias of brotherhood, fraternity (yep!), and understanding, a world where both spike head and Izod might coexist and even help a brother with his load, especially seeing as how they'd both ended up addicted to the same drug. It's a lovely portrait, but I'm afraid I just can't quite yet link arms with the joyous masses marching and singing down that golden Freedom Highway to the Wizard's castle. It seems I have at least one problem that nothing I've known can lick. I just don't like people. But that's okay too; I imagine they'll probably be able to get along on their own, without my succor. After all, they are the sons and daughters of the ruling class.

Previously Unpublished, November 1980

California

California has become so easy to kick around in the last few years you almost hesitate to join the snot-chained mob. It does absolutely nothing to redeem itself, but the virulence of our scorn ultimately reflects nothing so much as the quashed ineluctable admission that our New York cartoon is just about as bad. Like when I talked to my nephew in San Diego, who works in a roller-skate store, on the phone a few months back and he said, "Yeah, I know what Manhattan's like. I've seen all those Woody Allen movies."

You know something? I hate Woody Allen worse than anybody in the whole state of California. Woody Allen (with some help from Neil Simon, the media in general, and myself and most of the rest of the population of Edward K.'s[12] provincial little burg) has turned me into a second-class citizen. *I'm* not like that, I want to scream, but it's too late—I *know* my nephew's not a hot-tubular biofed granola cruncher because I knew him when we were both chillen and he hated everything even *then,* just like me, but it was me what up 'n' moved to this place where the streets are paved with gold and the Great White Way even goes out of its way to mount productions celebrating the virtues of minority groups—with one conspicuous exception, that is. I mean, can you imagine a B'way hit entitled *Marin's a Groove After All?* No. We hate, and thus are hated. Which serves us right, since there really is nothing going on anywhere else, except, damn, with so little going on *here,* how 'bout some recognition on the part of the rest of the nation

[12] At the time, Edward Koch was mayor of New York City.

that we frenzofried Nyawkers are as vacant and bewildered as the last leisure suit in Keokuk?

Nope, it's never gonna happen: we've been too snotty too long. We've bought our death, and the best we can say is that we're enjoying it (as opposed to Keokuk, which remains largely unmoved by the brand of irony stamped in the genes of anybody who's ever been knocked down in the subway by an ostensible human which could pass for their grandmother. Only here, not Keokuk, not nowhere else, do grannies become Charles Bronson death-units grinding up the tracks atcha. Or so we have been led to believe by popular folklore.) Last night my shrink concluded our session by saying, "Go home and do something *positive!*" I had absolutely no idea what he was talking about. He cured cancer (literally) in a patient the other day. I stare at the wall, pore over *TV Guide* as if the thirty-fifth reread of the day's skeds will reveal some cinematic gem I unaccountably missed instead of more reruns of *The Love Boat* in the middle of long nights getting longer when you're afraid to call anybody because you don't want to wake them up even though in reality they're all doing 'zackly what you're doing, making their peace with Mary Tyler Moore and the nine-thousandth rerun of General MacArthur's lifetime on *Biography,* so you have a whole city crammed with pathetic wretches lonelified out of their skulls but cowering before their phones because they actually believe that somebody else around this amphetamine skillet occasionally *sleeps!*

Yep, it's a great joke all right, but don't expect anybody else to get it. Like right after the "positive" bit my shrink (who really does understand me, it's just he refuses to support my eternal Will To Do Nothing) says, "Well, what gives you pleasure?"

"Pleasure?" I stare at him bug-eyed, repeat the word with amazement. He swears it's true, but reader, can any of you actually tell much less substantiate for me that there is such a thing extant hither or whither yon as "pleasure"? Sensation, yes. Relief from anxiety, certainly, if you're lucky. But pleasure? That's almost as big a canard as

"happiness." All these things, of course, are tissues constructed from straws randomly plucked from the wind and deposited in works of fiction written in other centuries when, as is well known, the emotions and experiences they purport to represent were even more alien from the human race than they are now. At least we've got child labor laws and TV. At least we've got fast food franchises and an endless supply of magazines reassuring us that the new "celebrity" aristocracy is every bit as miserable as us. Hell, this is the Garden of Eden! As I said to Richard Hell one time re his usual life-is-not-worth-living spiel: "Shit, buddy, a hundred years ago you woulda been behind a plow."

California flies in the face of all such wisdom, though, which is the main reason we hate it so ardently. California has in the course of the Seventies managed to convince itself and at least part of the rest of the world that this "pleasure," "happiness," "contentment" stuff might actually be attainable on a day-to-day basis. All you have to do is sign an affidavit foreswearing forever any resistance to being a moron. It's the real blank generation. We may be a shuddering heap of ostentatious neuroses, but they are eggs with the yolks surgically removed. One must conclude that they are worse, not only because one is a masochist but because one KNOWS deep in the gut that deep in their guts they all hate and want to kill too. We can proudly point to David Berkowitz as a man unafraid of following his most primal instincts, whereas they would probably have to dig back as far as Charles Manson (a whole decade) to come up with an action totem nearly as impressive. They have nothing, certainly not conscience, as is proven by the fact that so far they have failed to ship all their Valium scripts they don't need to us so's to make Hell a wryer vista for those ten days or so each month when so many of us (the author of this article, for instance) have used up ours and are climbing the walls and tic-twitching funkadelically.

Because they withhold this balm from us, they all deserve to be killed. Perhaps even before the next seven random strangers in our own neighborhoods. Someone perhaps should look into the matter of booking charter flights to run hourly for those of us (all of us) who've had enough. Not only would we not have to go through the guilt of knowing we'd killed human beings instead of mutants, but we'd get out of town for a while, which of course means that this place would look every bit as beautiful as it actually is when we got back. It would be the solution to all our problems except our mayor, and we could kill him before departure, wondering in idle coastal whimsy whether our return would find him replaced by Stanley Siegel or Joe Franklin. Reagan's obviously the next president, and in matters of showbiz and politics nothing combats fire quite so well as fire. While we're out there eliminating the populace and making the area safe for sagebrush and hodad-free surf we certainly could also see to it that there was never to be a chance of Jerry Brown succeeding Mr. Reagan as Big Kahuna to the fifty fading states. Even remotely considering the prospect of Linda Ronstadt as First Lady is realizing that earthquakes rendering Nevada the last thing before Japan notwithstanding it's them or us, sooner or later.

I know this because I was just out there for ten days, first time I worked up the nerve for such a trek since 1976, and hell, I was *born* (Escondido) and *grew up* (San Diego) in the damn place. In fact I thought it was wonderful for years, and didn't begin to recognize I was actually homesick for Detroit, a city accurately summarized by Ray Bradbury as several thousand miles up the rhinoceroses' anus. These days I think of Detroit the way many others think of California: as a place to cool out from the anxieties of this town, inasmuch as there has been, is, and will be in perpetuity absolutely certifiably Nothing going on there. As all New Yorkers know, Nothing is the only place where any modern citizen can relax. It is the Californian's inanely niggling insistence on a Something that initially makes you want to invest in a rifle with telescopic sights and a couple of .44 magnums; it is the further assertion deflecting all reasonable argument that this Something is not the worst thing in human history since Hitler or *Petticoat Junction* that makes you want to mow down every sentient being at the end of the jet shuttle.

I was actually afraid to go back to California. I was afraid that all the men would look like Robert Conrad or Richard Gere or both at once, and all the women of course like Farrah Fawcett, that every soul I met would talk like the zombies on TV, that my congenital hostility would be pushed so far past any line of socialized containment that I would end up murdering every living thing in my line of sight instead of coming back to New York and building a terrorist army of concerned citizens like the adult I thought I was.

As it happened, it wasn't nearly so painful as I'd imagined. In fact, it was not long before I found myself being blatantly seduced by all of the most decadent aspects of the region. It is that insidious. I had been in San Francisco a total of three days when I agreed to enter a hot tub with three other naked humans. My will, not to mention my mind, had eroded that much already. But what residues clung to this brainpan were still too much for most of the natives. Everywhere I went in that state, I was told: "You're so *definite*. . . ." The response of almost everyone I met in any of the cities I visited to most any external stimulus perhaps calling for some sort of decision or value judgment was "Whatever . . ."

I got into arguments with two people in two separate cities, one in San Francisco and one almost a week later in Los Angeles, over whether or not est was an evil thing. Both were intelligent, hip, charming, attractive, modern citizens who otherwise would give me no call to look askance, neither was an adherent of said cult, both were "open-minded."

I was learning by the second episode of this sort that on the whole it would be more politic to simply drop the subject and ingest heaping further helpings of whatever drugs we happened to be shoveling into our systems at the time. I should also mention here that it was not on this trip that I first learned that a great many Californians, especially in

L.A., have somehow achieved a psychophysical state in which they can soak themselves in every kind of dope known to man for years on end and come out absolutely unchanged, the exact same human configuration that entered the chemical labyrinth perhaps a decade or more previous. For this I hate them all, even if everything else about them were perfect.

In San Francisco I said to a young woman whom I liked a great deal, "Do you mean to tell me you actually don't sit in your apartment for days on end, staring into space depressed out of your mind, thinking life's not worth living but lacking the will to even turn on the gas?"

"No," she laughed, "I'm *happy*."

"Then you must be a sick dog," I said.

The next day we rode around town in her car. It was the only automobile I've ever been in which had a device installed in it which purported to remove the negative ions from the air, or is it to shove more of 'em in, I forget but anyway it was a mechanical addendum designed, advertised, and guaranteeing to create Good Vibes for whoever was lucky enough to be riding around with it. I was depressed out of my mind the whole time. So depressed, in fact, that after I'd left I called her back just to make sure that what I just described was, in fact, the purpose of this device. Sure, she laughed. I didn't have the heart to ask how much it cost. When I got back to New York I told all my friends about it, it was my supreme California story, till I encountered one friend who'd owned one herself: her husband had been a terminal cancer patient, and they'd tried *everything*. He died, of course.

I did not see anyone die in California. They didn't need to, being wedded to Stasis. I'm not sure why the disco-headphone roller skaters of Venice were more obnoxious than the ones in New York; I think it might have something to do with the fact that, as I first realized in 1974, it is possible to be *too* healthy, so healthy that one becomes obscene. I had the constant sensation that everybody at *my* table was all right, but we were surrounded by Them. Later I found out some of Us weren't so all right as I thought.

Of course my musical tastes hit a brick wall everywhere I went out there. In San Francisco, I was invited to guest-deejay at a new punk club called the City. I played Lydia Lunch, Teenage Jesus and the Jerks, the Contortions, Public Image Ltd., Richard Hell and the Voidoids, and my own single. I cleared the dance floor. They hated absolutely all of it, except (this is not self-promotion, believe me) my single, which has a sort of funk riff, which brought two couples onto the floor: one was a straight couple who'd obviously wandered in here thinking this was a disco and this was the closest thing to disco music they'd heard all night—all I remember about them aside from their jerky dancing was that the guy wore a red vest and reminded me of a bartender in a particularly low-rent swinging singles joint; and, way across the floor, there was this one psychotic girl who'd been dancing this horrendous amphetamine-OD mutation of the Grateful Dead ecstasy dance to every record anybody played all night, by herself of course, and when I put on "Let It Blurt" some slimy guy jumped up and started dancing after her, trying with zero subtlety to engineer some kind of pickup. I think he actually succeeded, in fact. Which reminds me that I didn't meet anyone in either Frisco or L.A. who was involved in any kind of ongoing, stable, monogamous relationship. Not so different from New York, of course, except that out there they think it's just ducky that they are apparently congenitally depersonalized, which may or may not be better than the neurotic flare-ups that occur from time to time in this town when people attempt the impossible, i.e., getting truly close to any other human. It occurs to me now that I actually heard less of that nauseating talk about the need for "space" out there than I ordinarily do here (just to get the set straight, let me say that I have never and will never use that word in that context/application: to me "space" is one of two things: where astronauts are, or a word preceding "out" and meant to describe how I am often feeling; the wretched hovel where I type these grousations is not in any sense my "space"—it's my *apartment,* and don't you forget it)—probably because there's so much more of it out there that you could walk around the most densely settled urban areas for days without ever encountering so much as a human asteroid.

The last leg of my trip took me to San Diego to visit my family. My mother is aging and ailing and endeavored to manipulate me into feeling guilty for those facts. After all the "whatever" ozone I'd experienced in San Fran and L.A., such ground-level neurosis was a positive breath of fresh air, and I greeted it wryly. I also spent a couple of evenings drinking beer with my nephew, who proudly showed me his collection of heavy metal LPs by groups like the Scorpions. I was speechless. Finally I managed to stammer out something about New Wave. "You mean *punk* rock?" he spat. "I *hate* that *shit!* I read all this garbage all you rock critics wrote about it and you fuckheads actually managed to convince me to go out and buy an album by some group called Devo! It was a piece of shit! I'm never buying a 'New Wave'/'punk rock' album again!"

I tried to explain to him that rock critics were not exactly a united front, that I hated Devo too, that he might find that he liked, say, the Ramones and Clash if he checked them out—"I *especially* hate the Clash!" he hissed. "All that *bullshit* written about them in all those magazines! All that 'You're out of it if you don't like this' horseshit! All that 'the only group that matters' crap! I never wanta hear those fuckers! And it's *your fault!*"

I gave him a copy of *London Calling* anyway. His response: "I'll file it under 'C'."

Oddly enough, he *did* like *The Metal Box* by Public Image, Ltd. But then, at that time, he had never read or heard anything about them, had no idea who they were. "Sounds kinda like a cross between the Doors and Terry Riley," he said, "Not bad." He probably hates them too by now.

I took my mother to the doctor in San Diego and then took a walk down the street. There was nothing there, blocks and blocks of nothing. Not a bookstore, not a record shop, not a bar you'd care to enter, nothing but car washes and taco-stand franchises and supermarkets and parking lots and everything clean clean clean as if all them damn autos were farting out Windex. Finally I wandered, half-dazed by now, into a liquor store. Liquor stores in California are not like the ones in New York. They carry beer, which is good, but they also carry all sorts of other nonalcoholic detritus which renders them almost more like Kmart or a cross between a drugstore, a 7 Eleven, and a hardware store than any place a self-respecting drunk would want to be seen. I got confused, and wandered the aisles aimlessly. The manager, sitting in some vast arena behind his cash register and four-sided counter, began eyeing me with open suspicion and hostility. Plainly, I was a Suspect, a possibly dangerous and certainly anomalous Character not from these parts and up to some kinda nogood for sure. An Outlander. I was dressed at the time in jeans, a normal shirt, sneakers, and with a brand-new haircut that I'd thought a little too short, though certainly not in the least punkish. I thought I looked like Andy Hardy. My mother said it best, probably, for the guy in the liquor store and who knows who else around them parts: "You look like an overgrown hippie."

Went to a record store in midtown San Diego I used to cut school to ride the bus to when I was a teenager. The same guy worked there as I'd first met in 1962. I think it was either the '73 or '74 trip when I first realized that he was gay. I used to wait for those days when I'd ride that bus up El Cajon Boulevard with an armload of albums that I'd then sell for a dollar apiece, buying others from him for two dollars or walking a few blocks to plunk down a fin for the then-new *Let Freedom Ring* by Jackie McLean, *Tijuana Moods* by Mingus, or anything by Ravi Shankar. I'd always said hello to this guy, every time I'd entered his store before, going back at least a decade and a half. This time I didn't. I didn't buy any records there, either. I live in New York now. I've got everything. I walked out depressed.

One of my other nephews did manage to find a used 8-track to play in his machine as we cruised the freeways beering, though: Jimi Hendrix's *Electric Ladyland.* As I popped another Coors and listened to all those wah wah pedals while staring out at the bay and the shopping centers and missions and almost cloud-free sky, it suddenly occurred to me that Jimi had been dead only a few months shy of a good decade by now, and here we were still listening to this stuff.

Worse than that was my other nephew's house, where my mother was living. When I walked in they were watching the Olympics on TV; I thought it was the Ice Capades. There were incomprehensible magazines about how to spruce up your condo on the coffee table. My mother kept asking me if I wanted a tuna sandwich. Sometimes I said yes, sometimes I said no. Barely a word was exchanged between me and my nephew's wife the whole time I was there. I made one painful attempt to make a conversation happen between me and their daughter, who I used to carry around on my head and is now just about to become whatever sort of incomprehensible creature the adolescents of the Eighties might be; she resolutely refused to respond to anything I threw out. I finally decided I hated her. Conversation with my mother was intermittently enjoyable, as long as she didn't start in again with that wheedling tone. She was all right, she was old. I became like child is father to the man in a way. But during the days, when my nephew was at work at the roller-skate store and I was stuck there in that house with the three of them, the absence of connection in the air sometimes congealed pretty chilly. Whenever that happened I'd just go downstairs and play records. "Albatross" by PiL was the theme song of my entire trip. I also listened to Jimmy Reed and the first Velvet Underground album, and of course the latter sounded like the most beautiful thing I'd ever heard and made me incredibly homesick. I only stayed there two days, which was fortunate, because if I'd hung around any longer I might have developed another kind of illness I certainly didn't need: their house was on a hillside overlooking the bay, which meant I guess that some kinda fog or sea wind or whatever came in at night, making the room I slept in horribly cold and damp. I woke up two days in a row feeling feverish, shivering; I'd get out of bed and put on my underclothes, shirt, pants, socks, shoes, two sweaters, and a jacket, and walk out into the living room still shivering. Look out the window and it's a beautiful day. Then I'd walk out the front door and immediately begin to sweat buckets because it was damn *warm* under that California sun. There must have been a twenty- or thirty-degree difference at least between the temperatures inside and outside that house. So of course I'd have to immediately peel off the jacket, sweaters, maybe even the shirt. I considered myself lucky to escape from the damn place without getting pneumonia.

I'd decided to use up my five-hour plane ride back reading *Fools Die.* The newsstand at the San Diego airport didn't have it. It apparently wasn't popular enough. The only book they had that I imagined I might remotely be able to relate to was *The Matarese Circle.* So I bought it, and later discovered that half the people on the plane were reading it. It was terrible. When I got back to New York and was riding the cab into Midtown, I thought of something Bob Quine said to me once in 1977. I don't remember the context, but with great emphasis and a totally straight face he stated: "I'm spiritually *dead.*" I laughed out loud at the memory. It was people like that, I realized more than ever, that I wanted to be around. And though some of them have emigrated to California, they're bitter about it, which takes all the fun out of the anomie, of course.

Previously Unpublished, circa late 1979/early 1980

\\\ ///

RAVING, RAGING, AND REBOPS

/// \\\

Admit It, You Like to Kick Cripples, Too (Especially if You Are One)

Eventually one finds oneself in a perpetual state of institutionalized walking sleep, this diagnosed—however erroneously—by the patient as not disease, but no less than a lifestyle. But all lifeforms need food. Hence heavy metal.

I saw the sun come out and blanched in sorrow at its incredible gall. I had made a journey to the middle if not the end of the night, and had accustomed myself to the conceit that I was in fact living through death on the installment plan. Didn't the Velvets say it way back in 1970, just when heavy metal was peaking: "Who Loves the Sun?" Damn right, i.e., nobody Jack, and that's why Black Sabbath.

In the fall and early winter of 1971–72 I lived in the living room of a wretched farm in Walled Lake, Michigan. Walled Lake, if you care—and you shouldn't—is kinda like Dogpatch without the charm. It's the sticks, and when you're in the sticks in Michigan there is no romance attached, brother. I got laid exactly once that whole winter and for that I had to import a Canadian veritable infant who had her life changed by reading *The Sensuous Woman.* The rest of the time I masturbated and pursued numbness. I was just starting at a rock 'n' roll magazine called *Creem* at the time, and it being 1971 and the mag being at least ostensibly poor we all lived communally, i.e., I slept on my publisher's couch. Well I don't wanna put your collarbone outa joint crying on your shoulder, but I will say that one night I fell asleep quite drunk listening to Nico's *The Marble Index* through headphones, and when I woke up seven or so hours later not only was it still playing but I was all wound up bondage-style in the headphone cords. Plus which we were so goddamn communal that I couldn't even go into the bathroom to jerk off to *Playboy* (best around then and there) without having Dave Marsh (I'm sure you've all heard of him) bust in on me just when I was trying to get willie to rise to paper. He was at least polite about ducking out, but the point is *I couldn't even jerk off in peace,* no spuzz-spizz forthcoming that nite.

The solution/alternative? Well, alcohol helped. But alcohol, as strong as its rep is, will not save you from Middle American death drag: you need something more obliterative than any drug, or at least copacetic with prefrontal spongism. Ergo: heavy metal, which I had sampled previously, but found extensive recourse to that miserable winter. Every night that season I had a ritual: About five o'clock I'd head down to the "party store," pick up a half gallon of Gallo Port, then back to the old farmhouse to consume it while listening to all of Black Sabbath's first three albums in a row. This was my regimen for months. It worked, too.

Later I even found it within myself, that following spring when I'd discovered Quaaludes in the way *People* magazine discovers new Wonder Bread faces today, to trumpet and even actually like Grand Funk. Deep Purple—you bet, Pops! All of 'em . . . oh, 'twas a grand season indeed, best typified by the fact that one of the biggest AM hits was "Slipping into Darkness" by War, then *Exile on Main Street* came out and confirmed all our retreats into the murk, and heavy metal was the Sound of the Hour and also the answer because when you want to shout but can hardly speak it's mighty handy to have all them loud machines do it for you as you wham out, however sluggishly, your own nullasthenic frustration in what somebody less decimated and hence a sucker might deem "power chords." Ahh, but the power is all in our nerves, and being the troopers we are when they are shot we just catarrh on. Dig it, I know fairies wear boots but the only heavy metal album that broke the mold and shot down an entire generation was the Stooges' *Raw Power.* I said it then and history has been kind to my fat mouth. But for some of us who pass for you and I in the guise of some united generation, for those of us who lived it, heavy metal will live forever, like the first time we realized that listening to our records and splintering them under our stomping boot heels and eating the black shards might be one and the same thing. An iron lung filled with smog, oppression/depression cultivated like Mister Charlie's cotton field by willing handkerchief heads, it was a party to end 'em all, *La Dolce Vita* without pillow fights.

Gig, November 1977

Everybody's Search for Roots (The Roots of Punk, Part 1)

The "roots" of punk. Hah! That's what we've come to. It's kind of like including *Scooby-Doo, Where Are You?* in the *Encyclopedia Britannica.* Looked at in one way, you could assume (perhaps much to your relief) that the mere existence of articles like this means that punk is dead and gone. It's like Leslie Fiedler, author of *Love & Death in the American Novel,* wherein he postulated that all American literature from Melville and Twain on down was closet-homoerotic (Huck and Jim were asshole buddies y'see, and I don't have to tell you what goes on amidships while Ahab waits for sperm whales like Godot). (His next book was called *Getting Busted:* it was about pot; at the rate he was going he should be writing this article instead of me.) As I was saying Mr. Fiedler sat down one day to review four massive tomes on the History and Significance of Comic Books in Contemporary American Culture for the *New York Times Book Review,* and after giving each its just deserts, he wrote something along the lines of so here I sit with these four tomes piled by my typewriter, and I wonder just what it means, and why why why why why . . .

In other words it's harder 'n hangnails to be a deviant or even have a little moronic fun these days without some codifying crypto-academic or (worse yet?) the fashion industry (seen the recent Macy's ads for punk couture?) swooping down to rape your stance and leave you shivering fish-naked in the cultural welfare line. So I wouldn't blame you for hating me for this article at all, but on the other hand, having been around long enough to see at least three generations of punk rock come and go, I figure you're all just slavering for a sense of *tradition,* or your *roots,* or history, for God's sake!

No? Well that's what I thought, in fact that's why I'm doing it, because I want to make you all terminally self-conscious or at least irritated. It's not so much that I'm prejudiced against the younger generation for not appreciating the subtleties of the Seeds as opposed to the Buzzcocks—it's that I didn't know there was a younger generation. I read this article in *Newsweek* which quoted me to the effect that punk was here to stay and since I didn't remember giving any such quote or anything else for that matter I figured now's the time to cash in on my typical rock critic's oppressively musty store of useless cranial trivia so you'll all know that nothing you're doing is new whatsoever so you'll all get demoralized and forget about it and we can go back to Jackson Browne wanking his tears. I am not a punk and never was (too literate, besides no jazz fan can be a punk), but I gained a certain amount of notoriety exploiting the phenom before *Newsweek* knew there was one so here I am beating a dead horse, of which one advantage you certainly can say is that it's not going to resist. Besides which I'm a dilettante and want to *come on* like a punk so I can be respected by the publisher of *New Stiletto Bund Gazette* and other similar fine publications, so the punkiest thing I can think of to do is put down everything going now by comparing it disfavorably to shit that happened a decade or more ago. I admit it's childish, but like I said it's hard to be deviant these days—just think of it as like buying a brand-new black leather jacket and going out of your way never to put a single crease in it.

All right, that's enough of that, this article is getting slack. Time to tighten up. Lessee, how can I accomplish such a feat. Archie Bell and the Drells are in Philadelphia and incommunicado since all the discomatzos realized they *could* stop dancing with impunity, so I'm going to have to think of something imaginative. How about this: "It is the phantom spirit of an amphetamine age, gushing forth his geysers of grotesque gargoylerie upon the hapless heads of a public so numb they can scarcely respond with a piteous terminal twitching. . . ." That was written by Marvin H. Hohman, Jr., in an article entitled "Purging the Zombatized Void with Alice Cooper," in the summer 1970 issue of *Creem.* It was the first article ever published anywhere about Alice, and his first magazine cover. Marvin obviously had a vision; now he reviews jizrackjob fusions for *Downbeat.* Sic transit. And sic transit punk (and magazines as well), eh amigos? Let's take for instance the Shadows of Knight: did you know that one of them was once caught in a motel room in Chicago *in flagrante delecto* with either Question Mark or one of his Mysterians? And this in 1966 yet! Obviously proof of Iggy's contention that those boys were ahead of their time. Unlike, say . . . shit, I was gonna pick the biggest hip / u'ground name right now and nick some cranny of slipup from their genius to slander 'em, but was stopped by the fact there is no name out now worthy of that. Everybody knows Patti's problems, Bruce Springsteen's been unemployed, Bowie's not worth mentioning except his white on white hair and face ensemble looks like a test pattern without the test, Iggy I can't say anything bad about because I'm giving him one more album before I dump ten tons of slag on his puny pretensions, I mean who's left? I suppose you really wanna talk about punk rock. Okay, you tell me what punk rock is—in this space:

See, I told you so. Oh, but I'll show you the roots of punk. The roots of punk was the first time a kid ended up living with his parents till he was 40. The roots of punk was the first time you stole money out of your mother's purse and didn't know what to spend it on because you weren't old enough to buy beer. The roots of punk was the first time your father got so frustrated with your intransigence he almost raised his fists against you, and you not out of high school yet, and you didn't even care, you just wanted to drift a few blocks away and get fucked up. Punk may (may?) be essentially passive. Punk is stupid proud consumerism. Punk is oblivion when it isn't any fun and unlike winos you do have a choice in fact; you're young. Punk is bleared out of your mind watching Lancelot Link at 12 noon on Saturday and having no idea of what you're seeing. Punk is getting up early Saturday morning to jack off to Isis.[13] Punk is vomiting all over your "motherfuckers"/John Sinclair liner notes version of *Kick Out the Jams* and not particularly caring. Punk is ten thousand tattered skin magazines under your bed but never getting any satisfaction from masturbation not the kind that leads to languorous rest anyway so you exist on a thin hot prostate wire of tension and jack off three, four times a day, knowing it's stupid and pointless and hating it for that more than submerged guilt but doing it because there's nothing else to do but get drunk. Punk is having favorite girlfriends in the skin mags you come back to again and again. Punk is finally getting a girlfriend and then treating her shitty because you're too stupid, drunk, and self-absorbed. Punk is being a girl and fucking your husband/boyfriend while watching TV over his shoulder as he gets his gun. Punk is not punk, because it has become too codified. Punk is sitting in a half-dark room alone wishing you had Valiums with an indifferent record playing wanting to claw the stuffing out of the chair but feeling futility in your fingernails. Punk is hating poeticization of your condition. Punk is vague dreams of carnage and

[13] Lancelot Link and Isis were two beloved Saturday-morning kiddie-show heroes; the former was a "super chimp," while the latter was a "super woman."

bloody revenge when you can barely swat a comatose fly. Punk is wine stains across the grooves of *Between the Buttons* and "Sister Ray." Punk is pointlessness. Punk is ripping up articles like this one. Punk is lacking the energy or interest to bother ripping them up. Punk is reading this article mechanically because there's nothing else to do and the words glide by like cinders. Punk is hurling the magazine across the room, dropping your hands into your lap, idly scratching your dick or clit wondering if you wanna jerk off again, deciding it's not worth the trouble, staring blankly into space. Punk is thinking maybe we should go to the movies tonight and not having the energy or self-discipline to get up and walk across the room to pick up the daily paper. Punk is talking back to situation comedy rerun syndicated characters on afternoon TV. Punk is seeing girls in TV commercials and croaking "Take off yer clothes . . ." when you haven't been laid in two years. Punk is running out of beer at 5:30 A.M. and taking three Chlor-Trimetons to see if they'll exacerbate what's left of it. Punk is waking up in the morning and not having the energy or motivation to get up and turn on the soap operas on the color TV atop the dresser across the room from your bed. Punk is starting to jerk off, getting a hardon, thinking oh fuck it what's the use, and giving up. Punk is putting on a record you love, lying down on the couch, rolling over and trying to go to sleep at four in the afternoon or seven at night just because you want that state of twilight consciousness which is better than drugs. Punk is being so lazy you want girls to jack you off or suck you instead of bothering to fuck. Punk is being willing to eat pussy while dreaming of some record you wanna buy. Punk is laziness at apogee with no apologies. Punk is saying fuck rock 'n' roll. Punk is saying fuck punk rock. Punk is treating your 2,000-plus LP collection like dirt. Punk is *passé.* Punk is just a word dug by media. Punk is anything you do that should have consequences but either doesn't or you ignore them. Punk is a meaningless word that everybody is sick to death of purporting to represent a state of mind and lifestyle which while not so very complex cannot be reduced any further than it has been already in inchoate preverbal practice. Punk is something worth destroying posthaste. Hopefully this article will speed that process. Punk is being old and smart enough to know that your girlfriend is too young but not having the balls to kick her out. Like when she keeps saying "Oh, I DON'T KNOW WHAT TO DO WITH YOU" everytime you say some ridiculous alkie crazy thing only Bukowski has a right to, and instead of attacking her or just withdrawing you chuckle indulgently. Punk is playing father to teen pussy when you should be a shark but haven't got the teeth. Punk is getting stuck months later like the old curmudgeon as she chases local deejays at press parties in front of you and all you can say is maybe she'll grow out of it because you love the taste of her twat and the fact that no other woman will fuck all nite to "Raw Power." Punk is when you throw her over and pick up a barfloozy same day take her home drink gin fuck and in the nite she menstruates all over your bed and in the morning you drink more gin. That is when you know you are growing from punk into what some people think of as a man. At least some blood marks the spot, like Grauman's prints or the hollows of Pompeii. You don't feel like such a punk no more with all that history under you. I suppose that's when you grow up to Jon Landau productions. Either that or a dusty window and an eye that needs a toothpick.

New Wave, August 1977

Back Door Men and Women in Bondage

There is a very good reason why I am writing and you are reading the reels of jabowock verbiage you are presently feasting your faded eyes on. The reason for me is that I am totally and terminally fed up with all the established regular commercial paying better distributed Rock magazines because none of them will allow me to jack off in print which obviously is a crime against true nature. *Creem* has become a repository of clumsy gibberish written by people who really haven't got the chops nor have they (I'm not afraid to say it) paid the dues necessary to make any reader but maybe their mothers and nursemaids actually purgatory their eyes with the flattened jiz they're publishing in there, in other words (I'm not ashamed to say this either, in fact I have no shame about anything at all, because I have no ego, you should see me sing my songs onstage some time but I'm not gonna use this space to hype myself because John Mendelsohn was pathetic enough to be a lesson to the next thirteen generations so hopefully you'll just be lucky to see me vomit up my fantasies on one of your local stages sometime) . . . where was I, I'm getting lost . . . that's one reason (one more) I like writing for rags like this, I can get lost and nobody cares, because you were lost in the first place, otherwise you wouldn't even be publishing a magazine like this, I mean what do you think "punk rock" and all attendant flapdoodle is about if not being lost and not only being upfront about it but actually *proud* . . . like this gay Junior College Speech Professor said to me one time with a knowing gleam in his eyes, "I've had some of my best times when I was *lost*" and that ain't what I mean either, I mean don't misread into it because I ain't paranoid but obviously your magazine is not directed at the *After Dark* audience, which is good, straights direly need some intimate organ of communication besides Dear Abby which as any fool knows is not straight at all, in fact one of the most inspiring things to me about the proliferation of new fanzines is not only that they're supporting all the great new groups all over the world but that I know they're written published art-directed linotyped printed proofread etc. by people who spend a considerable amount of their waking hours jerking off, be they men/boys or women/girls. Which by the way if we really all don't want to ever grow up we better concoct some new descriptive nouns for our persuasions—how about puds and bitches? I realize puds ain't too glorioski but I don't know a single woman who wouldn't be proud to be known as a bitch; like take Helen Wheels whom I'm sure most of you've all heard of NYC punk rock and Blue Öyster Cult lyrics fame . . . she's just basically a nice SWEET girl who wouldn't (couldn't) hurt a dying katydid if she was ordered to by Sandy Pearlman . . . but she likes to pass herself off as a black leather badass macho toughchick feralteething molteneyed stilettopalmed BITCH straight & drooling rat venom from the lower depths of the IRT . . . she hangs out with Hell's Angels and other subhuman trolls to reinforce this "image," not only that and speaking of which she actually wears a jacket upon the back of which is emblazoned the stigmatic spinal marquee "SUBHUMAN" but what's even worse she had the godawfullest tattoo that looks shit man I dunno like some hood ornament on a '53 Oldsmobile in red green and bile imprinted forever all the way around one of her wrists and that's something she'll carry to her grave which hopefully will welcome her approx 120 years from now if she eats enough yogurt, it's like Lenny Bruce said about being Jewish and having to get buried with a tattoo, your relatives would rather you just cut off your arm and buried it in the East River before the funeral, but by now if they've got a gander at some of her masculine companionados I imagine Helen's folksies would feel only slightly less mortified if she deported herself to a nuclear silo buried 40 miles underground in North Dakota, which only goes to show that in spite of manifold and pervasive evidence to the contrary it still is not all that hard to be an out-and-out all-American deviant at least in the eyes of Dom 'n' Mad in the year of our bored gumsgnashings 1977 so I hope all you ponque kidleets out there take proper inspiration from this twice-told talke of Helen Wheels and stop feeling so goddamn sorry for yourselves that both me and Phast Phreddie[14] would just as soon put you to death at this point. Either that or tie you to your high chairs and make you listen to *The Idiot* for the next eight years, by which time we'll have another prezidunce who hopefully will be a Republican and a criminal as well so we can all relax and go back to feeling cynical about the basic fact of being alive and everything else from there on up and not have to bear the onerous brunt of thinking that maybe rock 'n' roll and you and me and all the other warpos are not dead after all so things might actually get better if we pulled our paging fingers out our buttholes and got around to applying ourselves again like we did starting in 1963 or thereabouts as soon as that jock creep JFK caught a skullful of era's end and everybody thenceforth went berserk till Nixon got in but have ya ever noticed how even berserkness travels in cycles, shit it's almost enough to make ya go back to throwing the I Ching. Notice I didn't say where you should throw it; I threw mine out the window after it told me I was gonna marry a short blonde girl I went to high school with in 1963 when there were no blondes in my high school and all the vergingly verdant womens there were six feet eight inches tall which meant I could eat pussy without having to fall on my knees which did a hell of a lot for my masculine ego which by the way reminds me if Cherie Currie is reading this I'd love to fuck you even though I know you're nothing but a stupid bitch who thinks Quaaludes are the apogee of Western technological civilization, I'd like to tongue your clit till you screamed

[14] Esteemed *Back Door Man* publisher Fred Patterson.

and then make you suck my cock till I bled joy and then I'd kiss your pouty lips just once just to show how sensitive and compassionate I am and then I'd bite your pathetically teeny titties and maul and twist 'em around with my practiced mouth until you screamed louder better in real nonschmaltzy unromantic pain kinda like a Russian intellectual being tortured in a Soviet mental institution for writing poetry that didn't hype the proletariat and then I'd hunch crawl and maybe even grovel down trailing drool across the pale tender white breath trampoline between your titties and your cute li'l belly, I'd trail drool like a snail on his pilgrimage to a vat of salt, fact I'd fizz up just that gruesome just to lick the Fowley rust out of the inner circles of your eyeballs, your blasted bruised broasted irises which are like the eighth and ninth circles of Hell, speaking of which if you wanna go there read *Maldoror* by Comte de Lautreamont because Satan and nobody else wrote it and it proves for all time that Satan is most definitely not a punk rocker, then I'd suck out the knotted strands of your untied navel till last Tuesday's tuna sandwiches came streaming from your cunt-wide bleeding gut along with half-digested Percodans and I'd slop up that whole mess too, then down down down with monomanical obsessiveness because I really mean to devour you toenails to platinum dye Cherie, so down I snark to loll and brrble moleing and foaling in the Caledonian forest of your pubic hair, meaning before I get to eat your poosy I will slobber all over what grows like a victory garden just above it in fact worse than that I will bury my phlegmootic fool's face in the Hansel & Gretel forest of your bush and nuzzle to my mania's content, after which quite naturally I will take your ruby glistening and by now obviously primed clit upon the end of my totally schooled and ferally furious tongue and holding back the final fury of my two years at least nursed desire I will play taps and "Till There Was You" on that fine little kernel of your basically gelatinous self, I'll tongue you tentatively on purpose till you scream like a disemboweled dog and slam your fists against the wall over above behind your twisted head repeatedly until both your hands are bloody pulps fit for stomping wop grapes into rotten but reasonably priced wine that blazered swingers who read *New York* magazine are proud to serve their guests always making sure to get the pronunciation so exactly right you know in front they have no idea what they're serving or whether it's anything but swill, and swill is what I want from you Cherie, the swill that roils up inside your writhing cunt as I plunge my maddened mottled speed-cracked wine-drenched tongue just as deep into your mysterious eternal gushing flushing rushing timeless arching expansively contracting deliriously shivering soulhole as I can possibly get it, I mean I'm going to eat you out you worthless slut like you've never been eaten before especially since I bet say Robert Plant was never so considerate, that faggot probably just wanted you to blow his puny limey puckledrop after which he rolled over without another word (not that there was one in the first place) snored off hugging his pillow like you wished he'd hug you as he honks out flatted fifths that pass for Z's dreaming of stairways to heaven which in his benighted beleaguered budgie's brain is just a place where hippies don't lose their looks when they turn 35 and as nature will always have it the old jowls begin to sag just like any businessman approaching middle age, I mean shit Cherie if you can fuck a pathetic accountant like that putz you can certainly open wide your sugarbunny icecream spliceyummy for a destiny-driven madman like me, I ain't proud, I'd just like to taste the sweet sweet core of your honeybuns, been thinking about it ever since I saw the cover of your first album, I didn't even care that applying all habitual rock critic standards I think all your music sucks syphilitic rodents that have been dead in the backstreet gutters of Tijuana for nigh ten years now, excepting "Born to Be Bad" that is, I like that song, but who cares about songs anyway? Do you care about my songs? Of course not. You want to suck my cock and/or (take your choice as per matters of which approach goes first or later) feel it pulsing madly back in the USA which is only the deepest regions beyond time beyond lust beyond human citizenship beyond Mercury Records even who can't fuck you over any worse than they did the Dolls, way back heart attacking deeply plunged up there in the neverlevered land of your panicked palpitating pussy which after the fuck is over will get up drained and spent and wrecked and bent from the hotel room bed where I will be watching your ass wobble like Tina Louise's whole body on any old episode of *Gilligan's Island,* I will see you there naked and vulnerable defenseless and somehow slightly sad as all humans are in the dawn light after sex, I will watch you walk away from my spent joyjuice delirium through Egyptian-coin lidded eyes, I looking like someone shuttered and boxed by the heaviest of drugs not even invented yet, drugs that will make heroin look like the Fat Albert Show, and you with your tight white little ass disappearing from my yearning yet basically jaded because knowing (have known) eyes, across the room, into the half shadows of the distant oh so long-gone hopeless land between the closet where your halter top hangs and the bathroom where inside the medicine cabinet are Percodans and Valiums I'm gonna need badly as ever in about 20 minutes, because this is a hangover for the books, that's why I'm publishing it in this one, I have drunk cognac of your slushing slit and drunk on the realization of this dream I realize there is nothing left for me now in life at all by listening to old Neil Young and Strawberry Alarm Clock albums at 78 on a turntable that rotates counterclockwise, you have murdered my heart by gobbling my cock Cherie, so I will drink the sweat off my eyeballs in my cupped palm as I watch you walk across the room, step lithe as the child you are which is why I wanted to defile you in the first place, into your purple silk panties with the little face of Dewey Duck on the pudendal mound (Huey and Louie grew up to turn out homos, they're on Fred Halsted ballcruncher jockstraps worn by Sylvester Stallone because it's the only way he can get it up to fuck Ernest Borgnine who is his personal fantasy), I see you step lightly like a ballerina as Van Morrison said in *Astral Weeks* an album you're too stupid to appreciate, into the barely Kleenex-thick foliage designed to hide your own holy vibrant foliage, then into your hip huggers which I wish you wouldn't wear because they look so square but baby I don't care, I wouldn't love you if you weren't corny as hell and at least seven years behind the times, then into the closet reaches your pale thin arm for that halter with the Fonz's face in living color on it right between your tits because just like any other patriotic all-American girl you're religious and render unto Caesar the tremulous titty-banners that he only deserves, followed of course by the passage of your delectable heels which not 15 minutes ago I licked like they were the snocones of heaven into your high-heeled stiletto pumps which are as red as the blood of Idi Amin's victims who were found stuffed up in the dam of Lake Victoria with their rubbery water-rutted decomposing bodies swaying gently in the silent ever-slowing currents of the pitiless undersea, I see those suckable sintwinkle toes slide into them pumps like a switchblade into a Spanish sheath contrived by a Puerto Rican assassin of Rockefellers and Beames and hidden deep in his belt lining or interior boots were made for walking, where you out now out the door I see you walking strutting like a minxlynx sheena banshee bitchess rape-job expert leaving another decimated cock in your wake, and as you close the door behind you to go be interviewed by *Rolling Stone* and tell Ben Fong-Torres what a great lay I am I roll over in ennuidal despair and close my eyes tight as canned laughter just so I can open my mouth and let out a moan so long and low and lonely they could hear it over their Cheerios in Topeka. George Jetson, recently migrated to manage a Kansan Q-tip dispensary, dropped his spoon into his breakfast bowl where it splashed thru soggy cereal to smack commemorative JFK in the face at the bottom, and with tears in his eyes said to his wife Irma (he divorced the one on the cartoon show when he found out she was a lesbian disco deejay with pierced nipples depending rusty "I Like Ike" buttons) (you wouldn't wanna suck tits like that either, admit it) (besides her twat was blocked by a full color print of a Carter Family—not the ones that married into Johnny's Cash but yes them rubes down White House way—all blowing each other while reading *The Watchtower*) (enough to make any man or lesbian lose interest), he stopped masticating his fodder and said unto his spouse "Jesus' lice, Irma, did you hear that? Lester Bangs finally got to fuck Cherie Currie and he isn't even happy about it. What's the matter with those Hollywood hotshots anyway? It's enough to make you cancel your subscription to *People* magazine!" His wife didn't say anything; she was a deaf-mute; in fact that's why he married her; he didn't mind her predecessor's odd sexual proclivities so much as that she just couldn't keep her trap shut. But Irma, like so many deaf-mutes, blazed a Magna Carta phlegmspew of crystalline eloquence in the stalagtite nether reaches of her mutist's mind. She thought that Lester was just bored because he knew like she knew that to get back to the original subject of this aggressively pointless article Cherie Currie could never in an aeon of holidays be one-third the fuck that Helen Wheels was and is with one labial lip tied behind her ears which is why they're still wet and all the boys wanna lick 'em. And Irma, as usual, was right.

Back Door Man, July–August 1977

liner notes to *It Falleth Like Gentle Rains from Heaven—The Mekons Story*

The Mekons are the most revolutionary group in the history of rock 'n' roll. They are also the finest artists ever to have graced this admittedly somewhat degenerate form with the grace of their aesthetic sensibilities, rarefied as a glimpse through a butterfly's wing. The muses gobbled cantharides for these fellows. Collectively they comprise a kind of Sistine Chapel ceiling 'neath which the pathetic mess of pottage, which is commonly snickered off as the "rock scene" from PiL to Black Oak Arkansas, can but swash buboed forearms cross their offal-crusted snouts and recommence to grovel together in the La Brea–trackless depths of corporate swill.

Remember that scene in Lina Wertmüller's *Seven Beauties* where the concentration-camp inmate commits suicide by swan diving into a vat of festeringly clotted human excrement approximately the length of Troy Donahue's pool at the La Cienega pad he owned in the summer of 1963? And all because he would rather drown lungs full of shit than endure one more moment of this travesty posing as existence? Well, that's how John L*d*n told me he felt after hearing this new LP by the Mekons. "I must give it up," he wailed, knocking over his bottle of Tetley's AND NOT BOTHERING TO GET ANOTHER ONE! He took his vial of crystal meth and poured it out the open window of Virgin Records' offices, where it was quickly devoured by a passing train of abbesses who began to frug frenetically while lamenting as one keening dolorous wind-chilled whine their ignorance of the current whereabouts of "Killer" Joe Piro, as well as Monti Rock III. . . .

"Man! I thought I had 'em conned with that Public Image shit but these cats called my bluff! I'm a washout!"

Meanwhile the planet Earth is rid of yet another sniveling ingrate. The Mekons may now assume their proper place in the highest bowers of the hallowed Halls of Rocque (co-leased by Wolfman Jack and Sid Bernstein). THEY ARE BETTER THAN THE BEATLES. They are even better than Budgie and REO Speedwagon combined. They come not to bury the recording industry but to gourmandise it. They gave me fifteen hundred dollars for writing these notes. All their daddies are rich which is why they get to keep putting out this swill. I have never heard this album. I never will. I have better things to do, such as misting my begonias or playing Eno's *Music for Pizzerias* to my goldfish to wean him from his Valium habit. Music is all worthless garbage as obsolete as a lorgnette at a destruction derby in South Carolina. I never listen to it and neither do the Mekons. They make it instead. Everybody has to do something. My advice to you is to kill yourself. But buy this record first. It will make a nice coaster for your grieving relatives to put their Bushmill's and water on.

January 1981

Every Song a Hooker

This column is testament and deposition I did purchase one single 45 rpm record called "Bette Davis Eyes" by Kim (I *think* it's Kim) Carnes. I forget what label it's on, you can go look it up somewhere if you care. You can find it if you try hard enough. I have also seen Ms. Carnes perform this song on a videotape on TV. It was a gothic/Nouveau Romantic/s&m/etc. little strip of tape wherein Ms. Barnes, I mean Carnes, a blonde of apparent Irish extraction, wanked in the third person about all the sultry come-hithers she or someone could yank up outa her li'l ol' bod, while the camera slowly panned back to reveal several tiers on which women dressed in black were slapping the faces of men dressed in white or vice versa I forget which, anyway it was on the beat.

Although I live in Manhattan, I must confess a certain ignorance of some of my neighbors' more rarefied leisure-time activities. If anyone reading this magazine saw the same video strip and can explain to me what those people were doing would they please get in touch? Will reply immediately. Discretion assured.

As for Ms. Carnes, I am now informed that she does not holler, she does not shake them on down. She is a discrete modular woman who keeps her tresses fresh: immediately prior to entering the New Wave guignol where aforesaid vidtape was made she had very successfully completed and delivered a "duet" LP with Kenny Rogers. If the Mets win the World Series next year she might sing the National Anthem, and if Idi Amin is elected president of the United States in 1984 she may whistle tunes of ancient Cathay among his pale concubines. She's the drapes, but what's she framing?

Hooks, that's what. Fuckin' *dockloads* of 'em, buddy. And I am further informed that hooks are only the *magic secret element* that if you cram as many of them as you can into any one single it just might light up *Billboard.* YEA TEAM! A HIT!!! Dionne Warwick points and smiles. This is good. Yes.

Now you might get uppity and ask, "Just what the hell are these so-called 'hooks' and whence their derivation?" Cut to location footage. The withered black man is duly wheeled on-screen, at bottom of which the words "Aberdeen, Mississippi" appear.

"Mr. White, when you first wrote the words and adjacent notes to 'I'm looking far in my mind, and I believe I'm fixing to die,'[15] did you have any idea of the fabulously incremental hook therein?"

"Shit, are you kiddin'? Whadda you think I am, a local curiosity or somethin'? First we did extensive demographic surveys, which revealed to us that there was a mood of nihilism in the land owing to concurrent Depression conditions that might be tapped for big bucks if we screw the right set o' chords and words together! People always want to turn it into some kind of apocalypse when it's just their own pitiful little culture going down the drain, know what I mean? So I sat down and wrote it in the appropriate mode, and lord knows we cleaned up!"

"Were there any other hooks in said song, Mr. White?"

"Of course, fool. We made sure to stick in some shit about 'families' and 'mother' and all suchlike to keep the suckers thinkin' they were gettin' that 'personal' touch," he laughs.

Listen, I hate hooks. The first time I saw the word "hook" was in a review of a Shocking Blue album in *Rolling Stone* in 1969. The author

[15] That would be Delta bluesman Bukka White, whose 1940 "Fixin' to Die" is a primo example of his melodically simple and rhythmically treacherous style.

had evidently discovered that songwriters sometimes used it and now informed us that the bass riff was the almighty "hook" in their hit "Venus," that one irresistible little melodic or rhythmic twist that'll keep you just coming back and back and back to buy and buy and buy.

I went out one Friday afternoon more recently and bought *Sucking in the Seventies.* Now *there's* a hook. The Stones hadn't counted on a Moral Majority–type backlash against the title affecting sales, but they knew they could count on people like me. I knew the record was a piece of shit but there was some part of me that lied to some other part of me and said just maybe somewhere down in there it mighta held some of that primal Stones grit, as well as revelations previously untapped concerning the present lay of the *mores,* indications of what we might be up to. Aw hell, okay, I paid six bucks for the damn thing partially because I thought, I actually believed, that when Mick sang "New York, get up, get out, get into something new" in "Dance (Part One)" on *Emotional Rescue,* then in "Dance (Part Two)" (ONLY available on *SITS,* of course) Mick was actually gonna tell us all what that something new might be. So now I can be officially stamped and certified: MORON. Or really just a sucker but that's just one of the Stones' hooks. The Stones confess they sucked for most of the decade, but we sucked too, hey just one big happy family, except guess who sucked the bigger one? I tell ya, they got a million of 'em, even allowing for energy crisis.

I bought "Bette Davis Eyes" too, just like you did. While I think it's a hideous little ditty and want my money back immediately so I can go buy a quart of Sunkist sodee-pop, still it's this hook business that's really got me down. Partially I must confess this is sour grapes, because I write songs and not long after I started a friend (and fellow rock critic, y'oughta see our Old School ties!) informed me that: "Your songs are just poems set to music. They don't have any hooks." And then he pulls out his copy of Elvis Costello's *Armed Forces* and slaps it on the turntable: "Now here's an example where every song has hooks all over the place."

I listened. Still sounded like some limey gettin' an F in Bruce Springsteen class and throwing a wildly inflated snit about it, sounding like Springsteen sounding like a real bad but slicked-up imitation of the Band, with maybe some Gary Lewis and the Playboys thrown in, *pee-yew,* which reaction I also had to the likes of Graham Parker, poor bleeder. So maybe you can just mark it down not only to sour grapes but also I got bad taste (never liked *Layla,* either, so that clinches it).

On the other hand, just maybe somewhere over the years I heard one hook too many, or the same hook recycled once too often. Maybe you did too. I have also been informed along the way that hooks could take all sorts of other forms besides a change in the music or a line in the lyrics, could be a special sigh, x-tree li'l rhythmic fillip, or even thrown-in whizzer tweezer buzzers for all I know. It's been known to work. And if you mentioned something like "Leader of the Pack" by the Shangri-Las, I would happily concede that *there* was a song with hooks aplenty that blew you out of the car. But what people mostly mean by hooks today is catchy licks that worked for the Beatles or whoever so why shouldn't they work for *us?*

As for that one hook too many, I have not listened to the radio, of any sort, since "Band on the Run" was a hit and driving in my car I heard it for the 983rd time and got irritated for some reason and just turned off my radio and left it off in perpetuity. You are reading the words of a music critic who at this exact moment or any given time has absolutely no idea what the Top Ten albums and singles in this country are. Well, some idea—if I see Bruce Springsteen or REO Speedwagon release new LPs, I know they'll be in there, although I don't know what REO Speedwagon sounds like, or rather I wouldn't recognize them if I heard them but do know what they sound like and say no thanks. The charts do pass my eyes occasionally, but when I try to scan them they turn immediately into a blur. Last time I was on top of them Southern Boogie was questionable re whether holding or starting to slip into regional guaranteed sales, so you can see I am hopelessly out of touch.

The real question, though, is does either of us *want* to know about it? Do you leave the radio on just out of habit? Do 90 percent of those songs mean anything to you? The record industry has experienced massive sales slippage, but just maybe that's because they're putting out records that nobody can hear. I don't *want* to hear or know about songs like "Bette Davis Eyes" because their very existence makes me sick because of what it implies about the purveyors' attitude toward the target audience, which basically boils down to the corporate assumption that everybody's a creep. Or as P. T. Barnum etc. And the image of the hook implies seduction (and betrayal?) of the listener anyhow. Believe me, the musicians and studio technicians making this stuff, not to mention the deejays who have to play it all day, have just as much contempt for it as I do, and if you buy it they have even more contempt for you.

The music business was always cynical, but the cynicism of the music business as it stands today is awesome, surreal. I know it's hardly the first time they've managed to work an ad onto the *front cover* of a magazine, but I for one sure did appreciate that recent issue of *Rolling Stone* where Tom Petty was holding up a dollar bill while winking at the camera, thus implying that if YOU (The Consumer, ever alert) buy HIS NEW ALBUM, which I hear he ordered the Big Boys to knock a dollar off the price of or not raise it to $9.95 for 10 li'l toons in a cardboard sleeve, if you jes up an' buy thet sumbitch, why partner you be's cookin' with gravy even thank the lawd. Tom Petty'll like ya, clap ya on the shoulder, MCA will nod approvingly, *Rolling Stone* will love you for already having spent more than the dollar on them and dish up an even more stupefying insult in two weeks which everybody who likes to think they're hip will claim to have ignored while secretly knowing it's at least as good as *People* for the bus or subway—Christ, you gotta have something!

And as Tom himself steps into Them Boots of Next Springsteen (some people still think the world never needed the first one) you have practically committed a patriotic act by going out and buying not just *Rolling Advertisement* but also that worthless album where it all sounds like recycled Byrds/Stones and the omnipresent SPRINGSTEEN . . . some of the songs being short stories Tom started but couldn't think of a plot. Some grimy guy in a hotel room, you know the stuff, a song about transients, that stuff's big now too just like Mr. White said about the Thirties, or some girl or maybe various girls he's really pissed at but he never says why so you never can even figger out whether 'twas one dame done him bad or a whole parade of them . . . Christ, is this stuff pathetic. But. Somebody somewhere thinks he got that Certain Glow. Look, he went to the trouble to screw the hooks ripped straight outa the guts of the most obvious mid-Sixties standards right into them diesel carbines 'neath which his band be huff-puffin' away. That was good enough to get him on the cover of *Rolling Stone,* so it oughta damnsure be good enough for you. Even if I still can't get up an exclamation point about said product, you better not listen to my elitist babble and by all means keep your eye on that boy. He's gonna go places in this world. Somebody has to.

Music and Sound Output, March/April 1982

Bad Taste Is Timeless

Some excerpts from the diary of a crank . . .

I would like to clarify recent statements made here and elsewhere concerning nostalgia and listening habits, because I think both I in my last column and many other folks have recently gotten into the habit of confusing/misusing the word "nostalgia." For instance, I wrote in another publication: "What I did (in 1981) was what almost everybody else . . . did: listened to old music, when I listened at all." So I get a letter from one kid berating me for listing Beck, Bogert & Appice as a listening preference over, say, X or Joy Division: "How can you be so nostalgic? Don't you know there are all kinds of great *new* groups like the Fall, Fad Gadget, the Dickies, Clock DVA, and Orange Juice?" Another reader writes, "Why don't you just break out your hookah and your Blind Faith albums and hang it up, you old fool?"

The answer to that last one is I never liked Blind Faith in the first place, and marijuana makes *everything* sound like Fad Gadget and the Fall. These people are confusing nostalgia with taste, a not uncommon error these days. Ever since the advent of New Wave, it has been considered uncool, if not an outright admission of collapse in the face of future shock, to admit to liking anything recorded pre-1977 over the latest fab waxing from Blighty or your local garage. The editor of *New York Rocker,* for instance, writes to tell me that my stance reminds him of hoary old jazz critic Leonard Feather's cowlike intransigence in the face of Ornette Coleman's *Free Jazz* 20 years ago. I wrote him back: "Unfortunately, all that cowplop you tell your readers to run out and buy every month is not some ineluctable avant-garde that threatens everybody now but they'll all look back in 10 or 20 years and realize how vital it was. It's a bunch of nothing that challenges no one."

That's why I'd rather listen to Hank Williams or Beck, Bogert & Appice or Charlie Parker or the Royal Guardsmen. I have to say that the champions of the current New Wave "avant-garde" are largely trendies, and I can guarantee you there will be no Throbbing Gristle repackages from Japan in the year 2000. It's not even that big of a controversy right now, since most critics are afraid to put very much of this stuff down and 99.9 percent of the public is indifferent.

But listening to music recorded 20, 30 years ago is not living in the past, is not nostalgia. According to my dictionary, nostalgia is "homesickness . . . a longing for something far away or long ago or for former happy circumstances." The truth is that the Sixties, not to mention the Fifties, sucked in the first place and you wouldn't like it if you were back there in a time when people did things like informing you you were mentally ill or worse if you didn't wanna take a toke on the doob. The Fifties was a time when you couldn't walk down the street without bumping into some pissed-off frustrated repressed ugly cretin looking to beat the shit out of somebody (like you) because he wasn't getting any from his girlfriend. No one in his right mind would want to return to either of those eras, which is why the lie in rosy confections like *Grease* and *Beatlemania* is despicable. But preferring Hank Williams or Charlie Parker or the Sun Sessions or the Velvet Underground to Squeeze and Rickie Lee Jones and the Go-Gos and the Psychedelic Furs is not nostalgia, it's good taste. Just like listening to Beck, Bogert & Appice or Clock DVA and the Fall are bad taste. So I'll take my bad taste and you're welcome to yours, and maybe someday something will actually happen again and then we'll both be happy.

I know that by writing these columns I've put myself in danger of coming off as a crank. Why, an esteemed colleague in a crosstown publication even accused me of "crotchety nagging," by which I take it he refers to the fact that I no longer support the doctrine of teenage hegemony (didn't when I was a teenager, either), and think 99 percent of current music is worthless. But I suspect that some of my readers may have become cranks also. When was it: the day you let all those rock critics talk you into buying *Strength Thru Oi,* or the day you read your last exegesis on Elvis Costello's lyrics?

Vis a vis nostalgia, here are some capsule reviews of recent (mostly British) rock acts:

Bow Wow Wow: sounds like Sergio Mendez and Brazil '66 with Burundi drum machine.

Fad Gadget: lousy imitation of the Doors.

Rip, Rig & Panic and *Pigbag:* crappy jazz-rock—or as a friend said, "Remember when Savoy Brown had horns?"

Blurt: worthless sub–James Chance (no nasty edge) take on Sixties Coltrane-Ayler-Shepp honk.

Blue Rondo a La Turk: unbelievably lame samba band.

Konk: two and a half minutes of 1957 Shorty Rogers rhythm track outtakes with the melodies mixed out.

The Lounge Lizards: in which 1950s TV private-eye soundtracks with all the heat sucked out are mistaken for bebop.

Fingerprintz: the Lounge Lizards go disco.

The Gun Club: dull attempt to punk Robert Johnson blues.

The Blasters: in every song you immediately recognize where they stole the riffs, and most of them were stolen from Top Ten hits of the Fifties.

I recently appeared on a radio show with critic Robert Christgau and critic/DJ Pablo "Yoruba" Guzman of Manhattan r&b station WLIB-

AM. I told Pablo: "Black music has no soul anymore. You know it's true! I just figured you'd appreciate a white person coming on here and telling you. It doesn't have one iota more passion than all that New Wave garbage Christgau writes about. Do you really listen to it?"

Christgau says: "I don't consider intense emotionalism a valid criterion by which to judge music." (He had just finished saying: "I think there's more good records out now than ever!")

Pablo says: "Well, I went to a couple of concerts recently that I thought were really moving."

"Who was that?"

"Kraftwerk and Devo."

I was flabbergasted. What do you say to something like that?

"It was beautiful," he said, "to see all those black and white kids getting together like that." (Notice he didn't say the *music* did anything to him.)

"Yeah," I said, recovering, "that's because both races wanna be robots. Devo are just a bunch of wormy little wimps who think if they get rid of their personalities their neuroses will go too. And everybody knows it's been downhill for Kraftwerk since *Autobahn*—though "Showroom Dummies" was good. Did you see all those idiots in those discos dancing to that song? 'Ve are show-room *dahm*mies, *show*-room dummies.' 'Yeah, that's me!' "

He brightened. "Yeah, okay, that's what we wanted: some of that Lester Bangs controversy!"

I asked my friend James Marshall if he thought the current dismal state of music was likely to improve. "No," he said. "It's got to get worse, because everybody's into their own thing and doesn't wanna know. Pretty soon every band will have no more than three fans, and nobody will even have any friends. Then after that you'll start resenting the other guy *because* he likes the same thing you like: it's your turf! How dare he encroach? So then people will start killing each other for appropriating each other's musical tastes and thus infringing on the neighbor's hipness space. How can you be smug about being the only person in the world cool enough to appreciate some piece of New Wave shit, or a blues band or arcane jazz artist for that matter, if you find out somebody else likes it? Don't dare *tell* 'em! Don't even tell your wife or girlfriend! Keep it safe inside your Walkman!"

Music and Sound Output, July/August 1982

An Instant Fan's Inspired Notes: You Gotta Listen

Hi there. Right now I bet I can read your mind. You're standing there holding this album, your curiosity perhaps mildly piqued, but wondering (and probably more dubious than not) whether an album as off-the-wall as this one appears to be might actually be a worthwhile addition to your collection that you'd play often because you actually liked to listen to it, just like a lot of rock or jazz albums or anything else. I know, because I've been in the same position so many times, and I'm actually sick of all the dreams I keep having about it. The alternative outcome of course, would be that you just paid hard-earned money for some oddball novelty item that might be good for one play, maybe, another at Christmas when the relatives are over, a couple lame Nazi jokes and then "Get it *off!*"

Most records, as we know all too well, aren't worth the vinyl they're stamped in. Who the hell wants a bunch of by-now-probably-dead Germans from the mid-1920's singing harmonies that're some weirdo combination of music hall, rathskeller, alpine folk strains and, most important to me and perhaps you as well, *American black blues, gospel, ragtime, and jazz influences.* Which makes it more than just another novelty right there. Because when these guys sing Duke Ellington, they mean it. Do they ever.

Still reading? Good. Don't feel sorry for Hannibal Records if they end up taking a bath on this passel o' cheery Jerries—feel sorry for yourself if you don't buy it. Because I'm gonna lay it on the line right here and now: I have never heard anything like the contents of this album before in my life. Which is saying something, because over the years I've become something of a musicologist with around 4,000 albums covering everything from Mamie Smith and Her Jazz Hounds to Teenage Jesus and the Jerks. I may have bad taste (for instance, I truly *like* Teenage Jesus and the Jerks), but at least I know the territory pretty well.

Now, the more I listen to this record, the more I'm impressed by two qualities it has in abundance: one is soul, and nobody has to tell you how hard that is to find in *anything* new being put out these days; the other is that, near as I can tell, *this record does not fit into the territory.* It creates its own turf and holds it masterfully. It's too steeped in jazz and gospel to be truly "German," but of course it's still European through and through, enough so that more than one listener has laughed out loud. But they were laughing with pleasure.

What's more, I'll admit in front that I have a special affinity for things that don't quite fit into any given demarcated category, partly because I'm one of those perennial misfits myself by choice as well as fate or whatever. By profession, I am categorized as a rock critic. I'll accept that, especially since the whole notion that one somehow has a "career" instead of just doing whatever you feel like doing at any given time has always amused me when it didn't make me wanna vomit. O.K., I'm a rock critic. I also write and record music. I write poetry, fiction, straight journalism, unstraight journalism, beatnik drivel, mortifying love letters, death threats to white jazz critics signed "The Mau Maus of East Harlem," and once a year my own obituary (latest entry: "He was promising . . ."). The point is that I have no idea what kind of a writer I am, except that I do know that I'm good and lots of people read whatever it is that I do, and I like it that way.

These notes may seem discursive but bear with me, we're going somewhere, and you're going to like it. This "career" business, like whenever somebody sees me playing music and says, "Is this going to be your new career?" always reminds me of an old Charles Bukowski story called "Would You Suggest Writing as a Career?" It's about how he gets up one morning with a terminal hangover, vomits, staggers off to make some godawful dawn flight to some Bo-Weevil U located in the Lower Left Dustbowl corner pocket where the li'l Cessna now verging on Aeroflot vomitorium is about to touch down in one of the quaintest, cutest, most dilapidatedly rustic little burbs in America: We Eat Outlanders, Utah, our nation's last remaining dry college town. After showing the great poet (it is a fact that both Genet and Sartre have called him the best writer in America) his lodgings for the evening (a gunny sack in the bottom of a defrosted ice chest), they usher him with all proper pomp, circumstance, and puncturing of left eardrums with Ticonderoga pencil lead into the Main Hall, where he commences to befoul the lobes of these assembled pilgrims who never progressed by reading about an hour and a half's worth of deadpan monotone descriptions of cunnilingus, fellatio, missionary positions (well, of sorts) with 80-year-old landladies blind in one eye and palsied on the knee and one little 4-year-old lass who I hope fervently was a product of his imagination rather than reminiscence, as well as every kind of drug-sex-drink-orgy and an exhaustive catalogue of various methods by which one may so Stradivarize the heartstrings of the L.A.P.D. that those dapper gentlemen will actually consent to put you up in a quite exclusive private club they have established for the edification of just such connoisseurs of the Cabernets and Beaujolais of Life as yourself.

The audience, who had never been past the outer rim of the Bowl in their lives, were properly appreciative of these picaresques set in such exotic locales as Pismo Beach, Hialeah, and the East L.A. Blood Donors' Center. Mr. Charles Bukowski, America's greatest living poet, born in Andernach, Germany, around the time these recordings were made, the toast of France since he went on its version of the Dick Cavett show drunk, refused to wear his translator's headphones, asked a literary critic there if he could slobber all over her calves on national TV, and told the assembled frogmatik culture vultures that they should have dropped a hydrogen bomb on themselves the day in 1961 that Louis-

Ferdinand Celine died inasmuch as they had not produced a single writer above Peugeot ad-copy level since; this man, author of 33 published books so far, including *Confessions of a Man Insane Enough to Live With Beasts, Poems Written Before Jumping Out of an Eight-Story Window, Notes of a Dirty Old Man, The Days Run Away Like Wild Horses Over the Hills, Doing Time With Public Enemy Number One, Nut Ward Just East of Hollywood, A .45 to Pay the Rent,* and *Twelve Flying Monkeys Who Won't Copulate Properly,* now sat back in his worn swivel chair, relit his stogie, unpopped another Colt .45 and surveyed his audience. Dustbowl residence apparently did not do too much to encourage proliferation of barefoot boys with cheeks of tan. But that was all right; enough master races already. No, these sandlocked little lubbers looked positively bloodless, not unlike the specimens one may observe any day of the week buzzing, beeping, chirping, and peeping through the tubes traversing Greater Boston (if there is such a thing)—they don't call 'em WASPs for *nothin'!* But these were not wasps. These were chiggers. And at length one of them raised one of his bloodless yet febrile and oddly clawlike little hands:

"Mr. Bukowski?"

"Yes?"

"Um . . . we . . . uh, um . . . *would you suggest writing as a career?"*

That's your punch line. Just imagine asking Archie Shepp, "Would you suggest free jazz as a career?" Charles Bukowski worked in the Post Office, with unpaid overtime, for 14 straight years. Eventually he got desperate enough that one night he stopped off on the way home and bought a fifth of whiskey, two six-packs of beer, and two packs of cigarettes; as he himself put it later, "I wanted to be a writer and I was scared." That night he got dead drunk and wrote 30 pages. The next night he got dead drunk and wrote 40. Most of what he found on the sofa in the morning, a good deal of which you may be sure he had no memory of composing, was not only usable but good. Literature, even. Many writers try to duplicate experiences like this, since they've bought the myth that to write well you must be a drunken wretch. I'm glad they bought it because most of them are terrible writers who will end up on skid row instead of bothering the rest of us in some capacity or other. Bukowski wrote a novel called *Post Office* in 21 nights. It has been in print for 10 years and gone through several editions. I've read it five times. It's not one of my favorite works of his. Charles Bukowski does not have a career.

You may wonder what all this could possibly have to do with the Comedian Harmonists. Aside from shared national/geographical origins, which is pure chance, and the fact that I suspect Bukowski would like this record very much, the point I am concerned with here is that there are certain types of creative productions: records, books, plays, monologues, jokes even, call them what you will, but one of the most significant things about them for me is that *they fit into no genre.* Why? Because they are too original. Or too prescient. Or just plain quirky.

But let me ask you a few questions. What is *Sketches of Spain* by Miles Davis and Gil Evans? Is it jazz, since Miles plays on it and even (gasp!) *improvises?* Is it classical, since it does include awesome renditions of works by the Spanish (all this arbitrary nomenclature is going quotes from here on out) "classical" composers Joaquin Rodrigo and Manuel de Falla? You haven't a clue. Good. That's the way I like to see you. O.K., let's try something in rock, not too arcane—say, *Astral Weeks,* by Van Morrison. On it, Van plays acoustic guitar and sings original songs in an outpouring of poetry that as far as I'm concerned would do Walt Whitman proud, and kicks ass on anything Allen Ginsberg's managed to come up with in upward of 20 years. Musical accompaniment is provided by the likes of drummer Connie Kay of the Modern Jazz Quartet, bassist Richard Davis, who played with Eric Dolphy, and guitarist Jay Berline, whose only previous LP exposure to my knowledge was Charles Mingus's ultimate masterpiece, *The Black Saint and the Sinner Lady,* itself yet another unclassifiable work, featuring flamenco guitars, Duke Ellington horn charts, yearning waltzes, gutbucket NYC streetlife blare like a fusillade of lava: taxicabs honking, babies being born, people crying, dying, making love, tenderly comforting the wounded beloved one. . . . It's all life, is what it is, which is what I think all the best music is, or writing, for that matter, or anything. Mingus made a point on the front, back, and inner sleeves of *The Black Saint and the Sinner Lady:* where the usual logo read, "The New Wave"—that's what they called it!—"of Jazz Is on Impulse!" Mingus saw to it that all over that album the word "jazz" was deleted and "Ethnic Folk-Dance Music" emblazoned instead. A trifle clunky, maybe, but it gets at least part of the point across. And, babe, if you've ever heard that record, you sure do know you can dance to it. Across the crest of the sun.

As I may have said earlier, over the years I have noticed that the music that has meant the most to me, whether in terms of plain old garden variety association (you know, romance and all that stuff), the deeply personal identifications that occur when that magic confluence causes a certain piece of music to come along at a certain time, and—guess what?—it turns out to be better medicine for heart/soulache, balm for shredded nerves, them jetstream tropic mambo rumpus when spring breaks out in you lubricious unto delirium in any old time of the year—somehow, always, I end up with music, the soundtracks to whatever latest escapades ('cause I am truly obnoxious, carry armloads of albums with me everywhere I go), refusing to fall into your generic categories which, by the way, have you noticed in the stores they getting 'em ever-narrower defined till one day we're gonna wake up and the only way to tell *The Heartbreakers Live at Max's Kansas City Vol. VII* from *Chuck Mangione Plays Rupert Holmes Gorillas for UNICEF* will be by dat big old black-n-white PRICE CODE slapped right on the front of every album? Cover art? Who needs it? We gotta veritable New Hebrides among computer filing systems what don't give diddley iffen you think y'all just gonna barge in here splitting who-cares hairs such as *por exemplo* Judy Holliday and Billie Holiday now wasn't they sisters somewhere back there in the corncrib we'll file 'em together anyhoo they're both *dead* after all.

And that's the present and future state of the art of the music business, which is why I am more than merely proud to be associated with this set. I'm honored because, friends, if you'll just take my little words here on good faith, buy this sucker, take it home and slide it on that turntable, I guarantee you gonna have a listening experience like unto you never previously suspected existed in this galaxy at least. And they didn't even have to fall back on no "Star Wars" synthesizer gimcracks. Nope. This music sounds like it was recorded in the ballrooms of Heaven, and that's right, I'm talking about that place where all those peculiar emanations plop theyselves on stray cloudlets and Hendrixify just a tad now and then on all them golden harps. Here, you have one too, easy to play, ain't it?

But, I still hear you screaming, where in God's name did this stuff COME FROM? The answer is that I don't know. Haven't the foggiest. I do know that it was recorded in Germany pre-Hitler, mid-Twenties to early Thirties, that everybody in the band is white, that they've absorbed black soul, gospel, blues, ragtime, and SOMETHING ELSE AFRICAN that *really* sproings the chilly willies up your spine (eat your hearts out Byrne 'n' Eno, these kraut kats only beatcha by about 55 years!). Also you'll hear plenty purely Germanic trills bitten and uvular shim-sham, often corkscrewing through at the oddest moments conveying palpable deja views of secondary blear from the most vintage cartoons made in the same era and neck o' the globe this music was. Which is another good thing about it, its completely unexpected diversity of appeal. Why, you could slap this on the box and sit some dopesmokin' ponytailed Grateful Deadheads right knee-to-knee with the brittlest herringbone-cheeked SoHo artiste nouveau-punquelettes *and they wouldn't even claw blood and de-snaggletooth each other!* Not one hincty snoot lanced for drill even. Comedian Harmonists promote Peace & Love wherever, whenever they play!

And if you want to know why I'll tell you. Because of what I was talking about before: what you are holding in your hands ain't no career. These guys didn't record, say, "Creole Love Call" (my far-and-away absolute favorite cut; I think this truly sounds like it could have been recorded on some astral plane) because they'd heard Duke Ellington was hip and maybe moving some product in the States so they'd cover it quick cross the pond. They recorded it because they loved Duke Ellington so deeply and were so moved by the original that they just had to say thank you some way and this was fortunately for us the best way they knew how. I can't speak or read German, and almost all music I've heard from that country since these sides were cut makes me nervous at best. But I've been listening to music and at least trying to keep my ears open for the real thing amid the tides of dross long enough that I think I can still tell when something is done up not only professionally and technically but with pure hearts collectively welling for a long-awaited outpouring of love for their mentors, their accompanists, each other, whatever audiences (and of whatever kind!) they may have had, and most of all, for their music. When was the last time you heard someone sing for joy? Unalloyed.

What I'm interested in is people with musical obsessions they're driven to work out. In the cases of the Comedian Harmonists, I just kinda suspect they were a bunch of nice, unsuspecting German guys who some smartass slapped upside the head with their first blast of black American music one day, which musta been some kinda religious experience for them (I know it was for me, and I was *born* here), after which they were never quite the same again. Admittedly, it musta been more than a little schizo at times. Because there is, all delicate political questions aside, a certain kind of emotionalism in American music, a passion of a particular kind, and I am not even just talking about black music, that seems absolutely antithetical to everything German music is about structurally, conceptually, attitudinally. But believe me, there is something deep in the, well, *soul* of that society, national identity or whatever, that shoots off a hotline emergency interrupt call straight down to the gut every time that big American beat starts up again, the Voice of Control, where it issues from sepulchrally intoning booty-defamations leaden with dread, fear, and God knows whatall else.

One of the things I like best about this album is the way it transcends the usual inevitably somewhat sickly trappings of "nostalgia"-oriented disks. I'm sorry, but I had one childhood, one adolescence, and (particularly re the pube phase) once was *more* than enough. Maybe it's my age, but I have absolutely no referents for this music. Yet it sounds somehow familiar. There's nothing creepy about it, don't get paranoid you're gonna look up all rosy-cheeked and blanch at Hitler leering in the wings. It has nothing to do with Cabaret-style decadence chopped 'n' channeled into mass-marketable kitsch, either (always hated that play). Like I said, this music is from outer space. That's just about the only way I can begin to convey the effect it has on me. Brian Eno once said the same thing about his exposure to American a cappella doo-wop groups of the early '50s he heard when he was a little boy growing up near an American military base in the Midlands in England. So maybe even in a curious way it's tit for tat: we gave them the Five Satins, and they gave us this; *but whatever on earth are we going to do with it?*

Like those old doo-wop records that made li'l Eno's wig flapjack, these recordings serve perhaps their most important and heartening message in reminding us yet again that they can invent all the synthesizers, computers, phase shifters, distortion boxes, 980-track boards, and what have you they want—I use all that stuff myself, whenever somebody's foolish enough to let me get my hands on some of it—but there never has been and never will be any substitute for the pure soul and directness of the human voice, rolling up outta that throat so tremulously glad to be the official megaphone for that temple of unending mysteries and delights simply known as you and me. So spend those few bucks on this (if ever there was) one-of-a-kind platter, check in on these sauerbraten bashos' stopsout pearlpure whoopup, then let yourself loose, throw back your head, and yawp out a joyful noise unto the Lord or whoever else you wanna annoy. I'll be right there beside you.

Written 1980 as liner notes for Comedian Harmonists'
album that went unreleased until 1999.
(Published posthumously in *The New York Times,* September 5, 1999)

Bye Bye Sidney, Be Good

Since he's now finally dead, and I never met him outside of watching him stumble waxen-eyed through police headquarters while I played investigative reporter for *The Village Voice* the day Nancy Spungen died last October, my main memory of Sid Vicious remains what it was then: something photographer Joe Stevens said to me while Johnny Rotten was staying at his apartment in the aftermath of the Pistols' American tour almost a year ago: "Well, Sid is kinda like this giraffe you throw the pills up to. A dying child."

Joe is a friend of mine, more or less, but I couldn't help noting at the time how offhandedly he said those words. And believe me, I'm not saying I was less offhanded than anyone else. When Sid finally did what he had been trying to do to himself for years, I immediately called up Robert Christgau at the *Voice* to see if I should write about it, which might have paid my rent, although I did say that I had deeply mixed feelings. Christgau said he thought the whole matter as re the *Voice* should be over and done with by a couple of paragraphs he was about to write himself, and that was that. But Sid died Friday, I'm writing this on Monday, and I do feel I have something to say. I'm probably not going to pay my rent anyway till the landlord turns up the heat in here.

We all had a bit of Sid's hide I guess, but wasn't he such a willing victim? The Gary Gilmore of rock 'n' roll. I was taking care of a former girlfriend who was down with bronchitis this last weekend, and she observed: "This thing has really affected you, hasn't it?" I guess it had.

So we watched the news, which locally runs for about an hour and a half in New York, and no mention of Sid. We started to joke about it: "Well, I do guess gas station fires in New Jersey and how to grow your own organic artichokes are more important." Later we caught him doing "My Way" on Cronkite's nightly national spot. Walter told us that Sid's manager had said he was going to be "the next John Travolta" (and of course Malcolm McLaren would and did say that) but Walter, father figure to a nation of media junkies, summed it up unequivocally: "Punk rock died before Sid Vicious did."

I thought Bob Quine of Richard Hell's Voidoids put it better back in October. I called him up after hearing Dead Boys and other CBGBites muzzle on about how death and attendant publicity might put a damper on their scene. Bob said yeah Richard was all upset. Susan Springfield of the Erasers later wrote me a letter re my *Voice* piece: "How can you use this poor guy to pay your rent," etc. etc., and in fact I *did* use that money to pay the rent, big deal, in fact big deal to the whole thing because as Quine put it: "So some psychopath killed his girlfriend—so what?"

So what? If Sid Vicious had been a dishwasher in Queens the Nancy Spungen murder would have amounted to one paragraph in one day's edition of the New York dailies, which instead covered the case in predictable tones: "Sid Vicious, former bassist with punk rock band the Sex Pistols, famed for swearing, stomping, vomiting and spitting on their audiences, yesterday was arrested for stabbing his negligeed go-go dancer girlfriend after both succumbed to heroin fits"—not a precise quote, but that sort of thing.

I am probably as guilty of this as anybody. While I was covering the case for the *Voice,* I ended up on the day after Nancy's Thursday murder down at the NYC courthouse at 100 Centre Street with all the other journalists, and while Malcolm just laughed at me when I inquired about the possibility of an interview with Sid, Murray Kempton, a pipe-chomping "liberal" of some renown, did take the time to pick at what I was so willing to blab up. He followed me across a parking lot, I guess I looked authentic or something to him, and of course I waxed quotable like any stupe. The next day I saw it in his column in the New York *Post,* which might be the single worst daily in the USA, under the headline "The Awful Return of Sid Vicious: He Lived Up to His Name" (all the local TV newscasters summed it up with those exact words by the way): "Lester Bangs, a wise man there present, said: 'People are gonna say punk rock leads to this. Nothing leads to this. This was just babies beating each other and this time it went too far.' "

Of course swell Murray left out the part I told him about the Pistols being a great rock 'n' roll band ("The thing that gets me," he said that day on the courthouse steps, "is that there didn't seem to be any *talent* involved in the first place!" Which I guess indicates his priorities, not that they are that different from Malcolm's, or any of us when you get down to it. We wanted a geek run amuck, and Sid was happy to oblige), and when I saw myself thus quoted in that rag the next day I almost dropped my own piece entirely. Because suddenly one thing occurred to me which seemed to invalidate everything, or at least my own involvement on any level: I had been going totally under the assumption that Sid was guilty, that he had in fact stabbed Nancy to death, no, I'll go further, I *wanted* to believe it. Just like everyone else? Why? Oh, I dunno, the *name* of the guy or something . . .

In case you ever wondered whether America really was the land where, just like in *Perry Mason,* you were innocent until proven guilty . . . well if the cops and courts and lawyers most of whom are corrupt by definition don't kill you, the press down to what remains of what was once called "underground"/"alternative" will be glad to oblige.

I just broke off writing this to call up the District Attorney's office. I got Assistant District Attorney Sullivan, whom I'd been referred to by the Third Homicide cops who originally booked Sid; after introducing myself, I said: "I was just calling to find out whether in the aftermath of Sid Vicious' death the Nancy Spungen murder case was still being pursued, or . . ."

He seemed genuinely surprised that anyone would even think of such a question. "No. Why should it be?"

"So then you are fully convinced that Sid and he alone was responsible for the girl's death."

"Sure."

"But how can you be that certain? From everything I've heard, I don't think even he knew whether he killed her or not, and there was an awful lot of talk about a third party in the room, as well as all their money being missing . . ."

"Look, he killed her. We know it. We've got witnesses."

"*What* witnesses? Look, unless there was a third party in there the only two witnesses are dead!"

He began to lose patience. "Listen, I don't have all day for this. I'm telling you, he killed her, he confessed to it, and we've got witnesses. The case is closed."

There didn't seem to be much else to say, so I just hung up. I thought about calling Rockets Redglare, a buddy of Sid's who supposedly had all kinds of information about a dope dealer who'd been hanging around the Chelsea and Sid and Nancy and made himself scarce as soon as her death was discovered. Rockets used to call me up all the time when I was covering the case for the *Voice* and even after that, drooling on in his methadone monotone about dope dealers and Sid and Nancy's personal, chemical, and sexual habits, but a lot of the stuff he was saying seemed to make pretty good sense at the time. He said the cops flipped out when he drew a picture for them of a knife belonging to this one particular dealer. But who among us would it serve for me to inflict Rockets on myself one more time? The State of New York has decided to let what I imagine to be a confluence of convenience and public opinion dictate their handling of the Nancy Spungen murder, and if Sid was in fact innocent, then that's just tough shit for whoever cares about it which is almost nobody at this point. It's a disposable culture, and there's no reason why jurisprudence shouldn't conform to the mores of the rest of society; we all got our kicks off Sid, and now that there's nothing left to suck out it's only customary to toss him on the garbage heap, especially since he was human garbage in the first place. He served his purpose and got to enjoy his 15 minutes; all that's left now is to go scouting around for a new kickboy.

If it makes any difference to anyone now, there's a pretty good chance Sid actually did kill her. I spoke to Joe Stevens at the CBGB bar about a month ago, and between bitter recollections of how Malcolm stiffed him for a phone bill in the thousands of dollars and of being pretty much totally frozen out by the entire New York recording industry for his involvement with Sid, he gave me his part of the lowdown. I said, "Shit, I'm just sick to death of this whole sordid mess. I don't know if he did it, he doesn't know if he did it. . . ."

"He did it," Joe cut in. "He told me so. Sid is a very nice guy—he just gets kinda twitchy sometimes." And that might just sum it up, in a way. Sometimes I think one of the hardest things in the world is to recognize the psychopaths in our midst. They float so freely, meld so comfortably with the society as it prevails. Because they are instinctual chameleons. Nobody I talked to in New York that knew him believed he killed her, but then our whole image of murderers has been so warped by the modern screen that I doubt if we'd recognize the face of the beast until the knife was coming down our own guts. And of course there is still the possibility that he really didn't do it, that he might have just said that to Joe in one of his well-documented spews of macho rubbish.

What I do think is that Sid was just that, rubbish, and not in a way the *uber*society portrayed him. From all accounts I can gather, he was just an asshole. Certainly he was a patsy. (I wrote that in the *Voice* article, and Stevens told me when Sid read it he said, "What's a patsy?" Joe explained to him, and Sid said, "Yeah, that's what I am." Any old port in the storm, I suppose.) His death is the ultimate coup in terms of his patsýhood for McLaren, a man some people are still defending though he looks to me like the compleat slime. His *compere* Vivienne was so sensitive as to make up that shirt with Sid's mug: "She's dead, I'm alive, I'm yours," and now Malcolm's got the perfect ending for his movie, which of course everyone me included will rush out to see. I have always believed that McLaren was not so simple as your average Allen Klein strata slime, that he was indeed also a Sex Pistol and the money aside really in his heart of hearts wanted to live to see anarchy prevail and (British, at least) society blown to bits by at least some variant on these prototypically plug-ugly subhuman Visigoths.

But then you have to ask yourself, all morally and socially left-wing concerned as you fancy, whether you would really like to see things reduced to the level of rubble that people like Malcolm dream of. It's true that none of the old rules apply and no one has thought of any better or even as good to take their place—that's simultaneously why we may be facing a new dark ages, why now might be the most exciting time to be alive in human history, and for sure why Jim Jones was able to get all those suckers to off themselves and their babies down Guyana way. But when you get right down to it was the Guyana incident (for despite all the media flap, that was really all it was, I mean Gilles de Rais would laugh) all that different except in sheer quantity of deaths from the Sex Pistols phenomenon and all it represented? Both were about human manipulation under the guise of social change. "No future for you" was powerful not only because it was great music but because there was something awfully true about it, but did any of these people ever take the time to even try to posit some alternative? Richard Hell used to go onstage in a T-shirt that said "Please kill me," and that finally sums up 90 percent of the punk phenomenon for me.

I've defended this scene a million times, saying stuff like "Well at least they went halfway, at least they said 'Everything sucks!' instead of pretending everything was just a whoopie party like those disco creeps." But even then I was not so sure I was right. Because for one thing those disco creeps who are no more a united front than the punks, who still haven't resolved the fact that most American punks think the British are too self-righteously political and most British think the Americans spoiled dunderheaded dilettantes—those disco creeps, whom American punks have all written off with the homophobic slogan "Disco Sucks," have come up at times with material far more affirmative on the basic *humanistic* level than most anything punk has to show for itself. When I got up this morning the first thing I played was "I Love the Nightlife," by Alicia Bridges, which is not as I first thought just another cheerlead to empty solipsistic club-hopping hedonism, but in fact a feminist self-determination anthem. Let's line up Gloria Gaynor's "I Will Survive" and Richard Hell's "Who Says? (It's Good to Be Alive)" and see which one makes more sense in twenty years.

Richard's come in for an undue share of bad press, especially from such professional wanknoses as Tony Parsons, and I believe the first Voidoids album will someday be looked back upon as a rock masterpiece akin to *White Light/White Heat* and *Raw Power* that got lost in the shuffle of 1977 punk-overload, but Jesus Christ, man: I believed in Richard Hell and still do, as musician, poet, and I guess I'll have to be corny enough to say Philosopher (theoretician), but yesterday I had a friend over who is 19 years old and brilliant, a writer/photographer who came to New York from Michigan, lives on food stamps, sits in his room every day staring into space, thought he was a sadist for a while because the first girl he ever laid asked him to slap her around a little, has played around with Satanism and been committed by his parents at the age of 16 to a mental ward where the fave song of all the kids there interred was Lou Reed's "Kill Your Sons," committed almost solely because he happened to say one day that he didn't think the American high school system had much left to teach him so he didn't think he was going to go anymore, which was grounds for electroshock treatments according to everyone around him with any power at the time—I played this kid Richard's "Who Says? (It's Good to Be Alive)" and he just laughed. "That guy's stupid," he said. "No," I said, "don't you see, that he's at least going halfway toward some resolution with reality, that that's an important question to ask at a certain point in your life?" "Gimme a break," he said. "That's a question that should not even arise."

Which might well, when all is said and done, be the summation of the Sex Pistols. When it looked like Sid was gonna have his day in court I wouldn't have dared write something I'd felt in my guts and nervous system for months: that I am not at all convinced that there wasn't something in the Sex Pistols' music that *did* or would inspire acts of wholly unpremeditated random violence. I can recall more than one evening over the past couple of years, sitting around with a friend or two, listening to those singles and live bootlegs and the *Bollocks* album which didn't even work as an album when you get right down to it—we'd sit and stoke ourselves with that stuff, until we were filled with this consuming sense of blinding rapacious rage, and we realized at the time that *there was absolutely no place to take it.* I mean what good is rampant hatred of the status quo if it's all a closed system, if all this noise-spew does is churn up the bile inside you until you run for Valium? Forget it. There was something deeply amoral in the whole Pistols trip.

I knew women who said the song "Bodies" was somehow refreshing after all the feminist cant and masculine hypocrisy they'd been subjected to the last few years, but when you get right down to it all he was really saying was "Yeah I fucked you you fucking worthless bitch, and now you're pregnant with a baby that quite probably is mine, but I couldn't care less because you're just a trashy slut anyway." Mick Jagger would have to go some to top that one, not to mention sluggards of Bad Company ilk. Jeez, and I thought all this cock rock was something we were going to wipe away.

Oh, sorry, I forgot—punk rock was antisexual if anything, okay let's take what I believe was the very next song on that album, wherein Jonathan went on about how he had no feelings for anyone except his precious preening self. Well, all that ever said to me was "You can't hurt me." Another closed system. More solipsism too, and what I believe is that whatever musical, cultural, or social rubric you file it under, solipsism is the disease of this age, in America certainly. It is the currency, we have to deal with it and aside from the Clash I can think of few punk rockers who have offered anything but appeasement which makes them no different and possibly worse than the discoids. "Cause the world a person lives in is his brain/Well mine just gives in," or how about "I got no emotions for anybody else/You better understand I'm in love with myself." To which the obvious logical response is "So what?" "Thanks a lot, assholes" is giving them too much credit, the credit that they even made a gesture in the first place.

But oh what gestures they made! In other departments. Like putting nude almost pubescent boys with half-hardons on their T-shirts. Wonderful. I lay in there with my old girlfriend watching for Sid in the news the other night, and recalling that T-shirt she said, "I've gotta say that I just don't care what happens to any of those assholes. What I'd like to know is where is that kid they put on that T-shirt today and how does he feel?"

Oh but we can overlook little things like that, I mean so what if a few fingers or maybe genitals get burned in service of the great media scam/rock 'n' roll swindle? Fuck 'em. They were suckers for buying it in the first place. Johnny Rotten onstage at Winterland in San Francisco: "Ha ha haaa—ever get the feeling you've been *taken?*" Photographer Bob Gruen told me that on that tour he couldn't make Rotten out at all: "The guy would sit on the bus all day smoking dope and talking about a society based on love, then walk out and when a kid hands him a copy of his album to autograph he coughs up phlegm and spits on it. And then the kid says, 'Thanks!' "

I've had it up to here with bullies. School was bad enough, where you were a fag if you read books or some asshole might just decide to beat the shit out of you if he even *imagined* you took a sidelong glance at his girlfriend—at 30 years old OR ANY AGE do I need this? I think the one thing that might have impressed me most when I was in England covering the Clash tour in '77 was the unspoken but manifest gentleness and decency of everyone in the band and almost all their friends and fans. I'd gone expecting nigh-cannibalism, having been suitably brainwashed by American NBC reports which I'm sure Malcolm himself had no small hand in, and what I ended up concluding was that punk was a form of passive resistance.

One that was bound to fail, to be sure, though I was loathe to say that in the article I wrote at the time, but still it was all inspiring as the Clash are still so deeply inspiring to me that I'm not even sure I should write about them anymore because I might start looking like some of those guys that give out all that gush on the likes of Jackson Browne. But then, the Clash don't celebrate destruction, they merely report passionately on what is going on in the world or whatever's itching them at the moment. I could do without Strummer's Mott-like (but really almost like Ian Hunter at his soppiest) stop-picking-on-us harangue in "Cheepskates," but he has yet to come out with lines the likes of "You never listened to a word I said" or "You never realized I took the piss out of you."

Thanks a lot, Johnny, how can we ever repay your royal highness for letting us know where it was at. The *Queen* made you a moron? You made yourself a moron in front, and I question your intentions all down the line. Sorry. Like I kept hearing you guys were gonna get rid of all this "superstar" stuff, until I read in *Punk* magazine's definitive (by the lights of me, who admittedly wasn't there) account of the Pistols' American tour how some girl came up to you in the Winterland dressing room, stuck out her hand and said "How do you do?" and you started ranting about how "How do you do?" was an invalid statement. Righto, boy. Just keep that stuff up, as it looks like you're gonna. I realize "Public Image" (the song) is about media manipulation, but who's Gepetto and who are the puppets? Truly, has there ever been a more self-serving song in history?

I have to say that if one of my best friends was involved in a band with me and it was obvious that he was going to kill himself or try to *even whether or not he stayed in the band,* I'd do everything in my power to encourage him to get the hell out of this media mess and go someplace where he might begin to detox or at least sort his head out. And I don't care if this sounds self-righteous but I can say that because I went through something similar with Peter Laughner, one of the founders of Pere Ubu who undoubtedly would be a figure on the New Wave scene today if he hadn't died from years of combined alcohol and amphetamine abuse in 1977.

Oh but of course Sid was so *entertaining,* he made such great *copy.* You and Malcolm knew the dailies loved it when he went onstage with "Gimme a Fix" written in blood across his chest, or gouged himself for the 88th time that day. Of course no one is his brother's keeper, but the fact remains that he was your brother, possibly closer than flesh and blood, and whether you were helping him kill himself to make yourself famous or deliver a revolutionary polemic to the world makes absolutely no difference. You were everything you claimed to detest and supposedly sought to overthrow.

But look at what happened here. This was supposed to be a piece about Sid Vicious, and as usual I've ended up going on and on about the superstar instead of the fall guy. Perhaps because, ultimately, I'm just as lame as everybody I'm belittling, because I can't confront the reality of Sid either. A month before he died, I walked into Max's one night and saw him slumped at the bar, where I was told he could be found just about any night of the week, staring through blasted eyes down into his drink while punkettes came up whispering blandishments probably about some dumbhead's notion of s&m into his ear and his ever-watchful buddy Rockets Redglare, who took full advantage of his 15 minutes of post-Nancy fame, hovered nearby. Sid looked too gone to even be aware of any of them.

I felt a bit guilty myself, because here was this guy I had done a story on and never met, and I didn't even have the nerve to go up and introduce myself and try to maybe find out just what kind of cat he might be behind all the media bilge I kept hoping I hadn't contributed to. It wasn't that I was afraid of him, more that I had absolutely no idea on earth what I might say to someone as gone as that. So I ended up feeling like a bit of the dilettante. But what really killed me was all the time he sat there and I voyeurized his death-puddle, little 19-year-old proto-Sids dressed and sunglassed to the max staggered all around us, having gotten their fabgear Johnny Thunders smackstumble down just so *perfect* (you wouldn't even wanna guess whether they might actually be on the stuff or not). Jeez, I thought, here's this totally broken, flattened human being, a half-living testament to where all this shit really leads, and these assholes don't even *see* him.

But I was probably being self-righteous. Probably because I don't think I really saw him either. While I was doing the article for the *Voice,* talking to everyone who had known him and rereading every bit of Pistols press I could find, I had caught myself, in the midst of this mountain of incontrovertible evidence of what a fuckup if not psychopath this guy was, *still* somehow feeling somewhere inside that there was something charismatic, romantic even, about him. When now I really wonder if he deserved my or anybody's sympathy. That interview in Fred Vermorel's book *The Sex Pistols: The Inside Story,* where Sid goes on about how he doesn't read, hates TV, can't stand the movies, laughingly brags that the only thing in the world he cares about is heroin—"I spend every ha'penny I make on it!"—while Nancy laughs along with him . . . there was a part of me that responded to that, identified with it, admired it even. I've never taken heroin, partly because I've abused every other drug I've ever gotten my hands on and knew I'd like it too much, partly because I figured nothing could be as good as Burroughs' description of it, partly because of the human evidence of its effect that began to accumulate around me like so many half-ambulatory scrapheaps over the years. I hate it, I think it's evil, I don't want to work or even hang out much with anybody who is into it on any level, I think it's just something that should be recognized for what it is and then abhorred and avoided, just like fascism, racism, and Scientologists. *But the hours I've put in daydreaming, fantasizing, romanticizing about it over the years.* I mean anyone would have to admit that it does simplify things in a quite concrete and mathematically predictable way. Junkie life devolves to hassling in the street, copping, fixing, nodding, then repeating the cycle. Of course it eliminates all such little botherations as the unpredictabilities and indeterminancies of romantic or sexual pursuits. You can also forget about your neuroses on all levels—since you have effectively ceased to be human, you now lack the qualifications for any kind of personality much less neuroses in the first place. William Burroughs said he never met a psychotic junkie, but I wonder if that's not begging the question somehow: I mean, how could a doorknob or a kickstool be psycho?

But there's more to the Sid fixation, not to mention the junkie romanticism, than that. For one thing, the reality obliterated half of the myth in front: Sid and Nancy were possibly two of the most pathologically tortured humans on the face of the earth. The heroin didn't stop Sid from acting out, whether he actually did kill Nancy or not; there's also that night he slashed Patti Smith's brother. I think the really insidious element here is that looking at someone like Sid, no matter how fucked up he might get right unto death, in the face of all the evidence otherwise, his way just looks easier than yours. Because in whatever measure, by choosing not to be cowardly as Sid finally (always) was, you let yourself in for the myriad petty and huge contradictions of life as most of us are forced to live it. And now the question of choice enters the picture, which is perhaps the bottom line to the whole thing. Was Sid just a victim, or does *everybody,* even (to take the most extreme example I can think of) a person in Auschwitz, have certain options?

Sid was an asshole, as he himself would have been the first to tell you. Let's say not a doomed lost soul, not a societal or subcultural casualty, let's just say a simple mediocre asshole. Beyond all poses. So somewhere between fate, media conspiracy, and literally terminal assholism we are going to have to try to find some understanding of what this guy's 21 years amounted to and why. If we really even care, that is. I mean, he obviously didn't, not to even mention Malcolm, whom I would just as soon never see mentioned again anywhere.

Okay, let's say Sid was a product of his environment. I mean, Christ, look at his mother: what the hell was that bitch, with her tricolored hair and the interview she's going to sell Murdoch sheets worldwide, doing *crying* in front of the cameras at the little shithead's funeral?

And of course absolutely no one had anything good to say about Nancy. The general consensus around the New York punk scene seemed to be that she was just a bitch so who cares or maybe even good riddance. A charming little thing who calls herself Trixie Plunger even said to me: "I actually think it's kinda cool in a way, that he killed his girlfriend, and I liked her a lot!" Steve Jones' comment was also interesting: "Good, maybe now the album will sell a few more copies." (Yeah, Steve, and think how much more product you'll move now Sid's offed him*self!* You lucky dog! And say hi to Zsa Zsa for me.) Of all the people I talked to in the days after her death, absolutely the only person that had anything nice to say about Nancy Spungen was, ironically enough, the supposedly misogynist Stiv Bators: "They really loved each other, and she took better care of him than he'd ever take of himself. I think all that shit people said about her was just pure jealousy."

But maybe I'm begging the question again. Like, is, say, *Stiv Bators* a product of a corrupt society, or just an exhibitionist with masochistic tendencies more or less affected? And perhaps I can begin to consider that by telling you about some kids I knew when I lived in Detroit. They're all about Sid's age now, or would have been had they lived, and sometimes I wonder whether Sid even in death (or especially in death) might not have been the ultimate extension of their dreams.

Shirley (I'm changing their names, though they probably wouldn't care) only cared about two things in the entire world: the New York Dolls and *Pink Flamingos.* Divine was her hero, and one day she paid ultimate testament to her devotion by having a pink flamingo three inches long tattooed on her thigh. It looked to me like a blatant act of self-defilement, but she seemed proud of it. She has since attempted suicide, I'm not sure how many times. Works at odd jobs in small shops. When you see her she's always smiling but her eyes, which are pretty glazed anyway, don't ever seem quite to be looking at you. In fact, you're never quite sure what exactly they might be looking at. She's rather plain, but that doesn't entirely account for her never having had a boyfriend. I don't know what accounts for it, and I don't think she does either.

Her friend whom I always knew by the nickname Noodle used to take acid every day when he was in eighth grade. This went on for two or three years and then he got into junk. His eyes were just totally gone, not there, worse than Sid's. He always had girlfriends, but it didn't seem to matter. Neither did much of anything else. He was kind of like a shell with curdled smoke inside. He finally got off junk a few months ago, and last week he was killed in a motorcycle accident.

Jane, who was half in love with him and lived with him and Shirley in a kind of basically asexual communal unit (they were delighted when I referred to it as their "new family") is a brilliant photographer. She has that rare knack for capturing people at that precise instant that defines them, whether it's Lou Reed or a haggard crone in a luncheonette. She obviously has a much better chance than Noodle or Shirley, but they and people like them keep trying without even knowing it to drag her down. And her ignorance about certain things is so staggering that I was immediately reminded of her when I opened up a British punk fanzine early in '77 and saw this article where some kid actually wrote something along the lines of: "Well, since everybody's been wearing swastikas and stuff lately I got out this history book or encyclopedia or whatever and looked this guy Hitler up, and you know what? He was a bad guy!"

And then there is Mike, whom I mentioned earlier in relation to his disinterest in Richard Hell. Aside from all the stuff I already listed, he keeps intersecting with paranoia, and I keep telling him that things don't always really have the patterns they sometimes seem to. His eyes are almost too sharp, and there is real and well-grounded fear in them. Aside from Jane, whom he fell in love with and was rejected by, most of the girls he's come in contact with seem pretty much like trash, and punk trash at that. He says he doesn't care. He says he's beyond suicide. He says he feels dead, blank, null, void. It's not a pose. He got rid of all his records because he says they remind him of things he doesn't want to think about. About all he has in his apartment is one Diane Arbus pic of some retards on the wall. Since dabbling in Crowley Satanism, he's been freaked: he thinks the spirits are after him, and maybe they are. The other night he cut open his arms with a razor blade, not too deep, just enough, and put food coloring in the wounds. When I asked him why he said he just wanted to see what would happen. Which reminded me of the time I was on the phone with Rockets Redglare while doing my Sid 'n' Nancy story for the *Voice.* The subject of s&m came up, everybody from their friends to the cops seeming to be in agreement that Sid and Nancy's version of the bondage trip was really kiddie pennyante stuff (one friend in fact told me that they had quite a normal sex life; she said that was the only stable part of the relationship). Rockets blabbed on about which little kinks Sid and Nancy were into, but then he came out with the most amazing thing: "Yeah, but I can see how she coulda stabbed herself, or he coulda accidentally stabbed her. Y'know, like one night me and my girlfriend were fucking, and we took a razor blade to bed with us. We were just making little surface cuts and like that, but then we really got to fucking and forgot the razor blade was still in the bed and her elbow went back into it up to the bone. Somethin' like that sobers you up real quick."

I didn't say anything. All could think was, what on earth do these assholes think they're doing? I thought the stuff he was describing was more disgusting than real-life heavy-duty s&m—I mean, Christ, at least that's *honest.* This was real dilettante shit, except they were hurting themselves anyway because they were so fucking lame, and what's more disgusting than somebody who doesn't basically have them *toying* with somebody else's pathological compulsions, just because they think it's chic or cool? Wouldn't *you* be pissed off if you were a righteous grade-A certified pervert, and a bunch of little assholes come along rippin' off your scene without even manifesting the balls to actually get more than a toe in the water or asshole more precisely? That's one reason I always hated David Bowie, because James Williamson told me that Bowie was never the slightest bit gay in the first place, but affected it because he thought that was the way to make it in the music business. And *that's* the true perversion: consciously going against all your basic human instincts in the name of fashion.

So as far as I'm concerned on that level people like Sid and Nancy and Rockets are just creeps, and Mike simply doesn't know any better. I remember in the old days when we used to see Iggy maul himself while hurtling through the audience: it was sick, he was sick, we were sick for endorsing it, but at least there was something real about it. It was honest self-hatred. By 1977 we'd gotten to the point where well take your pick of groups but the ultimate for me was this bunch of wanks from Toronto who called themselves the Viletones and showed up at CBGB's one night. The lead singer had christened himself Natzee Dog, and dog was just what he made like, groveling on stage, scraping his scarred flesh across it, swinging from the rafters, gouging himself, etc. etc. etc. ad tedium. I just walked out, not even offended. Because he wasn't crazy like Iggy—he was just *trying* to be. Which of course is probably actually sicker than Iggy, but in a totally different and far more reprehensible way. Oh, I'm sure the guy's got some real bonafeed masochism down in him somewhere, but it's plain to see he wanks it up and milks it for all it's worth. By the end of the show, his arm was cut open literally in one great red line almost from wrist to shoulder, and he had to go down to the hospital and have about 883 stitches put in so he could show them off at the next gig. I think they should have refused him admittance; they've done as much to winos that friends and I have found in the streets and reported because we suspected they might be dying. And as far as I'm concerned winos deserve a hell of a lot more consideration than snotnoses who lacerate themselves so they can get famous.

Somewhere between a more extreme form of Iggy's pathology and Natzee Dog's jerkoff pose we might be able to find Sid Vicious. But at this point I'm beginning to wonder if it's even worth all the trouble. He was the Gary Gilmore of rock, but as with Gary Gilmore, when somebody wants to die that bad you might just end up saying So what, go ahead. I think of the line from *Naked Lunch,* The Judge to Bradley the Buyer: " 'I would recommend that you be confined or more accurately contained, but I know of no institution suitable for a man of your caliber. Therefore I must reluctantly order your release.' 'That one should stand in an aquarium,' the arresting officer said."

Gee, I guess that's pretty insulting to Sid's memory, isn't it? I mean, this was a *human being* we're talking about. Especially when you consider how the American and I'm sure the British press portrayed him after Nancy's death: like I said, a patsy, worse, a scapegoat. American society in the late Seventies is cancerous to the pit of the soul it no longer seems to have, and almost nobody wants to talk about it or even admit it, so there have got to be scapegoats. Each season brings a new one: in '76 it was Gilmore, '77 David Berkowitz hit the charts, and I guess you could say '78 was Sid's year. But, perhaps like Berkowitz and certainly like Gilmore, Sid's not only helped dig his own grave, he encouraged everyone else alive to think he was just as cretinous, subhuman, verminal, disgusting, and brutal as they were so delighted to portray him.

So the bottom line as far as I'm concerned is that he's dead and I just don't give a damn. I don't think Sid Vicious jokes are in bad taste, because his life as he chose and was suckered into living it was a monument to bad taste. Even when he tried to commit suicide when out on bail in October, that line he came out with: "Nancy, Nancy, I'm gonna kill myself, I wanna be with you!" Like, what bad soap opera did he pick that one up from while nodding to afternoon TV? The best thing you could say is that what happened to him might serve as a warning to others, but as already indicated I don't think there's too much likelihood of that. So fuck him. Let's forget he ever existed and move on to something else. Because when all is said and done people do have some element of choice.

Someone I dearly deeply love was committed to a hospital mental ward and almost the bigtime cuckoo's nest last year; I went barging out there like some halfassed Sir Lancelot, she eventually got herself out, but when I walked into that place I saw the most graphic evidence of what society can do to people, and just how totalitarian this supposedly free society can get when some administrator arbitrarily decides that you're not quite fit to mingle with the rest of the herd. What I saw in there was a whole bunch of people who as far as I was concerned were not crazy at all. Well, there was one guy who thought George Benson was sending him telepathic messages, but then that guy used to get raped by his uncles every day when he was about four years old while his father just sat there and cried. What I'm saying is that what I saw in there was a whole bunch of people who were just frightened literally out of their wits, and with good reason. There are some people who are like dogs who have just been beaten and beaten and beaten until it really seems kind of awesome that there's anything left at all.

Meanwhile the staff in there treated them with a mixture of contempt, condescension, and bored patience. There were all kinds of little Catch-22s: I took the person I'd gone there to see a bunch of jazz records, really nice stuff that wouldn't freak anybody out, albums by Bill Evans and Duke Ellington and like that, but she wasn't allowed to play them at an audible volume in the day room because they supposedly would disturb the other patients, and she wasn't allowed to have headphones because that was deemed "antisocial." There were all kinds of pointless little rules, and if you rebelled against them at all that was a strike against you and guarantee of more time inside, and if you obeyed straight down the line they'd tell you your attitude was "too positive," that you must be faking.

One guy in there used to play with Hank Williams. He was a poor old broken down alcoholic hillbilly with eight kids he could barely manage to feed and clothe and a 300-pound wife, and he'd had terrible luck with jobs to the point that all of them were going hungry half the time, so one day he just sat down and tried to kill himself. Possibly a perfectly logical and defensible reaction, under the circumstances. Cowardly, one supposes, but who is to say that there is not a point beyond which life becomes so awful it's just not worth the trouble anymore? No one. No one but the people who locked him in this place. Well, I looked at the guy and thought, "You know, people like Rockefeller just come right out of his hide." And countless others like him.

Johnny Rotten and Malcolm McLaren's slimy movie which we're all gonna go see anyway and the careers of Steve Jones and Paul Cook though they probably weren't aware of it and all the photographers who were only too happy to cop hot pix of Sid showing off his latest wound and winking and all the hype in rockmags down to articles like the one I wrote on the Pistols in *NME* and perhaps even what you are reading right now came out of Sid Vicious' hide. I guess it could be said that under the circumstances he made the same existential choice as that old hillbilly. I'm sure he was as suckered all down the line. But there are plenty of people in the world who have been beaten and whipped and raped and tortured and defiled and given zero chance to make it out of the pit, who have had a dose of all that every bit as heavy as Sid's if not worse, and some of them, a lot of them, are trying to do something about it besides crumple. It's like that scene in *Fat City,* where Stacy Keach goes to see his ex-girlfriend who's now living with a working-class black guy in some shitty tenement room. She's in there drinking and crying and the black guy says to Keach, "Look man, don't come 'roun no more, she's a juicehead and it wigs her out." And then, almost as an afterthought, "You know, she's had a bad life and all that shit."

Which is what I think about Sid Vicious and the whole Sex Pistols media-scam when you get right down to it: alienation, societal disintegration, anomie, and all that shit. You've heard it all before and you're gonna hear it all again from some other bunch of assholes, but if you stand there and keep listening after the first few familiar refrains you're not gonna find me standing next to you. Because I've had it. I'm not saying I'm any better. Directly the opposite, in fact—inasmuch as I had even as minuscule a part in helping shape the Sex Pistols saga as I did. I must accept some portion of the complicity in Sid's death and possibly Nancy's as well. And under such circumstances I feel the least I can do is try to stay aware enough to see something coming like this a little sooner in the future. And then avoid, boycott if not actively oppose it.

While I still don't wanna hear how everything is hunky-dory like a lot of those disco people and Barry Manilows are trying to sell us, I'm just completely fed up with cheap stupid nihilism especially when it starts acting trendy. I know society is sick and life is getting more complicated by the second, but if all you've got to say is get fucked life sucks you stink I stink who cares I'm bored whip me beat me kick me there's nothing else to do then I think you and everybody else would be a lot better off if you just kept your fucking mouth shut in the first place, not to mention your self-destructive habits to yourself instead of parading them around like The Red Badge of Courage or something. And this isn't like If You Can't Say Anything Nice Don't Say Anything At All, it's more like . . . why restate what's been said and refuted already?

The trouble beyond all the sleaze and manipulation with the Pistols was that like a lot of other (most?) punkers they *only* went halfway: they did say everything sucks, which needed to be said even though it isn't necessarily true, but they never took that next step of saying, "However, we have another idea over here. . . ." They never even began to *try* to find out what valid non-copout alternatives there might be. Which actually is a lot harder than screaming random abuse and groveling and retching and fixing and mutilating yourself. But there are bands around who *are* searching, in highly intelligent and methodical ways, for those alternatives previously mentioned. They're alternatives we all urgently need to explore, because the hour's getting late and outside things just keep getting uglier and uglier. I hope you will forgive me if I've gotten a little preachy or I hope not self-righteous herein; it's just that I and everybody else I know are fed up. We don't want to discuss Sid Vicious or any of that shit ever again beyond the simple word, "No." We think it's time for a change.

Written 1979

Published posthumously in *Throat Culture #2,* November 1990

from All My Friends Are Hermits

Local workers, toilers mortar 'n' pestling out this new politic so selflessly it brought a tear to any eye, grubhawgs racking up 60, 80, 120, 180 hours per week with no pay just because THEY BELIEVED . . . these became the New American Heroes. Or rather prototypes of a whole new type of American. It grew like Topsy, quite naturally turnin' the Feds every way but loose. "Uh, wha . . . ?" both Mr. Reagan and Mr. Carter were heard to respond in separate states that same campaign day, on being informed that a growing groundswell of the American public found not only them but the whole government irrelevant to immediate realities, it seemed America was starting over, rediscovering itself. The public was willing as ever to respond to Gallup and other polls even though everybody knew the polls were bought by one or another of the large political parties, General Foods, or whoever, every time. Americans turned on their TVs to hear the results of the latest surveys. Because the polls themselves had changed: sensing which side of the toast the average American family unit or citizen (single unit) was gonna slap his butter to this time, the polls opted for following public opinion, indicating to their more distant observers that soon now there might be no government left in America at all save whatever might issue up from a public preoccupied with local concerns of every sort. Somehow, while nobody was watching, decentralization had turned to complete fragmentation overnight. Nobody even bothered calling 'em states anymore, and to say "I am an American . . . ," well, a joke's a joke but they do get stale especially when every drunk you meet thinks he just made it up. Reagan and Carter held a five-hour private meeting together in the East Wing of the White House, then issued a joint statement to what was left of the press, and, they hoped, to the nation: "Listen to us or the hostages in Iran will die. And don't interrupt or we'll send in the National Guard, who have been instructed in the art of severing hands at the wrist. America, our Great Republic, the Union which inspired the World and don't forget is all that stands between you'n yours slaving away like sharecroppers without any blues to sing even in the rank weeds and sewage-stunted rivers of Soviet satellites, this America, our America, the America of the Great Bald Eagle and Karl Malden's Gibraltar-solid traveler's check reassurances; of Walt Disney and Norman Rockwell yet strong enough to permit the ideological syphilis of such as Black Panther Parties to gain their equal voice in the free marketplace of ideas—"

"*People* magazine?" somebody within hearing distance of the podium quipped.

Breaking off his and Mr. Reagan's address in midstream to extemporaneously contend with a rippling outbreak of druggy giggles from one section of the room Mr. Carter grimly intoned: "I see there are some of you who think this is funny. Well, I am as fond of a good joke as the next fellow. For instance, why did the chicken cross the road?"

He waited. Complete silence throughout the nation. *Though not a few found themselves thinking, If only, if only he comes through just this one time, shit, I'd vote for a man who could tell a good joke on network TV and get people to laugh without cue cards . . . maybe there's still hope, maybe he's got some sass to burn after all . . . a pinch of pepsin in the cornea . . . a regular guy who knows his way around . . . yeah, that'd be nice . . .*

Suddenly the nation's TV screens went red. Many thought it was a Red Alert, something they had heard about so often over the years that they were absolutely helpless, buffaloed when it came to dealing with such an eventuality . . . camp silhouettes of bomb shelter openings . . . the last time they watched *Dr. Strangelove* on the late late show . . . forget it. What it was was the back of Rosalynn Carter's red alpaca sweater, and what the whole nation heard her whispering urgently to their ostensible leader in that moment was: "Jimmy, *what do you think you're doing?* . . . This isn't the *Playboy* interview—"

"Wish it was," drawled Jim the Prez. "That was fun, even if it did get me in trouble."

"Well, it's not and the sooner you realize that what is happening at any given moment is just exactly that and not some rerun of a four-year-old prime-time hit the better. . . . No matter what the punch line of that joke might be, there's bound to be people out there gonna be offended by it. God, haven't you learned *anything?!* Look at Ronald Reagan: do you see *him* telling jokes?"

"That's 'cause he don' know any."

"Yes, but he speaks very seriously and it strengthens his campaign as long as he doesn't ad-lib. Same goes for you. Christ, we've got the best writers in the country working on this stuff: Vonnegut, Pynchon, Irving, Doctorow! By election day you'll be certified folklore! Dan'l Boone!"

"Rather be Grizzly Adams," replied Jimmy dreamily. "He gots modern conveniences. I ain't livin' in no wickiup . . . less o' course the National Mood 'n' the People git ta callin' for it . . . hell what these damn people don't realize is, I'd eat cowshit just to make 'em happy, if that's what it takes to make 'em happy . . ."

"But that's just the *point!* They don't want you to eat cowshit! They want you to get the hostages back! They want you to get the economy moving upwards again! They want you to act like a LEADER! Even if you keep on doin' nothin', even if it's all just empty gestures, tears 'n' flapdoodle, makes no difference at all, just *motion, motion, motion,* that's what they wanna see! Look at JFK! Didn't do shit 'cept the Bay of Pigs! A tadpole of a president! Course he died just in time! But when he did nothing, he did it with such élan! Such style! Such *savoir faire!* That nobody noticed! Nobody! Anywhere in the world! You had a shot at that! And you blew it! Remember all those pix in *Newsweek* back in '76, you jogging along the seashore with your damn hound muddlin' along beside you? What in the hell did you think that was all about? Glamour! And remember when you first got into office, all the columns in the magazines and newspapers: 'Never in all my years as a Washington correspondent have I seen so much hugging, kissing, and always good-natured yet overtly physical communication between the sexes, right out in the open, like a love-in practically! It's a particularly refreshing breath of life-giving air after the grim, ashen, drawn austerely sexless quality of the Nixon years. . . .' Shit Jimmy, they laid it right in your lap!"

"So why can't I tell 'em a joke or two now?"

"Because that was then and this is now besides which you're supposed to be the cool unflappable serious leader with your mind if not your hot li'l mitts on the helm of the ship of state at all times . . . let *them* tell the jokes, that's what they're good at!"

"Hey," said Reagan, "I'm about to die of boredom not to mention disgust over here! I can see who wears the pants in *your* family! C'mon, you can't bait me and who knows how many million other Americans and then leave us hanging, just like that! Let's hear the punch line, dammit!"

"Well . . ."

Jimmy was unsure. It was how he felt most of the time, but now as ever he didn't feel bad about it. He knew that feeling unsure meant that he was actually dealing with the problem, whatever it might be, rather than avoiding it with pat solutions or outright dismissal. He treated all problems brought to him this way, from Amy's broken backyard Water Wiggle ("Just turn the hose all the way up," he'd told her. "To hell with Water Wiggle. You're getting too old for it anyway.") to the Iranian crisis: he thought, pondered, mulled, analyzed, compared, reviewed, contemplated, meditated, regarded, slept.

For he only dreamed of affairs of state, except for the odd phosphene-surging liaison with Jane Fonda in the arms of Morpheus, which always followed a rigid script: she came to the White House to ask for a special dispensation granting legal abortions at low fees to

California women, because the entire state was addicted to smoking heroin via cigarette-ends and she was horrified at the prospect of an entire generation hooked from birth; he said, "Come with me into my private study, I need to consult my law book as well as . . ."

"You mean . . . ?"

". . . yes . . . Him . . . The Man Upstairs . . ."

"*You're* subletting too! Wow, the economy really is in a fix!"

"No, no, that's not it!"

"Wait, lemme guess . . . it's to Kissinger, right? No? Well then, uh, ah . . . y'know, I wouldn't put it past you to dig up some old has-been from the Sixties and hide him up there like some kind of secret weapon . . . *Robert McNamara!*" She looked triumphant.

He looked back at her triumph, or assumption of same. I give you this, *you owe me one.* He grinned. "Shucks, Jane, old LBJ shoulda learned his own damn self . . . cain' nobody fool you . . ."

"That's because I've discovered something wholly new, revolutionary, a technique that has changed not only my life but those of everyone around me. Now, I know the name Werner Erhard may—"

He snapped back into customary pose. The chief executive, after all, cannot go chasing every California beach ball that bounces past him on the sand. For a fleeting moment he had an image of himself at the beach, Malibu, in full dress suit, vest, the works, looking down and flushing at how silly his wing tips looked in all that sand. But no, this was his turf, his time, his—he grabbed her, held her in a clinch redolent of Dick the Bruiser's finer moments.

"Why . . . why, JIM . . . Jimboy . . . *what* are you *do*-ing . . . ?"

She wanted it, the bitch. Not like that dyke Joan Baez, who'd simply kneed him in the balls: "Ever hear that Neil Young song, Jimmy? 'Welfare mothers make better lovers.' Well, turn it around. I'm particular. Fuck off."

He ran his hand around and around those gorgeous gams, those calves he'd drooled at in so many movies. They were a little, just a winter tad fat, but when his big palm and knowing fingers moved up, swollen and glowing with lust like some mutant carrot, the heel of his palm brushing her thigh set off subterranean blasts of ricochets of lust in them both.

"But my hus-band . . ." she mewled weakly, and then gave up.

"*Barbarella*!" he hissed, which in real life would have turned her off quicker and surer than just about any other word in the English language, but this was his fantasy, only one he had in fact, so he could do anything he wanted and make whoever else behave likewise—"Like Hitler!"—he thought, sniggering like a little Catholic boy who has just masturbated at the statue of the Virgin Mary in a back pew without getting caught, now wondering where to put the handkerchief that caught the cum—so she got even more excited, ravenous, hot and wet like a tawny animal, in fact that's what she turned into, a horse, a pony, a sweatsweet dusktawny mochabeige shetland pony, and imagining her thus he took her from behind, slipping his arms up around to entwine with hers, entwining his own legs like he always did when he fucked and never knew why, sliding it in the slick wet hot hallelujah rumbleseat jungle of her, where he tarried awhile, thinking of the New York Mets and what he was gonna do about Koch in both the short and long runs, thinking about anything, really, but what he was up to, so's to make it last longer, having had enough of Rosalynn's scorn ("Well, now I know what William Burroughs meant by 'the flash bulb of orgasm'! An' he was a damn *fag!*") years ago, leaving her to Ham Jordan when the singles bars didn't pan out as they hadn't at all lately for some reason, he wondered idly if they were having an affair, that'd be funny, Jane ARCHED and let out a low catrrrrrrhhhhh-growl, henbane wildcat slashing its paws to shreds on the razor shale of a precipice, a jagged ledge over an expanse that could have been the Great Plains themselves swallowed whole right here, ten thousand foot drop down, and this motherfucker PUSHING HER . . . she screamed. "Wuzza matter?" quoth Jimmy. She said nothing. Arched again, hissed, dug her turquoise-lacquered nails into his back again and again. *Damn,* he thought, *if Rosalynn sees them 'uns* . . . shit. I liked Jane better in the

Sixties, when she was counterculture: clipped nails, no polish, no hairspray, whole lot less bullshit on every level . . . and everybody else thought exactly the opposite . . . 'course, it is nice having her shave her legs again . . .

He realized the extent of his detachment, wondered if he oughta give up altogether. What the fuck was the difference? Suddenly Jane shuddered, a deep coruscating *shoooom* from the bottom of her belly, and writhed. And writhed. Thrusting up against him, biting his neck—*hickeys! Rosalynn'll see them for sure!*—tearing his back to shreds with her nails, wrapping her great hamhock olde stock America legs like two mighty clampdown-nuggets around his back thighs and ass, rolling, swaying, riding, riding, squelching the screams that died in her throat because after all you never did know who *might* just happen to wander in . . . but it was good for her. It was the best. He knew that. That was the part he liked. When she had finished, he spizzed up two little zipgun mortarspits, making sure as always that his mouth was closed so the snorkel squonks of his nose, amphibious noises denoting ultimate passion from the man's not to mention the presidential side of the barbwire fence, came thru. Yes. It was good. She was a tigress. She was a wench. She was holy. She was a woman. And he was the President of the United States, so even if he turned up impotent, as happened often enough, it didn't matter, because Power was Sex was Power was Sex was Power. As everybody knew.

Jane sat up in bed and lit a Lucky Strike. "My husband—"

"—should be driving a Good Humor truck. Can that shit. Every damn time we fuck I gotta listen to the pitch. Whyncha lemme enjoy my afterglow for a change?"

"How can you have an afterglow when there was no fire to speak of in the first place?"

He hit her then, hard, backhand, straight across the face, a bone-bluing brutal jackhammer reaction. It was so full of hate he even shocked himself a little. She rolled on her side and into a fetal ball facing the wall all twinetimed in Amy's sheets—why did they always seem to end up making love in this room, this bed?—covered with smiling faces from *Sesame Street:* Kermit, Ernie, Oscar the Grouch, the Cookie Monster. If only he knew a woman with a disposition like Ernie's. No, lessee . . . political sense like Rosalynn's, sexual hysteria like Jane's, and every so often a reprise, respite in the form of Ernie . . . the perfect woman . . .

"I once got gang-banged by a PLO batallion," she said.

He didn't say anything. Ernie.

"The 43rd guy, after all that nightmare with the 42 before him, excited me more than you."

And even better if he could have Ernie for vice president as well! Though Bert did have his good points. The only thing he couldn't figure out was what excuse he could contrive to keep watching the show. Amy had long since outgrown it, it was a ritual between the two of them, and *she* was starting to give him weird looks.

"Another time I was caught in a napalm attack on a Vietnamese village. I ducked inside the nearest hut. There was a Cong crouching there in the shadows, black pajamas and all. He was terrified. He thought the Americans were going to bomb everything that moved, then land their planes and machine gun everything else, down to the newborn babies, dogs, and cats. 'Search and destroy,' he kept saying, his voice breaking, till it sounded like a mantra. 'Search and destroy.' They were the only three words in English he knew. He was trembling more violently than I've ever seen anyone shake before or since in my life. I moved into the corner with him, somehow signaling that I meant no harm even though I was obviously American. I began to caress him, first the hair behind his ears, the light fingertips down his sides under the pajamas, trickling along his ribcage, then up again. With what was probably the gentlest gesture of my life I brushed the tips of my three most prominent fingers on the left hand against his lips, for one second only. Then I kissed him on both eyelids, because his eyes were closed. He was sure I was going to kill him. Just another American trick, I could read his mind, it was too easy, so easy it was pathetic. A sluice of napalm hit the other side of the tent and tore away half of the whole dwelling in one bite. I looked out. You could see fires and hear screaming everywhere. Right across from us a man was burning to death. But he wasn't screaming. He didn't make a sound. He just stared at us with no interest, we just happened to be in his line of vision. There was a mound of molten rubble beside him with a few hairs and some shards of skin beside it. He kept picking at it, the base of it, with his fingernails, digging away. Eventually what was there became visible. It was the head of a little girl, I guess his granddaughter. Squashed flat, mulch of brain, blood, flesh oozing out the sides. Like a deflated tire almost, except with eyes. But they were closed. The rest of her was under the rubble. The hair kept falling out of her head into his palms, he was grabbing up huge hunks of it that he didn't seem to know what to do with. He looked at them. They didn't register any more than we did. I looked around us once more. In every direction, everything around us seemed to be on fire. A strong fierce white fire, not about to go away, thick steady stalks of white flame poised over razed houses, shattered bodies, broken bicycles, bits of metal and brick and glass and flesh. I turned back to my prisoner. He was somewhat calmer now. I looked into his eyes and he looked back, quizzically for sure. He was still ready at any second for me to kill him. 'No,' I said, 'I don't want to do that, I *love* you!' He didn't understand a word of it, of course. I felt like a prize fool. I felt the most intense shame commingling with the most overpowering lust. I slipped my hand into his pajama bottoms, and—ha! Sure enough, he was hard! Faker! Playing games, just like any asshole in New York! With my other hand I took one of his and guided it down a bit, then he took the cue, began to stroke me between my legs, occasionally sticking a finger, sometimes two or three into the hole, I was wetter than I was hot, I mean we were in the middle of an inferno, and I felt kind of guilty with so much death around us . . . but then I rationalized: how better to reaffirm life? Especially given who or what we were. Corny I know, but god did I get excited. I think it was the death around us more than anything else that excited me. I pulled his cock deep into me and we made love there, just like that, for a long, long time. Fierce, regal, Mau-Mau love. There was definitely a sense of ritual about it and we both knew it. The old man kept staring through us. We must have fucked for an hour. When we came we screamed at the top of our lungs, both of us coming at once because we'd known almost from the first moment of motion that we could control it that good and way beyond, but when we came all control went rampaging out the window, we were helpless, we were monsters, we were ashamed, we were in love, our screams rose with the smoke and mingled with the screams of the dying. It made us scream even louder. When we were done, we literally fell apart, he upon his back, I on mine. I couldn't look him in the eye after that. We sat there in awfulness for a while, listening to the death. Then I heard a noise and a Jeep came tearing through the fire, pulled up sharply and stopped almost on top of us. One of the hosts who'd been my guide through my whole tour of North Vietnam was sitting beside the driver. He was really pissed. 'You wandered away from the group,' he said, grim and dead and censorious and flat as all get out. I felt like a schoolchild caught playing forbidden games in the yard. I turned crimson with shame. 'You know that is not allowed,' he said. I couldn't look at him either. 'Get in the back,' he said. I climbed up in the Jeep. I still hadn't looked at the Cong's face since we'd fucked. We drove out of there. I didn't look back. Later I was censured in front of the whole group. They said I was an absolutely classical object lesson in selfish, spoiled, American embourgeoisement, and what was worse, they said, utterly lacking any sense of the stupefying extremity of my own decadence. Of course they didn't know what else I'd done. To them I'd just run away from the group. I had defected just a little bit, for just a little while, which for them meant I defected totally. They said I was living proof why Americans were too far gone for socialism and would have to be all killed or put in reeducation camps, at least until a new generation arrived not so polluted by capitalism and the cult of the individual. The criticisms were specific and uniform. Everybody knew the rules. I did too. Yet I broke them. Consciously. After a bit they turned gentler: 'Don't you see the foolhardiness of walking alone in the jungle? Even if there were no war, you would be foolish to do that. As it was, you were almost burned alive by your own countrymen. Was that what you wanted? To be some kind of martyr? Well, that was foolishness too. Who would have known? After the napalm, all bodies look the same. You would have been described in American news as having "disappeared into Communist North Vietnam." People would no doubt concoct elaborate fantasies that we had tortured, brainwashed, and finally murdered you. Your schoolgirl notions of "martyrdom" would have succeeded in setting us back! Played right into the hands of your leaders' schemes for deceiving and lying to the American people. Just another story for them to exploit, just more propaganda.' I knew they were right, of course, and felt ashamed. When it was over, they weren't mad at me anymore, everyone spoke of other things. But I couldn't lose my shame. They forgot all about it, while I carried it like stigmata for the rest of my stay."

As she was finishing her story, she heard a honk, a stopple of gander goose noise. She stabbed out her cigarette and looked down and over. Jimmy had fallen asleep in the middle of the tale. He was smiling, looking very boyish that way, cowlicked and remnants of freckles even at his age. It had been a lullaby for him. She had never told anyone else this in her entire life, not even her husband. Especially her husband. But it was okay. She knew Jimmy. He didn't believe in Vietnam. He remembered the years it encompassed, but he'd always said that it was part of the past and the best thing all of us could do was try to put it as far from us as possible. In campaign speeches in '76, he'd said: "I think America should *forget* Vietnam ever happened." Privately, to her, he'd said, "That's the only way. Just push and push it away until it disappears, dies, becomes a myth like the Battle of New Orleans or the *Monitor* and the *Merrimac.* Make it history. When it is history, when it really is, we'll be able to handle it. Not now. We have to erase it so we can go on. Either that or wallow in it. Make tasteless violent movies, dozens of them, bathing in the blood until it all becomes meaningless. One way or the other, we got to get it off our backs."

"What about all the crippled vets," she'd said, "or even the guys who just felt displaced, like they lost years out of their lives? Which they did."

"They're all on heroin anyway," he'd said. "They don't count."

She felt a sudden sense of revulsion that stormed through her body in one rancid wave: revulsion with their sex, with him, with herself, her memories, with life in any form, with how coldly life can be snuffed out and how the survivors continue, choosing consistently to block out what's in front of their eyes, because otherwise they would all go mad. *Yeah, go crazy,* she thought sarcastically. *That's the answer. Then when they've got you they can really do a job on you, open-ended.* She jumped up and pulled on her clothes as quickly as possible. Checked herself in the mirror: a slightly rumpled, near middle-aged schoolgirl. Well, there were worse things to look like. She clambered off the bed and crossed the room with a brisk, firm stride, out the door, down the marble stairs, into the clear black-lined sunlight of Washington, D.C., a ghost town. A few minutes later, driving past the Lincoln Memorial, trying to keep from staring at the tourists trooping solemnly up to pay their respects and cuff their kids into doing the same, she thought: And now even the ghosts are retiring. They prefer not to cast their shadows on the likes of us.

Previously Unpublished, 1980

Trapped by the Mormons

No it's this way! Why in the hell do you think everybody else does it exactly alike? What are you, a moron? There's rules for reasons and they're the only way anybody that knows anything does it! So grow up! Be a professional! Look sharp! Get your act together! Shave off all the loose ends! Learn the hairstyle! Fix those nails! Knot that tie right! That shirt's not Arrow, you're a loser! Mind that blow-dryer! Wrong cologne! You wore WING TIPS! Here's that gum that spurts in your mouth! Just grit your teeth, smile, and be polite! Where's your condo? Where's your Trans-Am? Where's your BABIES? Laugh sincerely! He's important! She's got money! There's a good job! Chance of a lifetime! Grab it now, it's never coming back! No you damn fool that electric guitar's not played that way! How I know? I been to school! Do it like this! Just like this! Practice makes perfect! Over and over! On forever! So what if it's the same solo? Can't you hear those TASTY LICKS! Just like George Benson! You're the greatest! You'll go far! No, you can't sing! Don't even try! You'll be a laughingstock! Stick to what you know! What you're good at! Stop playing around with all this nonsense! Some people WORK for a living you know! In fact, everybody does! Only Commies don't have bosses! So what if he's an asshole! I gotta take his shit too! You'll get a pension! Those jeans are OUT this year! You're such a fool! Now THEY all know! Act unconcerned! Don't let her know you like her or you'll lose her! That's just the way it is! Everyone's like that! No exceptions anywhere! Take it, shut up, there's nothing else! You're no artist, that's for queers! You'll never make a living writing books unless you're Harold Robbins! And you're not so give it up! Nobody will publish that! Exhibition? Those'd get you laughed out of every gallery in Soho! Your band can't play and you can't dance like Mick Jagger! Get off the stage! Back to the hardware store! Those clothes don't match! What, no American Express! You're dead buster! Stay with the tour group! Don't wander off alone, you might get lost! That's not the right unreadable magazine to be carrying, sorry! Get a nose job! That'll do it! Your career will zoom! Why are you talking to them, they're not important! Brownnose this one! He can HELP you! You'll thank me for this some day! By the way, you could still stand to lose about three and a half pounds! Then you'd look just like the new girl everyone's talking about! Stop laying around daydreaming! Up an' at 'em! Nice guys finish last! Get the Racer's Edge! Our bank's got Clout! Fly this airline you can board two minutes ahead of the next wretch! You'll be better! Buy this shit too! People will be jealous! They'll envy you and think you're cool! They'll hate you 'cause they didn't buy it first! Do it for the good of the team! We gotta pull together or we lose the damn race! Yeah I know who you are, you're 261! Now move that ass! We got a pyramid to build here and when it's done you'll get to live inside! No, don't thank us now! You didn't wash your hands after you pissed before you brushed your teeth this morning! That's dangerous! I read it in a magazine! They don't lie! If you don't go to school you'll never learn anything! Bookworm, why doncha get out and learn about REAL LIFE? That's not music! It says so right here! This guy's an expert, he's met lots of rock stars! A Bob Ezrin production would fit you just fine! Put you in the Top Ten! Otherwise you're dead! You'll never work again! But a word to the right people and you're in! Make up your mind! It's not selling out, it's for the good of the band as a whole! Okay, just watch us get famous faster than you! You'll never be anything! Everybody knows it! They're all laughing! Think you're bigshit! This is the only crowd in town, run with us or you don't exist! See that one? Yeah, that's right that one over there! That's the ass you gotta kiss! But don't worry you'll only ever kiss just this one! From then it's roses! But kiss it good! Like you mean it! They can tell!

Contempo Culture, December 1980

Permissions

Grateful acknowledgment is made to the following for permission to reprint previously published material:

"MC5: *Kick Out the Jams*," © 1970 Rolling Stone LLC; Charlie Haden: *"Liberation Music Orchestra,"* © 1970 Rolling Stone LLC; "Canned Heat: *The New Age*," © 1973 Rolling Stone LLC. All rights reserved. Reprinted by permission.

"Dandelions in Still Air: The Withering Away of the Beatles," copyright the Phoenix/Media Communications Group.

"Kind of Grim: Unraveling the Miles Perplex," copyright Greg Shaw, originally published in *Phonograph Record Magazine*. Reprinted by permission.

"Everybody's Search for Roots (The Roots of Punk, Part 1)," copyright *New Wave* Magazine and Howard Klein. Reprinted by permission.

"Back Door Men and Women in Bondage" appears through the courtesy of *The Back Door Man* Collective: DD Faye, Tom Gardner, Freddie Patterson, and Don Waller.

"Anne Murray: *Danny's Song*," by Lester Bangs from *Creem Magazine* (September 1973) © 1973 Creem Media Inc.; "Blood Feast of Reddy Kilowatt! Emerson, Lake, and Palmer Without Insulation!" by Lester Bangs from *Creem Magazine* (March 1974) © 1974 Creem Media Inc.; "Helen Reddy: *Long Hard Climb*," by Lester Bangs from *Creem Magazine* (August 1974) © 1974 Creem Media Inc.; "Death May Be Your Santa Claus: An Exclusive, Up-to-Date Interview with Jimi

Hendrix," by Lester Bangs from *Creem Magazine* (April 1976) © 1976 Creem Media Inc.; "Killer Frogs in Transatlantic Blitz: A Franco-American Chronologue Starring Les Variations," by Lester Bangs from *Creem Magazine* (February 1975) © 1975 Cream Media Inc.; "Deaf-Mute in a Telephone Booth: A Perfect Day with Lou Reed," by Lester Bangs from *Creem Magazine* (July 1973) © 1973 Creem Media Inc.; "Monolith or Monotone? Lou Reed's *Metal Machine Music*," by Lester Bangs from *Creem Magazine* (September 1975) © 1975 Creem Media Inc.; "Patti Smith: *Horses*," by Lester Bangs from *Creem Magazine* (February 1976) © 1976 Creem Media Inc.; "Innocents in Babylon: A Search for Jamaica Featuring Bob Marley and a Cast of Thousands," by Lester Bangs from *Creem Magazine* (July 1976) © 1976 Creem Media Inc.; "Bring Your Mother to the Gas Chamber!" by Lester Bangs from *Creem Magazine* (July 1972) © 1972 Creem Media Inc.; "1973 Nervous Breakdown: The Ol' Fey Outlaws Ain't What They Used to Be—Are You?" by Lester Bangs from *Creem Magazine* (December 1973) © 1973 Creem Media Inc.; "State of the Art: Bland on Bland," by Lester Bangs from *Creem Magazine* (July 1976) © 1976 Creem Media Inc.; "I Only Get My Rocks Off When I'm Dreaming: So You Say You Missed the Stones, Too? Cheer Up, We're a Majority!" by Lester Bangs from *Creem Magazine* (January 1973) © 1973 Creem Media Inc.; "C'mon Sugar, Let's Go All-Nite Jukin' with Wet Willie," by Lester Bangs from *Creem Magazine* (October 1974) © 1974 Creem Media Inc. All rights reserved. Reprinted by permission.

Excerpts from *Joey* by Donald Goddard, copyright © 1974 by Donald Goddard. Reprinted by permission of HarperCollins Publishers, Inc.

Excerpts from the song lyrics "Rocks Off," words and music by Mick Jagger and Keith Richards, © 1972 (Renewed 2000) EMI MUSIC PUBLISHING LTD. All rights for the U.S. and Canada controlled and administered by COLGEMS-EMI MUSIC INC. All rights reserved. International copyright secured. Used by permission. Excerpt from the song lyrics "It's Only Rock and Roll (But I Like It)," words and music by Mick Jagger and Keith Richards, © 1974 EMI MUSIC PUBLISHING LTD. All rights for the U.S. and Canada controlled and administered by COLGEMS-EMI MUSIC INC. All rights reserved. International copyright secured. Used by permission.

ALSO BY LESTER BANGS

PSYCHOTIC REACTIONS AND CARBURETOR DUNG

The Work of a Legendary Critic: Rock 'n' Roll as Literature and Literature as Rock 'n' Roll

Edited by Greil Marcus

"With affection and rudeness and fury and mockery, with prose that moved in gusts and swirls and pratfalls, he showed how music could be—for him as well as for less articulate, less self-conscious fans—an arena of moral choices. . . . Bangs was one of the best writers ever to appear on newsprint." —*The New York Times*

"A great American writer who happened to write about rock and roll . . . wild and funny and utterly unpredictable . . . Lester's prose pulsated with rock's own rhythms . . . a superb collection." —*Rolling Stone*

"Magnificent." —*The Village Voice Literary Supplement*

Music/0-679-72045-6